THE POETICS OF LATIN DIDACTIC

The Poetics of Latin Didactic

Lucretius, Vergil, Ovid, Manilius

KATHARINA VOLK

OXFORD
UNIVERSITY PRESS

Great Clarendon Street, Oxford, OX2 6DP
Oxford University Press is a department of the University of Oxford.
It furthers the University's objective of excellence in research, scholarship,
and education by publishing worldwide in

Oxford New York

Auckland Bangkok Buenos Aires Cape Town Chennai
Dar es Salaam Delhi Hong Kong Istanbul Karachi Kolkata
Kuala Lumpur Madrid Melbourne Mexico City Mumbai Nairobi
São Paulo Shanghai Singapore Taipei Tokyo Toronto
and an associated company in Berlin

Oxford is a registered trade mark of Oxford University Press
in the UK and certain other countries

Published in the United States
by Oxford University Press Inc., New York

© Katharina Volk 2002

The moral rights of the author have been asserted

Database right Oxford University Press (maker)

First published 2002

All rights reserved. No part of this publication may be reproduced,
stored in a retrieval system, or transmitted, in any form or by any means,
without the prior permission in writing of Oxford University Press,
or as expressly permitted by law, or under terms agreed with the appropriate
reprographics rights organization. Enquiries concerning reproduction
outside the scope of the above should be sent to the Rights Department,
Oxford University Press, at the address above

You must not circulate this book in any other binding or cover
and you must impose the same condition on any acquirer

British Library Cataloguing in Publication Data

Data available

Library of Congress Cataloging in Publication Data

Data applied for

ISBN 0-19-924550-9

1 3 5 7 9 10 8 6 4 2

Typeset in Baskerville
by Regent Typesetting, London
Printed in Great Britain
on acid-free paper by
T.J. International Ltd.
Padstow, Cornwall

PARENTIBVS OPTIMIS

PREFACE

Many of the most famous literary works from Greek and Roman antiquity—for example, Hesiod's *Works and Days*, the poem of Lucretius, and Vergil's *Georgics*—are didactic poems. Still, while these texts continue to be read and studied, their generic status is not typically the object of scholarly investigation, and neither is the genre of ancient didactic poetry as a whole. This may have something to do with our wariness of anything that is or purports to be 'didactic'; as a matter of fact, the student of this genre is not infrequently faced with miscomprehension on the part of classicists and non-classicists alike ('Didactic poetry? Sounds awful.'). Nevertheless, by understanding what it is that sets a particular body of texts apart as a specific genre, we are able to appreciate better the qualities of the individual texts, and especially in the case of a comparatively neglected type of literature such as didactic poetry, attention to generic characteristics can contribute in important ways to our interpretation even of otherwise well-studied works.

In this book, I both provide a discussion of the genre of didactic poetry as a whole and examine in detail four great Latin didactic poems, Lucretius' *De rerum natura*, Vergil's *Georgics*, Ovid's *Ars amatoria* and *Remedia amoris* (which I treat as a unity), and Manilius' *Astronomica*. My object is to show that there are certain defining characteristics of the genre and to trace the permutations of these features through the individual texts. Special attention will be given to the 'poetics' of these works, that is, to what each didactic poem has to say about its being poetry and how it presents the relationship between poetic form and didactic subject matter, or, to quote Manilius, between *carmen* and *res*. Contrary to popular associations of didacticism with the dry and prosaic, it will turn out that ancient didactic poetry is in fact especially self-consciously 'poetic'.

The book is a revised and expanded version of my 1999 Princeton Ph.D. thesis and would never have been written without the support of my adviser Elaine Fantham and the other members of my dissertation committee, Andrew Ford, Stephen Harrison, and Robert Kaster. In addition, I am grateful to Greta Austin, John Cooper, Richard Hunter, and René Nünlist for enlightening discussion of individual matters and to Ryan Balot, Joseph Farrell, and the late Don Fowler for allowing me to use and cite unpublished material. My editor at Oxford University Press, Hilary O'Shea, has been extremely helpful, as have Enid Barker, Lucy Qureshi, and Jenny Wagstaffe; I should also like to thank Rowena Anketell for her diligence in copy-editing the manuscript and the two anonymous readers of the Press for their comments. I am grateful to Oxford University Press for permission to cite from the *Oxford Classical Texts* of Lucretius (ed. Bailey, 2nd edn. 1922), Vergil (ed. Mynors 1969), and Ovid (amatory works, ed. Kenney, 2nd edn. 1994) and to K. G. Saur Verlag for permission to quote the *Teubner* text of Manilius (ed. Goold, 2nd edn. 1998). Special thanks go to my husband Joshua, whose love and expertise have accompanied this work since its beginning. Finally, the book is dedicated to my parents, who have taught me a lot without ever being didactic.

KV

Lewisburg, June 2001

CONTENTS

Abbreviations	xi
Note on Texts	xiii
Introduction	1
1. 'Tell Me, Muse': Characteristics of the Self-Conscious Poem	6
2. 'Improbable Art': The Theory and Practice of Ancient Didactic Poetry	25
2.1. Ancient Views of Didactic Poetry	26
2.2. Didactic Poetry as a Genre	34
2.3. The Development of Didactic Poetry up to Lucretius	44
2.4. Perceptions of Didactic Poetry in the First Century BC	60
3. The Teacher's Truth: Lucretius' *De rerum natura*	69
3.1. The Teaching Speech	73
3.2. The Poem	83
3.3. Poetry and Philosophy	94
4. The Poet's Choice: Vergil's *Georgics*	119
4.1. The Farmers and Maecenas	122
4.2. The Poet's Career	139
5. The Poem's Success: Ovid's *Ars amatoria* and *Remedia amoris*	157
5.1. The *praeceptor amoris*	159
5.2. Simultaneity	173
5.3. Poet and Persona	188
6. The Song of the Stars: Manilius' *Astronomica*	196
6.1. The Teacher of Astrology	198
6.2. *Vates mundi*	209
6.3. The Heavenly Journey	225
6.4. *Carmen et res*	234

Conclusion	246
Bibliography	250
Passages cited	268
Index	284

ABBREVIATIONS

Throughout the text and bibliography, references to classical texts typically follow the style of abbreviations of the *Oxford Classical Dictionary* (3rd edn.). A list of abbreviations for periodicals and other publications is appended.

A&A	*Antike und Abendland*
AAWM	*Abhandlungen der Akademie der Wissenschaften in Mainz, Geistes- und Sozialwissenschaftliche Klasse*
AC	*L'Antiquité classique*
AGPh	*Archiv für Geschichte der Philosophie*
AJPh	*American Journal of Philology*
ANRW	W. Haase and H. Temporini (eds.) (1972–). *Aufstieg und Niedergang der römischen Welt: Geschichte und Kultur Roms im Spiegel der neueren Forschung*. Berlin: de Gruyter
A&R	*Atene e Roma*
ARW	*Archiv für Religionswissenschaft*
ASNP	*Annali della Scuola Normale Superiore di Pisa*
BICS	*Bulletin of the Institute of Classical Studies of the University of London*
CB	*Classical Bulletin*
CGF	G. Kaibel (1899). *Comicorum Graecorum Fragmenta*. Berlin: Weidmann
CH	A. Nock and A. J. Festugière (eds.) (1946–54). *Corpus Hermeticum*, 4 vols. Paris: Les Belles Lettres
CJ	*Classical Journal*
CPh	*Classical Philology*
CQ	*Classical Quarterly*
FPL	W. Morel, K. Büchner, and J. Blänsdorf (eds.) (1995). *Fragmenta Poetarum Latinorum Epicorum et Lyricorum* (3rd edn.). Stuttgart: Teubner
GIF	*Giornale italiano di filologia*
Gramm. Lat.	H. Keil (ed.) (1855–80). *Grammatici Latini*, 8 vols. Leipzig: Teubner
GRBS	*Greek, Roman and Byzantine Studies*
G&R	*Greece & Rome*

Abbreviations

HSPh	Harvard Studies in Classical Philology
ICS	Illinois Classical Studies
LCM	Liverpool Classical Monthly
LSJ	H. G. Liddell, R. Scott, and H. S. Jones (eds.) (1996). *A Greek English Lexicon With a Revised Supplement* (9th edn.). Oxford: Oxford University Press
MD	*Materiali e discussioni per l'analisi dei testi classici*
MDAI(R)	*Mitteilungen des Deutschen Archäologischen Instituts (Römische Abteilung)*
MH	*Museum Helveticum*
OLD	P. G. W. Glare (ed.) (1983). *Oxford Latin Dictionary*. Oxford: Oxford University Press.
Pauly-Wissowa	A. F. von Pauly, G. Wissowa, and W. Kroll (eds.) (1894–1980). *Real-Encyclopädie der classischen Altertumswissenschaft*. Stuttgart and Munich: Metzler/Druckenmüller
PCPhS	*Proceedings of the Cambridge Philological Society*
PQ	*Philological Quarterly*
QS	*Quaderni di storia*
RAL	*Rendiconti della Classe di Scienze morali, storiche e filologiche dell'Accademia dei Lincei*
REA	*Revue des études anciennes*
RFIC	*Rivista di filologia e di istruzione classica*
RhM	*Rheinisches Museum*
RLAC	T. Klauser (ed.) (1950–). *Reallexikon für Antike und Christentum: Sachwörterbuch zur Auseinandersetzung des Christentums mit der antiken Welt*. Stuttgart: Hiersemann
SICF	*Studi italiani di filologia classica*
SO	*Symbolae Osloenses*
SVF	H. F. A. von Arnim (ed.) (1903–24). *Stoicorum Veterum Fragmenta*, 4 vols. Leipzig: Teubner
TAPhA	*Transactions and Proceedings of the American Philological Association*
WJA	*Würzburger Jahrbücher für die Altertumswissenschaft*
WS	*Wiener Studien*
YClS	*Yale Classical Studies*

NOTE ON TEXTS

The editions used for the major works discussed in this book are as follows:

Lucretius, *De rerum natura*, ed. Cyril Bailey (*Oxford Classical Text*, 2nd edn. 1922). Reprinted by permission of Oxford University Press.

Manilius, *Astronomica*, ed. George P. Goold (*Teubner*, 2nd edn. 1998), © K. G. Saur Verlag. Reprinted by permission of K. G. Saur Verlag.

Ovid, *Amores, Medicamina faciei femineae, Ars amatoria, Remedia amoris*, ed. E. J. Kenney (*Oxford Classical Text*, 2nd edn. 1994), © Oxford University Press, 1961, 1994. Reprinted by permission of Oxford University Press.

Vergil, *Opera*, ed. R. A. B. Mynors (*Oxford Classical Text*, 1969), © Oxford University Press, 1969. Reprinted by permission of Oxford University Press.

bina mihi positis lucent altaria flammis,
ad duo templa precor duplici circumdatus aestu
carminis et rerum.
> Manilius, *Astronomica* 1. 20–2

Introduction

> ... wie schwer es sei, ein Werk aus Wissen und Einbildungs-
> kraft zusammenzuweben ...
>
> Goethe, *Über das Lehrgedicht*
>
> omne tulit punctum qui miscuit utile dulci.
>
> Horace, *Ars Poetica*

Poetry that undertakes to lay out a branch of knowledge or teach a practical skill is likely to meet with suspicion on the part of modern readers. After all, in our bookshops the poetry section is clearly distinct from the one that offers 'how-to' or 'self-help' books, and what we are looking for in the one, we definitely do not expect to find in the other. Even professional classicists, who are somewhat more accustomed to poems that treat, say, the phenomenon of volcanism or remedies against snake-bites, tend to feel uneasy about what Alister Cox has described as '[t]he improbable art of harnessing poetry to severely technical instruction' (1969: 124). Occurring at the beginning of an introduction to Greek and Latin didactic poetry, this phrase is revealing, and what follows is even more indicative of Cox's, and other scholars', misgivings: didactic poetry 'originated almost accidentally in Greece, blossomed near-miraculously in Rome, and was never afterwards to be convincingly revived ... many would now claim that the art-form is defunct because it is in principle impossible (resting upon the fusion of incompatible elements)' (ibid.).

It is easy to see what is wrong with didactic poetry: to our feeling, it is a contradiction in terms. Poetry is not meant to be instructional, and teaching is certainly not expected to be poetic. Thus, to quote Goethe, '[d]ie didaktische oder schulmeisterliche Poesie ist und bleibt ein Mittelgeschöpf zwischen Poesie und Rhetorik.'[1] It is likely that this negative view is to a great extent due to the modern,

---
[1] Goethe, *Über das Lehrgedicht*, Weimar edn. 41. 2. 225. See also the quotation, from the same essay, used as an epigraph to the Introduction.

specifically Romantic, idea that true poetry (as opposed to an unsatisfactory hybrid like didactic poetry) is the expression of the poet's subjective feelings, a definition that is not generally applicable to any ancient poetry, as classicists are well aware. However, to worry about the status of didactic poetry is not just a modern preoccupation. As a matter of fact, the Greeks and Romans themselves found the combination of poetry and teaching problematic, at least from a theoretical perspective. For the most part, such poems as Hesiod's *Works and Days*, Empedocles' *On Nature*, and Vergil's *Georgics* were not regarded as constituting a genre in their own right, but rather as belonging to epic, with which they shared the hexameter. Aristotle, however, perceived a striking difference (*Poet.* 1447^{b}13–20): unlike, for example, the Homeric poems, Empedocles' text was not 'mimetic' and therefore, according to Aristotle's definition, could not be called poetry at all. Later critics tried to revoke this verdict and define didactic as a specific type of poetry after all, but a general consensus was never reached and didactic poetry continued to be a 'Problem der Poetik' long after antiquity.[2]

In this book, I approach the same problem, but from a different point of view. Instead of asking, How does didactic poetry fit into a given definition of poetry? or How can poetry and didacticism be reconciled?, I examine a number of Latin poems commonly labelled didactic in order to see what they themselves have to say about their status as poetry. My goal is to uncover the *poetics* of these texts,[3] specifically the ways in which they construct the relationship of poetic form and didactic content, of *carmen* and *res*.[4] The reason why I think this endeavour will be fruitful is the observation that didactic poetry—this marginalized and supposedly 'unpoetic' genre—is in fact especially self-consciously 'poetic'. Didactic poems typically present themselves explicitly as poetry and often show a

[2] See the title of Fabian 1968. A more detailed discussion of theoretical approaches to didactic poetry in antiquity will follow in Sect. 2.1.

[3] In current literary studies, the word 'poetics' is used in a number of different senses (see Brogan 1993: 929–30). Originally referring to the 'study or theory of poetry', it can also be employed to mean the 'theory of poetry implicit in a given text'. Thus, when I speak of the 'poetics' of a certain poem, I mean 'what the poem has to say about its being poetry or about poetry in general'.

[4] See the quotation from Manilius used as the epigraph to the book. Note that my association of poetry with form and didacticism with content is nothing more than a convenient shorthand in talking about the relationship of poem and subject matter and that I do not wish to imply that my texts generally present the relationship of *carmen* and *res* in these terms.

high degree of metapoetic reflection. The first-person speaker or persona of these texts, who is always clearly identified as the poet, is usually very prominent and almost never fails to comment on his role as the creator of the poem, often at great length. This self-referential tendency is a characteristic of didactic poetry rarely remarked upon in scholarship and one that I think is worth investigating.

I have chosen to focus on Lucretius' *De rerum natura*, Vergil's *Georgics*, Ovid's *Ars amatoria* and *Remedia amoris*, and Manilius' *Astronomica* as representatives of didactic poetry as a whole, in particular because these works constitute an important phase in the history of the genre. Lucretius' *De rerum natura*, a monumental work of a length unparalleled in earlier Greek and Latin didactic poetry (see Toohey 1996: 10 and 87–8), started a fashion in Latin poetry. Vergil's *Georgics* reacts to the Lucretian model, while the poems of Ovid and Manilius in turn show themselves influenced by both Lucretius and Vergil. A comparison of these works is thus especially rewarding for the very reason that each of them is meant to be held against its predecessor(s). Furthermore, the fact that, with the exception of the less popular *Astronomica*, the chosen poems are some of the best-known classics of Latin literature should add to the general interest of the inquiry.

Before examining the single texts in detail (Chapters 3–6 deal respectively with Lucretius, Vergil, Ovid, and Manilius), I provide in the first two chapters an introduction to some issues that I think are of importance for the investigation of the poetics of didactic poetry. In Chapter 1, I discuss typical characteristics of what I call self-conscious poems, that is, poems that present themselves explicitly as poetry. While this more theoretical treatment will at first appear to have little to do with my main topic, the insights gained from it will ultimately be crucial to the interpretation of the texts. Chapter 2 will survey the theory and practice of didactic poetry up to Lucretius and will attempt to arrive at a working definition of the didactic genre.

One point that I wish to stress already here is that in trying to assess the role attributed to poetry within the didactic process, I shall stay firmly on the level of the text. I shall examine what the single texts, that is, their first-person speakers, have to say, but I shall not draw inferences from this as to the intentions of the poems' actual authors. The vexed question of whether, for example, Vergil really wanted to teach farmers with his *Georgics* and how he himself viewed his role as didactic poet will not find an answer in my work; indeed, I remain sceptical as to whether problems of this kind can be solved in a satisfactory way. My approach is thus rather different from that of Effe 1977, which remains the best general treatment of ancient didactic poetry. Effe's famous distinction of three types of didactic poetry is explicitly based on the 'Intentionen der Autoren': if the author has the sincere intention to teach, the poem is 'sachbezogen'; if he uses his topic only as a pretext for verbal virtuosity, the poem is 'formal'; and if he pretends to teach one thing, but really wants to get across another, the poem is 'transparent' (1977: 26–39). This method falls prey both to the so-called intentional fallacy (where attitudes of a poem's persona are attributed to the author)[5] and to impressionistic subjectivity (where the author's 'hidden agenda' is 'reconstructed' by the interpreter), therefore failing, in my eyes, to add to the understanding of didactic poetry as a genre.

By contrast, my focus is not on the author and his reader (extra-textual), but on the speaker or persona and his addressee (intra-textual), and I shall strive to avoid mixing up these two separate categories, which are all too often confused in literary scholarship.[6] Thus limiting my interpretation to the world of the text, I do not wish to suggest that I generally regard poetry as in any way autonomous or cut off from its historical context (a point of view associated with scholarship in the tradition of New Criticism). I believe that in the case of ancient didactic poetry, as with any other type of literature, questions regarding the social, political, and cultural background are well worth asking (as are questions concerning the personality and intentions of the author). However, I myself do not feel confident to answer even the most basic questions of this kind, let alone offer new insights on the issues involved. For example, I do not presume to exactly place Vergil's *Georgics* within

---

[5] The term 'intentional fallacy' was coined by Wimsatt and Beardsley in their seminal 1946 article. While I cannot follow the authors in their radical exclusion of any consideration of historical context from the interpretation of literature, I shall certainly strive to adhere to their principle that '[w]e ought to impute the thoughts and attitudes of the poem immediately to the dramatic *speaker*, and if to the author at all, only by a biographical act of inference' (1946: 470). See also my discussion in Ch. 1, below.

[6] While I may, on occasion, not resist the temptation to speculate about the relationship between author and reader, I shall always clearly mark these forays into extra-textual territory.

Introduction

the so-called Augustan discourse (and allow myself to reserve some scepticism toward anyone who does), but I believe that I am competent to make pronouncements on the workings of Vergil's persona within the poem. As a result, this book does not deal with all interesting and relevant aspects of the didactic poems in question, just with certain ones.

As regards my use of critical terminology, my main goal in the following pages is to achieve both conceptual and linguistic clarity. I generally employ theoretical vocabulary not according to the jargon of any particular school, but in its 'common' sense, that is, in a way that I believe most literary scholars can immediately understand. I have tried to keep my terminology simple and to use Occam's Razor to eliminate unnecessary distinctions and subdivisions. Thus, for example, I employ the word 'poetry' the way most classicists do, that is, to refer to any λόγος ἔχων μέτρον (the definition of Gorgias, *Hel.* 9), despite the fact that nouns derived from the word ποιεῖν were used in this sense only from the fifth century and that earlier Greek verbal art, which was usually performed orally, is therefore perhaps more precisely described as 'song'.[7] Generally, I define all more controversial or ambivalent terms, not always when they first appear (this would have necessitated a host of footnotes already in the Introduction), but when they become central to the discussion.

Finally, as an aid to the reader, I have translated longer passages in Greek and Latin. I have tried to keep these translations as literal as possible, no doubt with the result that they often sound pedestrian. On more than one occasion, I have found that my translation simply cannot do justice to the complexity of the passage in question; in these cases, I refer the reader to my discussion in the main text, where I explore at greater length the ambivalences of a given quotation.

---

[7] See Ford 1992: 13–18 and *passim*; see also Kuhlmann 1906: 36–9 on the use of ποιητής in Greek. Note that I use 'text' likewise anachronistically.

1
'Tell Me, Muse': Characteristics of the Self-Conscious Poem

> Μουσάων Ἑλικωνιάδων ἀρχώμεθ' ἀείδειν.
>
> Hesiod, *Theogony*
>
> Therefore, my dear friend and companion, if you should think me somewhat sparing of my narrative on my first setting out,—bear with me,—and let me go on, and tell my story my own way:—or, if I should seem now and then to trifle upon the road,—or should sometimes put on a fool's cap with a bell to it, for a moment or two as we pass along,—don't fly off,—but rather courteously give me credit for a little more wisdom than appears upon my outside;—and as we jog on, either laugh with me, or at me, or in short, do any thing,—only keep your temper.
>
> Laurence Sterne, *The Life and Opinions of Tristram Shandy*

Almost everyone would intuitively agree that poetry is a kind of discourse distinct from ordinary, everyday speech.[1] However, where exactly the difference lies is not that easy to tell, and the question of the criterion by which to define the poetic has exercised critics since antiquity.[2] One approach is to conceive of poetry in purely formal terms. Thus, Gorgias declared, τὴν ποίησιν ἅπασαν καὶ νομίζω καὶ ὀνομάζω λόγον ἔχοντα μέτρον (*Hel.* 9; cf. Koster 1970: 22–4); that this connection of poetry and metre was perfectly commonplace in

---

[1] For my use of the word poetry, see the Introduction, above. Note that in the following survey of theoretical approaches to defining poetry, 'poetry' could often, and will sometimes, be glossed with 'literature', in the sense in which the term is used in modern philologies: 'English literature' means 'English novels, poems, plays, etc.', i.e., it refers to fictional writing; to the classicist, by contrast, any kind of written discourse usually qualifies as 'literature'. When it comes to ancient texts, 'literature' in the narrower sense is almost exclusively restricted to 'poetry' (discourse in verse), except for some comparatively late genres, such as the novel. Critics who have developed their theories apropos of modern forms of writing tend to speak of 'literature', but I believe that their approaches can be applied to ancient 'poetry', as well. Note that I have outlined some of the ideas developed in this chapter already in my article on Ovid's *Fasti* (Volk 1997), to which I shall from time to time refer.

[2] For the following discussion, see esp. Culler 1997: 18–42; see also Dalzell 1996: 12–18, esp. 17–18 and Dover 1997: 182–3, as well as the papers in Hernadi (ed.) 1978.

his time (and, we may surmise, throughout antiquity) becomes clear from Aristotle, who complains about οἱ ἄνθρωποι ... συνάπτοντες τῷ μέτρῳ τὸ ποιεῖν (*Poet.* 1447ᵇ13–14). In the twentieth century, the view that the *differentia specifica* of poetry can be located in formal characteristics, such as metre, formulas, or poetic language, was firmly put forward by structuralist critics, especially the Prague School. For example, Roman Jakobson in a famous article defined the poetic function of language as directedness toward the 'message', that is, the verbal sign itself (1960: esp. 353–6), and went on to discuss linguistic criteria for poetry.[3]

The formalist view of poetry was criticized already in antiquity. Its most prominent opponent was Aristotle, who regarded metre as a wholly unsatisfactory criterion and, taking up a concept found already in Plato (see esp. *Resp.* 3. 392c9–394c8), defined poetry as μίμησις (*Poet.* 1447ᵃ13–16). As is well known, this approach, too, has been extremely successful in the history of Western literary theory, even though modern critics often prefer to speak of fiction rather than mimesis, stressing not so much the fact that poetry imitates (Gk. μιμεῖσθαι) reality, but rather that in doing so, it creates (Lat. *fingere*) its own world.

It is obvious that both theories of what makes poetry special (or, to quote Jakobson 1960: 350, '[w]*hat makes a verbal message a work of art*') have much that speaks in their favour. As every reader knows, poems typically show certain formal characteristics, and they also usually exhibit the specific relationship to the extra-poetic reality that we call mimesis or fiction. However, as critics have pointed out, the same features can, and often do, apply to ordinary speech as well: if we do not want to label 'poetry' every utterance that accidentally takes the form of a verse or relates a made-up story, we are forced to admit that 'ordinary language' is not that ordinary after all, and our basis for the distinction between poetic and non-poetic discourse collapses (see Fish 1974; Pratt 1977: 38–78).

Still, we *know* that there is such a thing as poetry, and that it is somehow different from other forms of speech. In fact, this knowledge may turn out to be the best criterion available for a text's status as poetry (literature): a certain type of discourse is poetry because people regard it as poetry, and because they regard it as poetry, they will pay attention to certain formal characteristics or

---

[3] For a useful, though fiercely polemical, survey of structuralist theories of poetic language, see Pratt 1977: 3–37.

consider the story untrue. As Stanley Fish has phrased it, literature is 'language around which we have drawn a frame, a frame that indicates a decision to regard with a particular self-consciousness the resources language has always possessed' (1974: 24). In other words, poetry is an institution, a kind of speech that a society has marked as special, with special rules applying to its production and reception (see esp. Schmidt 1972). Obviously, this institution can be defined differently at different times and in different societies; thus, 'poetry' may be glossed for a certain context as 'divinely inspired song about gods and heroes', for another as 'carefully crafted piece of writing to delight an educated readership', and so on. The reason why I think it is useful to refer to these different manifestations with the same term 'poetry', is—apart from its convenience—the fact that, from a historical point of view, they all stand in the same tradition: at least since the fifth century BC, people have been talking about, and producing, 'poetry', even though they have meant quite different things by it.

This brief survey of different theories of poetry has brought us back to—and confirmed—the observation with which I started the chapter: poetry is a kind of speech that is set apart from ordinary discourse.[4] It is, to quote Stanley Fish again, language with a frame drawn around it. Typically, this frame is very clearly signalled. People recognize certain types of discourse as poetry, know the conventional markers that set this particular kind of speech apart. When at a public festival in Classical Athens a man holding a staff recited hexameters about the Trojan War, there was no way that the audience could have mistaken his words for, say, an eyewitness account at a jury court or a casual story told to friends. Likewise, when we pick up a book in the poetry section, we know that what we are going to read has a different status and functions according to different rules from, for example, the e-mail message that we received from a colleague yesterday. Poetry is different because people regard it as different, and they regard it as different because

---

[4] It must be stressed that this 'otherness' of poetry is not a concept unique to modern aesthetics, where a poem is viewed as an autonomous piece of art, but that it is characteristic also, and especially, of traditional and oral cultures. Compare the comments of Ruth Finnegan, who notes apropos of oral poetry that typically a 'poem is, as it were, italicised, set apart from everyday life and language' (1992: 25–8, at 25), and of Calvert Watkins (1995: 183), who in treating Indo-European poetics remarks that the 'total effect of all forms of poetic technique is going to be a *distancing* of the poetic message from ordinary human language' (here Watkins explicitly follows the Jakobsonian model).

there are certain markers that tell them to do so. These markers may include occasion (cult festivals, poetry readings), external form (books labelled 'poetry'), internal form (verse, poetic language), content (traditional stories, 'fiction'), and so on. Obviously there are always borderline cases (Jakobson 1960: 357 famously cites the American campaign slogan 'I like Ike'), but generally speaking, poetry is always recognized as such. Given this fact, however, two interestingly different possibilities open up: a poem (identified by its audience or readers as 'poetry', whatever it is that this means to them) can, in addition, explicitly present itself as poetry or, otherwise, choose not to draw attention to this fact. The former kind is what I have called the 'self-conscious poem', and it is to this phenomenon that I now finally turn.[5]

Consider, for example, the opening lines of Vergil's *Aeneid* and of Propertius' poem 1.1 respectively. The phrase *arma uirumque cano Troiae qui primus ab oris* not only identifies the content of the poem as 'arms and the man'; it also, with the help of the verb *cano*, clearly indicates that what we are reading is a poem and that the first-person speaker, who takes on the traditional role of the singing epic bard, is its poet. By contrast, *Cynthia prima suis miserum me cepit ocellis* gives no such indication, and neither does anything else in the poem; rather, the elegy styles itself as the genuine speech of the lovesick first person.

Now, obviously no one would be deceived into believing that Propertius 1.1 is not in fact a poem, but actually the real confession of an unhappy and tormented man. There are plenty of unmistakable signs that this is poetry, including the metre, the diction, and the fact that the elegy is found in a book which contains the works of Sextus Propertius, whom we know as a poet. As pointed out above, poetry is nearly always easily recognizable as such, and Propertius

[5] A note on terminology: I use 'self-conscious' to refer to poetry that explicitly identifies itself as poetry (as discussed in detail in the course of this chapter); a self-conscious poem is one that shows itself, as it were, 'aware' of its own being poetry. By contrast, I employ 'metapoetic' to describe any poetic utterance that I understand as making explicit or implicit reference to poetry, either to the particular poem or to poetry in general (thus, e.g., the Callimachean dictum οὐδὲ κελεύθῳ | χαίρω, τίς πολλοὺς ὧδε καὶ ὧδε φέρει (*Epigr.* 28. 1–2) can be taken as metapoetic, i.e., as implicitly making a comment about poetry). Finally, 'self-referential' denotes, not surprisingly, any utterance that refers to itself. Self-referentiality is not restricted to poetry, of course (neither, in fact, is self-consciousness; see below in the text), witness, e.g., the phrase 'I now come to the end' in speeches. There are obviously areas where 'self-conscious', 'metapoetic', and 'self-referential' overlap, and other scholars may employ these terms somewhat differently from the way I do, but I hope that my usage will be clear.

1. 1 is no exception. It differs from a work such as the *Aeneid* only in that the latter explicitly identifies itself as poetry and its speaker as the poet, whereas the elegy does not.[6] And it is poems that, like the *Aeneid*, show themselves to be 'aware' of their being poetry that are the subject of the following investigation.

Before we look more closely at some of the typical characteristics of the self-conscious poem, there is one question that arises from the preceding discussion. To talk about a poem that is 'self-conscious' or to ask what a poem 'has to say' is obviously a personification, a figure of speech convenient for any critic who, like me, wishes to avoid speaking of authorial intention. However, what I shall really examine in the following discussions of single texts, and what I have focused on in my short look at the two lines from Vergil and Propertius, are the utterances of the first-person speaker or persona. I use these two terms interchangeably to refer to a poem's 'I' (German scholarship poetically speaks of the *lyrisches Ich*), the fictional, intra-textual character who is understood as speaking the entire text of the poem, unless it is clearly indicated that he or she is reporting someone else's words.[7]

To ascribe the words of the poem's 'I' not to the actual author, but to a persona, has been customary in literary scholarship for a number of decades; however, it has never been uncontroversial.[8] Whoever wishes to identify a poem's speaker with its author can point first of all to the fact that to do so has been standard practice in literary scholarship since antiquity.[9] Thus, Plato and Aristotle,

---

[6] Note that lack of poetic self-consciousness does not mean lack of metapoetic potential (for the difference between self-conscious and metapoetic, see n. 5, above): there are many ways in which poems that do not explicitly present themselves as poetry can still be understood as implicitly commenting on their own being poetry and on poetry in general. Propertius 1. 1, for example, can be read as programmatic in terms of the speaker's role as not only an elegiac lover, but also an elegiac poet: it is a rule of the genre of love elegy that being a lover and being an elegist are presented as being just two aspects of the same way of life. Other methods of covert metapoetic reflection cannot be discussed here; as is well known, the phenomenon has been a popular topic in recent classical scholarship.

[7] Unlike some scholars, I will not use the term 'narrator' to refer to the speakers of the didactic poems I treat since I do not believe that these texts as wholes (as opposed to some of their parts, such as longer mythological digressions) can be classed as narratives. A narrative is typically the treatment of 'a chronological series of events caused or experienced by characters in a fictional world' (thus the definition in De Jong 1987 (glossary) of what narratologists refer to as the *fabula*), a description that does not apply to didactic poetry.

[8] For a survey of the history and fortune of the literary persona, see Elliott 1982; see also Clay 1998*b*: 13–16 on the discovery of the persona in classical scholarship.

[9] For the ancients' awareness (or, for the most part, lack thereof) of what we call the literary persona, see Clay 1998*b*.

for example, distinguish types of poetry in which 'the poet speaks' (as in dithyramb or the narrative parts of epic) from those where he introduces other speakers (as in drama or epic speeches).[10] In addition, the first person of a poem may even be identified with the author by name. Just within my small corpus of texts, for example, the speaker of the *Georgics* is called *Vergilius* at 4. 563, while the Ovidian *magister amoris* names himself *Naso* at *Ars amatoria* 2. 744; 3. 812; and *Remedia amoris* 71–2.[11]

The most compelling reason for the identification of author and persona, however, remains the fact that in a large number of poems, namely the ones that are 'self-conscious', the text itself makes this equation: *arma uirumque cano* unmistakably presents the speaker as the poet and thus invites the readers to understand that it is Vergil himself to whom they are listening.[12] However, readers know (and I believe that even the most naive readers do) that this invitation is treacherous: *persona*, after all, means 'mask', and masks can resemble the people who wear them or be completely different. There is no way to find out, if not backstage; and in the interpretation of ancient poetry, there is no backstage.

It therefore seems to me methodologically most sound to conduct my examination of poetry entirely on the level of the persona, without trying to look behind the mask. This is in my eyes the only way to make halfway verifiable claims in the field of literary interpretation in general; however, it is especially important in the field of poetics since the reconstruction of a self-conscious poem's 'idea of poetry' typically relies heavily on the first-person statements of the poet/persona.[13] Still, it should be stressed that the tendency of many poems to imply that their speakers are their actual authors is an important aspect of their poetic strategies, and one of which even the most 'anti-intentional' critics should at least

[10] Pl. *Resp.* 3. 392c9–394c8; Arist. *Poet.* 1448ᵃ20–4, 1460ᵃ5–11. Note Plato's very clear assessment of *Il.* 1–14: λέγει ... αὐτὸς ὁ ποιητὴς καὶ οὐδὲ ἐπιχειρεῖ ἡμῶν τὴν διάνοιαν ἄλλοσε τρέπειν, ὡς ἄλλος τις ὁ λέγων ἢ αὐτός (393a6–7). Cf. Clay 1998b: 23–8.

[11] Of earlier didactic poets, Nicander names himself at *Ther.* 957 and *Alex.* 629, while both Empedocles and Aratus may be hiding their names in puns (see Obbink 1993: 87–8 and n. 93 and Bing 1990)..

[12] By extension, even in the case of poems that are not self-conscious, readers have a tendency to automatically identify the persona with the author, unless there is a clear indication that the speaker is someone else.

[13] Note that while I use persona for the intra-textual character and author for the extra-textual historical figure, the term poet applies to both—even though I shall mostly employ it to denote the persona in his role as (purported) creator of the text.

be aware, even if they feel unable, as I do, to further investigate this relationship.

To return to poetic self-consciousness itself, it is obvious that poems can exhibit this feature to a greater or lesser degree. After the initial invocation to the Muse, the *Odyssey*, for example, does not explicitly mention its own status as divinely inspired song. The speaker of the *Iliad*, by contrast, returns to the Muses five more times (2. 484–93, 761–2; 11. 218–20; 14. 508–10; 16. 112–13) and on two occasions reflects on his own difficulties in telling the story (2. 485–6; 12. 176). Compared with the poem as a whole, these passages still do not amount to much. However, if we look at an epinician ode by Pindar or at Ovid's *Fasti*, we find that these poems dedicate significant space to the persona's talking about his poetic activity, with the result that this appears as one of the major concerns, if not as the most important topic, of the entire poem (see, specifically on the *Fasti*, Volk 1997).

Generally speaking, the use of poetic self-consciousness does not appear to be governed by fixed rules. Poems may or may not draw attention to their status as poetry (to do so is never necessary—a poem will always be recognized as such anyway), and they may do so more or less prominently. Nevertheless, there do appear to be certain tendencies, having to do with genre: some genres typically show poetic self-consciousness, others appear to discourage it. As has become clear from the short discussion of Propertius 1. 1, there are poems that try to give themselves the semblance of spontaneous real-life utterances and thus avoid drawing attention to their status as poetry. This is often true of shorter forms such as elegy or lyric, types of poems that purport to express their speakers' subjective feelings or attitudes.

By contrast, other genres stress that they are poetry, or song, because it is this very fact that gives them their cultural importance. This is typically the case for publicly performed choral lyric: Alcman's *Partheneion* or Pindar's victory odes (or, for that matter, Horace's *Carmen saeculare*) fulfil the function of being songs sung at a certain occasion where a song is called for. Not that what the song says is unimportant, but the most important thing is that it is a song, and it therefore highlights this fact.

Epic lies somewhere in the middle. Epic poems never fail to identify their speaker with the poet; however, they tend to keep their first person in the background and emphasize the story at the expense of the teller. This is what has been called 'epic objectivity', which does not, however, imply that the narrative cannot be focalized, that is, coloured by various points of view, including that of the narrator himself.[14]

As I have discussed extensively in my article on Ovid's *Fasti* (Volk 1997: 288–92), a text that presents itself explicitly as poetry and identifies its persona as the poet typically exhibits a further feature, which I have called *poetic simultaneity*. By this I mean the illusion that the poem is really only coming into being as it evolves before the readers' eyes, that the poet/persona is composing it 'as we watch'. Thus at the beginning of a poem, its composition is usually depicted as lying in the future or just about to begin:[15] the speaker of the Homeric epics asks the Muse to sing, which implies that the song is starting 'right now'; the *Homeric Hymns* often open with the announcement ἄρχομ' ἀείδειν (2. 1; 11. 1; 13. 1; 16. 1; 22. 1; 26. 1; 28. 1) or a verb in the future, such as ἄσομαι/ἀείσομαι (6. 2; 10. 1; 15. 1; 23. 1; 30. 1);[16] and Vergil's *arma uirumque cano*, with a verb in the present, implies a beginning just as much as Ovid's *tempora cum causis . . . | . . . canam* (*Fast.* 1. 1–2), with the same verb in the future.[17] At the end of a poem, the speaker may refer to the completion of his work, as the narrator of the *Metamorphoses* does in 15. 871–9: there, the phrase *iamque opus exegi* implies that the composition of the work is viewed as lying just about in the past; contrast the proem (1. 1–4), where to 'speak of shapes changed into new bodies' was only a wish of the speaker (*fert animus*, 1), and he asked the gods to assist his *coepta* (2), 'undertakings', literally 'beginnings'. Similarly, the narrator of Apollonius' *Argonautica* in 4. 1773–81 bids his heroes farewell since he is arriving at the end of their toils (ἤδη γὰρ ἐπὶ κλυτὰ πείραθ' ἱκάνω | ὑμετέρων καμάτων, 1775–6), and he imagines the future success of his song (1773–5).

---

[14] See De Jong 1987 on narrators and focalizers in the *Iliad*. The distinction between instances where the narrator's perspective, reactions, and opinions colour the narrative and those 'self-conscious' moments where he steps forward and identifies himself as the narrator/poet is very important and not always clearly drawn by scholars.

[15] Cf. Pfeijffer 1999: 33–43, specifically on Pindar.

[16] The *Homeric Hymns* probably functioned as real beginnings, or 'proems', in the performance of epic: they were the singers' more personal introductions that preceded the performance of the epic poems proper (see, e.g., Ford 1992: 23–31). Note that elsewhere in this book I use the word 'proem' more generally to refer to any kind of introduction to a poem.

[17] See Conte 1992: 147 on the liminal status of the proem: 'At the border between fully poetic speech and speech still outside of poetry, the proem—the preliminary announcement of a poem which follows—is already song and not yet song.'

In the course of a poem, too, the speaker may refer to the ongoing process of his composition. He can remind us of it only occasionally, as the speaker of the *Iliad* does in his internal invocations to the Muses (see above), especially at prominent moments such as the beginnings or ends of books, or in so-called 'proems in the middle' (such as *Aen.* 7. 37–45).[18] However, he can also choose to keep the readers aware of his poetic activity throughout the text. I have elsewhere tried to show this for Ovid's *Fasti*, where, as I have argued, the concentration on the speaker's production of the poem is so strong that 'what is usually called a poem on the Roman calendar might as well be described as a poem about a poet writing a poem about the Roman calendar' (Volk 1997: 291).

The *Fasti* may be an extreme example, but a large number of poems can be found that extensively exploit the concept of poetic simultaneity. Take, for example, Horace, *Odes* 1. 12 (*quem uirum aut heroa...*[19]). This poem praises a whole series of gods, demigods, and men, before culminating in the praise of Augustus, and for the first two-thirds of it, we are closely watching the poet/persona as he creates the song and following the choices that he makes. He begins by asking Clio 'which man or hero or god' his song will celebrate (1–3); after remaining unclear about his subject matter for the first three stanzas, he starts treating individual gods (13–24), demigods (25–32), and finally men (from 32), always reflecting on what he is doing. With the help of expressions like *quid prius dicam* (13), *neque te silebo* (21), *dicam* (25), and *Romulum post hos prius an quietum | Pompili regnum memorem an superbos | Tarquini fascis, dubito, an Catonis | nobile letum* (33–6), the drama of the poem's composition is unfolding before the readers' eyes.

A specific point that becomes apparent from *Odes* 1. 12 is that poetic simultaneity is not necessarily (in fact, only rarely) used consistently throughout a poem: in the last third of the text, the speaker no longer talks about his producing a song, but refers directly to his subject matter (the objects of his song no longer appear as accusatives, together with verbs of speaking in the first person, but rather as nominatives governing their own verbs). It is

---

[18] On proems in the middle as a typical place for metapoetic reflection in Alexandrian and Roman poetry, see Conte 1992.

[19] As is well known, this beginning is modelled on Pindar (*Ol.* 2. 1–2), to whom the poem may also in part owe its general stance of poetic self-consciousness.

quite common for the impression of simultaneity to lapse in the course of a poem: many poems have self-conscious proems; far fewer have epilogues.

Also, poetic simultaneity is hardly ever a case of cut-and-dried realism. Only rarely is the speaker convincingly presented as in the process of composing the poem for the duration of the entire text. For instance, the notion of the text as a finished, written object may come into conflict with the illusion that the poem is coming into existence—being sung—only right now. This is the case in the proem to *Fasti* 1, for example, where the speaker presents his work, paradoxically, both as a completed book that he dedicates to Germanicus and as a project on which he is embarking right now and for which he enlists Germanicus' help.[20]

Conversely, the notion of poetic simultaneity is so powerful that it can be used even when it is, logically speaking, inappropriate. Thus, Horace, *Odes* 3. 30 (*exegi monumentum aere perennius*), occurring at the end of the jointly published first three books of *Odes*, gives the impression of being spoken as the end of a unified, self-conscious poem characterized by poetic simultaneity, while in reality it is the last of a collection of clearly distinct and widely varying texts, few of which show poetic self-consciousness at all. Vergil's *Eclogues* present an even more striking case. The work is characterized by a multitude of voices; after all, half the poems are spoken by divers dramatic characters, who are often poets in their own right and perform songs, but who are not the poets of the songs in which they themselves appear. Despite this somewhat anarchic situation (note also that the work does not have a proem that would clarify matters), there sometimes emerges a persona who lays claim to being, as it were, the master poet and who pretends to have been singing what we have been listening to all along. Thus, for example, the famous opening of *Eclogues* 4, *Sicelides Musae, paulo maiora canamus!*, shows the speaker in the middle of the process of producing poetry, implying that the part at which we have now arrived will be somewhat 'grander' than what has preceded. Note also *Eclogues* 10, which the persona clearly presents as the conclusion of a work that has supposedly been going on for some time (see esp.

---

[20] See Volk 1997: 291–2, with further examples, as well as now Wheeler 1999: 44–8 (though I cannot agree with the author's contention that the *Fasti* generally presents itself as written text, in contrast to the supposed oral nature of the *Metamorphoses*). On the importance of 'orality' for the concept of poetic simultaneity, see below.

extremum hunc, Arethusa, mihi concede laborem, 1 and *haec sat erit, diuae, uestrum cecinisse poetam*, 70).

Poetic simultaneity thus turns out to be a pervasive concept in ancient poetry. In fact, it is so common that readers hardly notice it, and critics, too, generally fail to remark on it (though note the literature quoted in n. 29). Often, it is no more than a topos, a literary convention without larger consequence. However, it can also be employed to great effect, and especially poems that are very self-conscious and have a strong metapoetic tendency avail themselves of this feature. It is therefore worth while to enquire further into the nature of this poetic technique and to try to understand its origin and historical development.

Looking once more at the first line of the *Aeneid*, it is obvious, as mentioned above, that the poet/persona presents himself as a singer (*cano*), despite the fact that Vergil certainly composed his epic in writing and that, when the *Aeneid* was performed orally, it was read out or recited, not sung. The topos of the poet as singer is, of course, perfectly familiar and persists into modern times, and as has become clear from the preceding discussion, poetic simultaneity typically works along these same lines: the poem that is coming into being as it evolves is conceived of as a song *sung* by the poet; we are hardly ever given the impression that we are looking over the poet's shoulder as he is *writing*. The mention of writing usually occurs in reference to the already finished book and is thus not easily reconcilable with the notion of poetic simultaneity.[21]

The poet as a singer who in performing his song is creating it, composing it as he goes along—this is the scenario implied by poetic simultaneity, and a scenario that will sound oddly familiar to many classicists, especially Hellenists. With the same words I could have described the famous Parry–Lord theory of oral poetry, which revolutionized Homeric studies and according to which the oral poetry from which the Homeric poems arose was characterized by the simultaneity of composition and performance. To quote Lord

---

[21] One of the few examples of a reference to writing in the context of poetic simultaneity is Lucr. 1. 24–6, *te* [sc. *Venerem*] *sociam studeo scribendis uersibus esse | quos ego de rerum natura pangere conor | Memmiadae nostro* (see Sect. 3.2, below). Both the gerundive *scribendis* and the verb *conor* show that the speaker is only just starting on his poem. Another instance is Ov. *Fast.* 1. 93, *haec ego cum sumptis agitarem mente tabellis*, where the mention of the writing tablets has the main purpose of evoking the passage in Callimachus' *Aetia* prologue on which this scene is modelled (see Volk 1997: 295–6). Generally on 'singing' v. 'writing' in Greek and esp. Latin poetry, see Lowrie 1997: 55–70 (in the context of a discussion of Horace's *Odes*).

1960: 13, 'composition and performance are two aspects of the same moment'; therefore, an 'oral poem is not composed *for* but *in* performance'.

If what poetic simultaneity evokes is the composition-cum-performance of oral poetry, it is most reasonable to assume that this very traditional feature (found already in the *Iliad*) in fact originally goes back to oral poetry. In an oral performance, poetic simultaneity is not a topos, but a fact: the speaker's references to his ongoing singing are literally true, just as the speaker himself is not a persona, but the actual performer/poet. Once poetry ceases to be composed in performance, however, poetic simultaneity, with its traditional features, such as invocations to the Muses, turns into a mere literary convention.[22] Thus, those kinds of statements that originally served to refer to the actual external performance situation come to be used instead to create a fictive internal performance situation, a little intra-textual drama of the poet/persona's performing the song.[23]

As classicists, we are never interpreting an oral composition-cum-performance, but always texts, whatever exactly their origin, into whose making must have gone some of the premeditation involved in writing. I therefore suggest that in treating poetic simultaneity (and self-referential statements in general), we always regard it as a fiction, just as it seems reasonable to me to speak always of the persona, and not of the author. It should be noted, however, that while this principle might appear obvious to scholars dealing with Hellenistic or Latin literature, it becomes more controversial once we turn to the criticism of Archaic Greek poetry. After all, in this period, poetry was typically still performed (if not composed) orally, and critics therefore have an understandable interest in the aspects of a text's performance. Still, I would hold that it is difficult, if not impossible, to reconstruct a poem's performance situation on the basis of its self-referential statements. Even if a text was originally composed in performance, and its self-

---

[22] See Albis 1996: 8–9 on the convention of invoking the Muse(s) at the beginning of a poem: 'Even much later in the history of Greek literature, when poetry was no longer orally composed, inspiration was still associated with performance. When a poet invokes his Muse, he creates the impression that he is just then embarking on the process of composition, since divine inspiration is conventionally a necessary prerequisite for starting a poem' (9).

[23] Note that in principle, self-referential statements need not be literally true in the situation of composition-cum-performance either: even the actually performing poet can create a fictive speech situation.

referential statements were literally true, once it is reperformed, the self-referential statements come to refer to a fictive, internal performance situation.[24] If, as we have to assume for the majority of Archaic Greek poems, a text is composed in advance in order to be orally performed, there are two possibilities. One option is for the poet to devise the internal performance situation in such a way as to make it resemble as closely as possible the supposed external performance situation. He can do so by being very general in all his references to the singing of the song and its circumstances. Thus, in a song to be performed at a symposium, references to the ongoing drinking and the friendship among those present will almost surely be appropriate and make the song applicable to any similar situation (see Rösler 1983: 18–20). Conversely, the poet can try to be as specific as possible in his attempt to match the internal and external performance situations. This is possible, of course, only if information about the particulars of the performance situation is available beforehand.[25] Consider the case of choral lyric, specifically the kind where self-referential first-person statements are spoken in the voice of the chorus, such as the *partheneia* of Alcman and Pindar.[26] As Mary Lefkowitz has shown (1991: 11–25), texts of this kind abound in information about the ongoing performance, including references to such features as dress and choreography. To make his words fit the facts, the poet must have a detailed knowledge of the projected performance, if not in fact be himself involved in devising it.

However, the poet may instead decide not to have the internal performance situation match the external one and thus to stress its status as fiction. This, I would argue, is the case with the epinician odes of Pindar and Bacchylides, and it is already apparent from the

---

[24] Thus, to take a very simple example, Theognis 1. 943–4, ἐγγύθεν αὐλητῆρος ἀείσομαι ὧδε καταστὰς | δεξιός, ἀθανάτοις θεοῖσιν ἐπευχόμενος, which may originally have been an *ex tempore* composition-cum-performance at a symposium, can easily be reperformed even by someone standing left of the piper or without musical accompaniment—the listeners will automatically regard these words as a fiction. See also Nagy 1996: 59–86 on reperformance of the Homeric poems as a kind of re-enactment in which the rhapsode takes over the role of 'Homer', i.e., of the poem's 'I'.

[25] I here ignore the possibility of improvisation during performance, always a given, esp. in less formal settings.

[26] On the difference between the choral 'I' and the poet's 'I', see Lefkowitz 1991: 1–71. Note that texts of this kind exhibit a rather special kind of poetic self-consciousness not hitherto considered: they explicitly present themselves as poetry, but the speaker is not the poet, but the performer(s).

fact that these songs were, as is generally believed, performed not by the poet himself, but by a chorus, or otherwise a *komos*,[27] while (unlike in the *partheneia* discussed above) all self-referential first-person statements refer to the poet and his composition-cum-performance. Furthermore, the persona describes the process of creating the song in a way that is clearly unrealistic, positively fantastic. Take a famous passage from Pindar (*Ol.* 6. 22–8), where the speaker asks to be driven on the winner's mule chariot through the 'gates of hymns' (27), along the 'pure road' (23), to Pitane (28), a destination glossed as the 'origin of men' (24–5), that is, of the Iamidae. While the chariot is a real object and Pitane a real place, the 'gates of hymns', 'pure road', and 'origin of men' clearly belong to the realm of poetry alone. It is only inside the song that the poet goes on such a fantastic chariot ride (on this image, see more below); the real performance situation, whatever its particulars, will obviously have been wholly different.

Once oral performance has lost its importance and poetry is mainly written for readers, poetic simultaneity can no longer even attempt to refer to a real situation. Any reference to the speaker's composition-cum-performance is clearly recognized as fictive: everyone knows that, for example, the *cano* in *Aeneid* 1. 1 is just a topos. Without any real connection to the actual conditions of the poem's composition and reception, poetic simultaneity turns into a sophisticated metapoetic technique, employed by authors who wish to present their poems as self-conscious works of art. It may even be argued that it is in a literate culture, where poetry is mainly read, that poetic simultaneity comes to be used most extensively. In the case of purely oral composition-cum-performance, there is no real need to refer to the ongoing process of the poet's singing, even though the individual artist may choose to do so, especially at crucial moments in the course of the performance. However, once a *writer* wishes to create the illusion that the poem is only coming into being (through the agency of the poet/persona) as it is unfolding before the readers' eyes, he or she must make a much greater effort to establish this fictive situation and keep it up throughout the book.[28] For example, Apollonius' *Argonautica*, a typically 'bookish'

---

[27] On the controversy over 'Who sang Pindar's Victory Odes?', see the (necessarily partial) survey in Lefkowitz 1995. As will become clear from the following, I am extremely sceptical as to whether this question can be answered on the basis of the texts.

[28] We may compare the use of addresses to the audience; Finnegan 1992: 118 notes that

Hellenistic poem, not only exhibits poetic simultaneity, but, as Robert Albis has shown, specifically attempts to recreate the performance situation of Archaic Greek epic: Apollonius is striving to give the impression 'that his studied poetry is composed spontaneously and that this composition constitutes a performance'.[29] As a result of this, however, the *Argonautica* ends up a far more self-conscious poem than the Homeric epics that are its model, and it is the speaker's loquaciousness about his poetic activity and his very posing as an inspired bard that make it all too clear to which period the poem really belongs. Poetic simultaneity may have its roots in the most archaic oral poetry; however, it flourishes in the sophisticated and learned written literatures of a later age. To utter *cano* smacks of the *uates*; but it is also a trademark of the *poeta doctus*.

I wish finally to have a look at some of the imagery typically associated with poetic simultaneity. The metaphors I shall discuss are extremely archaic, but like poetic simultaneity in general, come to enjoy special popularity in Hellenistic and Roman times, and they remain topoi throughout the Middle Ages and beyond. Poetic simultaneity means to conceive of poetry as a process, a lengthy activity undertaken by the poet (whom we are watching), with a clear beginning and an end. An image that suggests itself—that is, in fact, already implicit in my use of the word 'process'—is that of a journey: during his composition-cum-performance, the poet travels on a certain route or along a path. 'Path of song' appears to be the meaning of οἴμη, used three times in the *Odyssey* (8. 74, 481; 22. 347) to refer to 'a specific epic tale';[30] note also Hesiod, *Works and*

---

these are rather uncommon in oral poetry. This might appear surprising, but then, in an oral performance, it is always clear that the poet is performing for an audience, at which his words are directed. By contrast, the reason why, e.g., didactic poetry typically abounds in direct addresses to the student(s) (see Sect. 2.2, below) is precisely the fact that the entire teacher–student constellation is a fiction that is *constituted*, not reflected, by these repeated addresses.

[29] Albis 1996: 10; see ch. 1 *passim*. Albis comes close to a treatment of the phenomenon that I call poetic simultaneity (when I wrote my article on the *Fasti*, the book was not yet known to me), but, since he focuses exclusively on Apollonius, he does not take account of the wider implications of his argument. The same is true for Wheeler who, in his narratological study of the *Metamorphoses*, observes that 'Ovid presents his poem as a fictive viva-voce performance' (1999: 3), apparently without realizing that many other (esp. epic) poems work along the same lines. Cf. also Pfeijffer (1999: 34) who aptly writes about Pindar that he is 'at pains to create the illusion that his odes take shape at the very spot, fictionally representing the process of composition'.

[30] The etymology of οἴμη is unclear, but it appears reasonable to connect it with οἶμος 'path' (itself of obscure etymology), which is first used metapoetically in *Hymn. Hom. Merc.* 451 (οἶμος ἀοιδῆς); see Chantraine 1968–80 and Frisk 1960–72 s.vv. οἴμη and οἶμος.

Days 659, με . . . λιγυρῆς ἐπέβησαν ἀοιδῆς [sc. *Μοῦσαι*], and the phrase μεταβήσομαι ἄλλον ἐς ὕμνον in the transitional (!) formula at the end of a number of *Homeric Hymns*. The use of the path metaphor (not only as an image for poetry, but also in other contexts) in Archaic and Classical Greek literature was studied extensively by Otfried Becker in his monograph *Das Bild des Weges* (1937), and Marcello Durante (1958), in particular, has demonstrated that to picture the poetic process as a journey is a concept that goes back to Indo-European times.

The examples from Homer and Hesiod just quoted imply that the poet is travelling the path of song on foot. However, it is more common to picture the poetic journey as either a chariot ride or a sea voyage. Both images can be shown to be extremely old (see Durante 1958: 8–10 for Vedic parallels); they also remain popular throughout antiquity and into modern times. Since these metaphors are familiar to classicists and have been treated extensively by other scholars, there is no need for me to discuss them in detail.[31] I wish simply to demonstrate, with the help of two examples, how journey metaphors go together with poetic simultaneity and by their nature tend to bolster the illusion that the creation of the poem is an ongoing process. The first is a famous passage in Pindar's *Pythian* 4, where, in the middle of recounting the story of Jason's winning the Golden Fleece, the speaker interrupts himself with the words,

> μακρά μοι νεῖσθαι κατ' ἀμαξιτόν· ὥρα γὰρ συνάπτει· καί τινα
> οἶμον ἴσαμαι βραχύν.
>
> (247–8)

(It is far for me to travel on the road, for time is pressing, and I know some short path.)

While on his poetic journey, the poet suddenly decides to change his route and take a short cut: he summarizes the remaining story of Jason and Medea only very briefly (this is the οἶμος βραχύς) in order

---

[31] In addition to Becker 1937 and Durante 1958, see now esp. Asper 1997: 21–107 (with special focus on Callimachus) and the comprehensive treatment of Nünlist 1998: 228–83. See in addition Giannisi 1997 for the idea of 'speech as progress' in Greek culture; Kuhlmann 1906: 20–2 and 24–6 for a collection of Greek passages; Ford 1992: 40–8 on the 'topical poetics' of Homer; Steiner 1986: 76–86 on the path metaphor in Pindar; Wimmel 1960: 103–11 on the 'Symbolgruppen des Weges' in Callimachus and his Roman followers; Norden 1891: 274–6 specifically on the chariot metaphor; and Lieberg 1969 and Curtius 1948: 136–8 on seafaring imagery.

to move on quickly to his new topic. All this goes on in plain view, as it were, of the audience or reader: a true instance of poetic simultaneity.

My second example involves the ship metaphor and comes from a text wholly different from the Pindaric ode just cited. At the end of the first book of Ovid's *Ars amatoria*, the speaker signals a break:

> pars superat coepti, pars est exhausta laboris;
> hic teneat nostras ancora iacta rates.
>
> (1. 771–2)

(Part of the undertaken task remains, part is over. Let the thrown anchor detain our ships here.)

The poet is halfway finished with his voyage, that is, with his poem, and stops for a moment on the open sea. Shortly afterward, he cautions the young man, his student in the art of love, that they have completed only half their journey:

> quid properas, iuuenis? mediis tua pinus in undis
> nauigat, et longe, quem peto, portus abest.
>
> (2. 9–10)

(Why are you hurrying, young man? Your ship is sailing in the middle of the waves, and the port to which I am steering is far away.)

Again, the poem's coming into being is portrayed as an ongoing process that the reader is following: the middle of the work is the middle of the poet's journey.[32]

It is interesting to note that the connection of poetry and travelling may go back to the close association of the two in magical, specifically shamanistic, practice. Over sixty years ago, Karl Meuli argued in a fascinating article (Meuli 1935) that epic poetry arose from the songs and narratives with which shamans in different cultures accompany the toilsome and adventurous journeys (often to the Underworld) that they experience once having fallen into a trance. Certain story patterns found in traditional narratives, especially those concerning heroes who travel to fabulous lands in order to fulfil some task, might thus reflect the original shamanistic journey and journey narrative (Meuli 1935: 164–76).

For this primeval notion that travelling and singing or story-

---

[32] On these Ovidian passages, see also the discussion below in Sect. 5.2.

telling are at some level connected, we may compare Bruce Chatwin's book *The Songlines*, which explores the myths of the Australian Aborigines that 'tell of the legendary totemic beings who had wandered over the continent in the Dreamtime, singing out the name of everything that crossed their path—birds, animals, plants, rocks, waterholes—and so singing the world into existence' (1987: 2). Modern-day Aborigines still go on journeys along these Songlines, resinging the original songs of their Ancestors, which are inexorably linked to their invisible tracks across the landscape of Australia (see Finnegan 1992: 116). It is not that the song describes the journey, but that the journey and the song are one.

Having come this far in our exploration of the self-conscious poem, it is time to leave the area of general poetics and to turn, more specifically, to didactic poetry. However, I wish to end this chapter by pointing out that the discussed features—'self-consciousness', 'simultaneity', and the use of journey metaphors—are by no means restricted to poetry, but can be found in different genres of prose as well, and even in everyday speech. Take, for example, this book: it is clearly self-conscious, that is, I have on numerous occasions explicitly drawn attention to the fact that this is a book and that I am the one writing it. As the sentence at the beginning of this paragraph shows, the text also operates along the lines of simultaneity and even uses a watered-down version of the journey metaphor ('having come this far'; 'it is time to leave'). None of this will strike the reader as out of the ordinary; in fact, he or she will be wholly familiar with rhetorical strategies of this kind. Not surprisingly, the same features regularly appear in Greek and Roman prose: speeches, for example, are often highly self-conscious and use self-referential statements to create the impression of simultaneity ('I now come to the end'; note also that Greek and Roman orators did not use scripts, which made the illusion of composition-cum-performance even more convincing[33]); the driest prose treatises exhibit simultaneity ('having discussed *x*, I now come

---

[33] It is interesting to note that in order to deliver long speeches without written notes, orators used a memorization technique that itself involved a mental movement through space (see Yates 1966: 1–26; Giannisi 1997: 139 and n. 20). As discussed, e.g., by Quintilian (*Inst.* 11. 2. 17–22), the speaker would in his imagination place the single details he wished to remember in certain places, e.g., inside a familiar house. In order to recall them in order, he would then have to 'walk' through this imagined location and 'pick them up'. Thus, to quote Frances Yates, '[w]e have to think of the ancient orator as moving in imagination through his memory building *whilst* he is making his speech, drawing from the memorised places the images he has placed on them' (1966: 3).

to *y*');[34] speech or narrative is often pictured as a movement in space;[35] and even the fancy chariot and ship metaphors are applied to prose as well as poetry.[36]

However, the fact that self-consciousness, simultaneity, and certain types of imagery are not unique to poetry does not, I believe, make them less interesting for the study of poetics. After all, many figures of thought and speech can be found in both poetic and non-poetic discourse (as pointed out at the beginning of the chapter, it may not even be possible to distinguish between poetry and non-poetry on purely formal grounds), and the crucial difference is simply the way in, and purpose to, which they are employed. To begin a text with 'In this book I examine the poetics of didactic poetry' makes it a self-conscious scholarly monograph; to start 'I sing of arms and the man' renders it a self-conscious poem.

---

[34] See Fuhrmann 1960: 28, 57, 69, 77–8, 97–8, 120–1, 142 and n. 2, and index s.v. 'Überleitungsformeln'.

[35] See Durante 1958: 3–4; Becker 1937: 101–16 (on the 'Weg des λόγος' in Herodotus). Compare in English the use of dead metaphors like 'come to', 'go over', 'leave aside', etc. to refer to speech.

[36] See Norden 1891: 274–5 (chariot) and Curtius 1948: 137 (ship).

2
'Improbable Art': The Theory and Practice of Ancient Didactic Poetry

> nam quam uaria sint genera poematorum, Baebi,
> quamque longe distincta alia ab aliis, nosce.
>
> <div align="right">Accius, <i>Didascalica</i></div>

> ἀλλὰ τορῶς ταῦτ' ἴσθι, θεοῦ πάρα μῦθον ἀκούσας.
>
> <div align="right">Empedocles, <i>On Nature</i></div>

The previous chapter treated a number of questions of general poetics that will be central to my discussion of the individual didactic poems in the later parts of this book. However, before the theoretical insights on the workings of self-conscious poetry can be applied to the interpretation of single texts, another preliminary question remains to be considered. Given that the topic of the book is the poetics of Latin didactic poetry, it seems reasonable to determine beforehand what didactic poetry is and how it is to be defined for the present purpose. Unfortunately, this is easier said than done. Trying to define didactic poetry takes us into the wild and dangerous territory of genre criticism, on a journey that is long and difficult, not only because the generic status of didactic was and is controversial, but also because it is not at all clear what we ought to understand by genre in the first place.

Genre appears to be a kind of necessary evil of literary criticism, classical scholarship included.[1] It is an immensely useful concept, employed widely by scholars as a way of differentiating among types of literature, that is, of understanding what connects, or distinguishes, individual texts. However, it is difficult to describe in theoretical terms what genre is, and it is next to impossible, on a more practical level, to draw up a comprehensive list of genres, define them, and distribute given pieces of literature among them. Even if such an experiment were restricted only to a very limited

---

[1] See the reasoned discussion in Dalzell 1996: 3–7. For the history of genre criticism, see Genette 1977; Dubrow 1982: 45–104; and Garber, Orsini, and Brogan 1993.

period of literary history, it is unlikely that any two scholars would agree on the exact distribution, let alone the definitions of individual genres. What they would all agree on, however, is that there is such a thing as genre and that it plays an important role in the production and reception of literature.

One of the main problems with genre is that 'built into its ways of working are difficulties that have ultimately to do with a version of the hermeneutic circle: how can we choose specific works from which to draw a definition of, say, epic . . . unless we already know what an epic is?' (Garber, Orsini, and Brogan 1993: 456). It is therefore inevitable that my discussion of the genre of ancient didactic poetry should describe a similar circular movement: the following observations that lead to a definition of didactic poetry would not be possible if I did not already believe that there was such a thing as the didactic genre and that it comprised a certain corpus of texts with certain characteristics. Additionally, since it seems impossible to define the didactic genre without first deciding what a genre is, I shall in the following also provide at least a working definition of genre; however, I would hardly be able to do so if I did not already have some concept of genre—which in turn is inevitably influenced by my thoughts about the specific genre in question, that is, didactic poetry. In the course of this chapter—in which I move from ancient views of didactic poetry and of genre in general (Sect. 2.1) to my definition of didactic poetry and of genre in general (Sect. 2.2), in order to then look at the historical development of the didactic genre (Sect. 2.3) and, finally, enquire into the way in which didactic poetry might have been perceived by poets and readers in the first century BC/early first century AD (Sect. 2.4)—I shall, by necessity, occupy various positions in the Hermeneutic Circle, in the hope that this procedure will ultimately lead to an increase of insight, instead of turning into a *circulus vitiosus*.

2.1. Ancient Views of Didactic Poetry

Starting from the assumption, shared by the majority of classicists, that there are literary genres and that Greek and Latin didactic poetry (that is, a certain body of texts[2]) constitutes one of them, it

---

[2] Apart from the Latin poems treated in this book and a large number of contemporary and later texts, which I shall not discuss (see Effe 1977 for a treatment of many of these lesser-known poems), the following works typically appear in a canon of didactic poetry: Hesiod's

seems a reasonable approach for a historically minded scholar to ask what the Greeks and Romans themselves had to say about this particular category. In order to arrive at an answer to this question, however, it is first necessary to enquire briefly into ancient views of genre in general since any given definition of didactic poetry can be understood only in the context of the more universal ideas of types of literature that underlie it. Now, ancient ideas of genre are no more unified than their modern counterparts.[3] For the most part, the Greeks and Romans, like many scholars today, appear to have regarded the distribution of individual literary texts among various categories more as a convenience than as a phenomenon worthy of theoretical investigation.[4] Thus, many writers throughout antiquity operate with such generic terms as epic, elegy, and tragedy in the same way that modern classicists do, that is, without reflecting overly much on the exact definitions of these categories. If these 'common sense' poetic genres are defined at all, it is first and foremost by their metres: thus, epic is written in hexameters, elegy in elegiacs, tragedy (mostly) in trimeters, and so on.[5] A second common criterion is content: epic, for example, is typically regarded as dealing with heroes and gods, 'kings and battles'. And third, a genre typically has a founder, a *primus inuentor*, who becomes the model imitated, and often explicitly invoked, by his successors (see Rosenmeyer 1985: 81–2). A nice combination of all three criteria is found in Horace's little overview of genres and their metres in *Ars poetica* 73–85; to demonstrate this, I quote just the first two lines, on epic (73–4):

Works and Days, the philosophical poems of Parmenides and Empedocles, Aratus' *Phaenomena*, and Nicander's *Theriaca* and *Alexipharmaca*.

[3] On ideas of genre in antiquity, see Rossi 1971; Russell 1981: 148–58; Rosenmeyer 1985; Conte and Most 1996; and, specifically on theories of epic, Koster 1970, as well as the literature cited in n. 1, above.

[4] See Conte and Most 1996: 631: 'Theory of genre as such is quite lacking in antiquity'; see also Russell 1981: 148–9.

[5] The Greek and Latin poets listed by Quintilian, *Inst*. 10. 1. 46–72 and 85–100 are ordered according to their metres, and Steinmetz 1964: esp. 455–9 traces this method of classifying poetry back to Alexandrian scholarship. The practice of defining genres by their metres must, however, be much older (see Steinmetz 1964: 462 and n. 8). It appears to be related to the view that poetry as a whole can be defined as discourse in verse (see the beginning of Ch. 1, above); if metre is the criterion of poetry in general, then it makes sense that individual genres should be recognized by individual metres. Cf. Koster 1970: 22–4, who, however, attributes this theory specifically to Gorgias; it seems more likely to me that it was a widely held, non-specialist view.

res gestae regumque ducumque et tristia bella [*content*]
quo scribi possent numero [*metre*], monstrauit Homerus [*founder*].

(Homer showed in what metre the deeds of kings and generals and grim wars might be treated.)[6]

This approach to defining poetic genres was certainly the most common way of conceiving of different kinds of texts in antiquity.[7] However, it was not the only one. As mentioned in Chapter 1, Plato and Aristotle famously distinguished three types of poetry: one where the poet himself speaks (exemplified by Plato, to the consternation of modern scholars, with the obscure genre of the dithyramb), a second where individual characters speak (as in tragedy and comedy), and a third, mixed, type (epic of the Homeric kind).[8] This division of poetry according to the 'situation of enunciation' (*'situation d'énonciation'*, thus Genette 1977: 394 and *passim*), though hardly mainstream at its time, was extremely influential in the subsequent history of Western poetics and came, mistakenly, to be regarded as the origin of the triad 'lyric-epic-dramatic' familiar from Romantic and modern literary theory.[9] It is important to understand, though, that, as Gérard Genette has shown, Plato's and Aristotle's idiosyncratic approach was by no means aimed at abolishing traditional concepts of genre, but rather accommodated them. Established genres such as tragedy, epic, or

---

[6] Here and elsewhere, Horace appears to imply that certain metres are, as it were, naturally appropriate for certain subject matters (see, e.g., *Archilochum* proprio *rabies armauit iambo, Ars P.* 79); as Russell 1981: 153 writes, '[f]or Horace the key is *decorum* (*prepon*): there must be a relation of appropriateness between form and content, and both terms are needed to characterise the "genre"'. This attitude is typical for what might be called the Augustan poets' 'obsession' with genre, that is, their continuous reflection on which genre to choose (highlighted in the *recusatio*) and subsequent worry whether the chosen genre is right for the purpose. See Conte 1994*a*: 122–5 and Sect. 2.4, below.

[7] Somewhat different, but basically reconcilable, is the practice of distinguishing types of poems by occasion, found already in the Homeric poems, where a song to celebrate a wedding is called a *hymenaios*, a dirge is a *threnos*, etc. This method (which is *mutatis mutandis* that of Cairns 1972) yields an unsystematic mass of poetic kinds, which can, however, be quite easily subsumed under larger genres. Thus, e.g., the Alexandrian philologists regarded Pindar as one of the great masters of the genre of lyric poetry, but divided his work into what we might want to call subgenres: hymns, paeans, dithyrambs, *prosodia, partheneia, hyporchemata, encomia, threnoi*, and *epinicia* (see Russell 1981: 153 and, for a useful definition of subgenre, A. Fowler 1982: 56 and 111–18).

[8] See Pl. *Resp.* 3. 392c9–394c8 and Arist. *Poet.* 1448ª20–4 (the differences in approach and terminology between Plato and Aristotle are of no concern here). For a discussion of these passages and their importance in the history of genre criticism, see Genette 1977: 392–9 and Rosenmeyer 1985: 75–81.

[9] Genette 1977 traces this extremely interesting development.

dithyramb fit more or less neatly into the new system of poetic 'modes' (Genette's term) and both thinkers recurred to them to illustrate their points: thus, the genre of tragedy, for example, was one example of the 'dramatic mode' (in which characters speak), but the genre and the mode were by no means identical or defined by the same criteria.[10]

The difference between the *communis opinio* about genre and the methods of distinguishing different types of poetry employed by such theorists as Plato and Aristotle is reflected also in the Greeks' and Romans' diverse ways of viewing didactic poetry.[11] For the most part, such poems as the *Works and Days*, the *Phaenomena*, the *De rerum natura*, and the *Georgics* were not in fact regarded as belonging to a distinct genre. Thus, Wilhelm Kroll rightly observed at the beginning of his *Pauly-Wissowa* entry on didactic poetry, '[v]on vornherein sei festgestellt, daß für die Alten das L[ehrgedicht] eine eigene Gattung nicht bildet; für sie sind die meisten L[ehrgedichte] einfach ἔπη' (1925: 1842). This general failure to recognize a genre of didactic is obviously in keeping with the widely held view, discussed above, that genres are distinguished in the first place by their metres. Since they were mostly composed in hexameters, the texts that we call didactic were in antiquity usually regarded as epic. Quintilian (*Inst.* 10. 1. 46–57), for example, lists Hesiod, Aratus, and Nicander together with Homer, Antimachus, Panyassis, Apollonius, Theocritus, Pisander, and Euphorion, a group labelled *epici* (51); in the discussion of Roman poets, Lucretius (10. 1. 87) appears in the same category as Vergil (85–6) and Ennius (88).[12] Apart from very few, and late, examples (see below), there is no evidence that the Greeks and Romans singled out the didactic poets as a specific subgroup, either of epic or of poetry in general.

If thus from the point of view of what I have called the common-sense genre theory of antiquity, didactic poetry was not a genre, it fared even worse at the hands of a somewhat more discerning critic, namely Aristotle. In contrast to οἱ ἄνθρωποι, who thought

[10] See Genette 1977: 417: 'cette relation d'inclusion n'empêchait pas le critère générique et le critère modal d'être absolument hétérogènes, et de statut radicalement différent: chaque genre se définissait essentiellement par une spécification de contenu que rien ne prescrivait dans la définition du mode dont il relevait'.

[11] On ancient ideas of didactic poetry, see esp. Fabian 1968: 68–74; Pöhlmann 1973: 815–35; Schuler and Fitch 1983: 2–21; and Lausberg 1990: 177–9.

[12] See Steinmetz 1964: 459–60; the mention of Tyrtaeus among the Greek epic poets (10. 1. 56) must be erroneous (Steinmetz 1964: 460 n. 1).

that poetry could be satisfactorily defined by its metre (*Poet.* 1447^{b}13–17; see the discussion in Chapter 1, above), Aristotle realized that Empedocles' poetry and that of Homer (both wrote in hexameters and therefore were, by common-sense nomenclature, ἐποποιοί) did not really have very much in common, in fact, nothing at all, except for the hexameter.[13] According to Aristotle, however, verse itself was not enough to make a text poetry; to him the criterion of poetry was mimesis, and unlike Homer, Empedocles crucially failed on this account. Since his work was not mimetic, he was, in Aristotle's opinion, to be called a φυσιολόγος rather than a ποιητής (*Poet.* 1447^{b}19–20).[14]

This Aristotelian verdict is usually quoted as the first recognition, however negative, of didactic poetry as a genre. However, it is important to note that Aristotle himself had no interest in distinguishing didactic from other types of poetry, or from epic specifically. His aim was to distinguish *poetry*, which included epic, from *non-poetry*, which happened to include what we call didactic, but which, in the context of the *Poetics* at least, was not only of no specific interest to Aristotle, but, in fact, decidedly a non-topic. Thus, our investigation of ancient views of didactic poetry has so far yielded the paradoxical result that, while the poems that we call didactic did for the most part not attain the status of a distinct genre and were lumped together with other hexameter texts under the rubric of epic, as soon as someone recognized their difference, they were demoted from the status of poetry and excluded from the study of poetics altogether. This dilemma, while apparently of little concern to the actual poets (didactic poetry flourished long after Aristotle), was clearly worrisome from a theoretical point of view, and for centuries to come, critics tried to solve this vexing 'Problem der Poetik' and to determine the exact status of didactic poetry.[15]

Two main approaches to the problem are known from antiquity. Both offer a positive theory of didactic poetry as a kind of *poetry* (*contra* Aristotle) that is *distinct* from other types of poetry (*contra* the *communis opinio*). Both are to a certain extent similar, both were highly influential in the subsequent history of the question, and

---

[13] *Poet.* 1447^{b}17–18: οὐδὲν δὲ κοινόν ἐστιν Ὁμήρῳ καὶ Ἐμπεδοκλεῖ πλὴν τὸ μέτρον. Aristotle was probably deliberately exaggerating: in the Περὶ ποιητῶν, he himself calls Empedocles Ὁμηρικός and praises his poetic talents (fr. 70 Rose).

[14] Aristotle's view is echoed most notably by Plut. *Quomodo adul.* 16 C.

[15] See the survey and discussion in Fabian 1968, as well as Albertsen 1967: esp. 10–39, and Schuler and Fitch 1983: 21–9.

both are rather difficult to date. The first is found in the so-called *Tractatus Coislinianus*, a tenth-century manuscript that contains an epitome of a Peripatetic work of literary criticism and deals mainly with comedy. The unknown author surreptitiously reverses Aristotle's verdict that, say, such 'physiological' works as that of Empedocles do not qualify as poetry; he does this, not by claiming that, somehow, such texts fall under the category of mimesis after all, but by simply and daringly positing a second type of poetry, one that is 'non-mimetic' (ἀμίμητος), next to the 'mimetic' (μιμητή[16]) one known from the *Poetics* (*CGF* 50 Kaibel). Mimetic poetry comprises narrative and drama; the non-mimetic kind is split into ἱστορική and παιδευτική, and the latter is further divided into ὑφηγητική and θεωρητική.[17] Thus, didactic poetry makes what is presumably its first appearance in literary criticism under the name ποίησις παιδευτική in this elegant, albeit somewhat subversive, attempt to solve the problem posed by Aristotle's one-sided definition of poetry. Note that in this schema, didactic and its supposedly closest relative, epic, belong to wholly different categories, for epic is clearly a representative of the narrative subgroup (τὸ . . . ἀπαγγελτικόν) of mimetic, as opposed to non-mimetic, poetry.

A second way of integrating didactic poetry as a distinct genre into a system of poetic types is found most prominently in the *Ars grammatica* of Diomedes (4th/5th cent. AD). While the *Tractatus Coislinianus* stands in the Aristotelian tradition, Diomedes takes up the originally Platonic tripartite division of poetic 'modes' (see above) and distinguishes three *poematos genera* (*Gramm. Lat.* 1. 482. 14 Keil) according to the mode of enunciation: the first is the *dramaticon . . . uel actiuum in quo personae agunt solae sine ullius poetae interlocutione* (17–18); the second is the *exegeticon . . . uel enarratiuum in quo poeta ipse loquitur sine ullius personae interlocutione* (20–1); not surprisingly, the third is the mixed type (κοινόν . . . *uel commune*; 23). While the latter comprises epic and lyric, and the dramatic type includes tragedy, comedy, satyr play, and mime, the narrative type is further divided into three subgroups, *angeltice, historice*, and, finally, *didascalice* (31–2). This last category is described as follows:

didascalice est qua conprehenditur philosophia Empedoclis et Lucreti,

---

[16] Kaibel suggests the emendation μιμητική, which is accepted, e.g., by Janko 1984: 22.
[17] The MS puts this division not under the παιδευτική, but under the ἱστορική, an error recognized and corrected by Bergk (cf. Kaibel's apparatus).

item astrologia, ut phaenomena Aratu et Ciceronis, et georgica Vergilii et his similia. (483. 1–3)

(Didactic poetry is the one under which is comprised the philosophy of Empedocles and Lucretius, likewise astronomy, such as the *Phaenomena* of Aratus and Cicero, and Vergil's *Georgics*, and things like this.)

This list, though not comprehensive, comes fairly close to what modern classicists would include in a survey of ancient didactic poetry. In Diomedes' theory, too, epic and didactic are regarded as two wholly different types of poetry.

The integration of didactic poetry into these two poetic systems must have been motivated by the realization that there was such a distinct kind of poetic texts that needed to be taken account of, *pace* Aristotle (and notwithstanding the indifference of earlier critics). While the *Tractatus Coislinianus* reacts to Aristotle directly, Diomedes circumvents the problem by taking recourse to the earlier, Platonic, division of poetry; both approaches inventively develop the theories of the two great thinkers in order to accommodate the various genres as they manifest themselves in poetic practice. What remains unclear is the date of these two instances of ancient genre criticism. The *Tractatus Coislinianus* is usually thought to be based on a Peripatetic treatise of the Hellenistic era, although its author could be as early as Theophrastus or as late as Andronicus of Rhodes (1st cent. BC).[18] Richard Janko (1984: esp. 52–90) has even boldly claimed that the underlying text is none other than Aristotle's lost second book of the *Poetics*, but this appears unlikely.[19]

---

[18] See the list of possibilities in Janko 1984: 43 and his subsequent discussion (though beware Janko's own solution, on which see immediately below). Note that, in theory, the *Tractatus* could have been composed even later and that if it combines material from a number of different sources, as has been suggested, the question of its date becomes more difficult yet.

[19] While I have no opinion on the discussion of comedy proper, which may or may not go back directly to *Poet.* 2, I cannot believe that sect. I of the *Tractatus*, with its division of poetry into mimetic and non-mimetic, reflects anything written by Aristotle himself. Janko realizes that the concept of ποίησις ἀμίμητος (which blatantly contradicts what is said in the *Poetics* as we have it) is a problem for his argument, but attempts to cut this 'Gordian Knot' with what he terms 'the sword of A.'s loose terminology' (1984: 132; see also 58, 81, 92, 121–33). However, it seems unlikely that Aristotle, after having endeavoured throughout Book 1 to drive home the crucial importance of mimesis, should suddenly be using 'poetry' in a wider sense and explicitly introduce a non-mimetic type—especially given that this is not at all needed for the discussion of comedy that follows. Note also that of the only ten words in the *Tractatus* that are not otherwise found in the extant works of Aristotle, two occur in sect. I and are used to describe didactic poetry: παιδευτικός and ὑφηγητικός. I do not think that this is chance: if Aristotle had had an expression ποίησις παιδευτική with the meaning 'didactic poetry', he

As for Diomedes, he is the first surviving author who explicitly makes didactic poetry as a genre an example of the kind of poetry 'in which the poet himself speaks'; however, the Platonic theory of the three τύποι λέξεως is so common in both Greek and Latin literary criticism that it seems unlikely that it should have been applied to didactic poetry only in late antiquity.[20] Egert Pöhlmann, following Hellfried Dahlmann, places the origin of Diomedes' view of didactic poetry in (early) Hellenistic times, a period that did, after all, see a renaissance of didactic poetry, especially in the works of Aratus and Nicander (see Sect. 2.3, below).[21] It is thus possible, though not assured, that by the time of the authors who are the principal subject of this book, there already existed a positive theory of didactic as a distinct genre of poetry.

On the whole, it seems that the story of the changing critical attitudes to didactic poetry in antiquity (and beyond[22]) is of greater interest to the historian of poetics than to the literary critic who attempts, as I do in this book, to understand the workings of Greek and Latin didactic poetry as an actual genre. There is no indication that any of the theories discussed had an impact on the practice of the authors who composed didactic poetry (an observation that probably holds true for literary theory and practice in general). It is often stated that Aristotle's verdict did not prevent didactic poetry from being composed or from being regarded as poetry by its authors and its audience (see, e.g., Dalzell 1996: 18–19)—quite the contrary, as I hope to show.[23] Likewise, there is no reason to believe

---

would surely have used it in *Poet.* 1447ᵇ16–20, rather than resorting to the awkward paraphrase, ἄν ἰατρικὸν ἢ φυσικόν τι διὰ τῶν μέτρων ἐκφέρωσιν (16–17).

[20] Janko 1984: 128–9 provides a list of authors who, like Diomedes, use the tripartite, Platonic schema (see also Dahlmann 1953: 149–58; Pöhlmann 1973: 825–32). Of these, only Iunius Philargyrius *ad Verg. Buc. Prooem.* 1I,12–2I,8 Hagen (quoted by Wendel 1914: 19) equates the *modus διδασκαλικός* explicitly with the *modus ἐξηγητικός*. Like Diomedes, also Servius *ad* Verg. *Ecl.* 3. 1 (29. 18–19 Thilo; see Wendel 1914: 21) mentions the first three books of the *Georgics* as an example of the type *in quo poeta ipse loquitur* (thus also Isidore, *Etym.* 8. 7. 11; see Wendel 1914: 12). In Proclus' *Prolegomena to Hesiod*, by contrast, it is, fittingly, the *Works and Days* that is used to illustrate the διηγηματικόν-type (*Poetae Minores Graeci* 4. 4 Gaisford). Descriptions of the three *poematos genera* almost identical to that of Diomedes (*Gramm. Lat.* 1. 482. 14–25 Keil) are also found in Dositheus' *Ars grammatica* (*Gramm. Lat.* 7. 428. 6–14, probably drawing on the same source as Diomedes) and Bede's *De arte metrica* (*Gramm. Lat.* 7. 259. 14–260. 2 Keil). However, these two works do not contain Diomedes' further division of the narrative type and his discussion of the *didascalice* proper.

[21] Pöhlmann 1973: 830, drawing on Dahlmann 1953: 158 n. 1.

[22] For the later history of the problem, see Fabian 1968: 74–89 and Schuler and Fitch 1983: 21–9.

[23] Effe 1977: 21 and n. 32 considers the possibility that the typical 'dichterisches Selbst-

that any known didactic poet was aware, or would have cared, that he was a practitioner of a 'non-mimetic' genre. Even the commonsense theoretical view of didactic poetry cannot have been too influential on actual poetic practice: after all, most didactic poems are quite unlike epic.

If the (admittedly rather few) known approaches to didactic poetry in antiquity fail to throw light on the poets' motivation, they also do not contribute much to the description and definition of the didactic genre, which, after all, is the goal of this chapter. We have learned so far that didactic poetry is somehow like epic, presumably mostly as regards its metre, but that, unlike epic, it is not mimetic in the Aristotelian sense. Furthermore, it is a kind of poetry in which 'the poet himself speaks', without interference from other characters. This is more or less all that we can glean from the ancient critics, and it is clearly unsatisfactory. It is thus time to turn away from theory and toward the poems themselves and to try to understand the genre of didactic poetry on the basis of the actual texts that constitute it.

2.2. DIDACTIC POETRY AS A GENRE

Since in the following I shall attempt to arrive at my own definition of the genre of didactic poetry, it seems appropriate first to comment briefly on my own use and understanding of the term genre. In the context of the discussion at hand, my concept of genre is largely heuristic. With hindsight, that is, many centuries after the fact, I perceive that during a certain period of literary history (Greek and Roman antiquity) a certain major body of texts exhibits a certain number of shared characteristics that distinguish it from other texts and that these similarities do not appear to have come about by chance, but must to a certain extent be assumed to have been intended by the authors and noticed by their audience.[24] To say that these texts belong to the same genre is nothing more than a convenient shorthand to describe the phenomenon. This empirical

---

bewußtsein' of didactic poetry (on which see more below) was a conscious reaction to Aristotle. This seems to me highly unlikely.

[24] That my perception and interpretation of literary history is not original, but rather influenced by predecessors (in this case, the entire tradition of classical scholarship) is not only unavoidable (the Hermeneutic Circle again), but also acts as some kind of guarantee: I would feel rather uncomfortable if I were the only one to believe in the existence of ancient didactic poetry!

approach to genre appears to me the most fruitful and secure, even though it may be criticized as anachronistic since, strictly speaking, by this understanding a genre can be fully recognized only in hindsight. To quote Genette, 'toutes les espèces, tous les sous-genres, genres ou super-genres sont des classes empiriques, établies par observation du donné historique' (1977: 419). It is thus not necessarily the case that the genres established by literary historians were perceived in exactly the same way by their practitioners at the time, especially not in those cases where a new genre was just being established, a process that may not have been obvious to those involved in it. The question of how authors and their contemporary audiences conceive of specific genres and genre in general is a question that is as interesting as it is difficult. I shall return to it at the end of this chapter, after first determining the characteristics of the genre of didactic poetry with the help of the empirical method just described and tracing its historical development.

Despite the fact that the ancients, as we have seen, mostly viewed didactic poetry as belonging to epic, it seems to me reasonable to regard it (more or less anachronistically) as its own genre and not, as some classicists are inclined to do, as a mere subgenre. According to the definition of Alastair Fowler, '[i]n subgenre we find the same external characteristics with the corresponding kind [*'kind' is Fowler's term for what I would simply call 'genre'*], together with additional specification of content' (1982: 56). Thus, if the novel constitutes a genre, the historical novel is one of its subgenres. Even though classicists sometimes speak of 'didactic epic',[25] Greek and Latin didactic poetry clearly does not qualify as a subgenre according to this definition. Vis-à-vis epic, the content of didactic poetry is not 'additionally specified', but usually wholly different. In fact, apart from the metre (though note exceptions like Ovid's *Ars amatoria*, in elegiacs) and, as a consequence, often a somewhat 'epic' diction and 'high' style, didactic poetry has generally very little in common with epic.[26] It thus seems reasonable to me, as it did earlier to Diomedes and the anonymous Peripatetic critic epitomized in the *Tractatus Coislinianus*, to recognize the sadly neglected category of didactic poetry as its own poetic genre.

[25] See the bilingual title of Schiesaro, Mitsis, and Clay (eds.) 1993; Toohey 1996 is called *Epic Lessons*.
[26] On the relationship of epic and didactic poetry, the differences and points of contact between the two genres, see Lausberg 1990; cf. also Schindler 2000 on didactic (v. epic) similes.

In order to do so, it is important to distinguish from didactic poetry proper the notion, widespread in Greek and Roman culture, that *all* poetry is, or has the potential to be, didactic (see esp. Lausberg 1990: 192–4). From the idea of Homer as the 'teacher of Greece' (on which compare Verdenius 1970) to Horace's famous dictum *aut prodesse uolunt aut delectare poetae* (*Ars P.* 333), the view that one can, or ought to be able to, learn from poetry remains commonplace throughout antiquity.[27] However, even if it is true that the *Iliad* can teach us about the Trojan War, and perhaps even about the art of generalship, as the rhapsode Ion contends in Plato's dialogue (540d1–541d7), this does not make it a didactic poem. Whether one can in fact learn something—anything—from a text is a useless criterion since by that token, there would be very few, if any, poems that could not pass as didactic. Still, it is clear that the time-honoured concept of the poet as teacher plays an important role in didactic poetry, being regularly exploited in the poems themselves and possibly lying behind the obscure origins of the genre as a whole.

To turn now to the positive characteristics of didactic poetry, it is clear to me that the criteria I shall propose in the following do not constitute the only possible way of defining this elusive genre, and that individual scholars, even ones who share my basic approach, may wish to put individual accents differently. It is also obvious that the actual Greek and Latin didactic works 'adhere' to my definition more or less closely; as will become clear in the following section, didactic poetry is a genre very much in flux and arguably reaches its 'ideal' state (that is, 'ideal' according to my definition) only after going through a number of permutations (see also nn. 33 and 67). Nevertheless, I believe that my definition captures the essence of both the 'didactic' and the 'poetic' aspects of didactic poetry and can serve, as I hope to show in the following chapters, as a useful key to the interpretation of the individual poems.

Of the four central features that in my opinion define didactic poetry, the first is the *explicit didactic intent*. A didactic poem either states clearly, or gives other strong indications, that it is first and foremost supposed to teach whatever subject or skill it happens to be treating. Thus, while we are free to imagine that Homer really

---

[27] The history of the thought is traced by Schuler and Fitch 1983, who do, however, not distinguish it properly from specifically didactic poetry and its exigencies; see also Kroll 1924: 64–86; Fabian 1968: 72–4; Russell 1981: 84–98; and Dalzell 1996: 8–12.

did wish to instruct his audience in strategy, the *Iliad* itself gives no sign of any such intent. By contrast, Hesiod's *Works and Days* clearly signals its didactic thrust, most prominently in the statement ἐγὼ δέ κε Πέρσῃ ἐτήτυμα μυθησαίμην (10). Obviously, the didactic intent can be displayed more or less prominently. In Aratus' *Phaenomena*, it is merely—but unmistakably—implied in the speaker's frequent addresses to his student. Ovid's *Ars amatoria*, by contrast, blatantly advertises its didactic potential already in the very first distich:

> si quis in hoc artem populo non nouit amandi
> hoc legat et lecto carmine *doctus* amet.
>
> (1. 1–2)

(If anyone in this people does not know the art of love, let him read this and, having read the poem, love as an expert [lit. as one who has been taught].)

It is important to note that the displayed didactic intent is not in the first place that of the actual author who wishes to instruct his audience—an intention that may underlie many works of poetry and that need not be made explicit (it is reasonable to state that, say, the *Theogony* teaches us the genealogies of the gods, even though it does not claim to be doing so, which is one of the reasons why it does not, at least according to my definition, qualify as a didactic poem). Rather, the poem's didactic intent is part of what might be called a little intra-textual drama, in which the speaker of the text teaches a student or students by means of the poem itself. This *teacher–student constellation* is the second defining characteristic of didactic poetry and one that has traditionally received much scholarly attention (see esp. the papers in Schiesaro, Mitsis, and Clay (eds.) 1993). It was observed already by Servius, apropos of Vergil's *Georgics*. His remark (which I left out of my previous survey since it is not in the first place concerned with genre criticism as such) is easily the most insightful statement about didactic poetry to have survived from antiquity:

hi libri didascalici sunt, unde necesse est, ut ad aliquem scribantur; nam praeceptum et doctoris et discipuli personam requirit. unde ad Maecenatem scribit [sc. Vergilius], sicut Hesiodus ad Persen, Lucretius ad Memmium. (*Praef. ad Georg.* 129. 9–12 Thilo)

(These books are didactic, whence it is necessary for them to be addressed to someone; for instruction calls for the roles of both teacher and student.

Thus (Vergil) addresses Maecenas, just as Hesiod Perses and Lucretius Memmius.)

Servius' list could easily be extended to include Empedocles and Pausanias; Aratus and his unnamed student; Nicander and, respectively, Hermesianax (*Theriaca*) and Protagoras (*Alexipharmaca*); Ovid and his *iuuenes* and *puellae*; and Manilius and his nameless addressee.[28] While the characters of these addressees can be developed to a greater or lesser degree (thus, we learn a lot about the unpleasant Perses, whereas, for example, Aratus' student remains purely generic), the frequent addresses to them are a feature that all didactic poems share and that is possibly their single most prominent trait.

By regarding the teacher–student constellation as a purely intra-textual phenomenon (cf. also D. Clay 1983*b*: 212–16) I do not wish to deny the possibility that characters like Perses, Pausanias, and Memmius existed and stood in some relationship to the author. I also do not mean to imply that, say, Empedocles or Lucretius did not actually compose their poems in order to teach, be it their addressees or their wider audience. Finally, I do realize that in the larger communication process between actual author and audience, the figure of the intra-textual addressee or student can play the role of a foil, with whom the readers or listeners can either identify or from whom they can distance themselves. This use of the addressee as a kind of dummy figure is extremely interesting, especially in such cases as those of Perses or Memmius, in which the reader can clearly not (wholly) identify with his or her intra-textual equivalent and has to find a way to negotiate this relationship.[29] However, the actual intentions of authors (Did Vergil really want to teach farmers?) and reactions of readers (Did people really read the *Ars amatoria* to learn the art of love?)[30] are extremely hard to assess and, as mentioned in the Introduction, my focus is instead on the purely intra-textual aspects of didactic poetry. I shall thus treat the teacher–student constellation in isolation from the author–reader relationship that it may, or may not, mirror, in the belief that this is

---

[28] Note that contrary to what Servius says, Maecenas does not function as a student figure in the *Georgics* the same way Perses does in the *Works and Days* and Memmius in the *De rerum natura*; his somewhat unclear role will be discussed in Sect. 4.1, below.

[29] See J. S. Clay 1993 and Mitsis 1993.

[30] Little scholarly work has been done on the reception of didactic poetry in antiquity itself, but note Christmann 1982 (on reactions to the *Georgics*) and von Staden 1998 (on Galen's attitude to didactic poetry on medical topics).

the only approach that will yield reliable results and not sway into mere speculation.

While the *persona discipuli*, to use Servius' expression, has been a focus of recent work on didactic poetry, the *persona doctoris* has been comparatively neglected. This is remarkable since in didactic poetry the speaker is even more prominent than the addressee. As Diomedes observed, didactic poetry belongs to the kind *in quo poeta ipse loquitur sine ullius personae interlocutione* (*Gramm. Lat.* 1. 482. 21 Keil). And not only does the poet speak himself, but he speaks qua poet and presents what he is saying explicitly as poetry. In other words, didactic poetry typically exhibits *poetic self-consciousness*, as discussed in Chapter 1, and often to a very high degree. This third characteristic of didactic has not usually been remarked upon in scholarship (though see Effe 1977: 21 and n. 32; Myerowitz 1985: 87), and its neglect may be due to modern prejudices against didactic poetry as unpoetic and to Aristotle's verdict. It is also a feature that strongly distinguishes didactic poetry from epic: as mentioned in Chapter 1, epic always exhibits poetic self-consciousness, but the law of 'epic objectivity' does not allow wide scope for reflection on the speaker's role as poet or the poetic nature of his words; didactic, by contrast, has the possibility to stress the persona's poetic activity and to reflect at great length on its own status as poetry. This difference is easily observed, for example, by taking just a brief comparative look at the *Aeneid* and the *Georgics*.

Since the poetic self-consciousness of Lucretius, Vergil, Ovid, and Manilius will be a main topic of the later chapters, it remains to be demonstrated only that their Greek predecessors, too, styled themselves as poets in their didactic works. The *Works and Days* is somewhat problematic in this respect (see Sect. 2.3, below), but the Hesiodic persona does invoke the Muses (1–2) and later refers to his profession as a poet (654–62). Empedocles' poem, by contrast, abounds in self-conscious references to its being poetry (B3, B4, B23. 11, B35. 1–3, B131); Aratus, too, invokes the Muses (16–18), and while Nicander conspicuously fails to do so, he uses the *sphragis* of his two extant poems to call himself Ὁμήρειος (*Ther.* 957) and ὑμνοπόλος (*Alex.* 629).

As poetically self-conscious texts, all didactic poems furthermore exhibit *poetic simultaneity*, their fourth and final central characteristic. They frequently comment on the process of the poet's 'singing', which in their case is at the same time the process of the teacher's teaching. It is thus often the teacher's addresses to the student that create the impression of the poem in progress: didactic poems abound with phrases of the kind, 'having sung of x, I shall now tell you y'. While scholars tend to marginalize them as transitional passages, it is such statements that actually create the framework of a didactic poem and constitute what has been called the didactic plot. Though not narrative in any real sense, a didactic poem does to a certain extent tell a story: the story of its own coming into being as a poem, which is at the same time the story of the teacher's instructing the student.[31] None too surprisingly, didactic poems also favour the journey imagery evocative of poetic simultaneity, such as the chariot and the ship metaphors.

To sum up: In the scheme that I have been proposing, the genre of ancient didactic poetry is defined by four main characteristics: (1) explicit didactic intent; (2) teacher–student constellation; (3) poetic self-consciousness; and (4) poetic simultaneity. Obviously, the four are closely related. A didactic poem could thus be described as the self-consciously poetic speech uttered by the persona, who combines the roles of poet and teacher, explicitly in order to instruct the frequently addressed student in some professed art or branch of knowledge. While, as Diomedes knew, didactic, unlike say, tragedy or epic, is strictly a kind of poetry in which only the poet speaks (with some justification, Diomedes thus apparently regarded the second half of *Georgics* 4 as aberrant (*Gramm. Lat.* 1. 482. 22 Keil)), it also shows some affinity with both drama and narrative. Even though the student never says a word (except sometimes in counter-arguments anticipated by the speaker, such as Lucr. 1. 803–8, 897–900; and perhaps 6. 673; and Man. 4. 387–9 and 869–72), his supposed presence adds dramatic immediacy to the text: he is there and could potentially do something, at least contradict. Likewise, while didactic poetry does not actually *tell* a story, it conveys a sense of plot: the audience can follow the development of the teacher's instructing the student, as well as the development of the poem itself. The observation of these features even led Manfred Erren to conclude that Aristotle had actually been wrong to dismiss didactic poetry as not mimetic: '[D]as Lehrgedicht hat eine mimetische Komponente, die Aristoteles offenbar übersehen hat: Der lehrende Dichter ahmt eine Belehrungstat so, wie sie zwar nicht geschieht,

---

[31] On the notion of the didactic plot, see esp. D. Fowler 2000; cf. also, specifically on Lucretius, the discussions in Schiesaro 1994 and Gale 1994*b*: 117–28.

aber geschehen könnte, nur nach, in einer... Handlungserfindung, in der er die lehrende Anredestruktur des Gedichts begründet' (1990: 185). Whether Aristotle would actually have been happy to speak of mimesis in such a case remains unclear, but Erren's description certainly captures the most important aspects of the didactic genre.

Apart from the central characteristics just discussed, it seems practical to distinguish, again purely empirically, between two somewhat different types of didactic poetry. This distinction can be found already in the *Tractatus Coislinianus*, where the kind of poetry that is παιδευτική is further divided into ὑφηγητική and θεωρητική. The second, 'theoretical', kind appears to be didactic poetry that lays out a science or branch of knowledge, such as the works of Empedocles or Lucretius. By contrast, poems that teach a practical art, such as the *Works and Days*, the *Georgics*, and the *Ars amatoria*, belong to the 'instructional' type. The main formal difference between the two is that, for obvious reasons, in instructional didactic poems, the addresses to the student(s) tend to take the form of actual advice or downright orders, which are understandably rarer in works of the theoretical kind.[32] Thus, the longer first part of Aratus' poem (Φαινόμενα, 1–732), for example, is a theoretical treatment of the constellations, while the shorter second part (Διοσημίαι, 733–1154) provides practical instructions in the art of the weather forecast. Tellingly, of the twenty-five imperatives addressed to the student, only six occur in the theoretical section (see the list in Bing 1993: 109).

By the definition expounded above, the following major texts qualify as didactic poems: Hesiod's *Works and Days*, Empedocles' *On Nature*, Aratus' *Phaenomena*, Nicander's *Theriaca* and *Alexipharmaca*, Lucretius' *De rerum natura*, Vergil's *Georgics*, Ovid's *Ars amatoria* and *Remedia amoris* (and, as far as we can tell from the fragment we possess, the *Medicamina faciei femineae*), and Manilius' *Astronomica*, as well as numerous other works in the same tradition from the late first century BC onward. One poem that is usually regarded as didactic does not fit the bill, namely that of Parmenides, as will be discussed in greater detail in the historical survey in Section 2.3. Likewise, a number of other works that are sometimes considered

---

[32] On orders to the student in (Latin) didactic poetry, see Gibson 1997, who argues that such commands take a form different from and more personal than those in comparable instructional prose treatises.

didactic poems or treated in the context of didactic poetry do not fulfil the postulated criteria.[33] Thus, Horace's *Ars poetica*, while clearly exhibiting didactic intent as well as the typical teacher–student constellation (the speaker v. the Pisones), does not show poetic self-consciousness (and therefore not poetic simultaneity either). Interestingly, the speaker is clearly a (professional) poet (see esp. 11; 24–5), but he never implies that the teaching speech he addresses to the Pisones is itself a poem. Rather, he ironically pretends that it is because of his lack of poetic *ingenium* that, instead of *writing* poetry, he is reduced to *teaching* it (301–8; esp. 306, *nil scribens ipse docebo*). This attitude is far removed from that of a typical persona of didactic poetry, such as, for example, the speaker of the *Georgics*, and generally speaking, the *Ars poetica* is much more reminiscent of Horace's own *Satires* and *Epistles* (which typically present themselves as *sermo*, that is, everyday speech, and not as poetry; see *Sat.* 1. 4. 39–42) than of the didactic poetry of his time.

Ovid's *Fasti*, too, cannot be called a didactic poem. It is true that the text exhibits poetic self-consciousness to a high degree, exploiting the concept of poetic simultaneity in an unprecedented fashion, and also that the speaker repeatedly addresses unnamed addressees in a manner reminiscent of didactic poetry.[34] However, there is no indication that the persona's main intent is to teach anyone about the Roman calendar, rather than simply to sing about it. In addition, the addresses to what one might call the anonymous students occur in an extremely random and unsystematic fashion and are interspersed with addresses to numerous other characters, especially to deities and other informant figures.

While the *Ars poetica* and the *Fasti* (as well as Parmenides' poem) are thus not didactic poems in the sense adopted here, they, as well as many other texts or parts of texts, obviously show a certain similarity to works that unequivocally belong to didactic poetry. We might say that they are written in the *didactic mode*, with the term

---

[33] By excluding certain works from didactic poetry as I define it, I obviously do not wish to imply that these texts are inferior or to deny that they share many characteristics with those poems that I recognize as didactic. It simply appears useful, for the purpose of this book, to define didactic poetry in the rather narrow way explained above. Anyone who favours a more inclusive definition of the genre is welcome to use 'didactic poetry' in a wider sense, but I would still maintain that the group of poems that I have singled out forms a set distinct from other texts, however comparable those may otherwise be.

[34] See Volk 1997: 290 n. 10 for examples. The relationship of the *Fasti* to didactic poetry has been examined by John F. Miller in a number of publications, most notably Miller 1992.

mode here being used according to the definition of Alastair Fowler: 'Mode . . . is a selection or abstraction from kind [*'kind'* = *'genre'*; *see above*]. It has few if any external rules, but evokes a historical kind through samples of its internal repertoire' (A. Fowler 1982: 56; see also 106–11).[35] Thus, a text in the didactic mode is reminiscent of a didactic poem by virtue of exhibiting characteristics typical of didactic poetry, most often by casting a speaker, at least temporarily, in the role of teacher. For example, Anchises' extended presentation of the future Roman heroes to his son Aeneas in Book 6 of the *Aeneid* (713–892) could be described as a speech in the didactic mode (cf. D. Fowler 2000: 206–7): Anchises expresses a clear intention to 'teach' Aeneas (esp. *te tua fata docebo*, 759; see also 716–18, 722) and repeatedly addresses him, using phrases similar to those employed by the speakers of didactic poetry in addresses to their students.[36] Obviously, this fact makes neither Anchises' speech nor the *Aeneid* as a whole a didactic poem.

To adopt A. Fowler's phrase and regard the didactic mode exhibited by many poetic texts as an abstraction of the genre of didactic poetry is convenient for the critic; however, it is important to understand that this view, like many ideas having to do with genre, is anachronistic. With hindsight, it may appear that texts in the didactic mode 'evoke' (Fowler's term) texts of the didactic genre; from a historical point of view, however, there almost certainly was a didactic mode before there was a didactic genre, and instead of the mode's being 'abstracted' from the genre, it is rather the genre that arises from a specific development of the mode. Thus, scenes of instruction, in which a speaker imparts information or advice to an addressee, are found in literatures all over the world. Greek and Latin didactic poetry is clearly part of this tradition, but at the same time a very specialized and more narrowly defined manifestation of it. The following short survey of the origin and development of didactic poetry will both illustrate this point and provide the historical background needed to judge and understand the Latin poets that are the subject of the following chapters.

---

[35] Note that this use of the term 'mode' is different from that of Genette, quoted in Sect. 2.1 in connection with Plato's and Aristotle's views of genre.

[36] *uides*, 760; *aspice*, 771, 825, 855; *uiden*, 779; *huc . . . flecte acies*, . . . *aspice . . .*, 788; *uis . . .* | *. . . uidere . . .*, 817–18. Note that while verbs of seeing are often employed metaphorically in didactic poetry, they are here used in their literal sense: Anchises is actually pointing out the characters he describes.

2.3. The Development of Didactic Poetry up to Lucretius

Hesiod's *Works and Days* is usually regarded as the beginning of didactic poetry as we know it. However, to assume that an Archaic Greek poet (whose very status as a historical person is under dispute) would simply 'invent' a genre is clearly unacceptable to Hellenists today, who have been taught, notably by Parry, Lord, and their successors, that every Archaic Greek poem draws on a wealth of poetic tradition or, to put it differently, that it is itself nothing but a manifestation of this tradition.[37] In the case of the *Works and Days*, one need not look hard for the underlying tradition. Scholars have long been aware of the similarities between Hesiod's work and what is usually referred to as Wisdom Literature, a tradition of instructional writing found in many cultures, most notably (from the point of view of Hesiodic scholarship) in the Near East.[38] These works typically consist of a series of pieces of advice, addressed very often by a father to his son, or otherwise by some wise figure to a king or prince. Many of the instructions imparted in such texts have parallels in the *Works and Days*: teachings on farming and on general moral conduct (such as those addressed by the Hesiodic speaker to Perses) and political advice (such as that imparted by the Hesiodic speaker to the 'kings') are staples of this type of literature.

While the tradition of Wisdom Literature thus sheds light on a number of features of the *Works and Days* and can help us understand the work in its historical and cultural context, it is not sufficient to explain all its characteristics. For in a crucial way, Hesiod's poem is quite unlike the wisdom texts usually cited as parallels. From the anachronistic point of view of the genre critic, we might say that while the Near Eastern and other instances of Wisdom Literature clearly exhibit the didactic mode, the *Works and Days* actually is a didactic poem in terms of the definition expounded above. Or, rather, while it may not quite yet be a standard didactic poem, it certainly is on its way to becoming one.

Let us briefly test the poem against the four criteria for didactic poetry. The *Works and Days*, as already mentioned, clearly shows

---

[37] For a radical formulation of this view, see Nagy 1990: 36–82, esp. 48, 71, 79.
[38] On Wisdom Literature in general, see M. L. West 1978: 3–25; Near Eastern wisdom texts are conveniently collected and translated in Pritchard 1969: 405–52.

Ancient Didactic Poetry

didactic intent (see esp. 10), a feature that it shares with Wisdom Literature as a whole. It also exhibits the usual teacher–student constellation: the Hesiodic speaker and his stubborn brother Perses are probably the most famous pair of protagonists of any didactic poem known from antiquity.[39] As pointed out above, the teacher–student constellation is inherent also in Wisdom Literature in general, where the advice or instruction imparted is typically addressed to one specific student figure. However, in these traditional texts, the actual teaching speech is often framed by an introductory narrative, however short, in the third person. Note, for example, the Sumerian *Instructions of Šuruppak* (quoted by M. L. West 1978: 3–4), where the actual advice is introduced by 'Šuruppak gave instructions to his son', a phrase that, as West notes, recurs a number of times throughout the text (ibid.: 4 and n. 1). Likewise, another Sumerian text, the *Instructions of Ninurta*, begins, 'In days of yore a farmer instructed his son' (ibid.: 5). Unlike Hesiod's *Works and Days*, and unlike all other Greek and Latin didactic poems that we have, these texts are clearly not ones in which 'the poet himself speaks'; rather, they take the form of mini-narratives whose main bulk consists of reported speech. Related to this phenomenon is a fact that constitutes the most important difference between the *Works and Days* and traditional wisdom texts: the latter, as far as I can tell from the examples in M. L. West 1978 and Pritchard 1969, never present themselves as poetry; in other words, they entirely lack poetic self-consciousness, the third defining criteria for didactic poetry. Hesiod's work, by contrast, is explicitly a poem—even though, as we shall see, its use of poetic self-consciousness is somewhat problematic.

Like the speakers of other didactic poems, the persona of the *Works and Days* is very prominent throughout the text.[40] Continually drawing attention to the ongoing process of his teaching, he creates a vivid sense of simultaneity (my fourth criterion for didactic poetry) with the help of self-referential statements such as ἐγὼ δέ κε Πέρσῃ ἐτήτυμα μυθησαίμην (10), εἰ δ' ἐθέλεις, ἕτερόν τοι ἐγὼ λόγον ἐκκορυφώσω | εὖ καὶ ἐπισταμένως· σὺ δ' ἐνὶ θρεσὶ βάλλεο σῆσιν

---

[39] On the teacher–student constellation in the *Works and Days*, see J. S. Clay 1993. The vexed question of whether Perses is to be regarded as a historical figure need not concern us here.

[40] By contrast, in the *Theogony*, once the proem is over, the persona, in standard epic fashion, remains completely in the background (the invocations to the Muses in 965–9 and 1021–2 no longer belong to the *Theogony* proper).

(106–7), and σοὶ δ' ἐγὼ ἐσθλὰ νοέων ἐρέω (286).[41] However, it is striking that the reference is always only to the speaker's *speaking*, never to the poet's *'singing'* or the like.[42] In this context it is interesting that, as scholars have pointed out, the rhetorical strategies and vocabulary of the Hesiodic teaching speech are reminiscent of certain speeches of Homeric characters, notably those of blame and advice (such as, e.g., Phoenix' speech to Achilles in *Il.* 9. 434–605; see R. P. Martin 1992: 16–19)—a kind of discourse that is not 'poetic' and that in its diction and structure likewise mirrors the traditional didactic mode exhibited in Wisdom Literature proper.[43]

Still, the *Works and Days* is more than the kind of rebuke a Homeric hero would address to an inferior or the advice a Near Eastern wise man would impart to his son. At least in the proem (1–10), the text presents itself as Muse-inspired song (in this respect resembling epic), and later in the poem, in the context of the advice on seafaring, the speaker mentions his victory at a poetic contest in Chalcis (654–9; this implies that he is a professional poet) and proceeds to declare that since he was taught by the Muses 'to sing godly song', he will (now) speak of 'the mind of Aegis-bearing Zeus' (661–2). These passages are the only instances where the persona's words are explicitly presented as poetry, and while they are enough to make the *Works and Days* qualify as poetically self-conscious, and thus as a didactic poem, it must also be admitted that they are extremely odd and do not fit in very well with the 'unpoetic' teaching speech of the rest of the poem.

As for the proem, the invocation to the Muses, who are explicitly asked to speak of Zeus (Δί' ἐννέπετε, 2), and the following address to the god himself make the audience expect that Zeus will indeed be the subject of the song to follow (cf. the proems to the *Iliad* and the *Odyssey*, where the topic of which the Muse is told to sing—μῆνιν

---

[41] See also 202; 316; 367; 403; 536; 603; 623; 648; 661; 687–8.

[42] We might say that the text for the most part exhibits self-consciousness and simultaneity, but not *poetic* self-consciousness and simultaneity (see Ch. 1, above, esp. n. 5, for the distinction).

[43] As just a single example of a parallel between the *Works and Days* and Homeric rhetoric, note the use of the formula σὺ δ' ἐνὶ φρεσὶ βάλλεο σῇσιν (*Op.* 107; see also 274), which occurs seven times in the *Iliad* (always prefixed with ἄλλο δέ τοι ἐρέω; compare the use of ἐρέω in *Op.* 202; 286; 661), nearly always in a speech with a somewhat aggressive tone: 1. 297 (angry speech of Achilles to Agamemnon); 4. 39 (angry speech of Zeus to Hera); 5. 259 (paraenetic speech of Diomedes to Sthenelus); 9. 611 (Achilles' answer to Phoenix); 16. 444 (angry speech of Hera to Zeus), 851 (final words of Patroclus to Hector); 21. 94 (Lycaon's supplication to Achilles).

and ἄνδρα respectively—is also the topic of the poet's song). However, in line 10 a sudden shift occurs when the speaker abruptly declares, ἐγὼ δέ κε Πέρσῃ ἐτήτυμα μυθησαίμην. As it turns out, 'saying true things to Perses' constitutes the contents of the following poem, while the Muses and their song about Zeus remain all but forgotten.[44] This is remarkably odd, and the problem is not solved if we assume, with M. L. West 1978: 136–7, that *Works and Days* 1–10a is a προοίμιον in the strict sense, that is, an independent introduction such as the *Homeric Hymns* or *Theogony* 1–104.[45] The transition between proem and actual song would be exceedingly odd: *pace* M. L. West 1978: 142, the phrase 'but I should say true things to Perses' is quite unlike the connecting formulas found at the end of the *Homeric Hymns*, and we would also expect another invocation to the Muses at the beginning of the song proper, such as that found in *Theogony* 105–15, where, after the end of the proem, the goddesses are now asked to sing the genealogies of the gods, that is, to begin the *Theogony* itself. Thus, whether one wishes to see *Works and Days* 1–10a as the proem or the invocation, there is a marked contrast between this poetically self-conscious address to the Muses and the ensuing teaching speech, which for the most part does not exhibit poetic self-consciousness and is uttered by a speaker who appears to rely on his own authority rather than on the goddesses of poetry.[46]

---

[44] Obviously, Zeus and the concept of justice elaborated in 3–10a are of great thematic importance throughout the *Works and Days*. Still, this hardly makes the text qualify specifically as a song about Zeus, in the way in which the *Iliad* can be said to be a song about the wrath of Achilles.

[45] On 'proems' in this sense, see Ch. 1 n. 16.

[46] Not all scholars share my reading that the sudden announcement ἐγὼ δέ κε Πέρσῃ ἐτήτυμα μυθησαίμην marks a contrast between the poetic discourse of the Muses and the ostensibly unpoetic one of the speaker. For example, Watkins 1995: 101 sees *Op.* 1–10 as a unity held together by a 'ring', namely the fact that the first word, MOUSAI, is echoed by and contained in the last word, MUthēSAImēn: 'The Muses—collectively the mind of the poet—are thus literally embodied in the poet's first person singular verb μυθησαίμην'. If Watkins thus regards line 10 clearly as part of the poetic discourse of the preceding verses, R. P. Martin, by contrast, takes the entire proem to indicate that the poet's 'composition introduces itself not as musical speech but as authoritative talk, or more exactly, instruction' (1992: 13). In his view, already ἐννέπετε (*Op.* 2), a verb typically coordinated with μῦθος, 'authoritative speech-act', in the Homeric poems (cf. μυθησαίμην, *Op.* 10), points to the fact that the following speech is not in the first place characterized as poetic. I remain unconvinced by either attempt at integrating 10b into what precedes: as for Watkins's reading, phonetic similarity does not yet guarantee semantic connection, and while I obviously agree with Martin that, on the whole, the *Works and Days* is presented more as authoritative speech than as 'song', I cannot believe that this is implied already in ἐννέπετε, given that the imperative is addressed to the Muses (who are associated with poetry) and that the same verb is used in the proem to the *Odyssey*.

The exception, of course, is 661–2, where the Muses—who were mentioned immediately before, at 658–9—appear as inspiring figures whose teaching enables the speaker to expound 'the mind of Aegis-bearing Zeus'. In the context of seafaring, as M. L. West 1978: 322 points out, Ζηνὸς νόον αἰγιόχοιο (661) must refer to the weather, and this is what the speaker treats in the ensuing passage. However, it is striking that the only time after the proem when the Muses are mentioned as having a part in the creation of the persona's composition is, again, in connection with Zeus—as though we had suddenly come back to the original song about Zeus that was begun in the first verses and then all but abandoned.[47] While it makes sense for the speaker to refer to the authority of the Muses at a point where he cannot sufficiently rely on his own knowledge (his experience with seafaring is restricted (660); nevertheless (ἀλλὰ καὶ ὥς), he will continue to speak about it, having been taught by the Muses (661–2)), the sudden return of the Muses is still something of a surprise. In epic, too, it is typical for internal invocations to the Muses to occur at points where the speaker is at a loss or has to deal with especially difficult material (e.g., the long appeal in *Il.* 2. 484–93, before the Catalogue of Ships), but there one usually has the feeling that the song of the Muses and the song of the poet have been moving along in unison (or, rather, have been identical), and not, as is the case in the *Works and Days*, that the speaker has gone off on his own discourse.

Hesiod's text remains ambiguous as to whether the persona's speech ought to be understood in the first place as Muse-inspired song or rather as the (not explicitly poetic) utterance of a wise man who relies on his own authority. The *Works and Days* (a work in any case not famous for its internal coherence) thus appears as a strange hybrid, in which the didactic mode found in traditional Wisdom Literature, as well as in certain Homeric speeches, has been combined, but not wholly reconciled, with the poetic self-consciousness of genres like epic. In this context it is interesting to note that, as R. P. Martin 1992: 22–7 and others have shown, Hesiod's poem also

---

[47] Note that the mention of the Muses three lines earlier (658–9, where they are said to have 'first put [the speaker] onto [the path of] high-pitched song') and the preceding narrative of the poetic contest at Chalcis (654–7) do not themselves constitute poetic self-consciousness and simultaneity respectively. That the speaker is a poet and was taught by the Muses does not necessarily imply that he is also uttering his actual words qua poet; note the case of Horace' *Ars poetica*, discussed above, whose speaker, though a professional poet, presents his *sermo* explicitly as non-poetic (*nil scribens*, 306).

incorporates elements of a number of other separate genres, such as the fable, the folk song, and the proverb. The work, which from our perspective just about qualifies as a didactic poem, is thus perhaps better described as a unique, and none too coherent, mixture of genres. To what extent this combination of various elements was the original work of a poet named Hesiod, or whether there was indeed an older tradition of poetry of this kind (and not just of the various genres and modes that make up its parts), cannot be ascertained. From the retrospective point of view of the literary historian, at any rate, the *Works and Days* is the first didactic poem and at the same time, not surprisingly, the most unorthodox one (see Cox 1969: 124–5).[48]

Surveys of ancient didactic poetry usually include Parmenides' philosophical poem, but as I have already briefly mentioned, this text is quite different from the other Greek and Latin examples and does not fit my definition of this genre. Like Hesiod, Parmenides made use of the traditional didactic mode in order to impart, not advice, but theoretical knowledge, and in doing so, he created a poem with a coherent and original conceptual and narrative framework. Unlike Hesiod, however, Parmenides did not 'start off' a poetic genre with his work; rather, his poem, for all its traditional elements, remains a unique creation.

As far as we can tell from the fragments, the poem fails the test for didactic poetry on all four counts. It does not itself exhibit didactic intent, for the person who wishes to teach is not the speaker, but rather the goddess, that is, a character in the narrative. The typical teacher–student constellation is likewise absent or, rather, it is reversed: instead of taking the role of the teacher, the speaker of the poem is in fact the student who receives instruction from the goddess, whose teaching speech takes up the greater part of the fragments. Furthermore, the text shows neither poetic self-consciousness nor poetic simultaneity: in fact, the whole notion of

---

[48] Other works ascribed to Hesiod, such as the *Precepts of Chiron* or the *Great Works*, do not throw much light on the history of didactic poetry since they survive only in fragments and cannot be dated with certainty. Note that one passage from the *Precepts of Chiron* (fr. 283) exhibits at least the didactic mode. Given the title, however, it appears unlikely that the instructions would have been spoken by the persona of the poet; one might imagine rather that, like many of the Near Eastern wisdom texts, the poem purported to be the speech of a wise man, in this case Chiron's instructions to Achilles. However, if fr. 283 really was the beginning, as Σ *ad* Pind. *Pyth.* 6. 22 claims, the poem lacked an introduction and started immediately with the teachings.

poetry is absent. The speaker never presents his words as 'song' or the like, and the text, as we have it, does not contain an invocation to the Muses, an announcement of topic, or any other proemial feature. Indeed, if the poem did actually begin with B1 (the description of the speaker's chariot ride and his reception by the goddess), as we are told by Sextus Empiricus (*Math.* 7. 111), it plunged right into the unmediated narrative.

Since the unnamed goddess provides information to the speaker, one might see her as a Muse-like figure, and it is certainly possible that the Muses and their function in epic might have given Parmenides the idea or have shaped his depiction of the goddess (cf. M. R. Wright 1997: 6–9). However, she is not called a Muse, and her speech is never described as poetry or singing. Likewise, the famous chariot ride at the beginning might make one think of the use of the journey metaphor for poetry. Again, however, there is no indication in the text that the chariot ride stands for the progress of Parmenides' poem; rather, it describes the speaker's journey toward knowledge, just as the path metaphors in the speech of the goddess (see esp. B2, B6, and B7 on the ὁδοὶ διζήσιος) refer to intellectual methods, 'ways' of looking at the world.[49]

Like the persona, the goddess, too, never presents her own words as poetry. However, her speech is extremely self-referential: she draws attention to the process of her own teaching (e.g., εἰ δ' ἄγ' ἐγὼν ἐρέω, B2. 1; see also B2. 6, B8. 60–1), addresses direct and indirect commands to her student (e.g., κόμισαι δὲ σὺ μῦθον ἀκούσας, B2. 1; see also B4. 1, B6. 2, B7. 2–8. 1), and creates the impression of simultaneity by indicating to which point of her speech she has come (e.g., . . . κρῖναι δὲ λόγῳ πολύδηριν ἔλεγχον | ἐξ ἐμέθεν ῥηθέντα [*reference to the preceding argument*]. μόνος δ' ἔτι μῦθος ὁδοῖο | λείπεται ὡς ἔστιν [*reference to the argument about to begin*], B7. 5–8. 2; see also B6. 3, B8. 50–2). Her speech thus sounds remarkably like a didactic poem—only without the poetry. In other words, it is an example of the didactic mode, the traditional teaching style, which Parmenides, unlike Hesiod, employs not for the speech of his persona, but for a character in that persona's story. In a sense, Parmenides' poem works like the traditional wisdom texts, only that the framing narrative is in the first person: not 'a farmer instructed his son', but 'the goddess instructed me'. As in these texts,

---

[49] On the chariot ride of Parmenides, see now Asper 1997: 73–8, who stresses that it is not to be understood as a metaphor for poetry; differently, e.g., Nünlist 1998: 260–1.

and unlike in Hesiod, poetry is not given a role in the teaching process.

The situation is different in Empedocles, whose *On Nature* is the first text that unequivocally fulfils my four criteria.[50] Singled out by Aristotle as the example of a poem that treats 'something medical or physical' (*Poet.* 1447ᵇ16) and chosen as a formal model by Lucretius, Empedocles' work appears to us as the first 'true' didactic poem, that is, as the first poem that exhibits those characteristics that we associate with later manifestations of the genre. The speaker's didactic intent and the teacher–student constellation, our first two criteria, are apparent from the repeated addresses to Pausanias, who is continually exhorted to pay attention to and learn from the persona's words, as, for example, in Παυσανίη, σὺ δὲ κλῦθι, δαίφρονος Ἀγχίτεω υἱέ (B1).[51] Like the persona of the *Works and Days* and the goddess of Parmenides, the Empedoclean speaker throughout the text refers to his ongoing teaching with such verbs as ἐρέω (B8. 1, B17. 1, 16) and λέξω (B38. 1). However, Empedocles' teaching speech also clearly exhibits poetic self-consciousness, the third criterion for didactic poetry: his persona is a poet inspired by the Muses, who can refer to his exhortations to Pausanias as ἡμετέρης . . . πιστώματα Μούσης (B4. 2) and who tells his student that he had better believe what he, Pausanias, has heard 'from a god', θεοῦ πάρα μῦθον ἀκούσας (B23. 11).[52]

Unlike the speaker of the *Works and Days*, who, after presenting

[50] I cannot enter here into the controversy over whether Empedocles' extant fragments all belong to one single work or whether the two transmitted titles, Περὶ φύσεως and Καθαρμοί, refer to two different poems; for a brief survey and discussion of the different views, see Obbink 1993, whose own opinion about the Καθαρμοί were a 'set of oracular-sounding selections from the larger poem *On Nature* that circulated as a separate text' (1993: 56–7 n. 15) I find rather attractive. Note that the new Strasbourg papyrus does not settle the question, either, but shows that B139, previously typically ascribed to the Καθαρμοί, was clearly part of the second book of Περὶ φύσεως (see A. Martin and Primavesi 1999: 114–19).

[51] On the student figure in Empedocles, see Obbink 1993, who on p. 72 provides a list of the direct addresses to Pausanias; to this we may now add three passages from the Strasbourg papyrus, a (ii) 21–2, 29–30, and d 10–11, as reconstructed by A. Martin and Primavesi 1999. Admittedly, the teacher–student constellation is made somewhat more complicated by the fact that in some of the fragments, the poet speaks to his audience in the plural (see Obbink 1993: 76–80), notably in B112, which is addressed to the citizens of Acragas. However, according to Diogenes Laertius 8. 54, this fragment constituted the beginning of the Καθαρμοί (see n. 50, above), which, if a work separate from the Περὶ φύσεως, need not have had the same addressee; if, as Obbink (1993: 77–8) suggests, it was instead a kind of anthology from the larger poem, B112 could have been added as a proem for purposes of (rhapsodic) performance.

[52] The reference is almost certainly to the Muse, not to the supposedly divine nature of Empedocles himself; see Kranz 1944: 77 n. 16; M. R. Wright 1995: 181.

himself as a poet in the proem (by means of his invocation to the Muses), does not dwell on this aspect of his activity and, for the greater part of the poem, appears simply in the role of the teacher, the Empedoclean persona, even in those few fragments that we possess, speaks of his undertaking clearly in terms of poetry, using elaborate metaphors reminiscent of the imagery of Pindar. Thus, for example, he prays to the gods to make a 'pure spring' flow from his mouth (ἐκ δ' ὁσίων στομάτων καθαρὴν ὀχετεύσατε πηγήν, B3. 2)[53] and asks the Muse to drive the εὐήνιον ἅρμα (B2. 5). These images, the flowing spring and the chariot ride, are evocative of poetic simultaneity, our final criterion, a concept clearly discernible in Empedocles' poem. Using another water metaphor, the poet marks his transition from one part of his teaching speech to the next as follows:

αὐτὰρ ἐγὼ παλίνορσος ἐλεύσομαι ἐς πόρον ὕμνων,
τὸν πρότερον κατέλεξα, λόγου λόγον ἐξοχετεύων
κεῖνον.

(B35. 1–3)

(But I shall turn back to the stream of songs that was my subject before, deriving this argument from that one.)[54]

While this passage is expressive of the poet's, and poem's, progress, the following prayer to the Muse gives a vivid impression of simultaneity by implying that the speaker's composition is going on right now:

εὐχομένῳ νῦν αὖτε παρίστασο, Καλλιόπεια,
ἀμφὶ θεῶν μακάρων ἀγαθὸν λόγον ἐμφαίνοντι.

(B131. 3–4)

(Kalliopeia, stand by me now again as I pray and as I show forth a good speech about the blessed gods.)

As he speaks, the poet is in the process of 'showing forth' his treatment of the gods, that is, presumably, his ongoing poem about physics (see Obbink 1993: 59).

Empedocles thus seamlessly combines the roles of teacher and poet, which in Hesiod still appear to exist somewhat uneasily side

---

[53] On water metaphors for poetry, see Nünlist 1998: 178–205, who quotes the Empedocles passage on p. 188; cf. also B35. 1–3, quoted below in the text.

[54] On 'watercourse, channel' *vel sim.* as the sense of πόρος required in this passage, see Becker 1937: 148–9 n. 22.

Ancient Didactic Poetry 53

by side. Doing so not only makes his poem more coherent, but also serves an important rhetorical function: the Empedoclean persona is not just a teacher who also happens to be a poet (or vice versa), but his authority as teacher derives from the very fact that he is inspired by the Muses. Listening to him, Pausanias is listening to the goddesses of poetry themselves, θεοῦ πάρα μῦθον ἀκούσας (B23. 11). By presenting his philosophy not only in poetic form, but explicitly as poetry, the speaker is able to exploit for his own purposes the powerful paradigm of divine inspiration (cf. also Most 1999: 353). In the work of Empedocles, poetry and teaching, *carmen* and *res*, are for the first time inextricably linked: poetry is the natural medium for the speaker's cosmological teaching; in fact, were it not for the poetry, there would be no teaching.[55]

More than a century lies between Empedocles and Aratus, and the history of didactic poetry during this period is hard to assess (cf. Wöhrle 1998). Still, despite the silence of our sources, it seems unlikely that, as some scholars have assumed, the genre died out and was not practised at all.[56] Aristotle's formulation in *Poetics* 1447[b]16–20 gives the impression that he mentions Empedocles only as one (outstanding) example of the kind of poetry that deals with 'some medical or physical topic' (16). While this is not proof, it is at least a strong indication that some kind of didactic poetry continued to be composed in the fourth century. As a matter of fact, we do possess considerable fragments of one of these works; however, it is fair to say that the *Hedypatheia* of Archestratus of Gela is anything but a typical didactic poem.

Thanks to Athenaeus' gastronomic interests, sixty-three fragments survive of what appears to be a systematic didactic poem on where to find and how to prepare the world's best foods.[57]

---

[55] Note that with this analysis of Empedoclean poetics, I do not intend to provide an answer to the question (tackled recently by Wöhrle 1993; M. R. Wright 1997; and Most 1999: 350–9) of why the historical author Empedocles (just as his near-contemporaries Parmenides and Xenophanes) chose poetry as the medium for his philosophy instead of prose; in fact, I am inclined to agree with Osborne 1997 (who is specifically responding to Wright) that this question would not have put itself to Empedocles, who may simply have regarded verse as the 'natural' form of his thought.

[56] See, e.g., Cox 1969: 132: 'Empedocles stood at the end of an era. Didactic poetry was soon dormant and apparently dead'.

[57] For the text and interpretation of Archestratus' poem, see now the new edn. of Olson and Sens 2000. The authors date the work to the first two-thirds of the 4th cent. (p. xxi) and estimate that the *c*.330 preserved verses 'represent at least 28 per cent of the text and perhaps considerably more' (p. xxiv).

Addressed to two students (Ath. 7. 278e), Moschus (5. 2; 28. 1; 36. 4) and Cleander (18. 3), the poem clearly shows didactic intent and, with the help of frequent references to the speaker's speaking, creates the impression of simultaneity; however, at least in the surviving fragments the persona never presents his words explicitly as poetry. While parodic elements are obvious throughout the poem, which has clearly some affinity to contemporary mock-epic (see Olson and Sens 2000: pp. xxxi–xxxv), it must be pointed out that the speaker himself takes both his subject matter and his didactic mission quite seriously (see Effe 1977: 235) and also that the *Hedypatheia* abounds in detailed and quite technical information. Olson and Sens 2000: pp. xxxv–xliii convincingly place the poem in the cultural context of a 'broad late classical literary interest in fine food and dining with roots in the Sicilian culinary tradition' (p. xliii) and point to tantalizing evidence that there existed in the same period other hexameter 'cookbooks', such as the work of one Philoxenus mentioned in fragment 189 of Plato Comicus. In their poetic treatment of specialist knowledge, these works thus appear as forerunners of Hellenistic didactic poetry.

Whether it had to be revived, or whether, in fact, it never ceased to exist, didactic poetry became fashionable in the Hellenistic period. Of the many works produced in this era, only Aratus' *Phaenomena* and Nicander's *Theriaca* and *Alexipharmaca* survive, but they allow us to form an idea of what the genre was like and for which reasons it was appreciated. Generally speaking, compared to both Empedocles and the later Latin works, the poems of Aratus and Nicander appear more technical and scientific, and less explicitly poetic. While Aratus was not an astrologer and Nicander did not have specialist knowledge about snakes and poisons, they based their poems on prose treatises on their respective subjects and thus, like their models, aspired to a certain comprehensiveness and scientific correctness.[58] A growing interest in science and technology must have contributed to the popularity of such poems, and

[58] The astrological part of the *Phaenomena* is based on a work of Eudoxus; the section on weather-signs probably goes back to a 4th-cent. Aristotelian treatise (see Hunter 1995; Fantuzzi 1996: 958). Both the *Theriaca* and the *Alexipharmaca* appear to be modelled on works by a certain Apollodorus (early 3rd cent.; see Gow and Scholfield 1953: 18). At least for Cicero it was a fact that neither poet was himself a specialist in the field that he had treated—quite the contrary: *constat inter doctos hominem ignarum astrologiae ornatissimis atque optimis uersibus Aratum de caelo stellisque dixisse . . . de rebus rusticis hominem ab agro remotissimum Nicandrum Colophonium poetica quadam facultate, non rustica, scripsisse praeclare* (*De or.* 1. 69; the reference is to Nicander's *Georgica*, which survives only in fragments).

while I remain sceptical about the claim in Schuler and Fitch 1983: 11–12 that Hellenistic didactic poetry constituted a serious attempt to popularize science, it is a fact that at least Aratus' work was read as a textbook on astronomy throughout antiquity and into the Middle Ages and was taken seriously enough to warrant a commentary by the famous astronomer Hipparchus (2nd cent. BC).[59] However, it appears that the main appeal of didactic poetry in the Hellenistic age lay in the very fact that poets attempted to tackle such unwieldy, unpoetic, technical subjects.[60] Learned authors and learned audience alike must have enjoyed the *l'art pour l'art* of a kind of poetry whose topics were the obscurest of the obscure (say, snake-bites) and which purported to give advice for situations in which no member of this urban society would ever find himself (thus, the *Phaenomena* is geared toward the needs of farmers and sailors, and Nicander's work tells you, for example, how to protect yourself against reptiles when forced to spend the night in the woods).[61]

I have in the preceding paragraph veered from the path of purely intra-textual analysis and speculated on the actual interests of the Hellenistic authors and readers, in the belief that these might be able to throw some light on the remarkably low degree of poetic

---

[59] It is somewhat harder to believe that Nicander's obscure poems were ever taken as science, let alone *popularized* science. See Dalzell 1996: 29–30, who also provides an amusing collection of what exasperated classicists have had to say about the Colophonian poet.

[60] For this widely held view, see, e.g., Kroll 1925: 1847–50 (cf. 1924: 185–8), who, for his part, is clearly disgusted by Hellenistic didactic poetry as he perceives it (e.g., on Aratus: 'So vermacht Arat der Nachwelt die Wahl eines möglichst unpoetischen und dem eigenen Verständnis fernliegenden Stoffes und die Ermächtigung, ihn unter rücksichtsloser Ausnutzung der theoretisch denkbaren Mittel gegen jedes gesunde Sprachgefühl in Verse zu bringen' (1925: 1850); this view of Aratus is combated by Effe 1977: 40–56). While most recent scholars will not share Kroll's negative attitude toward this kind of Hellenistic learned poetry, they do still tend to accept his analysis of Hellenistic didactic as 'Stilübung' and 'Bravourstück' (Kroll 1925: 1847; cf. esp. Effe 1977: 56–65, who exemplifies his 'formal type' of didactic poetry with Nicander).

[61] See Effe 1977: 42–3 and Bing 1993: 103–8 on the audience of Aratus. To explain the popularity of didactic poetry in the Hellenistic age, as I have just done, with reference to this period's notorious love of the learned and the obscure, is admittedly neither original nor particularly insightful. However, this somewhat banal view appears to me preferable to the widespread idea, expounded in detail first by Reitzenstein 1931: 41–52 (of later scholarship, cf. esp. Reinsch-Werner 1976: 1–23 and *passim*), that under the influence of Callimachean poetics, didactic poetry (a 'smaller genre') came to be seen as a preferable alternative to epic and that Hesiod was regarded as a model poet and therefore imitated, e.g., by Aratus. This theory can in my eyes not be proved (cf. Cameron 1995: 362–86, esp. 362–3) and appears to be based mainly on Callim. *Epigr.* 27, which, however, refers specifically to Aratus and need not be taken as making a general statement about poetry or the pros and cons of individual authors or genres.

self-consciousness in the didactic poems of the age. If readers really expected works like those of Aratus or Nicander to be scientific treatises in verse (the 'popularized science' thesis) or, more probably, to artfully imitate scientific treatises in the outlandish medium of verse (the *l'art pour l'art* thesis), excessive self-consciously metapoetic reflection would have either defeated the purpose or spoiled the illusion. Be that as it may, as the following short analysis will show, both the *Phaenomena* and the *Theriaca* and *Alexipharmaca*, despite what one may call their dryness, clearly do qualify as didactic poems according to our definition, which shows that by the Hellenistic age, the genre, which had reached its standard format with Empedocles, was firmly established.

Aratus' poem is exceedingly sparing with references to the speaker's speaking. Still, there is the proem (1–18), which clearly indicates a beginning (ἐκ Διὸς ἀρχώμεσθα, 1); the *praeteritio*, where the poet famously refuses to treat the planets (460–1); two points where he declares that he will not leave certain constellations unmentioned (179–80; 607–8); and the rhetorical question, τί τοι λέγω ὅσσα πέλονται | σήματ' ἐπ' ἀνθρώπους; (1036–7). These instances are enough to create self-consciousness and simultaneity; the sole invocation to the Muses (16–18), furthermore, indicates that the speaker understands his words explicitly as poetry. As mentioned above, the persona's didactic intent is never clearly expressed, but should probably be inferred from his frequent addresses to a 'you'.[62] The presence of this anonymous addressee enables us to claim for the *Phaenomena* the teacher–student constellation typical, and necessary, for didactic poetry; however, it should be noted that, despite some references to the student's potential interest in farming and sailing (collected by Bing 1993: 100 n. 3; here, and elsewhere, the influence of Hesiod is clear[63]), his character remains so undefined that one might in many instances take the 'you' simply to be a generic 'one'. Generally speaking, while the *Phaenomena* clearly exhibits all four criteria for didactic poetry, it makes strikingly little use of them. On the whole, the poem is more like epic, and not only because of its greater 'objectivity'. Note, for example, the fact that the work begins with a

[62] See the list in Bing 1993: 109, which also contains all occurrences of the first-person singular.
[63] For parallels (and differences) between the *Phaenomena* and the *Works and Days* (apart from general thematic and structural similarities, note esp. the figure of Dike and the myth of the Ages of Man), see Hunter 1995; Fantuzzi 1996: 958–9; and Kidd 1997: 8–10.

hymn, which is clearly reminiscent of the use of προοίμια in Archaic Greek epic performance.[64] Aratus' hymn to Zeus shares important features with the *Homeric Hymns*, such as the use of a form of ἄρχομαι at the beginning (1) and the greeting χαῖρε at the end (15); as in a proper rhapsodic performance, the actual song after the 'proem' begins with an invocation to the Muses (16–18) and an announcement of the topic, ἀστέρας (17).[65] It is therefore not surprising that, in contrast to Callimachus, whose opinion of the *Phaenomena* was that Ἡσιόδου τό τ' ἄεισμα καὶ ὁ τρόπος (*Epigr.* 27. 1), many ancient readers thought that Aratus was rather a ζηλωτής . . . Ὁμήρου (see Reitzenstein 1931: 43–4; Cameron 1995: 374–80).

Nicander's poems are more obviously didactic. Both the *Theriaca* and the *Alexipharmaca* are dedicated to named students, Hermesianax and Protagoras respectively, and these dedicatees are again and again addressed in the course of the texts. Also, the speaker continuously refers to his own speech and the process of instruction. Even more so than in Aratus, though, there is next to no explicit indication that the persona's words are to be regarded as poetry. Strikingly, both the *Theriaca* and the *Alexipharmaca* lack invocations to the Muses or, in fact, any mention of the goddesses at all (see Koster 1970: 153; Pöhlmann 1973: 847–8). In both proems, the persona simply declares that he will speak about remedies for snake-bites and poisons respectively. While the verbs used, φωνήσαιμι (*Ther.* 4) and αὐδήσαιμ' (*Alex.* 5), are evocative of poetic speech, this quality of the speaker's instructions is not made explicit. However, in each work the *sphragis* hints that what has preceded is in fact a poem, for when the speaker names himself Nicander, he qualifies his name, in the *Theriaca* with Ὁμήρειος (957), in the *Alexipharmaca* with ὑμνοπόλος (629). In my eyes, this is enough to attribute poetic self-consciousness even to the most technical and bizarre manuals of Nicander.[66]

[64] Cf. Kidd 1997: 161–2. Erren 1967: 9–31, esp. 14–15 sees the model rather in the ritual libations-cum-invocations at the beginning of the symposium: Aratus 'tut . . . so, als ob er bei einem Symposion spräche' (15). Hunter 1995 compares the hymn to Zeus at the beginning of the *Works and Days* (presumably for the content), but does not remark on the structural differences.

[65] Cf. Apollonius' *Argonautica*, which likewise begins with a hymn/'proem' (1. 1–4), while the Muses are invoked only later (1. 22). As Albis 1996: 6–8 has argued, Apollonius was trying to recreate the sequence of an Archaic performance of epic. So, apparently, was Aratus.

[66] Note that for all their dearth of poetic self-consciousness proper, the poems of Aratus and Nicander (and, as far as we can tell, that of Archestratus) are still vastly more explicitly poetic than, say, Horace's *Ars poetica*, which, as we have seen, goes out of its way not to

As this short survey has shown, Hesiod, Empedocles, Aratus, and Nicander are the main representatives of didactic poetry (as I define it) before Lucretius. Of the four, Empedocles most closely matches my definition of the didactic poem and is most similar to the kind of didactic poetry practised by the four Latin authors who are the subject of this book. The reason for this is, of course, that Lucretius chose Empedocles as his model, and Vergil, Ovid, and Manilius are, in turn, strongly dependent on Lucretius.[67] I shall trace this development in the following four chapters; however, there first remain to be examined what scant traces we have of the Latin didactic poems prior to Lucretius.

When Conte 1994*b*: 160 writes that '[u]ntil the *De Rerum Natura*, Latin literature had not produced fully serious works of didactic poetry', this seemingly correct observation is based not on our detailed knowledge of a body of early Latin didactic poetry, but rather on the near-complete lack of information, let alone texts, that might illuminate how writers of the Early and Middle Republic practised this particular genre, or otherwise failed to do so. Still, we have some indication that didactic poetry was written in Rome before Lucretius, and it is worth while quickly to review the admittedly patchy evidence. One might indeed be tempted to apply Conte's verdict, 'not fully serious', to the *Hedyphagetica* of Ennius, a poem about good food based on the work of Archestratus. It is interesting that the one surviving fragment (see Courtney 1993: 22–5), a list of fish, exhibits a number of features typical of didactic poetry, which make it likely that the entire *Hedyphagetica* was a 'standard' didactic poem that fulfilled all four criteria. The eleven lines are clearly addressed to some kind of student, who is given both practical advice on which fish to buy (*sume*, 4; *fac emas*, 6) and theoretical information on their quality (*scito*, 5). Furthermore, the persona refers to the process of his own speaking with the rhetorical question, *quid scarum praeterii cerebrum Iouis paene supremi?* (7), a phrase that strongly gives the illusion of simultaneity. There is no explicit

present itself as poetry. Thus, these works have such poetic trappings as proems and epilogues and present themselves as deliberately and systematically structured discourses in a way radically opposed to Horace's affected 'spontaneous' conversation style.

[67] Obviously, this is at the same time the reason why, with hindsight (and all speculation about genre takes place with hindsight, as I have argued), Empedocles' work appears to be such a standard didactic poem: my idea of the standard didactic poem is, of course, mainly based on those four Latin poets who, directly or indirectly, depend on Empedocles (the Hermeneutic Circle in full swing).

reference to the speaker's words as poetry, but that may be rather much to ask from a fragment of this length (though note the same phenomenon in the fragments of Archestratus; see above). We may thus comfortably regard the *Hedyphagetica* as a nice and early example of Latin didactic poetry; however, it should be kept in mind that the poem is an adaptation of an older Greek text (on the fragment's relationship to what we have of Archestratus, see Olson and Sens 2000: 241–5) and thus should perhaps not carry too much weight as a witness for the development of the genre in Rome (just as, for example, Livius Andronicus is not usually regarded as the originator of Roman epic).

On a more original level, we find tantalizing hints of what may or may not have been a kind of subgenre of didactic poetry popular in the second century BC, namely works of literary history and criticism. Lucius Accius, known mostly as a tragedian, also wrote a theoretical work of at least nine books called *Didascalica*, which was apparently concerned in the first place with questions of Greek and Roman drama (*FPL* 84–6).[68] It is usually believed to have been written in a mixture of prose and poetry, but this may be a mirage: the work may simply have been in prose throughout (thus, e.g., Courtney 1993: 60). In either case, the *Didascalica* cannot be regarded as a typical didactic poem; note, though, that fragment 13 (quoted as an epigraph to the chapter), which may be in sotadeans, addresses a student (*Baebi*), who is told to recognize (*nosce*) the various *genera poematorum*. It is a pity that, unlike Baebius, we no longer have the chance to find out how Accius distinguished between different poetic genres.

A similar concern with literature is found in the works of Porcius Licinus (*FPL* 97–100) and Volcacius Sedigitus (*FPL* 101–3; for both poets, see Courtney 1993: 83–96), whose surviving fragments treat mainly comedy, specifically Terence. Porcius Licinus writes in trochaic septenarii, and Volcacius Sedigitus' *De poetis* is in iambic senarii, and this makes their works look rather atypical for the mainly hexametric genre of didactic poetry (though see Kroll 1925: 1851 and 1853 for Greek didactic poems not in hexameters); it appears likely that the poets chose these metres in accordance with their subject matter (both occur in comedy), just as Ovid was to use

---

[68] The title of the work has nothing to do with didactic poetry (see the use of *didascalicus* by Servius, quoted in Sect. 2.2, above), but rather with the *didascaliae*, 'production notices', of plays (Gk. διδασκαλίαι).

elegiacs, an appropriately 'erotic' metre, for his *Ars amatoria* (see Sect. 5.1, below). Since the scanty remains of both poets' work do not exhibit any of our four defining characteristics, it is impossible to say whether these curious poems were in fact didactic in our sense or not.[69]

We are on more familiar ground once we come to the time of Lucretius himself. A certain Egnatius likewise wrote a *De rerum natura* in hexameters (*FPL* 143–4; Courtney 1993: 147–8), and Cicero (*Q Fr.* 2. 10. 3) mentions the *Empedoclea* of one Sallustius, which, in contrast to Lucretius' poem, he appears to find quite unstomachable.[70] The latter work may, of course, have been a translation of Empedocles' own poem, just as Cicero himself had in his youth created a Latin version of Aratus, an undertaking in which he was to be followed by Varro of Atax, Ovid, Germanicus, and Avienus. At any rate, it appears that by the beginning of the first century BC, didactic poetry like that of Empedocles and Aratus was not unheard of in Rome and was practised, in more or less original fashion, by Latin writers. Lucretius thus did not have to rediscover a forgotten Greek genre; his achievement was rather to create an original masterwork, *multis luminibus ingeni, multae tamen artis* (Cic. *Q Fr.* 2. 10. 3), in the confines of an extant type of literature that was at least reasonably well established in the Rome of his age.

2.4. Perceptions of Didactic Poetry in the First Century BC

This brief history of pre-Lucretian didactic poetry has finally brought us back to a specific problem of genre criticism I mentioned before only to disregard it. Tracing the development of a specific genre with hindsight, as I have done in these pages, is one thing. However, this approach disregards the question of how authors and audience experienced the phenomenon genre at the time. For example, was Lucretius aware that he was writing a

---

[69] The one exception is Volcacius Sedigitus fr. 1. 3, where a first-person speaker addresses a second person with a phrase that one might want to regard as a self-conscious reference to the speaker's teaching speech: *eum meo iudicio errorem dissoluam tibi*. There is, however, no indication that this speech is regarded as specifically poetic.

[70] *Lucreti poemata, ut scribis, ita sunt, multis luminibus ingeni, multae tamen artis; sed cum ueneris. Virum te putabo si Sallusti Empedoclea legeris, hominem non putabo* (for the interpretation of the last sentence, see the amusing discussion in Shackleton Bailey 1980: 191). On Egnatius and Sallustius, see Rawson 1985: 285.

'didactic poem'? Did his readers—Cicero, for instance—regard the *De rerum natura* as belonging to the specific genre that classical scholars believe they can isolate? What about Vergil? Centuries later, Servius could simply state about the *Georgics, hi libri didascalici sunt (Praef. ad Georg.* 129. 9 Thilo). Would Vergil himself have been able to describe his work in such a way? What about Ovid and Manilius? Note that the question of whether a particular genre was perceived as such at the time is especially interesting in the case of didactic poetry: as we have seen, at least the common-sense view of genre did not recognize a specific didactic genre; also, we do not have any independent testimony concerning ideas about didactic poetry from my four authors' time and place (Rome of the middle and late first century BC and early first century AD).[71]

To abandon the anachronistic view of genre and ask what a genre meant to the people who dealt with it at the time is important also in view of the fact that in genre theory, genre is often seen as a kind of contract that regulates the behaviour of both author and reader. In the words of Heather Dubrow,

[T]he way genre establishes a relationship between author and reader might fruitfully be labelled a generic contract. Through such signals as the title, the meter and the incorporation of familiar topoi into the opening lines, the poet sets up such a contract with us. He in effect agrees that he will follow at least some of the patterns and conventions we associate with the genre or genres in which he is writing, and we in turn agree that we will pay close attention to certain aspects of his work while realizing that others, because of the nature of the genres, are likely to be far less important (1982: 31; see also 2).

In Latin studies, this approach has been represented first and foremost by Gian Biagio Conte, who writes that genre 'proposes itself as a field of reference within which the addressee can recognize, by means of comparisons and contrasts, the specificity of the text' (1994*a*: 154 n. 2; see also 36). On this view, it is crucial that both author and readers know that what they are dealing with (the *Georgics*, say) is in fact a didactic poem—otherwise, there might be serious misunderstandings.

A second theoretical reason to enquire into contemporary

---

[71] Cicero's report that, according to general knowledge, Aratus and Nicander treated topics in which they were not specialists (*De or.* 1. 69) and his verdict that Lucretius' poem was good and Sallustius' bad (*Q Fr.* 2. 10. 3) do not throw much light on 1st-cent. views of didactic poetry in general.

perceptions of genre is the observation that in Latin literature of the first century BC, a number of genres were undergoing interesting developments (e.g., the short and vigorous flourishing of subjective love elegy), and that, consequently, questions of genre often became the explicit subject matter of poetry itself. This phenomenon, too, has been described perceptively by Conte, who writes that the 'whole development of literary production from Catullus to Ovid can be considered as a process of the construction of genres' (1994*a*: 115) and notes that one characteristic of Roman poetry of this time is 'its tendency to put the choice of language and of genre in "dramatic" terms, almost to "stage" the problem of the choice of literary form' (120). This is not the place to discuss in full this tendency, to which I have alluded earlier (see above, n. 6) and to which I shall return in the chapter on Vergil. To illustrate the point, let me mention only one especially striking example for the explicit reflection on a particular generic choice. In *Fasti* 2. 119–26, the Ovidian persona falls into a panic, faced with the task of having to treat the fact that Augustus was given the honorary title *pater patriae* on 5 February. He fears that the genre he has chosen—elegy—will prove too 'weak' for this undertaking and expresses remorse that he has not decided on epic instead (*quid uolui demens elegis imponere tantum | ponderis? heroi res erat ista pedis*, 125–6).[72] The 'staging' here is particularly dramatic; however, every student of Augustan poetry would be able to come up with numerous similar instances of metageneric reflection.

Given this fact about the poetry of the period in question, one might be hopeful that the works on which I have chosen to focus, too, might explicitly discuss the implications of their genre, in this case, didactic poetry. However, wholly unlike, say, elegy, the didactic works of Lucretius, Vergil, Ovid, and Manilius turn out to be not very forthcoming on the question of their generic affiliation. While it is not surprising that the poems are never called 'didactic' (the Latin of their time probably did not have a word for the genre; it was only later that grammarians like Servius and Diomedes borrowed *didascalicus* from the Greek), we might expect that they would express their generic allegiance by means of reference to their models or predecessors (cf. the view of Rosenmeyer 1985: 81–2 that genre is, synchronically, the *imitatio* of a literary 'father figure'; see Sect. 2.1, above). Indeed, the Lucretian persona praises the

[72] See Conte 1994*a*: 124–5.

poetic genius of Empedocles (1. 731–3), and the speaker of the *Georgics* famously declares, *Ascraeumque cano Romana per oppida carmen* (2. 176). However, it is quite obvious that the *De rerum natura* is not modelled solely on Empedocles, just as Vergil's poem is not simply an *Ascraeum carmen*. Both works abound in allusions to a multitude of other poets, not all of them didactic.[73]

As for the 'staging' of the generic choice, this is most developed in Vergil's *Georgics*. As I shall show in detail in Chapter 4, this poem exhibits prominently what Conte has described as the 'most characteristic, most constant element of Augustan poetry', namely the 'poet's insistence on letting us know that he could also be doing something else' (1994a: 123). However, the type of poetry actually chosen is not explicitly described in terms we would use to identify didactic poetry. Rather, the insistence that the poem, just like its subject matter, is lowly and humble (speaking about farm animals means *angustis . . . addere rebus honorem*, 3. 290; notice also the repetition of the keyword *tenuis* (1. 177; 4. 6)) puts the *Georgics* into the same category as other 'small' genres, such as elegy, that is, the type of poetry that Augustan writers are wont to defend in that dramatization of generic choice par excellence, the *recusatio*. Note also that when in the *Remedia amoris* the Ovidian speaker responds to critics of the *Ars amatoria* (*Rem. am.* 361–98), he defends his work explicitly as a representative of the genre of *elegy* (esp. 379–80), not of didactic poetry.

On the whole, the Latin works in question, for all their poetic self-consciousness, do not show themselves to be particularly aware of being specifically didactic poetry. There are three possible explanations for this phenomenon. First, we have to beware the intentional fallacy and keep in mind that the evidence of the poems cannot tell us what their authors really had in mind. It is possible that Lucretius, Vergil, Ovid, and Manilius had as clear a picture of the genre of didactic poetry as we do and simply chose not to make this aspect of their poetry part of their works' metapoetic reflection.

However, given that in contemporary criticism, too, the notion of didactic poetry was, at best, murky, one might come to the conclusion that our four poets were not in fact fully aware that the

---

[73] Ennius is evoked as a model in the *De rerum natura*, as is Homer (see esp. 1. 120–6: both epicists, it is implied, wrote *de rerum natura* and are thus predecessors of the speaker), while the *Georgics* at points presents itself as *imitatio* of, among others, Homer, Pindar, and Callimachus (on intertextuality in the *Georgics*, see the extensive study of Farrell 1991 and now Gale 2000); cf. Chs. 3 and 4, below.

works they were creating could be classified as a specific genre, which later critics, such as Servius and Diomedes, would come to recognize as 'didactic'. To postulate such a lack of generic awareness is not wholly absurd; as Alastair Fowler writes, 'generic operations are partly unconscious' (1982: 25; see also 43), and this must be even more true when there is no generally accepted theory of, and not even a name for, the genre in question. Thus, Lucretius, Vergil, and Manilius may well have regarded their works as some kind of epic;[74] Ovid, as we have seen, explicitly put the *Ars amatoria* in the category of elegy.

However, as a third possibility, a sceptic might argue that the poets' silence indicates that the whole notion of didactic poetry is nothing but an anachronistic construct, imposed on works to which such a classification is alien and which should instead be studied and understood in their own right rather than in the light of some later theory of genre. To this argument I would answer that, while my definition of didactic poetry with its four characteristics is obviously an abstraction made with hindsight, it is indeed striking that these three poets, as well as many others, adhere to it, consciously or not. Whether they had a clear concept of the genre (or even of genre in general) or simply followed some intuition (just as a parent who makes up a story for a child has a tendency to begin with 'once upon a time', thus entering the confines of the genre 'fairy tale') can no longer be assessed; what remains apparent, however, is that their works clearly share the same features—which is the very observation that led to the postulation of a genre 'didactic poetry' in the first place.

There is one passage in first-century BC Latin poetry that I believe demonstrates that poets of the time 'knew' what it took to write a didactic poem—whether this knowledge was based on some theoretical understanding of the genre or not. This passage does not come from one of the didactic poems of the period, but from a work that is, strictly speaking, to be classified as epic: Ovid's *Metamorphoses*. As is well known, this poem incorporates elements from a number of other genres (e.g., a love-letter reminiscent of the same author's *Heroides* (9. 530–63)) and in the extended speech of

---

[74] The short history of poetry that Manilius presents at 2. 1–48 appears to comprise only works in hexameters (i.e., epic poems, according to the common-sense view of genre), and it is likely that the poet considers himself part of this tradition, despite his immediately following claim of absolute originality.

Pythagoras (15. 75–478) presents what might well be classified as a didactic poem *in nuce*.[75] This monologue exhibits all four characteristics of didactic poetry. The speaker addresses an audience that he attempts to instruct (in this case, to convert to vegetarianism, an undertaking that also involves lengthy theoretical teaching on metamorphosis as the governing principle of the universe). This envisaged audience includes all mortals (see 75) and is usually addressed in the plural, but Pythagoras not infrequently speaks to a generic student in the singular (see 92, 186, 200, 293–4, 333, 362, 364); the form that these addresses take is greatly reminiscent of didactic poetry, especially of Lucretius (see esp. the use of the Lucretian formula *nonne uides*, 362, 382; cf. Schiesaro 1984: 150; Barchiesi 1989: 81). Furthermore, the speech is strikingly self-referential, with Pythagoras drawing attention to the process of his teaching with such words as *doceo* (172), *uaticinor* (174), and *referam* (308). Most interestingly, however, the sage presents his speech explicitly as poetry. Thus, in 143–7 he describes the inspiration that comes to him at this very moment (a true instance of poetic simultaneity) and causes him to 'sing' of the secrets of nature:

> et quoniam deus ora mouet, sequar ora mouentem
> rite deum Delphosque meos ipsumque recludam
> aethera et augustae reserabo oracula mentis.
> magna nec ingeniis inuestigata priorum,
> quaeque diu latuere, canam . . .

(And since a god inspires my speech, I shall, as is right, follow the god who inspires my speech, unlock my Delphi and the sky itself, and open up the oracle of a lofty mind. I shall sing of great wonders never investigated by the minds of earlier men and of things that have been hidden for a long time . . .)

This is not the place to interpret in detail this rich passage (or the one, just as interesting, that follows in 147–52). However, two things are especially worth noting about this portrayal of Pythagoras. First, to have the philosopher speak as a poet would not have been necessary and does in fact come as something of a surprise. Obviously, Ovid is playing with the similarity of prophetic enthusiasm and poetic inspiration: his Pythagoras is a *uates* in both senses (cf. *uaticinor*, 174). Note, though, that the 'inspiration' only

---

[75] See Barchiesi 1989: 77 and 80–1, Myers 1994: 133–47, and P. R. Hardie 1995 on the speech and its affinity to didactic poetry, esp. Lucretius and Empedocles; see also Wheeler 1999: 96.

occurs once Pythagoras has already been speaking for some time and that it changes the direction of his speech: what was a simple diatribe against the eating of meat turns into an ambitious didactic poem about natural philosophy. A sign that Pythagoras is speaking not just as a wise man, but indeed qua poet, is his use of the journey metaphors so popular in didactic poetry: indeed, both the ship (*et quoniam magno feror aequore plenaque uentis | uela dedi*, 176-7) and the chariot (*ne tamen oblitis ad metam tendere longe | exspatiemur equis*, 453-4) make an appearance.

The second interesting fact about Pythagoras' poetic self-consciousness is that it in a sense affords some poetic self-consciousness to the narrator as well. It is the speaker of the *Metamorphoses* who reports Pythagoras' speech, just as he reports many other speeches in the course of the poem, and just as in many of the other framed narratives, especially the longer ones, the voice of the primary narrator becomes blended with that of the secondary one. Additionally, as has often been pointed out, the content of the Pythagoras speech, with its stress on metamorphosis, is pointedly similarly to that of the *Metamorphoses* itself, and Pythagoras even mentions some of the phenomena previously treated by the primary narrator.[76] While the speech cannot have been intended as a kind of philosophical explanation of the events narrated in the poem,[77] it is nevertheless clear that the primary narrator and Pythagoras have an at least partly similar agenda, and the two characters nearly seem to merge when Pythagoras declares (418-20),

> desinet ante dies, et in alto Phoebus anhelos
> aequore tinguet equos, quam consequar omnia uerbis
> in species translata nouas.

(The day will come to an end and Phoebus will plunge his panting horses into the water of the sea before I shall encompass with my words all things that have been changed into new shapes.)

The joke is that these words could also have been uttered by the narrator *in propria persona*.[78] But then again, they could not have

---

[76] Note esp. 237-51 (four elements, cosmogony; cf. 1. 5-31), 262-9 (flood; cf. 1. 260-312), 319-21 (Salmacis; cf. 4. 285-388), and 416-17 (coral; cf. 4. 750-2).

[77] The main 'philosophical' difference is that according to Pythagoras, metamorphosis is a wholly natural process, whereas in Ovid's poem as a whole, it typically appears as an (often catastrophic) disruption of nature.

[78] Pythagoras' topic, *omnia . . . | in species translata nouas* (15. 419-20) is highly reminiscent

been. After all, the speaker of the *Metamorphoses* strictly adheres to the code of 'epic objectivity', limiting poetic self-consciousness nearly exclusively to the proem and epilogue of his poem. If he wants to make a self-conscious statement about the progress of his composition, he must do so through the mouth of a secondary persona, in this case Pythagoras.

To come back to the question of didactic poetry, it seems to me that Ovid intended the Pythagoras speech as the imitation of a particular type of poetry, which may not have had a name, but which had clear and recognizable characteristics.[79] While it appears that he wished in the first place to imitate—or, perhaps rather, parody—Lucretius (both in diction and content, the speech is close to the *De rerum natura*, while at the same time blatantly contradicting its philosophical view, most notably on the question of the soul's immortality), I still think that we can regard the Pythagoras speech as an indication that Ovid and his contemporaries had some concept of didactic poetry as a genre.

To conclude, the purpose of this chapter has been to isolate a corpus of ancient texts and to discern the features common to all of them that make it reasonable to regard them as a distinct group or 'genre'. While I have not approached this task in a wholly unprejudiced way (I have used the model of the Hermeneutic Circle to argue that one cannot attempt to make out and describe a genre without already having some preconceived notion of its nature), I believe that I have arrived at a theory of didactic poetry that, while it is only one way of conceptualizing the evidence (other scholars may define the genre differently), will prove useful for the interpretation of the individual works. As Chapters 3–6 will show, knowing what to expect from a didactic poem enables the reader to appreciate where a poet adheres to generic conventions, as well as where he decides to part from them, and thus adds in a crucial way to the understanding of the text as a whole.

I also hope to have provided in this chapter a meaningful narrative of literary history. While we first encounter other genres, such

---

of *in noua . . . mutatas . . . formas | corpora* (1. 1–2), the narrator's topic. Note also Pythagoras' repeated use of the word *corpora* at the beginning of a verse (76 (the second line of the speech), 156, 215, 363, 459), a mannerism that harks back to 1. 2.

[79] See Barchiesi 1989: 81, who maintains that the style of the speech 'assicura il riferimento non solo a una funzione communicativa, ma anche alla tradizione di un genere letterario'.

as epic or tragedy, in what many would argue is already their ideal form (Homer and Attic drama), with didactic poetry we have the chance to trace the development of a kind of poetry that underwent numerous permutations until it was finally recognized as a genre. I have argued that at least by the time of my four authors (and very possibly earlier), didactic poetry was established as a distinct literary type in the realm of poetic practice, even if it may not yet have been explicitly acknowledged by literary theory. The specific ways in which Lucretius, Vergil, Ovid, and Manilius availed themselves of this genre, employed its characteristics to their individual purposes, and, in doing so, influenced the idea of didactic poetry held by later poets and critics is the subject of the following chapters.

3
The Teacher's Truth: Lucretius' *De rerum natura*

> primum quod magnis doceo de rebus et artis
> religionum animum nodis exsoluere pergo,
> deinde quod obscura de re tam lucida pango
> carmina, musaeo contingens cuncta lepore.
>
> Lucretius, *De rerum natura*

> Haec et plura canens, avide bibat ore diserto
> Pegaseos latices; & nomen grande poetae,
> non sapientis amet. Lauro insignire poetam
> quis dubitet? Primus viridantes ipse coronas
> imponam capiti, & meritas pro carmine laudes
> ante alios dicam: dum scilicet ille docendo
> abstineat; nec mortifero, ceu perfida Siren
> gestiat ignaras cantu male perdere gentes.
>
> Cardinal Melchior de Polignac,
> *Anti-Lucretius sive de deo et natura*

In many ways, Lucretius' *De rerum natura* appears as the 'ideal' didactic poem, and Effe 1977: 66–79 chooses it to illustrate what he calls the 'sachbezogener Typ', that is, the type of didactic poetry that is actually serious about teaching its professed subject matter. There can be no doubt that the text exhibits strong didactic intent (my first criterion for didactic poetry; see Ch. 2, above) and that the teacher–student constellation (the second criterion) is highly developed and crucial to the structure of the poem. These features, which I shall discuss in detail in what follows, are so dominant and so obviously 'didactic' that it appears counter-intuitive to understand the poem rather as an example of the epic genre, as some scholars have done.[1]

While it is true that the *De rerum natura* employs a number of epic

---
[1] See Murley 1947; Mayer 1990; cf. also P. R. Hardie 1986: 193–219; Conte 1994*a*: 1–3; and Gale 1994*b*: 99–128, and 2000: 235–8.

motifs (surveyed by Mayer 1990) and differs sharply from earlier didactic poems (at least as far as we know them) by virtue of its length (cf. Toohey 1996: 87–8), it seems hardly warranted to construct the poem as a narrative of the heroic conquests of Epicurus or the like.[2] To be sure, Epicurus is described as some sort of military victor, especially in 1. 62–79,[3] but passages like this are few and far between, compared to the bulk of the poem. By contrast, the plot of the speaker's instruction of Memmius is prominent throughout the text, and it is therefore perverse to claim that Lucretius merely 'preserved some of the formal "signals" of didactic, such as the address to readers, and the appropriate material, the real world' (Mayer 1990: 36). Instead of being external relics, these elements are in fact the central features of the text.

In order to be able to view the *De rerum natura* as an epic poem, scholars have pointed to the fact that, as discussed in Chapter 2, the ancients typically did not make a distinction between epic and didactic (see Gale 1994*b*: 100–2). This is obviously correct, and, as I pointed out above in Section 2.4, Lucretius may well himself have thought of his work as epic. However, on this common-sense view of genre, 'epic' means nothing more than 'a longish poem in hexameters', which is a fair description of the *De rerum natura* but does not warrant taking the poem as an epic in the more narrow sense in which the word is used by classicists today.

It is likewise unnecessary, in my opinion, to invoke the famous 'Kreuzung der Gattungen' to understand the character of Lucretius' poem.[4] Didactic poetry obviously has a certain affinity to epic, especially as regards diction and metre, and epic motifs and techniques (such as, e.g., extended similes) are not out of place in the *De rerum natura* or alien to its genre.[5] Likewise, the fact that Lucretius is imitating Ennius and Homer does not make his work an epic; at any rate, as is generally agreed, his main poetic model is Empedocles, the Greek didactic poet par excellence and himself a writer whose subject matter was so 'unepic' that Aristotle refused to regard him as a poet, while still acknowledging that his work was in fact 'Homeric'.[6]

[2] See P. R. Hardie 1986: 195: 'Epicurus is the hero of the *De Rerum Natura*, combining the Iliadic *persona* of military leader with the Odyssean *persona* of wanderer'.
[3] On this passage, see Buchheit 1971; Graca 1989: 1–12.
[4] This is the strategy of Mayer 1990, who views the *De rerum natura* as 'heroic didactic'.
[5] See, however, Schindler 2000: 72–5 on the 'unepic' nature of Lucretian similes.
[6] See Arist. *Poet.* 1447^{b}17–20 v. fr. 70 Rose and the discussion in Sect. 2.1, above. On

I have begun this chapter by defending the *De rerum natura*'s status as didactic poetry because it seems to me that the modern attempts to classify the work as epic are an interesting continuation of ancient practice: as we have seen in Chapter 2, one reason why didactic poetry was hardly ever recognized as constituting its own genre was that it was lumped together with other hexameter poetry under the rubric of epic. As we have also seen, a different, but even more unfavourable, approach to this type of literature was that of Aristotle, who claimed that works like that of Empedocles did not even count as poetry. This view, too, can be paralleled in modern times: as mentioned in the Introduction, critics from the eighteenth century onward have often regarded the very concept of didactic poetry as a contradiction in terms, and Lucretius easily appears as a prime example for the problematic nature of the genre. He himself acknowledges that the subject matter of the *De rerum natura* is especially technical and difficult to treat in Latin verse (e.g., 1. 136–9), and readers have often found that Lucretius' poetic talents express themselves best in 'purple patches' such as proems and digressions, while the greater part of the poem, with its genuinely philosophical arguments, is dry and unrewarding.[7] The poetic form and the philosophical content of the *De rerum natura* may thus appear as two separate elements not easily reconciled;[8] Samuel Taylor

---

Lucretius' relationship to Empedocles, see now esp. Sedley 1998: 1–34 (cf. already Sedley 1989), as well as Jobst 1907; Regenbogen 1932: 44–5; Kranz 1944; Furley 1970; Rösler 1973: 54–7 and 61 (who doubts that Lucretius knew Empedocles' work first hand); Tatum 1984; Wöhrle 1991; and Gale 1994*b*: 59–74. For passages in the new Empedocles papyrus (*P. Strasb. gr.* Inv. 1665–6) that have parallels in Lucretius, see A. Martin and Primavesi 1999 index s.v. 'Lucrèce'.

[7] This was certainly my reaction when I first read the poem as an undergraduate, but similar views used to be generally accepted even among more informed scholars. Bailey 1947: 1. 168 writes, 'It has often been said that Lucretius has two styles, one the free style of the poet, in which he rises above the argument and writes sheer poetry, the other on a far lower plane, where the poet is hampered by his philosophy and the philosopher by his verse; the one, it is said, is poetry, the other "scanning prose" ' (see also the quotations provided by Regenbogen 1932: 2 n. 1 and Amory 1969: 145 n. 3). Bailey proceeds to demonstrate that the assumption of two separate Lucretian styles is misguided; cf. also the discussion in Amory 1969.

[8] There is, of course, the additional problem that for a long time, Lucretius' philosophy was regarded as wrong and dangerous (an attitude ridiculed by Lord Byron, *Don Juan*, canto 1. 43: 'Lucretius' irreligion is too strong | for early stomachs, to prove wholesome food'). Thus, Melchior de Polignac in his brilliant *Anti-Lucretius* (1747) could praise Lucretius as a sublime poet while vehemently combating his heretical doctrine (see the quotation used as an epigraph to this chapter). The conviction that Epicurean philosophy was obviously wrong is still a driving force behind H. J. G. Patin's 'Antilucrèce chez Lucrèce' theory (see below), which is very much motivated by the sentiment that it is a real pity that such a good poet as Lucretius should have squandered his talents on such an undeserving cause. Cf. Johnson

Coleridge summed up this view when he remarked, 'Whatever in Lucretius is poetry is not philosophical, whatever is philosophical is not poetry' (Letter to Wordsworth, 30 May 1815).

The relationship of *carmen* and *res* in Lucretius is further complicated by the fact that Epicurus—whose natural philosophy is, after all, the subject matter of the *De rerum natura*—was himself openly opposed to poetry.[9] This makes Lucretius' choice of medium appear problematic, and scholars have been worrying about the implications of this contradiction. The following quotation from Otto Regenbogen, for example, shows this critic's agitation at the perceived tension in Lucretius' work: 'Es ist wirklich die zentrale Frage des Lukrezischen Wesens und Werkes: Wie kam Lukrez zu seinem Stoff? Wie wurde der Epikureer Lukrez zum Dichter Lukrez? Wie waren beide zur Einheit, zur Deckung zu bringen? Gelang das? Konnte es gelingen?' (1932: 2). Regenbogen himself came to the conclusion, as did many other scholars, that Lucretius the Epicurean and Lucretius the poet were never fully reconciled; in his eyes, the *De rerum natura* was characterized by a kind of personality split, a 'tiefste[ ] und unaufhebbare[ ] Spannung' (1932: 81). This view of Lucretius as a kind of schizophrenic torn between poetry and Epicurean doctrine is itself a variant of the notorious 'Antilucrèce chez Lucrèce' theory (the phrase was coined by Patin 1868–9), according to which the (rationalist) Epicurean doctrine of the *De rerum natura* is (subconsciously) undermined by the (much more spiritual) poet himself.[10]

Reacting to this kind of psychological interpretation, scholars have in recent decades paid close attention to the poetics of Lucretius and come to the conclusion that, far from being in conflict, poetry and philosophy are closely aligned in the *De rerum natura*. Critics like Pierre Boyancé, Francesco Giancotti, P. H. Schrijvers, Diskin D. Clay, and Monica Gale have examined in detail the strategies by which Lucretius combines the roles of

---

2000: 79–133 on the reception of Lucretius in its changing contemporary contexts from the 17th to the 19th cent.

[9] The evidence for, and nature of, Epicurus' rejection of poetry will be discussed in Sect. 3.3.

[10] The assumption of any kind of personality split, between Epicurean and poet, rationalist and spiritualist, optimist and pessimist, etc. is made easy by Jerome's report of Lucretius' *insania* and ultimate suicide (*Ab Abr.* 1923, p. 149 Helm). The problem of the perceived self-contradictory nature of the *De rerum natura* has even been called the 'Lucretian question'; see Glei 1992: 82–7 for a nice *historia quaestionis*.

Epicurean teacher and poet and presents his work as a unified whole. They have made valuable contributions, and it is on their insights that I shall build in the following discussion.

For expository reasons, I shall first treat the form of the teaching speech addressed to Memmius by the persona (Sect. 3.1) and only then consider the fact that the speaker's words are clearly presented as poetry (Sect. 3.2). This will lead to an extended consideration of the relationship of poetry and teaching/philosophy and of the ways in which the two are combined (Sect. 3.3).[11]

3.1. THE TEACHING SPEECH

Reading *De rerum natura* is an intense experience. Far from providing an impersonal, disinterested exposition of Epicurean physics, the poem takes the form of a speech by the persona to the addressee, the tone of which is urgent, sometimes even aggressive. At no point are we allowed to forget that it is the teacher who is speaking, that he is speaking to the student, and that the subject he is teaching is one of enormous importance. The resulting effect is described well by Alexander Dalzell: 'The *De rerum natura* is from start to finish a long and passionate argument, carefully organized and pursued relentlessly. The reader is allowed no escape from the remorseless logic of the text' (1996: 56).[12]

While the speaker is continuously drawing attention to the process of his teaching (in the terminology developed in Chapter 1, we may say that the text shows *self-consciousness*; on this being specifically *poetic* self-consciousness, see Sect. 3.2, below), he provides nearly no information about his own person. We learn that he stays awake during 'serene nights' in order to write his poem (1. 140–5) and that his motivation for doing so is the *sperata uoluptas | suauis amicitiae* (1. 140–1) of the addressee, but this is the most personal touch in a character who throughout the text appears solely in his role as teacher (and, as we shall see, poet). He is not given a name either, by contrast to the student, who is addressed, or

---

[11] The text of Lucretius used in this chapter and elsewhere is the *Oxford Classical Text* of Cyril Bailey (2nd edn. 1922).

[12] Cf. also the incisive observations of Johnson 2000: 10–11 on the extreme sense of urgency created by the persona: 'the voice of the poem, the sum of all the speaker's teacherly moods and stratagems, is always on or near the boil' and '[h]e [the speaker] is on (the) edge, and wants us to be there'.

referred to, as *Memmius* eleven times in the course of the poem.[13] However, within the *De rerum natura*, Memmius remains as unspecific a character as the speaker. The most detailed information given is 1. 41–3, where he is said to be obliged to assist the 'common good' in *hoc patriai tempore iniquo* (1. 41), but this identifies him only as a politically active Roman citizen, which hardly amounts to adding a particularly individual trait.

Now, we know, of course, that the dedicatee of the *De rerum natura* can be identified as Gaius Memmius, the son of Lucius, a character known from numerous letters of Cicero, as well as from Catullus 10 and 28, and a minor player in the turbulent Roman politics of the 60s and 50s BC.[14] However, since Lucretius does not choose to provide the Memmius of his work with much of a personality apart from his being an—often reluctant (see below)—student of Epicurean physics, it appears unwarranted to ascribe to the addressee of the *De rerum natura* any of the more specific characteristics of his historical namesake, just as it would be impermissible to characterize the persona in terms of what is known of Lucretius' own life (that is, if anything were in fact known about it). We therefore have to understand Memmius primarily as an intra-textual character, a 'creation of the poem itself',[15] in other words, as one member of the teacher–student constellation typical of didactic poetry as a genre. Given that the student is addressed by name only eleven times in the course of the poem, but innumerable times simply as an anonymous second-person singular, it does not seem to me likely that Lucretius intended his readers to think of the addressee of his persona's teaching speech first and foremost as the man who was tribune in 66, praetor in 58, and so on.

I have in the preceding paragraph been assuming the identity of Memmius and the anonymous addressee, an interpretation I believe to be correct. I can therefore not follow G. B. Townend, who famously diagnoses the 'Fading of Memmius' (1978), arguing that Memmius 'disappears' in the course of the *De rerum natura* and is replaced by a highly impersonal addressee. While it is true that the name Memmius appears only in Books 1, 2, and 5 (which may,

[13] See 1. 26 (*Memmiadae*), 42 (*Memmi clara propago*), 411, 1052; 2. 143, 182; 5. 8, 93, 164, 867, 1282. On the distribution of these addresses, see below.
[14] On the historical Memmius, see Münzer 1931; cf. also the long discussion in Giancotti 1959: 91–131.
[15] D. Clay 1983*b*: 212; cf. the whole discussion pp. 212–16. On the teacher–student constellation in the *De rerum natura*, see also Johnson 2000: 4–11.

or may not, be an indication that Lucretius wrote these books first[16]), Townend's distinction among different types of second-person address is unconvincing (compare n. 28, below) and ultimately wholly subjective: how is the reader supposed to know in every single instance whether the person addressed is Memmius or not? In my view, all second-person addresses involve the same character, Memmius, the student figure of the *De rerum natura*, who is a continuous presence in the text. Far from fading, Memmius, in the words of Diskin Clay, 'is there explicitly from its [the poem's] beginning to its end' (1983*b*: 213).[17]

An exhaustive discussion of the characteristics of Lucretius' teaching speech and the various techniques used to structure the argument and involve the addressee could easily fill a book on its own; in the following paragraphs, I can merely provide a summary of the central features.[18] As mentioned above, Lucretius' poem exhibits both self-consciousness and simultaneity. The speaker is continually referring to his own speaking, as well as to the addressee's (ideally attentive) listening. He also clearly indicates that his instruction of Memmius is a process that—in the familiar illusion—is taking place 'right now'. When embarking on the teaching speech proper, the speaker creates a strong sense of beginning with the words principium *cuius hinc nobis* exordia *sumet* (1. 149),[19] and while the end of the *De rerum natura* is not explicitly marked as such,[20] the speaker signals at the beginning of Book 6

---

[16] Thus the influential hypothesis of Mussehl 1912, which is, however, based mainly on other observations (cf. the discussion in Bailey 1947: 1. 32–7). If true, this need not mean that Lucretius changed his conception of the addressee when writing the later books. Note also Keen 1985: 1, who observes that the overall number of second-person addresses in a given book of *De rerum natura* does not appear to depend on whether it is one of the 'Memmius books' or not; he concludes: 'Thus if Lucretius wrote 1, 2 and 5 first and Memmius was out of the picture after that, he continues to address his reader with almost the same frequency'.

[17] As Clay himself points out (1983*b*: 216–20), Memmius is most individual, most historical, and most 'Roman' in the proem and develops into a more generic student later on. Again, this is no reason to postulate the existence of more than one addressee: as Conte 1992: 147 observes, the proem stands '[a]t the border between fully poetic speech and speech still outside of poetry' and thus helps establish the relationship between the extra-textual and the intra-textual, i.e., in the case of the *De rerum natura*, the relationship between Lucretius, the author, and Memmius, the dedicatee, on the one hand and the speaker and his student on the other. Obviously, there is a real person Memmius, and it is the job of the proem, so to speak, to cast this real person in the role of the fictive character inside the text.

[18] A short but valuable discussion is Wiltshire 1974; see also Kranz 1944: 73–6 and Keen 1985.

[19] The pronoun *cuius* refers back to *naturae species ratioque* (1. 148); see Bailey 1947 *ad loc.*

[20] For a discussion of covert signs of closure at the end of Book 6, see P. Fowler 1997.

that his work is nearing completion.[21] Throughout the text, he shows himself aware of what has been said before and what is still to come.[22] Thus, for example, at the beginning of Book 4, he summarizes the material treated so far, before announcing the new topic on which he will start immediately: *sed quoniam docui* ... (4. 26) ... *atque* ... *quoniam docui* ... (4. 30) ... *nunc agere incipiam* ... (4. 33). He continually cross-references his own work, postponing the treatment of certain topics until later (e.g., *quae tibi posterius, Memmi, faciemus aperta*, 2. 182) or, much more often, referring to earlier discussion, frequently with set phrases such as *uti docui* (1. 539 and *passim*, with variations) and *quae paulo diximus ante* (1. 794; numerous variations in the course of the poem).[23]

The *De rerum natura* abounds in repeated formulas like these (others include *nonne uides*,[24] *nunc age, fateare necessest*), which help structure the speaker's discourse and lend a certain 'archaic' feel to the poem. Scholars have compared the oral style of Homeric epic, as well as the (obviously related) practice of Empedocles (Kranz 1944: 84–5; Gale 1994*b*: 63 and 116–17). However, Lucretius also repeats entire sentences and even short passages (a famous example is the simile of the children in the dark, 2. 55–61 = 3. 87–93 = 6. 35–41; the last three lines also occur at 1. 146–8), and there the purpose appears to be didactic and grounded in Epicurean practice (see the extended discussion in D. Clay 1983*b*: 176–85; see also D. Clay 1973).[25] Epicurus had his followers memorize the central doctrines of his philosophy (see, e.g., *Ep. Hdt.* 35–6), and similarly, Lucretius repeats important points in order to 'fix them indelibly in the mind of his reader' (D. Clay 1983*b*: 183).[26]

---

[21] See 6. 46: *quae restant percipe porro* and esp. 6. 92–5 (the invocation to Calliope), on which see Sect. 3.2.

[22] See the perceptive description of D. Clay 1983*b*: 36: 'as he moves forward, he takes pains to mark his process by reviewing the arguments on which the poem builds. The reader is never allowed to forget where he is, by what reasoning he has been brought there, and where he is going'. The self-awareness of the speaker who is wholly in control of the process of his argument is also apparent in the continuous use of such discourse markers as *principio, praeterea, denique, postremo*, etc., on which see Bailey 1947: 1. 160–1.

[23] See Amory 1969: 151 and n. 10.

[24] Perhaps the most famous Lucretian formula, *nonne uides* has even had an entire scholarly article dedicated to itself: Schiesaro 1984 shows, among other things, how because of its frequent use in Lucretius, this particular *iunctura* became so associated with didactic poetry that it was subsequently eschewed in other genres, such as elegy and epic.

[25] On the repetition of 1. 926–50 at the beginning of Book 4, see n. 50, below.

[26] On repetition in the *De rerum natura*, see also Bailey 1947: 1. 144–5 and 161–5 and Schiesaro 1994: 98–104. I cannot follow Deufert 1996: 27–224, who maintains that all repeated passages in the poem are due to interpolation.

This attempt to 'hammer in' (thus Bailey 1947: 1. 162) the fundamental principles of his work is but one of the methods the teacher employs to drive home his message. A central feature of the *De rerum natura* is the speaker's unchanging concentration on the addressee; as Carl Joachim Classen puts it, 'Lucretius shows immediate and continued concern for the attention, understanding, judgment . . ., consent, and active cooperation of the listener' (1968*a*: 96). Again and again, the teacher addresses the student, urging him to pay attention (e.g., *uacuas auris ⟨animumque sagacem⟩ | semotum a curis adhibe ueram ad rationem*, 1. 50–1, in the first address to Memmius[27]) and to accept the truth of Epicurean philosophy (see the recurring *fateare necessest* and similar formulas). He employs numerous strategies to involve the student in his argument, some of them very subtle. One is the repeated use of verbs and pronouns in the first-person plural in order to evoke the impression that speaker and addressee are taking part in a joint enterprise. Thus, the teacher declares toward the end of the first proem, *quapropter bene cum superis de rebus habenda | nobis est ratio . . .* (1. 127–8), implying that he and Memmius will investigate the phenomena of nature *together* (see D. Clay 1983*b*: 222–3). Of course, in Latin the first-person plural is frequently used to refer solely to the (single) speaker ('we' equals 'I'), or to make a statement about human experience in general ('we' equals 'one'). However, I would argue that in the *De rerum natura*, even the most unspecific use of the first-person plural serves to implicate the listener. Shortly after the use of *nobis* just cited, the speaker mentions another topic of the investigation to come:

> et quae res *nobis* uigilantibus obuia mentis
> terrificet morbo adfectis somnoque sepultis,
> cernere uti *uideamur* eos audireque coram,
> morte obita quorum tellus amplectitur ossa.
>
> (1. 132–5)

(And [we must examine] what thing frightens our minds, occurring to us when we are awake, suffering from illness, or buried in sleep, so that we seem to see and hear in person those whose dead bones the earth embraces.)

While the reference is to the kind of hallucinations and nightmares

---

[27] These may not be the very first words the speaker says to Memmius: most editors, including Bailey, posit a lacuna before line 50 in order to smooth the abrupt change of address from Venus to Memmius.

that everyone has and that the speaker is going to explain as a perfectly natural phenomenon (see 4. 33–45, 453–68), the formulation gives the impression that what is meant is really the bad dreams specifically of the speaker and Memmius. Whether he likes it or not, the addressee and his experience are already part of the teacher's discourse.[28]

A similar method of evoking a sense of *tua res agitur* in the student is the use of the ethical dative, a grammatical feature that is typically employed in discourse situations to signal personal involvement.[29] This is clear in the repeated phrase *ne tibi res redeant ad nilum funditus omnes* (1. 673, 797; 2. 756, 864), which implies not only that if one harbours wrong assumptions about the nature of the universe, 'all things will utterly return to nothing', but that if this happened, it would be of personal concern to the addressee. The expression is interesting also in another respect: strictly speaking, it is a metonymy, and 'lest all things return utterly to nothing' really means 'lest you allow for a system in which all things return to nothing', which is, of course, impossible from an Epicurean point of view (cf. Lucr. 1. 215–64); however, the argument is formulated in such a way as to evoke the literal disappearance of the physical world before the eyes of the addressee (*tibi*). It thus conveys a strong sense of urgency: if Memmius does not hold the right opinion about the natural world, all things will come to nothing—for him and, in a sense, because of him.[30]

This idea is part of a motif that recurs throughout the *De rerum natura* and that I have called the *creator* motif, borrowing an expression from Godo Lieberg. Lieberg 1982 discusses instances in Latin

[28] In my opinion, this is even more true of those cases in which the speaker uses a verb in the second-person singular in what might appear as a generalization ('you' equals 'one', as in English). Thus, a phrase like *praeterea nil est quod* possis *dicere ab omni | corpore seiunctum secretumque esse ab inani* (1. 431–2) might be translated, 'there is nothing that *one* could claim is either separated from the body or parted from the void'; however, the use of the second person implies that it is specifically the addressee who is unable to come up with a third principle. I can thus not agree with Townend 1978 that such 'impersonal' uses of the second-person singular are not directed at the primary addressee/Memmius.

[29] See Kühner and Stegmann 1955: 1. 323–4 (=§76,8c). As Katz 1998: 254–8 shows, the dative of personal pronouns, especially those of the second-person singular, is cross-linguistically extremely common in real speech, as well as in those genres of literature that, like didactic poetry, imitate a real speech situation.

[30] I even feel tempted to regard *tibi* as a kind of dative of agent. While this construction is typically found with gerundives and verbs in the passive (see Kühner and Stegmann 1955: 1. 324–5 (=§ 76,8d)), it can rarely also be used 'bei intransitiven Verben passiver Bedeutung' (ibid., Anm. 12), e.g., Luc. 2. 547 *Catulo iacuit = a Catulo prostratus est*. Is it possible likewise to understand *ne tibi res redeant* as *ne res redigantur a te*?

poetry where the poet is said to be doing what he is really only describing, as in this example from Vergil: *tum Phaetontiadas musco circumdat* [sc. *Silenus*] *amarae* | *corticis* (*Ecl.* 6. 62–3; see Lieberg 1982: 5). This technique, which creates a close connection between the poet and his subject matter, will concern us again in the next chapter, on Vergil's *Georgics*; it is not found in Lucretius, but I would argue that my *creator* motif is a variation of it. At points in the *De rerum natura*, we get the sense that, following the instructions of the speaker, the addressee is, as it were, creating the physical world. Compare, for example, the following passage:

> *neue* bonos rerum simili constare colores
> semine *constituas*, oculos qui pascere possunt,
> et qui compungunt aciem lacrimareque cogunt
> aut foeda specie diri turpesque uidentur.
>
> (2. 418–21)

(Nor determine that pleasant colours of things that are able to delight the eyes consist of similar seed as those colours that prick the eye and make it cry or those that seem dreadful and ugly because of their vile appearance.)

One has the impression that Memmius is actually 'making' the colours and that the speaker is warning him against getting it wrong.[31]

A final prominent method used by the speaker to involve the addressee in the argument is the creation of a quasi-dialogue. As Classen 1968*a*: 88 observes, 'The arguments are not simply presented to the listener; he is made to join the enquiry and to contribute himself, as in a Platonic dialogue'. Of course, as we have seen, didactic poetry is a genre that typically takes the form of a monologue (*poeta ipse loquitur sine ullius personae interlocutione*, Diom. *Gramm. Lat.* 1. 482. 21 Keil), but the speaker of the *De rerum natura* does his best to give a voice to Memmius. Rhetorical questions abound throughout the poem, and we are invited to imagine the student's answering with a humble 'Yes, of course' to the many instances of *nonne uides . . . ?* and similar expressions. The speaker also frequently anticipates the student's reactions (which he usually depicts as negative; see below), twice including a counter-argument of Memmius in direct speech (1. 803–8 and 897–900, both

---

[31] See also 2. 485–96, 755 (*proinde colore caue contingas semina rerum*), 834–6; 3. 626. On Manilius' use of the *creator* motif in the context of an allusion to Lucretius, see Ch. 6 n. 89, below).

introduced by *inquis*; see also 6. 673). There even is one instance where, it seems to me, Lucretius is self-consciously making fun of the conventions of the didactic genre. In 5. 1091, the teacher senses that his student wants to ask something: *illud in his rebus tacitus ne forte requiras*... The reason why Memmius is *tacitus* and does not voice his wholly reasonable question about the invention of fire is that he is the student figure in a didactic poem, where no one is allowed to speak except the poet himself.[32]

Of course, even in those instances where the teacher gives voice to the student, his questions, and his counter-arguments, the person we hear is not an individual character, 'Memmius', but rather a voice that has been constructed by the teacher himself.[33] The way in which he presents his student is rather interesting and, perhaps, somewhat surprising. For despite the fact that the teacher presents a philosophical system that will ultimately enable the student to live a 'life worthy of the gods' (3. 322), Memmius appears remarkably unsympathetic, unwilling to learn, and even plain stupid. The speaker continually anticipates his addressee's lagging attention and utterly misguided views. Already in his very first address (1. 50–61), the teacher urges the student to be attentive (1. 50–1, quoted above) and adds,

> ne mea dona tibi studio disposta fideli
> intellecta prius quam sint, contempta relinquas.
>
> (1. 52–3)

(Lest you despise and shrink from my gifts, laid out for you in faithful zeal, before you have understood them.)

Throughout the poem, the speaker keeps assuming that Memmius is getting it wrong and must be prevented from error; as a result, his speech is characterized by what Philip Mitsis has described as the 'aggressive, condescending tone of paternalism' (1993: 112; see also Schiesaro 1987: 47–8).

Mitsis's article is the most extensive study of what he calls the

---

[32] The line reminds me of the famous moment in Euripides' *Orestes* where Orestes answers a question for Pylades with the words, φησὶν σιωπῶν (1592). Pylades is silent (σιωπῶν, *tacitus*) because he is played by the fourth actor, whom tragic convention barred from speaking.

[33] Not only are the reactions ascribed to the addressee not those of the historical figure Gaius Memmius, but even within the text, the student figure is merely a creation of the teacher. Didactic poetry is not drama, and while it has two *personae*, as Servius recognized (*Praef. ad Georg.* 129. 9–12 Thilo; see Sect. 2.2 and cf. also the end of Sect. 5.2), the teacher–student constellation is always lopsided and controlled by the speaker himself.

'didactic coercion' of the *De rerum natura*. In his view, Lucretius' construction of the poem's student character as a stupid child functions as a kind of psychological trick in the extra-textual interaction of author and reader. Witnessing, as it were, the dialogue between teacher and student, readers will not wish to identify with slow-witted Memmius, and will therefore tend to accept the propositions of the intellectually superior teacher. With the help of the less-than-ideal intra-textual student, Lucretius creates his ideal extra-textual reader.[34]

I find Mitsis's reading very appealing and would on the whole agree with him that the negative depiction of Memmius forces readers continually to negotiate their own alliances: while the recurring addresses in the second-person singular serve to involve them in the instruction process and make them feel like students themselves, the apparent stupidity of the intra-textual addressee causes them to dissociate themselves from this character and side with the teacher instead (see Mitsis 1993: 123–8). However, since this question is beyond the scope of this book (see my methodological remarks in the Introduction), I shall now return to the purely intra-textual student character—even though questions of the poem's actual readers will continue to arise.

Mitsis's article, with its disillusioned view of the teacher–student relationship, reacts against a different reading of the *De rerum natura*, that of Diskin Clay, according to whom the teacher, as it were, emancipates the student in the course of the poem and teaches him to think for himself (1983*b*: 225).[35] Clay points to the speaker's practice of sometimes leaving arguments unfinished, trusting the addressee to fill in the blanks; mentioning other passages, he quotes especially 1. 402–3, where the teacher refuses to give more arguments for the existence of the void since he has left enough 'traces' (*uestigia*) for the addressee to figure out the rest for himself (see the entire passage 1. 398–417).[36] Clay also contends, as do many other

[34] This interpretation would even provide a reason why Lucretius chose as his addressee a man whom many scholars have regarded as a somewhat unlikely candidate for such philosophical instruction: his very lack of sympathy for the enterprise would have made Memmius the ideal foil for the real reader; see Donohue 1993: 116–22.

[35] Cf. Erler 1997, who traces 'meditative elements' in the *De rerum natura*, passages supposed to serve as 'starting points' for the reader's own reflection.

[36] It should be pointed out, though, against Clay, that the speaker has already spent 69 lines (1. 329–97) proving the existence of the void and that in 1. 411–17, he promises (or, perhaps, rather threatens) that, if Memmius is lazy and loses his concentration even for a moment (*quod si pigraris paulumue recesseris ab re*, 1. 410), he, the speaker, will flood him with

scholars, that the description of the plague at the end of the *De rerum natura* acts as a kind of test for the student: if he has absorbed all the teachings of the preceding poem, even this harrowing account of human suffering will not disturb his *tranquillitas animi*.[37]

To regard the end of Book 6 as a kind of final exam in Epicurean philosophy has great appeal in view of the fact that the grimness of the poem's finale would otherwise remain unexplained.[38] However, here as elsewhere it is of paramount importance to distinguish between the fictional addressee and the actual readers. If the plague does indeed serve as a test, it seems that it is one that can be passed only by the 'real' audience, not, however, by Memmius. Despite the fact that the teacher occasionally exhorts the student to think for himself, there is no indication that the addressee is actually making any progress in the course of the poem: if one trusts the speaker, Memmius is as stupid at the end of the *De rerum natura* as he is at the beginning.[39] The test-function of the end of Book 6 thus appears as a (possible) part of the extra-textual interaction of author and reader, not of the intra-textual teacher–student constellation.[40]

Since we cannot be entirely certain that Lucretius intended his poem to end in exactly the way it does, any speculation about the purpose of the finale as it stands is open to doubt.[41] Given the

---

arguments until the end of his life. It is thus hard to claim that this passage shows a high degree of trust in the student's self-sufficiency on the part of the teacher.

[37] This interpretation was first proposed independently by D. Clay 1976: 222–3 and Müller 1978: 217–21; cf. also Glei 1992: 94; Schiesaro 1994: 102–3; Erler 1997: 82–5; and P. Fowler 1997: 137–8.

[38] Simply pointing to the fact that the end of the work, with its emphasis on death, balances the beginning, with its emphasis on birth (cf. Subsect. 3.3.2), is hardly a satisfactory explanation in itself. Gale 1994*b*: 227–8 believes that the plague depicts the horrors of life without Epicurus, with religion being wholly unable to provide any relief of human suffering. However, I do not believe that this can be the point: even if the Athenians had all been Epicureans and gone about dying in a calm and disciplined way, it would still have been a painful, and thus, from an Epicurean point of view, undesirable situation.

[39] Keen 1985: 1–4 shows in detail that there is no indication of a learning process on the part of the addressee; cf. Mitsis 1993: 124 and n. 20.

[40] Even the real reader, though intellectually superior to Memmius, might find this final test hard to pass. As Peta Fowler writes, 'The reader who wants to make a "success" of the poem must read the ending in the spirit of an Epicurean convert. . . . To read the ending more pessimistically is an option available to the reader . . . but it is an option that inevitably makes the poem a failure' (1997: 138).

[41] While I believe that the *De rerum natura* in its present state can, and should, be interpreted as a meaningful and unified whole, I do think that there are signs that point to the fact that the poem was left unfinished (see also immediately below in the text and n. 50) and that it is reasonable to entertain the notion that the end of the poem, especially, might still have been modified by the author.

general structure of the *De rerum natura*, I find it surprising that the poem should end without any further reference to either the speaker or the addressee, that a text that is so self-conscious should finish with an impersonal narrative. Scholars have been fascinated with the 'open ending', at which major tensions remain unresolved—just as, say, at the end of the *Aeneid*. However, didactic is not epic, and it is interesting to note that the majority of Hellenistic and Roman didactic poems end with an explicit signal of closure, and in most cases with a highly self-conscious *sphragis*.[42] One would therefore expect the Lucretian teaching speech to finish on as self-conscious a note as it began, and it is hard to believe that the ever-present, 'coercive' speaker would suddenly step back and simply let his student go.

Ultimately, the issue of the end of the *De rerum natura* must remain unresolved. While it is impossible to determine exactly where the poem's teaching speech is going (Does it end with the abandoning of the intra-textual student, which enables the actual reader to step in, as it were, and pass the test of Epicurean *ataraxia*? Or will the speaker return to Memmius after his narrative tour de force and bring his instruction to an orderly conclusion?), I hope to have shown in this section some of the major characteristics of its working. It is now time to turn from teaching to poetry and to a discussion of the poetic self-consciousness of the *De rerum natura*.

3.2. THE POEM

The speaker of Lucretius' poem is a serious teacher. Absolutely convinced of the truth and importance of his mission, he goes about the conversion of Memmius with great zeal and dedication. However, he is also a serious poet, and there can be no doubt that he regards this aspect of his activity as equally important. In fact, it is not possible to distinguish his teaching from his poetry: after all,

---

[42] See Aratus, *Phaen.* 421–2 (final address to the student); Nic. *Ther.* 957–8 and *Alex.* 629–30 (*sphragis* with mention of the poet's name); Verg. *G.* 4. 559–66 (lengthy *sphragis* with description of the circumstances of the poem's composition and mention of the poet's name); and Ov. *Ars Am.* 3. 809–12 (clear indication of the end of the poem with mention of the students and of the poet's name). There are no certain counter-examples: the end of the *Works and Days* has been blurred through additions in the MS tradition, even though 826–8 (*makarismos* of the man knowledgeable in the choice of days), the end of the poem as we have it, certainly conveys a sense of closure; Empedocles' poem survives only in fragments; and Manilius' *Astronomica* may be unfinished. See P. Fowler (1997: 124–6, at 126) who states that 'there is clearly a tendency for didactic works to end with a formal conclusion'.

what I have been calling the teaching speech is a poem and self-consciously presents itself as one.

The poetic self-consciousness of the *De rerum natura* is obvious (cf. D. Clay 1976: esp. 205–6). Again and again, the speaker refers to his words as *uersus* (1. 24, 137, 416, 499, 823, 825, 949; 2. 529, 688, 690, 1013; 3. 36; 4. 24, 180, 909; 6. 83) or *carmen* (1. 143, 934, 946; 3. 420; 4. 9, 21; 5. 1; 6. 937) and describes his own activity as *canere* (5. 509; 6. 84). His double status as both teacher and poet is neatly expressed in the proem to Book 1, where he asks Venus for assistance with his work:

> te sociam studeo scribendis uersibus esse
> quos ego de rerum natura pangere conor
> Memmiadae nostro.
>
> (1. 24–6)

(I desire you to be my ally in writing the verses about the nature of things that I attempt to fashion for our Memmius.)

In these programmatic two and a half lines, the persona manages to mention his subject matter (*de rerum natura* functions as a (quasi-)title for the work[43]), as well as his addressee (*Memmiadae nostro*); to indicate clearly that the work in the making is poetry (*uersibus*); and to create a sense of beginning with the help of the gerundive *scribendis* and the verb *conor*, and thus to establish poetic simultaneity.

There are two somewhat unusual features about this invocation. First, of course, it is odd for Venus to play the role of a Muse.[44] The poet/persona explicitly mentions two reasons why he is asking the

---

[43] It is not entirely clear whether Lucretius' poem would have been known to its ancient audience as *De rerum natura*, given that ancient books did not have fixed titles in the modern sense (see Daly 1943; D. Clay 1969: 31–2 and 1983a: 82–3; and Erler 1994: 406). However, I tend to agree with Bailey 1947: 2. 583 that 'It is highly probable that *De Rerum Natura* was intended by Lucretius himself to be the title of his poem', esp. in light of the repeated use of the phrase *(de) rerum natura* throughout the poem (see below) and given that its Greek equivalent Περὶ φύσεως was the generic title of works on natural philosophy, including Empedocles' poem and Epicurus' magnum opus.

[44] The description of Venus as a Muse in the proem to Book 1 has its counterpart in the proem to Book 6, where the *callida musa* | *Calliope* (6. 93–4) is called *requies hominum diuumque uoluptas* (6. 94), a phrase that harks back to the address to Venus in the very first line of the poem, *Aeneadum genetrix, hominum diuumque uoluptas* (1. 1). The invocation of Calliope may be modelled on Empedocles' appeal to the same Muse (B131), just as Lucretius' Venus owes much to Empedocles' *Philia* (on the various aspects of Lucretius' imitation of Empedocles, see the literature quoted above in n. 6); see also Arrighetti 1997: 31–3, who suggests that Hesiod was a model as well.

help of this particular goddess.[45] The less important one is that Memmius appears to be a special favourite of Venus (1. 26–8);[46] the more important one is explained in the causal clause immediately preceding the invocation:

> quae quoniam rerum naturam sola gubernas
> nec sine te quicquam dias in luminis oras
> exoritur neque fit laetum neque amabile quicquam.
>
> (1. 21–3)

(Since you alone govern the nature of things, and without you nothing is born onto the shining shores of light and nothing joyous or lovable comes into existence.)

Venus is the goddess who governs nature (*rerum naturam*, 1. 21); she is therefore invoked to assist a poem whose subject matter is nature (*de rerum natura*, 1. 25). However, *rerum natura* can also be understood as the 'birth/coming-into-being of things', and this is Venus' field of influence as described in lines 1. 22–3 (nothing is born without her doing). It is therefore fitting that she should be asked to help with the coming-into-being of the speaker's poem; Venus will, so to speak, assist the *natura* of the *De rerum natura*.[47]

The second interesting point about the invocation is the fact that the speaker refers to the composition of his poem as writing (*scribendis uersibus*, 1. 24). As I discussed in the first chapter, texts that exhibit poetic simultaneity typically present themselves as oral compositions, while references to writing usually occur in the description of already finished works. Now, as we have already seen, the speaker of the *De rerum natura* also frequently styles himself as the more traditional singer (cf. the use of *carmen* and *canere*). Still, throughout the text there is a certain emphasis on the poem as a written artefact. This is apparent especially in the repeated analogy between the atoms and the letters (1. 196–8, 823–7, 907–914; 2. 688–99, 1013–22), where the speaker uses the example, not just

---

[45] As for the speaker's wish to have Venus act as his 'ally' (*sociam*, 1. 24), Gale 1994*b*: 137 suggests a bilingual wordplay: *socia* = ἐ/Ἐπίκουρος. O'Hara 1998 picks up this idea and proposes Simon. fr. 11. 21 West, where the poet invokes his Muse as an ἐπίκουρος, as the model.

[46] We gather from Verg. *Aen.* 5. 117–18 that the Memmii were one of the families that traced themselves back to Troy. This may explain their special veneration for Venus (cf. also the address *Aeneadum genetrix*, Lucr. 1. 1), which is also apparent from their coinage; cf., e.g., Boyancé 1950: 213–14

[47] On the meaning of *natura* here and elsewhere in Lucretius' poem, cf. D. Clay 1969. On the role of Venus, see also Subsect. 3.3.1.

of writing in general, but (in the second, fourth, and fifth of the five passages quoted) of his own work specifically, in order to demonstrate how larger units (words/natural objects) can be created by means of the combination of small elements (letters/ atoms). As I shall discuss in greater detail in Subsection 3.3.2, below, the analogy serves not only to illustrate the point at hand, but also to signal a strong affinity between the poem and its subject matter: if atoms are like letters, then both the poem and the world it describes are built according to the same principles.

A second reason why the speaker presents his poem as something written is, I believe, because he wishes to stress its similarity to the work of Epicurus. As Diogenes Laertius 10. 119 (= fr. 563 Usener) tells us, Epicurus held that the wise man should produce 'writings', συγγράμματα.[48] The philosopher himself was clearly not a 'singer'; rather, as the Lucretian speaker acknowledges, his *aurea dicta* (3. 12) are found in books (*chartis*, 3. 10). By indicating that he is a writer, too (striving to expound the *natura rerum* by means of *patriis chartis*, 4. 969–70), the persona thus places himself in a tradition that is not poetic. I shall return below to his *imitatio* of Epicurus, but note for the moment that this attitude clearly distinguishes the Lucretian speaker from an epic persona: the narrator of the *Aeneid*, for example, could never present himself as *writing* his poem, but has to adopt the more sublime stance of the inspired bard.[49]

The speaker's role as a proud and self-confident poet is played out most fully in the famous passage 1. 921–50 (1. 926–50 are repeated, with minor changes, as 4. 1–25[50]). He describes himself as

[48] Note that συγγράμματα is specifically used for prose works as opposed to poetry (see Dover 1997: 183–4): Epicurus (who also thought that the wise man should not compose poetry; cf. Diog. Laert. 10. 121 = fr. 568 Usener) thus regarded prose as the appropriate medium for philosophy; see Asmis 1995: 21 and the beginning of Sect. 3.3, below.

[49] The only epic narrator I can think of who presents his work as writing is the speaker of the *Batrachomyomachia*, whose references to the technical aspects of writing (he mentions the first σελίς, 'column', of his poem (1), as well as the fact that it is contained in δελτοί, 'writing tablets' (3; this line appears to be modelled on Callim. *Aet.* fr. 1. 21–2 Pfeiffer)) are in keeping with the parodic tone of the work. The epilogue of Statius' *Thebaid* (12. 810–19), which asks whether the poem will still be 'read' in the future, is addressed to the already finished book and therefore does not violate epic decorum; the same is true, *mutatis mutandis*, for the prediction in Ov. *Met.* 15. 878, *ore legar populi*.

[50] Unlike some scholars (now most notably Gale 1994a, who provides a detailed *historia quaestionis*), I cannot believe that the doubling of this passage can reflect the author's intention. As discussed in Sect. 3.1, repetitions in the *De rerum natura* can often be understood as serving a didactic purpose, but these lines do not contain any basic Epicurean doctrines or other material that the speaker might wish to impress on the student again and again, and the passage is also considerably longer than any of the other repeated passages in the poem. As

struck by a kind of Bacchic frenzy, inspired not only by 'sweet love of the Muses' (*suauem . . . amorem* | *musarum*, 1. 924–5), but also by 'great hope for fame' (*laudis spes magna*, 1. 923). Scholars have been disturbed by the idea that Lucretius would be interested in such an un-Epicurean good as glory and have tried to circumvent the problem by claiming that the *laus* the poet is seeking is really only fame as a disciple of Epicurus (thus Giancotti 1959: 47–50) or the praise he will earn from Memmius once the latter has been converted to Epicureanism (Gale 1994*b*: 146–7). However, in the context of the passage it appears obvious that what the speaker aspires to is fame specifically as a poet.[51] A great part of his achievement, as he describes it, is the novelty of his work:

> auia Pieridum peragro loca nullius ante
> trita solo. iuuat integros accedere fontis
> atque haurire, iuuatque nouos decerpere flores
> insignemque meo capiti petere inde coronam
> unde prius nulli uelarint tempora musae.
>
> (1. 926–30)

(I roam through the pathless realm of the Pierides, never before trodden by any foot. It is pleasing to approach untouched fountains and drink there; it is pleasing to gather new flowers and win for my head a crown of fame from a spot from which the Muses have wreathed the brow of no one.)

As scholars have pointed out, this passage is clearly indebted to Callimachean metaphors for poetry, as well as probably to Ennius, who was himself influenced by Callimachus.[52] Lines 1. 926–7 are reminiscent of Apollo's famous advice in the *Aetia* prologue (fr. 1. 25–8 Pfeiffer) to avoid crowded roads and to choose instead κελεύθους | ἀτρίπτους (27–8; cf. *nullius ante* | *trita solo*, Lucr. 1. 926–7), while the untouched fountains (1. 927–8) appear to allude to the small and pure spring presented as a poetic ideal in Callimachus,

---

for the question of the original position of these lines, I am weakly inclined to place them in Book 1 (since this is the most overt manifesto of the speaker's poetics, one would like it to occur comparatively early in the poem, and the passage is well integrated in the context of Book 1, as Lenaghan 1967; Deufert 1996: 81–9; and others have shown), but a case can be made for Book 4 as well.

[51] See Boyancé 1947: 95: 'Incontestablement il a voulu la gloire poétique de l'artiste'. Schrijvers 1970: 34 points out that the idea of glory is implicit already in the speaker's prayer to Venus to grant aeternum . . . *leporem* to his verse (1. 28).

[52] See Kenney 1970: 369–70; Brown 1982: 80–2; Graca 1989: 67–70; and Donohue 1993: 35–48.

Hymn 2. 110–12.[53] As for the crown that the poet hopes to win (1. 929–30), this harks back within the *De rerum natura* itself to the description of Ennius, *qui primus amoeno | detulit ex Helicone perenni fronde coronam* (1. 117–18).[54] Note that while Ennius was the first (*primus*) to bring home such a *corona*, the Lucretian persona, too, rejoices in looking for a crown *unde prius nulli uelarint tempora musae* (1. 930).[55] As I shall discuss more extensively in Subsection 3.3.3, below, the poet here employs the so-called *primus* motif that is well known from other Latin poets: he claims to be the first to have attempted a certain type of poetry, the implication being that he is the first Roman to practise a genre already extant in Greek literature (just as, on this model, Ennius was the first Latin poet to write epic in hexameters, a type of poetry previously composed only by Greeks, most notably Homer). We shall see below that Lucretius uses this trope with a certain twist and that his envisioned Greek forerunner (not mentioned in this passage) is a rather unlikely candidate to play 'Homer' to this 'Ennius'.

To return to the text at hand, it is obvious that the image of the poet's wandering through 'pathless places' (1. 926–7) is an instantiation of the journey metaphor that we have seen in Chapter 1 to be typical of texts that exhibit poetic self-consciousness and poetic simultaneity.[56] In fact, this metaphor is pervasive throughout the *De rerum natura* and even appears in its traditional form as the

---

[53] While earlier critics liked to think of Lucretius as an archaizing poet untouched by the ideals of the 'new' (Neoteric, Callimachean) poetic ideals of his time, recent scholars have rightly pointed out his debts to Callimachus and Hellenistic poetry in general (see the authors quoted in n. 52, above; contrast, however, now Knox 1999).

[54] Lucretius' claim that Ennius brought a crown down from Helicon has been used as a major source for the reconstruction of a *Musenweihe* in the style of Hesiod and Callimachus in the proem to *Annals* 1 (this may also have included Ennius' drinking from the Muses' fountain, cf. Prop. 3. 3. 5–12), in addition to the more unequivocally attested encounter with the shade of Homer, which Lucretius describes in 1. 124–6 (see Suerbaum 1968: 55–61; Skutsch 1985: 147–8 is more sceptical). On Lucretius and Ennius, see also Gigon 1978*a* and my further discussion in Subsect. 3.3.3, below.

[55] There is a certain contradiction here, which can hardly be resolved with the argument that Ennius got his crown from Helicon, while the Lucretian speaker wins his in Pieria (thus D. Clay 1976: 210 and 1983*b*: 44–5). Rather, as Hinds 1998: 52–63 discusses, Latin poets have a tendency to assert their own being 'first' by means of allusion to their predecessors' claim to the same effect. Of course, in one sense the novelty of the Lucretian persona's enterprise consists in his subject matter, which is different from Ennius'. See also my discussion immediately below in the text and in Subsect. 3.3.3.

[56] As just pointed out, the formulations in this passage are specifically indebted to Callimachus. However, Callimachus' imagery is itself based on older, traditional metaphors; see now esp. Asper 1997: 21–107 on Callimachus' use of journey metaphors.

image of the chariot. In 6. 46–7, the speaker, whose work is nearing completion (Book 6 is the last book), tells the student to listen to 'the rest' (*quae restant percipe porro*, 6. 46). He continues, *quandoquidem semel insignem conscendere currum* (6. 47), a line that is unfortunately followed by a lacuna.[57] The identity of the chariot and the purpose of its mention remain thus unclear; however, less than fifty lines later we return to the image of the poet charioteer:

> tu mihi supremae praescripta ad candida calcis
> currenti spatium praemonstra, callida musa
> Calliope, requies hominum diuumque uoluptas,
> te duce ut insigni capiam cum laude coronam.
>
> (6. 92–5)

(As I race toward the white mark of the last finish line, show me the course ahead, clever Muse Calliope, respite of men and pleasure of gods, so that led by you, I may win a crown with illustrious praise.)

Here the speaker presents himself as entering the final phase of a chariot race and asks the Muse for assistance; the *corona* he hopes to gain has changed from a wreath acquired in the *Musenlandschaft* (1. 929–30) into a trophy won at the games, but just as at the beginning of the poem, the poet is still highly interested in glory (*laus*, 6. 95; cf. 1. 923).[58]

A number of scholars have pointed out that the journey metaphor in the *De rerum natura* does not only, or even in the first place, refer to poetry.[59] The learning 'process' of the student is likewise presented as a journey along a path, as becomes clear already at the beginning of the poem, where the speaker anticipates a hostile attitude on the part of Memmius (the first of many similar instances; compare my discussion in the previous section):

> illud in his rebus uereor, ne forte rearis
> impia te rationis *inire* elementa *uiam*que
> *indugredi* sceleris.
>
> (1. 80–2)

(In this matter, I am afraid lest you believe yourself to be entering the introduction to an impious philosophy and embarking on a path of crime.)

---

[57] On Manilius' imitation of this verse, see Ch. 6 n. 56, below.

[58] On the chariot metaphor in *De rerum natura* 6, see Henderson 1970, who suggests a line of Simonides (*Anth. Pal.* 6. 213. 4) as the model for Lucr. 6. 47.

[59] On the path and journey metaphors in Lucretius, see esp. Schrijvers 1970: 18–26; see also Gale 1994*b*: 58, and 2000: 236, and D. Fowler 2000: 208–15.

However, Memmius apparently overcomes his fears, the teaching begins, and by 1. 156–7, the speaker can describe (with the typical use of the first-person plural) himself and his addressee as being on the same track: . . . *tum quod* sequimur *iam rectius* inde | *perspiciemus*. Still, Memmius remains prone to error (e.g., 1. 332, *errantem*), and the speaker must make sure that he does not lose his way:

> illud in his rebus ne te *deducere* uero
> possit, quod quidam fingunt, *praecurrere* cogor.
>
> (1. 370–1)

(In this matter, I am forced to run ahead, lest that which some people make up lead you astray from the truth.)[60]

The plot of the student's instruction by the teacher can thus be described as a common journey; as Schrijvers 1970: 25 writes, '[L]e poète et le lecteur suivent ensemble le chemin de la *vera ratio* tel qu'il se déroule du début à la fin du poème'.

Memmius' journey toward knowledge and the related poetic journey of the poet are also closely connected to yet another journey, that of Epicurus. In the proem to Book 1, the achievements of the *Graius homo* (1. 66) are described as follows:

> ergo uiuida uis animi peruicit, et extra
> *processit* longe flammantia moenia mundi
> atque omne immensum *peragrauit* mente animoque.
>
> (1. 72–4)

(Thus the lively force of his mind prevailed, and he marched far beyond the flaming ramparts of the world and travelled through the immeasurable universe in thought and mind.)

As we have seen, the verb *peragrare* is used of the poet in 1. 926;[61] it is applied to the addressee in 2. 677, *cetera consimili mentis ratione peragrans*. Their travelling is thus associated with Epicurus' journey of the mind, his transcending the boundaries of the known

---

[60] The pervasiveness of the path metaphor in the *De rerum natura* is in part due to the fact that many terms for intellectual activity and discourse are in fact lexicalized, 'dead', journey metaphors (cf. English 'I come to', 'let us move on to', etc.; see also the end of Ch. 1), which are, as it were, brought back to life by being put in context with more elaborate and unique path images. A prominent example of this strategy is the frequent use of *errare*, a dead metaphor whose original meaning is revived through juxtaposition with such non-lexicalized phrases as *auius a uera longe ratione uagaris* (2. 82).

[61] See D. Clay 1976: 209; Cabisius 1979: 243; Graca 1989: 8; and Gale 1997: 61 and n. 13.

world.[62] And there still is a fourth path in the *De rerum natura*, one that is of crucial importance to the other three: ultimately, Epicurus, the speaker, and Memmius are all concerned with the right 'way of life', the *uia uitae* (2. 10). While so many people are looking for it in vain (2. 9–10: . . . *alios passimque* . . . | *errare atque uiam palantis quaerere uitae*), Epicurus was able to show mankind the right path:

> exposuitque bonum summum quo tendimus omnes
> quid foret, atque uiam monstrauit, tramite paruo
> qua possemus ad id recto contendere cursu.
>
> (6. 26–8)

(He expounded what the highest good is for which we all strive and showed the way on which, as on a short path, we might move toward it on a straight course.)

The path metaphor is one example of the extreme versatility of Lucretius' imagery. The figurative journeys described are not all one and the same, but are connected to and associated with one another through the use of the same expressions. By this technique, the speaker manages to present his poetry, his instruction of Memmius, and his subject matter (Epicurean philosophy) as having similar structures and being bound up in similar processes. The same is true for another set of images, the metaphors concerning darkness and light. At the end of Book 1, the teacher promises the student that in his learning process, one insight will lead to the next (this is one of the few encouraging addresses in the entire poem):

> namque alid ex alio clarescet nec tibi caeca
> nox iter eripiet quin ultima naturai
> peruideas: ita res accendent lumina rebus.
>
> (1. 1115–17)

(For one thing will become clear from another, and black night will not interrupt your journey and prevent you from seeing the furthest reaches of nature: thus will things kindle lights for one another.)

The journey (*iter*, 1. 1116) of the student thus appears as a journey

---

[62] For the motif of the 'flight of the mind', see Jones 1926 (who quotes Lucretius on p. 112) and Kerényi 1930: 392–5, as well as my discussion in Sect. 6.3, below.

from darkness to light.[63] Again, the same metaphor is applied to Epicurus, who is the one who 'enlightens' mankind:

> e tenebris tantis tam clarum extollere lumen
> qui primus potuisti inlustrans commoda uitae.
>
> (3. 1–2)

(You who were first able to raise such a bright light out of such great darkness, throwing light on the blessings of life.)

As the speaker repeats four times in the course of the poem (1. 146–8 = 2. 59–61 = 3. 91–3 = 6. 39–41), it is not the sunlight that will cast out the 'terror and darkness of the soul', but rather *naturae species ratioque*, that is, the understanding of nature according to the teaching of Epicurus.[64]

And, not surprisingly, the poet, too, is concerned with creating light out of darkness: . . . *quod obscura de re tam lucida pango | carmina* (1. 933–4). However, there is a catch: the *obscura res* that the speaker illustrates with his 'bright songs' (cf. also 1. 136–7, *nec me animi fallit Graiorum obscura reperta | difficile inlustrare Latinis uersibus esse* and 1. 921–2, *nunc age quod superest cognosce et clarius audi. | nec me animi fallit quam sint obscura*) is nothing other than the doctrine of Epicurus, himself associated with the bringing of light.[65] Now, in a sense, Epicurean natural philosophy is 'dark' merely because it treats things, notably the atoms, that are hidden and invisible (Gk. ἄδηλα; the Latin word used is *caecus* 'blind; dark; invisible', see, e.g., *corporibus caecis igitur natura gerit res*, 1. 328), and poetry 'throws light' on them simply by pointing out their existence.[66] However, it is hard to see how *obscurus* would not, at the same time, have the simple connotation of 'obscure, strange, difficult to understand': while this may be part of his condescension toward the addressee, the speaker shows himself fully aware that his subject matter is difficult, and he has the ambition to make it as clear as possible.[67]

---

[63] See esp. D. Fowler 2000: 213–15, who draws attention to the fact that the progress from darkness to light is also an intrinsic element of initiation into mystery cults: one of the 'plots' of the *De rerum natura* is thus Memmius' initiation into Epicurean natural philosophy; cf. also Graca 1989: 11–12 and 25–6.

[64] Bailey 1947 nicely translates *naturae species ratioque* as 'the outer view and inner law of nature'; on the meaning of the phrase, which combines sense-perception (*species*) and theory (*ratio*), see D. Clay 1969: 43, and esp. 1983*b*: 105–8, as well as Sedley 1998: 37–8.

[65] Cf. Waszink 1954: 252–4; Arragon 1961: 372–3.

[66] See Schrijvers 1970: 41–2; Cabisius 1979: 242; D. Clay 1969: 44–7, and 1983*b*: 107–8.

[67] The poet may also be implicitly criticizing the 'obscure' prose style of Epicurus, whose works are indeed anything but easy to understand; compare the speaker's lack of sympathy

Thus, Epicurean philosophy can be described as both 'light' (it 'enlightens' mankind) and 'dark' (it deals with invisible matter and may be hard to understand), and I would argue that this is a typical example of 'discontinuity in Lucretian symbolism'.[68] Throughout the *De rerum natura*, Lucretius uses imagery, not in a strictly logical way (*x* refers to *y*, and only to *y*), but as a means to create certain sets of associations (*x* is associated with *y*). This gives him the possibility, not to make points, but to create very subtle impressions. Thus, for example, the various instances of the light–dark metaphor combine to convey a positive image of the speaker's poem that is associated with light (a force with positive connotations) throughout: both the light of Epicurean reason that casts out the darkness of the human mind and the light of clear diction that illuminates even the most obscure teachings of philosophy.[69]

I shall return to the question of Lucretian symbolism at the end of the chapter. After having determined in this section that the speaker of the *De rerum natura* presents himself self-consciously as a poet and that the process of his teaching and the development of his poem are not only practically identical, but also connected through common imagery, I shall now move on to the question of the relationship between poetry and philosophy. Does the poem gives us any indication of how we are to understand the relationship between poetic form and philosophical content, between *carmen* and *res*? What makes this question especially interesting in the case of Lucretius is, of course, Epicurus' well-known hostile attitude toward poetry.

---

for the riddling language of Heraclitus (1. 638–44), whom he ridicules with the oxymoron *clarus ⟨ob⟩ obscuram linguam* (1. 639).

[68] This phrase is borrowed from Anderson 1960, who, however, uses it in a more restricted sense. D. West 1994: 43–8 and 79–93 likewise comments on the 'fluidity of imagery' in the *De rerum natura*, but does not draw more general conclusions from his observations.

[69] Furthermore, Asmis (1995: 33–4, at 34) suggests that by stressing the clarity of his verse, the speaker 'asserts, paradoxically, a continuity of his method of teaching with that of Epicurus, who regarded σαφήνεια as the only quality of good speech (Diog. Laert. 10. 13 = fr. 54 Usener; see Asmis 1995: 21); see also Fögen 2000: 125–9. *Mutatis mutandis* the same idea is developed at greater length by Milanese 1989: 107–25, who discusses Lucretius' *obscura de re tam lucida . . . carmina* in the context of both Epicurean theories of style and contemporary Roman rhetorical terminology.

3.3. POETRY AND PHILOSOPHY

We do not possess a comprehensive treatment by Epicurus of the value (or lack thereof) of poetry, but we can glean from the surviving fragments and testimonies that, at least as far as its didactic potential was concerned, the philosopher regarded poetry as useless at best and pernicious at worst.[70] For the attaining of *eudaimonia*, traditional education (including poetry) was unnecessary and could thus be discarded, an attitude neatly summarized by Cicero: *nil opus esse eum, philosophus qui futurus sit, scire litteras* (*Fin.* 2. 4. 12; cf. frr. 117, 227–30 Usener).[71] In addition, however, poems could be downright dangerous because of their subject matter. According to the allegorizing mythographer Heraclitus (*Quaest. Hom.* 4. 2 = fr. 229 Usener), Epicurus rejected poetry summarily, decrying it as ὀλέθριον μύθων δέλεαρ. Obviously, the philosopher, whose aim it was to provide rational explanations for natural phenomena and to free people from their fear of the gods, could not but have a wholly negative attitude toward myth, and since this was what poetry mainly dealt with, his hostility extended to poetry as well.

If Epicurus thus emphatically denied poetry educational value and, as a result, regarded it as a medium unfit for philosophy (see above, n. 48), it is just about possible that he nevertheless thought it was acceptable as long as it was aimed solely at entertainment. Owing to the paucity of our sources, this point is extremely controversial.[72] However, it is clear that later Epicureans, notably Lucretius' contemporary Philodemus (who was, of course, a poet himself), took a positive view of the pleasure derived from poetry, while still adhering to Epicurus' view that it did not afford any

---

[70] For Epicurus' views of poetry, see esp. Asmis 1995, as well as Gale 1994*b*: 14–18; cf. also Boyancé 1947: 89–94; Giancotti 1959: 15–90; and Arrighetti 1997: 21–6.

[71] See Erler 1994: 169–70.

[72] The argument hinges mainly on Plutarch's report that according to Epicurus, 'the wise man enjoys sights and takes pleasure in Dionysian spectacles like everyone else' (φιλοθέωρον μὲν ἀποφαίνων τὸν σοφὸν . . . καὶ χαίροντα παρ' ὀντινοῦν ἕτερον ἀκροάμασι καὶ θεάμασι Διονυσιακοῖς, *Non posse* 1095 C = fr. 20 Usener). Asmis 1995: 19–21 concludes from this that Epicurus welcomed poetry as entertainment (see also Giancotti 1959: 15–90, and 1960, who, however, makes the further claim that Epicurus disapproved only of mythological poetry and would have been in favour of a poem like Lucretius'), while, e.g., Gale 1994*b*: 15 believes (cf. also Boyancé 1960: 441–2, and 1962: 404–7, who reacts specifically against Giancotti) that Plutarch's statement does not invalidate the impression given by our other sources, namely that Epicurus objected to poetry in general.

moral instruction.[73] Philodemus even went so far as to completely exclude considerations of didacticism from the judgement of poetry: if a poem happened to be useful from a philosophical point of view, this had nothing to do with its poetic quality and was purely accidental.[74]

Whether viewed before the background of Epicurus' original rejection of all poetry (if this was indeed his attitude) or judged in the light of his latter-day followers' separation of the entertainment of poetry from the edification afforded only by philosophy, Lucretius' decision to write a long didactic poem on Epicurean physics appears equally unorthodox. The question of how the actual author reached this decision, and to what extent he himself found his undertaking problematic, is a question that we cannot answer. What we can do is look at the attitude of the intra-textual persona and ask what this poet has to say about his divergence from Epicurean orthodoxy.

First of all, the speaker of the *De rerum natura* does not himself explicitly present his choice of medium as a problem. As we have seen, he appears as a self-conscious and self-confident poet throughout the text and does not give the impression that there is anything strange or untoward about this fact.[75] The only point where the persona might appear apologetic is in 1. 935, the line that introduces the honeyed-cup simile. After having claimed that he composes 'bright songs about a dark subject matter' by 'drenching everything in the Muses' charm' (*musaeo contingens cuncta lepore*, 1. 934), the speaker declares, *id quoque enim non ab nulla ratione uidetur*. This phrase can be taken very weakly to mean 'this does not appear wholly unreasonable'; however, given the associations of *ratio* in the rest of the poem, it can also be understood as making the claim that the speaker's act is not against Epicurean reason specifically.[76]

---

[73] See Asmis 1995: 22–33; cf. also Gale 1994*b*: 16–18. For the discussion of various aspects of Philodemus' poetics, see the papers in Obbink (ed.) 1995. Note that despite the fact that what appears to be a papyrus of Lucretius' poem has been found in the Villa dei Papiri in Herculaneum (see Kleve 1989 and 1997), we cannot be certain that Lucretius and Philodemus were acquainted or that Philodemus himself (as opposed to later inhabitants of the Villa) knew the *De rerum natura*.

[74] See *On Poems* 5 col. 32. 17–19 Mangoni: κἂν ὠφελῇ, καθὸ ὃ ποήματ' οὐκ ὠφελεῖ, 'and even if (poems) are useful, they are not useful qua poems'.

[75] By contrast, the speaker openly reflects on the problems inherent in the use of myth, another feature highly suspicious from an Epicurean point of view (see esp. the Magna Mater episode, 2. 600–60, and the discussion in Gale 1994*b*: 26–32).

[76] See Bailey 1947 *ad* Lucr. 1. 51 on *ratio* in the *De rerum natura*. The word is used with a

The following simile (1. 936–50) is the most explicit discussion of the relationship of poetry and philosophy in the *De rerum natura*. However, there are a number of other passages that appear to have a bearing on the question, and I shall treat a selection of them in what follows. I have arranged the material in three subsections, each of which deals with one technique employed by the speaker to depict the close relationship between his poem and his subject matter. While Subsections 3.3.1 ('The Poetics of Pleasure') and 3.3.2 ('Letters and Atoms') are mainly summaries of the work of other scholars (the poetics of Lucretius has been a favourite topic in Latin studies for decades), Subsection 3.3.3 ('*Imitatio Epicuri*') will treat what I believe is a hitherto unrecognized strategy of the Lucretian persona to present himself as a thoroughly Epicurean poet.

3.3.1. The Poetics of Pleasure

The honeyed-cup simile (1. 936–50 ~ 4. 11–25) is the speaker's own explicit explanation of why he has chosen the medium of poetry and how the poetic form of his teaching relates to its philosophical content. Scholars have always regarded it as a key passage and used it as a starting point for a more general reconstruction of Lucretius' poetics, and a certain interpretation has emerged over the last fifty years or so that can now safely be regarded as the *communis opinio*. This view, which I label the 'poetics of pleasure', appears to me basically correct and able to explain what is perhaps the most important aspect of the interaction of poetry and philosophy in the *De rerum natura*. However, since it is well known, it will suffice to give only a brief summary.[77]

The obvious meaning of the honeyed-cup simile is that poetry, the 'sweet honey of the Muses' (1. 947), is the sweetener that attracts the student and induces him to swallow the bitter draught of Epicurean philosophy, the attractive means by which the teacher conveys the (at least superficially) less-than-attractive truth. The comparison with doctors who smear honey around the rim of the cup in order to make children take their medicine implies that poetry plays a subordinate role vis-à-vis the teaching of philosophy: it is a means to end, and what ultimately counts is the 'medicine',

---

number of meanings, but often refers specifically to the Epicurean system; cf. also Gale 1994*b*: 142–3 and my n. 79, below.

[77] Variants of the 'poetics of pleasure' view are found in Boyancé 1947; Waszink 1954; Giancotti 1959; Classen 1968*a*; Schrijvers 1970; Glei 1992; and Gale 1994*b*.

Lucretius' De rerum natura

the saving gospel of Epicurus.[78] It is thus fair to say that poetry for Lucretius is an *ancilla philosophiae*. Note, however, two things: first, while poetry is subordinate, it seems that the speaker still regards it as absolutely necessary. Just as the children may utterly refuse to take their medicine without the honey rim, the student (who has a tendency to spit out the bitter truth; see 2. 1040–1, *desine quapropter nouitate exterritus ipsa | exspuere ex animo rationem*) may not accept Epicurean philosophy unless it is presented in an attractive form. Even so, the teacher is rather hesitant about his success, witness the tentative *si* forte *animum tali ratione tenere | uersibus in nostris possem* (1. 948–9).[79] Second, the supporting role played by poetry in the honeyed-cup simile is set off by the preceding passage 1. 922–30 (discussed above in Sect. 3.2), where the speaker ecstatically celebrates his own achievement simply as a poet, without even mentioning his role as a teacher. The combination of poetry and philosophy is introduced only in 1. 931–4:

> primum quod magnis doceo de rebus et artis
> religionum animum nodis exsoluere pergo.
> deinde quod obscura de re tam lucida pango
> carmina, musaeo contingens cuncta lepore.

(First because I teach about great things and proceed to free the mind from the tight knots of religion; second because I fashion such bright songs about a dark subject matter, drenching everything in the charm of the Muses.)[80]

---

[78] As scholars have noted (e.g., Schrijvers 1970: 40–1; Mitsis 1993: 111–14), the honeyed-cup simile seems to imply that there is an inherent element of deception in poetry (after all, the children do not know that they are taking medicine). In Mitsis's view (cf. Sect, 3.1, above), this is another example of the speaker's patronizing and 'coercive' attitude toward his addressee. Note, however, that in this case, the 'doctor' gives away his trick and avows openly the function of the 'honey rim', i.e., his poetry. He appears unconcerned that this might diminish the success of his treatment, presumably counting on the fact that even adults prefer to take their medicine with a little honey. On the Epicureans' specific predilection for medical imagery, see Konstan et al. 1998: 20 with n. 49.

[79] Note the shift of the meaning of *ratio* in the simile (another example of Lucretius' use of the same expressions with changing connotation: there is an amazing, and in my eyes purposeful, discontinuity, not only of symbolism, but even of regular reference in the *De rerum natura*; cf. the end of the chapter): in 1. 935, it means simply 'reason' (with a flavour of specifically *Epicurean* reason; see above in the text and n. 76); in 1. 946, it refers to the 'system' of Epicurus; but in 1. 948, *tali ratione*, 'this way', refers to poetry—poetry, which at the beginning had to be defended as being reconcilable with *ratio*, but which now is a *ratio* itself.

[80] The syntactical connection of these lines with what precedes is somewhat loose (cf. Schrijvers 1970: 30 and n. 6; D. Clay 1976: 224 n. 9), and it is not quite clear what the causal

And while the speaker's mission as a teacher is mentioned first (*primum*), the description of his creation of bright and sweet poetry is given an equal number of lines. It thus seems that while poetic form is ultimately subordinated to philosophical content, the persona actively tries to stress and elevate the role of poetry as much as possible.

The psychagogic function of poetry, as developed in the honeyed-cup simile, has been linked by P. H. Schrijvers to Epicurean theories of perception. Just as human beings cannot perceive an object unless their attention is directed toward it (see Lucr. 4. 802–15), the student will not be able to perceive the truth of Epicurean physics unless his attention is grabbed by the attractive qualities of the poem (see Schrijvers 1970: 87–147). However, it is not necessary to take recourse to the rather complicated *simulacra* theory in order to explain the function of poetry in the teaching process of the *De rerum natura*.[81] Another, more obvious, model is rhetoric, which, after all, also aims at gaining the listeners' attention and making them well disposed toward the argument, and which likewise uses verbal beauty to help win over the audience.[82]

Lucretian scholars have long recognized that the honeyed-cup simile harks back to the proem of Book 1, another programmatic passage. When in 1. 934 the poet describes himself as *musaeo contingens cuncta lepore*, this is reminiscent of 1. 28, where he asks Venus to grant *aeternum . . . leporem* to his verse. This *lepos*, 'charm', is obviously the sweet, attractive quality of poetry, the honey on the rim of the cup (*musaeo contingens cuncta lepore*, 1. 934, becomes *musaeo dulci contingere melle* in 1. 947). It is also a characteristic of Venus, who uses *lepos* to incite the animals to procreation: *ita capta* lepore | *te sequitur cupide quo quamque inducere pergis* (1. 15–16). If the animals are thus captivated by Venus' *lepos*, it is to be hoped that Memmius will likewise be attracted by the *lepos* that she grants to the verses of the speaker.

Venus' role as the giver of charm and sweetness makes her help

quod refers to: the speaker's joy (*iuuat*, 1. 927, 928, the main verb of the preceding sentence) or the novelty of his poetry (1. 929–30).

[81] While I can see the attraction of regarding the *De rerum natura* as a 'poème qui expose les doctrines d'Epicure d'une manière épicurienne' (Schrijvers 1970: 140), I doubt that this case can really be made (see also Subsect. 3.3.2 and the end of the chapter). And even with special pleading, writing a poem in the first place can hardly be called 'Epicurean manner'.

[82] On the rhetoric of the *De rerum natura*, see esp. Classen 1968a; Schiesaro 1987 is specifically concerned with Lucretius' relationship to contemporary oratory.

crucial to the poem, whose success relies on its power to please the student. Now, if we look at the very first line of the poem, Venus is herself identified as *hominum diuumque uoluptas*, a highly significant designation in view of the fact that *uoluptas*, ἡδονή, is the highest (or, rather, only) good according to Epicurean ethics. Venus can thus be regarded as, among other things, the personification of Pleasure, and it is as such that she is asked to assist the poem and to make it charming, sweet—in a word, pleasurable.[83]

The association of poetry with pleasure runs through the entire poem. Poetry is repeatedly described as sweet (*dulcis*, *suauis*, and *suauiloquens*), and as the honeyed-cup simile shows, it is this sweetness that helps win over the student to the truth of Epicureanism (there may even be an etymologizing pun with *suauis* and *suadere*; see Schrijvers 1970: 36–7). However, poetry is pleasurable not only for the addressee, but also for the poet himself. While in 1. 140–2, his motivation for writing poetry is the *sperata* uoluptas | suauis *amicitiae* of Memmius (thus, pleasure is anticipated only for the future), in 1. 924, the poet is inspired by suauis *amor musarum*, and in 1. 927–30, he is 'enjoying' his wanderings through the realm of the Muses (note the emphatic double *iuuat*, 1. 927 and 928).

A poetry that is sweet and gives pleasure is a poetry described in Epicurean terms, and Monica Gale, among others, has convincingly suggested that the Lucretian speaker is deliberately attempting, as it were, to 'Epicureanize' poetry, that is, to present this problematic medium as something that makes perfect sense from an Epicurean point of view (Gale: 1994*b*: esp. 138–55). Note that instead of making an explicit argument to this effect, he proceeds at the much more subtle level of vocabulary and imagery. By associating poetry with honey, Venus with *uoluptas*, and *lepos* with both Venus and poetry, the poet has created a powerful nexus of concepts that works on the audience at a probably less than wholly conscious level. In a sense, it is a perfect illustration of the honeyed-cup simile: without ever fully noticing how we arrived at this conclusion in the first place, we may come away from the *De rerum natura* thinking that a poem about Epicurean physics is *non ab nulla ratione*.

---

[83] The first to put forward the identification of Venus with ἡδονή in any detail appears to have been Bignone 1945–50: 2. 136–44, who is followed by Giancotti 1959 (see Giancotti 1959: 193 n. 67 for a list of Bignone's forerunners). Boyancé 1947 apparently arrived at the same interpretation independently.

3.3.2. *Atoms and Letters*

While the preceding subsection dealt with what might be called the official poetic programme of the *De rerum natura*, I shall now discuss a more covert way in which the poem reflects on the relationship between its poetic form and its philosophical content. Already in Section 3.2, I briefly drew attention to the analogy between the atoms and the letters, a comparison found five times in the *De rerum natura*, each time in somewhat different form.[84] As seen clearly from the second occurrence of the analogy (1. 823–7), there are two respects in which letters and atoms are similar:

> quin etiam passim nostris in uersibus ipsis
> multa elementa uides multis communia uerbis,
> cum tamen inter se uersus et uerba necesse est
> confiteare et re et sonitu distare sonanti.
> tantum elementa queunt mutato ordine solo.

(Indeed, even in my verses themselves you see everywhere many letters common to many words, while nevertheless you must admit that the verses and words are different from one another, both in meaning and in sounding sound. Such an effect do letters have just when their arrangement is changed.)

Thus, just as the letters are the small particles that constitute the words and ultimately the poem, the atoms are the small particles that constitute the physical objects and ultimately the universe. And, just as the same letters can be combined to form a large number of different words, so, too, can the same atoms combine to form a large number of different objects, just by virtue of different combinations.

Apart from simply illustrating the behaviour of the atoms, the repeated comparison with the letters hints at a larger analogy: if the letters are like the atoms, then the poem is like the universe that it describes and the *De rerum natura* has a structure similar to that of the *rerum natura* itself. As I pointed out in Section 3.2, it is significant that in three of the five occurrences of the analogy, the speaker compares the atoms not to letters in general, but specifically to the letters of his own poem (see the extremely self-referential *nostris in*

---

[84] The passages are 1. 196–8, 823–7, 907–14; 2. 688–99, 1013–22. On the history of the analogy, which probably goes back to Democritus and Leucippus, and on its use in Lucretius, see most notably Snyder 1980: 31–51.

uersibus ipsis, 1. 823; 2. 688, 1013). Note also that the word *elementum* itself, just like the Greek στοιχεῖον, originally refers to the letters of the alphabet and is only secondarily used of the 'principles' or 'elements' in a physical sense (see Snyder 1980: 32–4). It can be argued (see Dionigi 1988: 11–38) that other expressions employed by Lucretius to describe the behaviour of the atoms (such as *concursus*, *motus*, *ordo*, *positura*, and *figura*; see Lucr. 2. 1021) are likewise derived from grammatical terminology, and that, to a certain extent, the physical world is thus depicted in the *De rerum natura* as though it were a verbal artefact. It is, then, no longer clear which system is the model for the other: is the poem imitating the real world, or is it the real world that is like the poem?

The speaker of the *De rerum natura* uses the analogy of atoms and letters, again, not to make an explicit point (since the explicit function of the individual passages is the illustration of the matter at hand), but to create the subtle impression of a close relationship between *carmen* and *res*, poetic form and philosophical content. Now, critics have started from this observation and proceeded in two different directions, establishing two minor trends in the recent study of Lucretian poetics. Both are interesting, though not unproblematic, and I shall briefly explore them here before turning to the next subsection.

The first approach goes back to a seminal article by Paul Friedländer (1941) and has been developed especially by Jane McIntosh Snyder.[85] It is an attempt to explain Lucretius' well-known propensity for wordplay and puns with reference to the atoms–letters analogy and to Epicurean views of language. If words are made of letters just as the physical objects they denote are made of atoms, and if objects of similar qualities consist of atoms that have the same form, then words that contain (some of) the same letters must have similar meaning. Thus, for example, *IGNis* and *lIGNum* denote objects that are in reality closely related (fire typically originates in wood; see, however, n. 87, below). Likewise, the similarity in sound of words like *TERra*, *MATER*, and *MATERies* points to the similar concepts that underlie these expressions.

On this view, the analogy between the poem and its subject matter would be even more pronounced and extend to the micro-level of the text. However, it is not entirely clear whether such an

---

[85] See Snyder 1980; cf. also Ferguson 1987 and Armstrong 1995.

explanation of the wordplays in the *De rerum natura* is actually consistent with what Lucretius says, or with Epicurean doctrine in general. Dalzell (1987; see also 1996: 66) has attacked what is sometimes called the 'atomology' theory (thus Friedländer's own pun) with the argument that the point of the atoms–letters analogy is that a 'rearrangement of the same, or similar elements produces something *qualitatively different*' (1987: 24), not something similar or related. Dalzell is certainly correct that this is the thrust of the analogy in each of its occurrences; however, it is also true that Epicurus' atomistic theory, in order to explain the variety in shape and quality of physical objects, relies on not only the combination of atoms, but also the existence of atoms of different shape (as expounded in Lucr. 2. 333–477; e.g., sweet-tasting things are aggregations with a preponderance of smooth and round atoms). One might therefore logically extend the atoms–letters analogy to argue that similar letters constitute, as it were, words of similar quality.[86] However, if this is the intention of the Lucretian speaker, he does not make it explicit,[87] and note that Friedländer's and Snyder's points about the use of puns stand even if we cannot explain this practice with reference to Epicurean physics.[88] Whether or not Lucretius wanted to make a strong second claim (in addition to the basic analogy) about the similarity of letters and atoms, it certainly appears that such puns as *callida musa* | *Calliope* (6. 93–4) and the ones cited above are meant to imply close semantic (or (pseudo-)etymological) connections between similar-sounding words.

[86] As far as I can tell, however, neither Friedländer 1941 nor Snyder 1980 advances a clear argument to this effect. I am very grateful to John Cooper for clarifying for me these and other matters having to do with Epicurean philosophy.

[87] In fact, at least the context of the third atoms–letters analogy (1. 907–14) rather appears to militate against such an interpretation. The speaker is arguing against Anaxagoras' *homoiomeriae* theory, according to which every single substance can be divided into smallest parts. Fire, for example, consists of little fire particles, and some such particles are also contained in wood, which explains why wood can burn (1. 870–2 and 897–900). From the Epicurean point of view, this theory is wrong: there is no fire in the wood (*non est lignis tamen insitus ignis*, 1. 901), and if wood burns, this is solely because of a rearrangement of its atoms (1. 902–12; esp. *eadem paulo inter se mutata creare* | *ignis et lignum*, 1. 911–12). This is where the analogy comes in: words, too, change, just by virtue of a rearrangement of their letters—e.g., *ligna* and *ignis* (1. 912–14). The passage ends with an assertion of how absurd it is to ascribe to the atoms the qualities of the objects of which they are part; if this were the case, atoms would also laugh and cry (1. 916–20).

[88] On puns in Latin poetry, see Ahl 1985. The fact that etymological wordplay is found frequently in many different authors implies that it is at least not necessary to look for a separate explanation for its occurrence specifically in Lucretius.

On the Friedländer/Snyder view, the comparison between letters and atoms is still basically an analogy: letters behave like atoms, and vice versa, but they belong to different spheres, and there is not necessarily an ontological connection between the two. By contrast, the second interpretative approach, to which I now turn, posits a much closer and more essential relationship between the poem and its subject matter. In the view of scholars like Eva M. Thury (1987) and Alessandro Schiesaro (1994), we have to regard the poem as a physical object in the Epicurean sense. Consisting of atoms, it 'functions as a *simulacrum* of the *rerum natura* in the technical sense, that is, . . . presents word-pictures or images of the real world that enter the mind of the reader and are susceptible to evaluation in the same way as the actual *simulacra* given off by material objects' (Thury 1987: 271). The *De rerum natura* is thus both a mirror image or microcosm of the universe that it describes and at the same time part of it, in all its physicality. Schiesaro takes this idea further, arguing that the poem, which, like the cosmos, is a conglomeration of atoms, obeys the Epicurean cycle of growth and decay, just as the cosmos does. Beginning with the description of spring and procreation and ending with the plague of Athens, the poem itself 'is born' and 'dies', only to be 'reborn' once the reader (if he knows the value of the Epicurean method of repetition; see Sect. 3.1, above) returns to the beginning of Book 1 and starts all over again (thus the title of Schiesaro's paper, 'The Palingenesis of *De rerum natura*').

There is a great fascination to this view, which wholly blurs the boundaries between *carmen* and *res* and regards both the poem and the physical world as part of the same infinite movement of atoms. However, I believe that it is problematic and ultimately misguided. First of all, it is not at all clear how Epicurus would have explained the physical process of reading and understanding a poem, and while it is a fair guess that such an explanation would involve *simulacra*, it is risky business to build an interpretation on a mere hypothesis of Epicurean theory.[89] Second, even if we can say that the poem somehow produces *simulacra* which are received by the mind of the

---

[89] Not only do our fragments and testimonies not tell us anything about how Epicurus would have understood the exact way in which a text—say, the *De rerum natura*—creates *simulacra* in the mind of the reader, but, as John Cooper points out to me, it is questionable whether he would even have cared. While Epicureanism is a materialist philosophy, its aim is not to explain every phenomenon and experience in strictly material terms, but only those which, if misunderstood, might cause unwarranted fears and thus prevent human beings from attaining *eudaimonia*.

reader, the poem is not identical with these *simulacra*, and there still is a clear boundary between what we would call the signifier and the signified. Schiesaro tries to gloss over this distinction, and this is where his clever interpretation ultimately fails: the poem may speak about birth and death, and it may evoke images of birth and death, but the poem itself does not die.[90] On the contrary, one might argue that at the very end, the *De rerum natura* reaches the material high point of its existence, its greatest physical extension.[91]

I would therefore argue that the analogy between the *De rerum natura* and the *rerum natura*, between poem and subject matter, is an analogy between two entities that belong to two separate spheres. Atoms and letters mirror each other, but they are not part of the same process, or, at least, this does not appear to be the point of the analogy. The Lucretian speaker is not interested in a possible ontological connection between his poem and the world it describes; what he conveys or, rather, hints at is the structural similarity between the two. The poem appears as the ideal medium to describe the Epicurean world, not because it consists of atoms (a quality it shares, after all, with all other objects), but because its 'elements' behave like atoms; not because it is born and dies (in the illusion of poetic simultaneity, we witness its birth, but not its death; rather, the speaker hopes that its *lepos* will be *aeternus*, see 1. 28[92]), but because it describes the alternation of birth and death and thus reflects nature's cycle of growth and decay (see, e.g., Minadeo 1969).[93]

[90] P. Fowler 1997, whose argument is similar to that of Schiesaro 1994 in a number of respects, notes that 'if the analogy [between poem and world] were properly followed through, the poem would end with a meaningless jumble of letters individually placed to mirror the disintegration of the compound into constituent atoms' (1997: 136); this is obviously not the case, but in Fowler's opinion, it can be shown that at least the 'words break down into their constituent syllables (*consanguineos* into *cum sanguine*, 6.1283–85; *morbus* into *mors*, 1250–51; *temptaret* into *tempore*, 1251)' (1997: 135). Note that Fowler favours the transposition of 6. 1247–51 to after 6. 1286, the last line of the poem as we have it.

[91] At least this would be true if poetic simultaneity were taken literally and we believed that the process of the poem's creation, even its creation as a physical object, is finished only once we come to its end.

[92] Of course, from an Epicurean point of view, this kind of eternity can last only until the end of this world, a thought wittily captured by Ovid (whose diction alludes to Lucr. 5. 95 and 1000): *carmina sublimis tunc sunt peritura Lucreti, | exitio terras cum dabit una dies (Am.* 1. 15. 23–4).

[93] As we shall see in Sect. 6.4, below, the speaker of Manilius' *Astronomica* likewise strives to give the impression that his poem is a microcosm of the macrocosm it describes; unlike in the case of the Lucretian persona, however, his Stoic creed enables him to claim an actual ontological connection between *carmen* and *res*. See also Osborne 1997: 31–5 for the idea that in the works of Empedocles and Parmenides, too, the poems' structure mirrors their subject matter.

The one real connection between the letters of the poem and the atoms of the world is the Lucretian persona. He is a part of the physical *rerum natura*, as becomes clearest when he describes typical human experience by means of the first-person plural (see Sect. 3.1, above); however, he is also the one who produces the poem *de rerum natura*, who is, in fact, according to the conceit of poetic simultaneity, producing this poem 'right now'. And this experience of composing the poem is itself part of the physical world that the poem describes; thus, the poet is able to use himself as an example of the phenomenon that people tend to dream at night of their activities during the day. Just as lawyers dream of being in court, generals of engaging in battle, and sailors of experiencing storms,

> nos [sc. uidemur] agere hoc autem et naturam quaerere rerum
> semper et inuentam patriis exponere chartis.
>
> (4. 969–70)

(But I always seem to do this: seek the nature of things and expound it, once found, on pages written in my own language.)

Clearly, researching nature, writing poetry about nature, and dreaming about both are all natural phenomena themselves and thus become the object of the poem *de rerum natura*.

3.3.3. Imitatio Epicuri

It turns out that the speaker of Lucretius' poem is not the only one to write *de rerum natura* (his main topic as mentioned already in 1. 25; cf. 1. 950; 4. 969–70): throughout the text, a number of people are credited with having treated the same subject. Thus, in 1. 124–6, Ennius' famous dream is paraphrased as follows:

> unde sibi exortam semper florentis Homeri
> commemorat speciem lacrimas effundere salsas
> coepisse et *rerum naturam* expandere dictis.

(Whence [from the underworld] he tells that the shade of ever-flourishing Homer arose, wept salty tears, and began to expound the nature of things with his words.)

This implies that both Homer and especially Ennius treated the 'nature of things' in their poetry,[94] a claim that has always

[94] Strictly speaking, Homer is credited only with speaking about *rerum natura* within

confounded scholars of Ennius since it is not entirely clear to which part of Ennius' work Lucretius could possibly be referring.[95] Since it is highly unlikely that the *Annals* contained an extended discussion of natural philosophy (as opposed to a brief summary of Pythagorean *metempsychosis*),[96] I suspect that Lucretius' claim that Ennius' Homer explicated the *rerum natura* is a deliberate exaggeration (note that *expandere* would seem to imply a treatment of some length) and serves simply to align both Homer and Ennius with the speaker's own project[97]—and with the work of at least one other author as well. In 3. 14–15, it is Epicurus who speaks about *rerum natura* (*nam simul ac ratio tua coepit uociferari* | *naturam rerum* . . .), just as he does in 5. 54, where his activity is described as *omnem rerum naturam pandere dictis* (note the verbal similarity to the description of Homer in 1. 126), which is, of course, especially apt since Epicurus' major philosophical work was in fact called Περὶ φύσεως.

The persona thus places himself in a tradition of writers on natural philosophy, a tradition that includes Homer, Ennius, and Epicurus, as well as Empedocles. While the last is not explicitly said to have treated *rerum natura* (note, though, that Empedocles' poem on natural philosophy was also known as Περὶ φύσεως), the description of his work in 1. 731–3 is highly reminiscent of the descriptions of Epicurus' achievements in the proems to Books 3, 5, and 6 (thus, e.g., Empedocles has a *diuinum pectus*, 1. 731, Epicurus a *diuina mens*, 3. 15; the *praeclara reperta* of Empedocles, 1. 732, are parallel to the *diuina reperta* of Epicurus, 6. 7; and the verb *uociferari* is used of both, 1. 732 and 3. 14).[98] While these four writers (three Greek, one Roman) appear indeed to be Lucretius' most important models, there is something strange about this group. Epicurus, who, one

---

Ennius' work, and the Lucretian speaker does not claim that the Homeric poems themselves deal with natural philosophy. Note, though, that Homer interacts with Ennius qua poet (after all, Ennius has literally inherited his poetic genius in the form of his soul), and knowledge about the *rerum natura* thus appears as part of his poetic expertise. Note also that on an allegorical interpretation, the Homeric poems themselves might well be understood as treating cosmic forces; see P. R. Hardie 1986: 25–9.

[95] See Suerbaum 1968: 96; Gigon 1978a: 177–8; P. R. Hardie 1986: 79–80; and Farrell 1991: 306–7.

[96] See Suerbaum 1968: 96 and n. 303, who points out that the genre of Ennius' poem makes the inclusion of a detailed discussion of the *rerum natura* rather improbable.

[97] See Cabisius 1979: 246; see also Gale 1994b: 106–14 for a more general discussion of Lucretius' relationship to Homer and Ennius.

[98] See Waszink 1954: 254–6 and Giancotti 1959: 79 (both of whom adduce further parallels), as well as Tatum 1984: 185.

Lucretius' De rerum natura

might argue, is after all the crucial source for Lucretius, is really the odd man out: a prose writer with an outspoken aversion to poetry, one might think he would hardly fit in with a triad of poets.

As I shall endeavour to show in the following pages, this juxtaposition is deliberate, and it is one of the major poetic strategies of the Lucretian speaker to portray Epicurus as though he, too, were indeed a poet and, consequently, to cast himself in the role of the literary successor who follows his model in an act of *imitatio*.[99] As we have seen, the use of *rerum natura* to denote the subject matter of not only Epicurus and the speaker, but also Homer and Ennius, and the similarity of the descriptions of Empedocles and Epicurus serve to create a connection between the prosaic philosopher and the poets.[100] There are a number of other instances where Epicurus is described even more clearly in terms appropriate to an author of poetry and where the speaker himself reflects explicitly on his own imitative relationship to his master.

As discussed already in connection with the journey and the light–darkness metaphors, the speaker throughout the poem presents his own achievements and those of Epicurus as parallel: thus, both are 'travelling', both 'enlighten' mankind (certainly Memmius), etc.[101] The proem to Book 3 provides the most explicit acknowledgement that the poet is following in the philosopher's footsteps:[102]

---

[99] Gale 1994b: 137 argues that the relationship of Lucretius to Epicurus is that of a poet to his Muse, a claim that I cannot follow. The speaker never invokes Epicurus to ask him for inspiration, information, or assistance, but he does invoke other Muses or Muse-like characters, such as Calliope and Venus. Far from treating Epicurus as a present, timeless deity, he describes him as a historical and—despite all his divine characteristics—now dead human being (see esp. 3. 1042–4). Thill 1979: 500–1 and 510–11 uses specifically Lucr. 3. 3–6 (on which see below in the text) to show that Latin poets conceived of imitation (of another author) very much in terms of inspiration (by a divinity), but this still does not make Epicurus a Muse.

[100] Note that it is Epicurus who is described with terms previously used for the poets, and not vice versa. The treatment of Epicurus' literary achievements begins only in Book 3, while Ennius, Homer, and Empedocles are discussed in Book 1; the reader is thus led to think, 'Oh, Epicurus is like Homer/Ennius/Empedocles/the speaker', not 'Homer, etc. is like Epicurus'.

[101] See esp. the discussion in Cabisius 1979. Other parallels between the speaker and Epicurus include that both are credited with being the 'first' (see 1. 926–30 for the speaker and, e.g., 1. 66 and 71 for Epicurus; of course, Ennius is *primus*, too, see 1. 117) and both are described as 'victorious', the speaker in his poetic chariot race (6. 92–5) and Epicurus in 1. 75–9 (*unde refert nobis* uictor *quid possit oriri*, etc.).

[102] For the following discussion, cf. esp. Graca 1989: 19–22; Tomasco 1999: 22–6; and Fögen 2000: 132–6.

> te sequor, o Graiae gentis decus, inque tuis nunc
> ficta pedum pono pressis uestigia signis,
> non ita certandi cupidus quam propter amorem
> quod te imitari aueo; quid enim contendat hirundo
> cycnis, aut quidnam tremulis facere artubus haedi
> consimile in cursu possint et fortis equi uis?
>
> (3. 3–8)

(You I follow, O glory of the Greek race, and put down my firm footsteps now on the tracks left by you, not so much desirous of competition as out of love, because I wish to imitate you. For how could a swallow vie with swans, or what could kids with trembling limbs achieve in a race to match themselves against the power of a strong horse?)

The wording of this description is such as to invoke the imitation of one poet by an another. The speaker uses the verb *imitari* (3. 6) to describe his preferred relationship to Epicurus; his inspiration for this *imitatio* is 'love', *amor* (3. 5; cf. 1. 924–5 *suauem . . . amorem | musarum . . .*), and he therefore eschews a more antagonistic engagement with his model (*non ita certandi cupidus*, 3. 5).[103] At any rate, he realizes that a competition between himself and Epicurus would be grotesquely uneven, as illustrated by the hypothetical contests between the swallow and the swans (3. 5–6) and between the kids and the horse (3. 7–8).[104] These two comparisons are extremely interesting since they involve animals that are typically used as symbols for poetic activity and thus help create the impression that not only the speaker, but also his model Epicurus, is a poet.

As for the first simile, in which the swallow stands for the Lucretian persona and the swan for Epicurus, it is hardly necessary to provide proof that swans are traditionally associated with poetry.[105] Additionally, the contest of two birds or other animals of different vocal ability is frequently used as a metaphor for the

---

[103] See Reiff 1959: 9–15; Thill 1979: 453–4, 460–1, 475, 494, and 500–1. Note that *imitari* (a word that does not have a strict technical meaning, but can be used to describe any instance where an author follows a literary model; see Thill 1979: 465) is here opposed to *certare*, a verb with the same force as *aemulari*, which often denotes a more ambitious form of imitation, presented in terms of a contest. See generally Reiff 1959 on the terms *interpretari*, *imitari*, and *aemulari* (cf. also Zintzen 1987: 17–22), but note Thill's critique of Reiff's system as being too schematic (1979: 451–70).

[104] I take it that the distribution of singulars and plurals in the two similes (*hirundo* and *equus* v. *cygni* and *haedi*) is merely poetical and *metri causa*.

[105] See now Nünlist 1998: 48–51, as well as Donohue 1993: 18–29, whose discussion also contains observations on the zoology of the mute swan and the whooper swan (only the former is indigenous to Greece and Italy, but only the latter actually sings!).

Lucretius' De rerum natura

uneven relationship between a superior and an inferior poet, especially between a 'classical' poet, who is seen as an unreachable ideal, and his latter-day imitator(s).[106] Already Lambinus in his 1563 edition of Lucretius (*ad* 3. 6) draws attention to Theocritus, *Idylls* 7. 39–41, where Simichidas declares,

> οὔτε τὸν ἐσθλόν
> Σικελίδαν νίκημι τὸν ἐκ Σάμω οὔτε Φιλίταν
> ἀείδων, βάτραχος δὲ ποτ' ἀκρίδας ὥς τις ἐρίσδω.

(And I do not conquer in song noble Sikelidas from Samos or Philitas, but compete like some frog against crickets.)

A few lines later in the same poem, the goatherd Lycidas agrees with this sentiment of the speaker, adding that he himself hates those Μοισᾶν ὄρνιχες ὅσοι ποτὶ Χῖον ἀοιδόν | ἀντία κοκκύζοντες ἐτώσια μοχθίζοντι (47–8).[107] Similarly, in Vergil, *Eclogues* 9. 35–6, Lycidas states:

> nam neque adhuc Vario uideor nec dicere Cinna
> digna, sed argutos inter strepere anser olores.

(For I do not yet seem to say anything worthy of Varius or Cinna, but am a cackling goose among clear-voiced swans.)

Another comparison between beautiful and less beautiful birdsong is found in the *De rerum natura* itself, at 4. 181–2 (repeated at 4. 910–11):

> paruus ut est cygni melior canor, ille gruum quam
> clamor in aetheriis dispersus nubibus austri.

(Just as the short song of the swan is better than the noise of cranes scattered in the sky through the southern clouds.)

As likewise first pointed out by Lambinus (*ad* 4. 181), these lines are a translation of part of an epigram of Antipater of Sidon that honours the poet Erinna (*Anth. Pal.* 7. 713): her work is short, but she is still superior to recent poets,

---

[106] See Thill 1979: 496–8. As far as we can tell from our fragmentary evidence, the motif in this form is only Hellenistic; by contrast, when Pindar speaks of the crows that croak against the eagle (*Ol.* 2. 86–8; *Nem.* 3. 80–2), the point is not that they are worse *singers* (see Steiner 1986: 105 and 107; Nünlist 1998: 57–8).

[107] See also Theocr. *Id.* 5. 136–7: οὐ θεμιτόν, Λάκων, ποτ' ἀηδόνα κίσσας ἐρίσδειν, | οὐδ' ἔποπας κύκνοισι.

> λωίτερος κύκνου μικρὸς θρόος ἠὲ κολοίων
> κρωγμὸς ἐν εἰαριναῖς κιδνάμενος νεφέλαις.
>
> (7–8)

(The short song of the swan is better than the croaking of jackdaws scattered among the spring clouds.)[108]

As these examples show, the bird simile in *De rerum natura* 3. 6–7 surreptitiously gives the impression that Epicurus is a poet, by means of identifying him with the swan, the most superior of singers, whom a mere swallow like the speaker cannot hope to emulate.[109] The second absurd contest, that between the kids with their trembling limbs and the strong horse (3. 7–8), has the same implication. We have already seen that the horse race is a traditional metaphor for poetry and one that is employed by Lucretius in 6. 47 and 92–4, where the speaker pictures himself as a charioteer approaching the finish line (see Sect. 3.2, above). Like the image of the competing birds, the race metaphor, too, is one specifically used to describe the phenomenon of literary *imitatio* (see Thill 1979: 494–6). Furthermore, it appears that the Lucretian speaker in this passage does not only, as before, refer to Epicurus with an image appropriate for a poet, but that he has a specific poet in mind with whom he wishes to associate his master.

---

[108] See Donohue 1993: 1–34; Schindler 2000: 142–5. Both Antipater and Lucretius compare the two sets of birds (swan and jackdaws/cranes) in two different regards, the length of the song and its sweetness. The same combination of criteria of quantity and quality is found in the rather similar imagery of Callimachus' *Aetia* prologue (fr. 1. 13–16 Pfeiffer): the speaker admits that the crane covers a long distance in flight and that the Massagetae shoot their arrows very far (quantity), only to add that 'even so, nightingales are sweeter' (quality); see Asper 1997: 199–201. I assume that at least Lucretius' lines are influenced by Callimachus; note the substitution of the Callimachean cranes for Antipater's jackdaws (see Donohue 1993: 31). The entire context in Lucretius is rather 'Callimachean': in the line that introduces the simile, the speaker declares that he will treat his next topic only briefly, but sweetly, *suauidicis potius quam multis uersibus edam* (4. 180 = 4. 909). As Thill 1979: 497 points out (cf. also Sedley 1998: 140; Schindler 2000: 144), it is rather interesting that the Lucretian persona here aligns himself with the swan, while in 3. 6–7 he is the swallow as compared to the swan Epicurus.

[109] See Donohue 1993: 148–9, who does not draw any further conclusions from this observation (see also Cabisius 1979: 242). Heinze 1897: 49–50 suggests that the swallow is specifically chosen to stand for the speaker because of this bird's association with 'barbarian' speech (cf., e.g., Aesch. *Ag.* 1050–1; Ar. *Ran.* 93; and LSJ s.vv. χελιδονίζω and χελιδών): 'vielleicht will L. damit seine φωνὴ βάρβαρος bescheidener Weise gegenüber der Stimme des *Graius homo* bezeichnen' (cf. Fögen 2000: 135–6). Note also Sedley 1998: 57–8, who points out, among other things, that *hirundo* is a Latin word, by contrast to the Greek *cygnus*, concluding that the poet is specifically drawing attention to the fact that he is a Roman imitating a Greek.

Yet again, it is Lambinus who, apropos of *fortis equi uis* (3. 8), points to a fragment of Ennius' *Annals* (522–3 Skutsch):

> sicuti fortis equos spatio qui saepe supremo
> uicit Olympia nunc senio confectus quiescit.

(As a strong horse that has often won on the last lap at Olympia is now resting, tired out by old age.)

As we learn from Cicero, *De senectute* 14, Ennius compared himself to this aged race horse.[110] The frequent victory at Olympia thus stands for the poet's literary achievements; since he says that the horse is now resting, we may assume that the passage stood in an epilogue, possibly at the end of Book 15, the original conclusion of the *Annals*.[111] It appears likely that the Lucretian phrase is meant to evoke the Ennian passage and that the speaker is thus creating yet another connection between Epicurus and the Latin poet who is said to have likewise been concerned with the *rerum natura*.[112]

The vocabulary and imagery used in *De rerum natura* 3. 3–8 help paint Epicurus as a superior poet and the speaker as his inferior imitator, and this impression is continued in the following lines (9–13), which praise Epicurus' work and describe the poet's method of appropriating it. Epicurus is the πρῶτος εὑρετής, the *rerum inuentor* (9),[113] whose *aurea dicta* (12) are available in *chartis* (10);[114] from

---

[110] It may be impossible to decide whether Ennius' horse was used to draw a chariot or rather carried a jockey (both disciplines were part of the Olympic games). As René Nünlist kindly informs me, in many instances where a poetic journey metaphor involves horses, it is impossible to tell whether the authors are thinking of horseback riding or rather of travelling in a chariot.

[111] See the extended discussion in Suerbaum 1968: 114–51 (specifically on the simile 120–34), as well as Skutsch 1985: 673–4. It seems that the simile is a conflation of the widespread motif of the ageing horse (cf., most famously, Ibycus fr. 287. 6–7) and of the more specifically metapoetic race metaphor.

[112] The allusion to Ennius is prepared in the preceding line (3. 7) by the phrase *tremulis . . . artubus*, which, as Bailey 1947 *ad loc*. points out, is modelled on Enn. *Ann*. 34 Skutsch, *et cita cum tremulis anus attulit artubus lumen*.

[113] The phrase *rerum inuentor* (on which see also Tomasco 1999: 27) should not be taken merely as the 'finder of the subject-matter', i.e., of the *res* that the speaker is treating in his *carmen*. As I argue in the text, Lucretius does not clearly separate philosophical subject matter (the field of Epicurus) and poetic form (the field of the speaker), but instead approximates the two. The *res* whose *inuentor* Epicurus is are rather the physical objects whose multitude forms the universe and whose behaviour is the topic of the *De* rerum *natura*. It is interesting that Epicurus is said to have 'found/invented' the *res*: of course, there was a universe before, but it was only really 'discovered' by Epicurus (cf. 5. 335–7, another passage that aligns the speaker with Epicurus: *denique natura haec rerum ratioque repertast | nuper, et hanc primus cum primis ipse repertus | nunc ego sum in patrias qui possim uertere uoces*; cf. also 4. 969–70, where the speaker himself 'seeks' (*quaerere*, 969) and 'finds' (*inuentam*, 970) the *rerum natura*).

[114] As mentioned above (Sect. 3.2), the stress on the written form of both Epicurus' and the

these writings, the speaker gathers the material for his own song, just as bees gather honey (*floriferis ut apes in saltibus omnia libant*, 11).[115] The bee is a traditional symbol for the poet (see, e.g., Pl. *Ion* 534a7–b3; cf. Nünlist 1998: 300–6); that the gathering of honey from a particular source can be used as a metaphor for the *imitatio* of one poet by another is clear from an anonymous Hellenistic fragment (*Suppl. Hell.* 1001), whose speaker describes himself as carrying honey that he has derived from Sappho, ἐκ Σάπφως τόδ' ἀμελγόμενος μέλι τοι φέρω (see Nünlist 1998: 62, 208, and 302). Lucretius' choice of this particular image, of course, also recalls the honeyed-cup simile. Interestingly, there the honey was the additional sweetener the poet had to apply to make the bitter truth of Epicurean philosophy palatable, whereas now the honey is derived from Epicurus' writings themselves (see Schindler 2000: 139–41), and it is perhaps even possible to understand the repeated epithet *aurea* [sc. *dicta*] (3. 12–13) as evocative of honey (see, e.g., *aurea mella*, Ov. *Fast.* 4. 546; cf. Waszink 1974: 22 and n. 37; Stokes 1975: 95; and Graca 1989: 21). Just like the speaker's song, Epicurus' works are thus associated with sweetness, as well as with light (by virtue of the shiny quality of gold (see Tomasco 1999: 29); the *aurea dicta* are not too different from the *lucida carmina*, 1. 933–4). Philosophy and poetry are no longer opposites, but the speaker has, purely by means of his diction, succeeded in surreptitiously approximating philosophy and poetry.

This strategy of presenting Epicurus, paradoxically, as though he were a poet is pursued further in the proem to Book 5. Here, the speaker relies wholly on his choice of words to give the impression that his activity and that of his model Epicurus are really the same sort of thing. The book starts with the rhetorical question,

---

speaker's work can be explained on the one hand with the fact that, after all, Epicurus was a prose writer and Lucretius could not very well refer to his work as 'song' or the like, even if he had wanted to, and on the other hand with the usefulness of the atoms–letters analogy (discussed in Subsect. 3.3.2, above), which would not be applicable to a poem conceived as oral. In this particular passage, it is possible also that the speaker wishes to present himself as a *poeta doctus*, one who, like the poets in Catull. 68. 33–6 and Ov. *Tr.* 3. 14. 37–8, needs a library in order to compose poetry; see Kroll 1924: 143; Thill 1979: 18 and n. 32.

[115] Thill 1979: 212–14 compares Hor. *Carm.* 4. 2. 25–32 and argues convincingly that the Augustan poet modelled this passage on Lucretius: like the persona in the *De rerum natura*, the Horatian speaker does not wish to compete with the 'swan', in this case Pindar, but is content with his role as a humble bee. The possibility of active competition, *aemulatio*, is excluded from the start.

> quis potis est dignum pollenti pectore carmen
> condere pro rerum maiestate hisque repertis?
>
> (5. 1–2)

(Who is able to compose with mighty genius a song worthy of the majesty of things and these discoveries?)

Bailey 1947 translates *pollenti pectore* somewhat vaguely as 'might of mind', but it seems that the meaning is rather more specifically 'poetic talent, *ingenium*'.[116] It is thus rather striking that only four lines later, the *praemia* (5. 5), 'achievements', of Epicurus are described as *pectore parta suo*, 'brought forth by his *ingenium*', and it is even more interesting that these *praemia* are also *quaesita*, 'sought out, chosen'. The latter would seem to refer to poetic *ars* and the long, laborious process of choosing the right themes and formulations.[117] Note that the speaker describes himself during his sleepless nights as quaerentem *dictis quibus et quo carmine demum | clara tuae possim praepandere lumina menti* (1. 143–4) and that he calls his songs conquisita *diu dulcique reperta labore* (3. 419).

In 5. 21, the teachings of Epicurus are said to be *dulcia . . . solacia uitae* that 'soothe' (*permulcent*) people's minds. Their sweetness is highly reminiscent of the sweetness of poetry—as we have seen, a leitmotif in the *De rerum natura*. Also, the fact that Epicurus spoke *diuinitus* about the gods (5. 52–3, itself a pun), while mainly intended to prove that the philosopher was himself 'divine', might also allude to the concept of the divine inspiration of poets. Finally, Epicurus' works are typically described as *dicta* (e.g., *aurea dicta*, 3. 12), a word that is repeated three times in the short passage 5. 49–54: *expulerit dictis*, 5. 50; *dare dicta*, 5. 53; and *pandere dictis*, 5. 54.[118] When in the very next sentence the speaker—who, again, presents himself as following in the footsteps of his master (*cuius ego ingressus uestigia*, 5. 55)—refers to his own activity as *doceo dictis* (5. 56), one has the very strong impression that his *dicta* and those of Epicurus belong to the same category, that the activity of the poet and that of the philosopher are really one and the same.

---

[116] Cf. the use of *pectus* in Ov. *Fast*. 2. 119–20, where the speaker wishes he had the genius of Homer: *nunc mihi mille sonos quoque est memoratus Achilles | uellem, Maeonide*, pectus *inesse tuum*.

[117] The standard view is that *parta . . . quaesita⟨que⟩ praemia* is a ὕστερον πρότερον with the meaning 'the prizes sought and won by his mind' (cf. Bailey 1947 *ad loc*.)—a rather dull and redundant expression.

[118] Heinze 1897: 50 suggests that *dicta* is a translation of φωναί and that the latter was a common term for the sayings of Epicurus.

By presenting Epicurus as a poet and himself as his follower, the Lucretian persona places himself firmly into a Latin literary tradition and employs what has been called the *primus* motif. Since Roman literature is nearly entirely modelled on Greek literature, a Roman poet typically constructs his own achievements through reference to his Greek model(s). His claim is not that he is the first to have practised a certain type of poetry—this fame will always go to his Greek predecessor—but that he is the first to practise it *at Rome*. This topos of poetic self-representation has been nicely summed up by Andrée Thill:

> L'usage littéraire latin veut que tout poète se trouve un répondant grec, et l'histoire de chaque genre commence par la question quand et par qui il a été introduit à Rome. Le poète latin est rarement l'*inuentor* ou l'*auctor*, il lui suffit d'être le *primus* et au mieux le *princeps*, c'est-à-dire l'introducteur et l'adaptateur d'un genre grec, le 'premier', voir le chef de file, mais seulement à Rome.[119]

The Latin poet is thus, paradoxically, on the one hand a 'first', on the other hand a latecomer, dependent on his Greek model. This contradictory state is apparent from the way Ennius presents himself in the *Annals* and from the way he is presented in the *De rerum natura*. As mentioned above, Lucretius describes the archaic poet as *Ennius . . . noster . . . qui* primus *amoeno | detulit ex Helicone perenni fronde coronam* (1. 117–18),[120] but a few lines later he mentions his encounter with Homer (1. 124–6), alluding to Ennius' claim that Homer's soul was now living in him and thus stressing the Latin writer's dependence on his Greek forerunner.[121] Ennius himself may have expressed his double role as an innovator, on the one hand, and a

---

[119] Thill 1979: 2; Thill's entire discussion on pp. 1–36 is extremely useful. On the *primus* motif, see also Regenbogen 1932: 22–3; Wimmel 1960: index s.v. '*primus*-Motiv'; Suerbaum 1968: 269; Zintzen 1987: 24 and *passim*; and Hinds 1998: 52–63.

[120] I wonder whether *noster* in Lucr. 1. 117 can be understood as limiting the claim of being first to 'being the first of our poets' (as though *primus nostrum*). At any rate, it is likely that already Ennius called himself 'first'; compare *Ann.* 206–10 Skutsch and the discussion in Suerbaum 1968: 265–82. Other famous instances of *primus*/*princeps* in Latin poetry include Verg. *G.* 3. 10–11 (primus *ego in patriam mecum, modo uita supersit, | Aonio rediens deducam uertice Musas*), on which see Sect. 4.2, below; Prop. 3. 1. 3–4 (primus *ego ingredior puro de fonte sacerdos | Itala per Graios orgia ferre choros*); Hor. *Epist.* 1. 19. 23–4 (*Parios ego* primus *iambos | ostendi Latio*) and *Carm.* 3. 30. 10–14 (*dicar . . .* princeps *Aeolium carmen ad Italos | deduxisse modos*).

[121] Hor. *Epist.* 2. 1. 50 calls Ennius *alter Homerus*; cf., e.g., Propertius' claim to be the *Romanus Callimachus* (4. 1. 64) and similar passages collected and discussed by Thill 1979: 4 and nn. 13–15. Ennius is unique in his use of what might be called the *poeta rediuiuus* motif in that he claims to be literally a reincarnation of Homer, according to the Pythagorean doctrine of metempsychosis (cf. Suerbaum 1968: 82–91).

follower of tradition, in this case Homer, on the other, by including in the proem to *Annals* 1 both an account of his famous dream-encounter with Homer, which stressed his being dependent, and a separate *Musenweihe*, which developed the theme of his being the 'first'.[122]

If we now turn to Lucretius, it turns out that the persona of the *De rerum natura* finds himself in the same paradoxical situation of being both a *primus* and a *secundus*, that is, a follower (from *sequor*). He chooses to highlight this contradiction by employing the same metaphor to describe both states, in two passages that are by now familiar: in 1. 926–7, the speaker walks on untrodden paths (*auia Pieridum peragro loca nullius ante | trita solo*), while in 3. 3–4, he follows in the footsteps of Epicurus (*te sequor, o Graiae gentis decus, inque tuis nunc | ficta pedum pono pressis uestigia signis*).[123] It is the typical dilemma of the Roman *imitator*: like Ennius, the speaker wins for himself a *corona* from the untouched landscape of the Muses, but like Ennius, he is deeply indebted to a Greek model. Interestingly, however, the *Graius homo* who is to the Lucretian speaker what Homer was to Ennius is not, say, Hesiod, the supposed originator of didactic poetry, or Empedocles, in many ways the true poetic model for the *De rerum natura*. Rather, it is Epicurus, the thinker who disapproved of poetry but who, in Lucretius' work, is subtly cast in the role of poet.[124]

Epicureans believed that one way of obtaining *eudaimonia* was to emulate the behaviour of their master, who they thought had succeeded in living a life worthy of the gods.[125] Thus, for example, Philodemus' treatise Περὶ παρρησίας makes it the most important principle of the Epicurean community to 'obey Epicurus, according to whom we have chosen to live',[126] and Seneca tells us that Epicurus advised his followers to always act as though he himself were observing their actions.[127] This practice of attempting to shape

---

[122] As mentioned in n. 54, above, it is controversial whether there ever was an Ennian *Musenweihe*; Suerbaum 1968: 46–113 makes a good case for it.

[123] See D. Clay 1983*b*: 9 and 40–5.

[124] In this context, note also that the description of Epicurus in 3. 1042–4 is probably modelled on an epigram in praise of Homer by Leonidas of Tarentum (*Anth. Pal.* 9. 24); see Gale 1994*b*: 140 and n. 41.

[125] On the worship of Epicurus as a god, see the testimonies collected by Pease 1955 *ad* Cic. *Nat. D.* 1. 43; cf. also D. Clay 1986.

[126] καὶ τὸ συνέχον καὶ κυριώτατον, Ἐπικούρῳ, καθ' ὃν ζῆν ᾑρήμεθα, πειθαρχήσομεν, 45. 7–11 Olivieri.

[127] '*Sic fac*' inquit '*omnia tamquam spectet Epicurus*', Sen. *Ep.* 25. 5; see also 11. 8–10 and 52. 3.

oneself in the image of the divine teacher is known as *imitatio Epicuri*.[128] The Lucretian speaker, too, believes that Epicurus was a 'god' (5. 8: *dicendum est, deus ille fuit, deus, inclute Memmi*) and he, too, wishes to imitate him (3. 6: *te imitari aueo*). However, his imitation is not ethical but literary, a practice that can be paralleled throughout the history of Latin poetry, and one whose aim is not the good life but rather the composition of a *dignum . . . carmen | . . . pro rerum maiestate hisque repertis* (5. 1–2).

To conclude: the speaker of the *De rerum natura*, who is both a dedicated teacher and a self-confident poet, employs a number of sophisticated strategies in order to suggest that *carmen* and *res*, his poem and its philosophical subject matter, are closely connected. While explicitly remarking on the role of poetry in the honeyed-cup simile—poetry is the sweetener that makes Epicurean doctrine palatable to the student—the persona also implicitly suggests, by means of vocabulary and imagery, that the sweetness of poetry and the pleasure derived from it are crucial elements in his enterprise and ones that are highly compatible with Epicurean thought and its stress on *uoluptas*. By repeatedly using the atoms–letters analogy, the speaker furthermore gives the impression that his poem *de rerum natura* and the physical world, *rerum natura*, that is its subject matter share a similar structure and behave in a similar way, with the result that the poem appears as a microcosm of the macrocosm that it is treating. Finally, by presenting Epicurus as though he were a poet and constructing an *imitatio* relationship between himself and his Greek model, the speaker manages to 'poeticize' Epicurus, just as he endeavours to 'Epicureanize' poetry.

As we have seen, the persona hardly advances any direct arguments concerning the relationship of poetry and philosophy (the only exception is the honeyed-cup simile), but rather operates on the level of association, making use of a technique that has been called 'discontinuity of symbolism' (Anderson 1960) or 'fluidity of

---

[128] Modern scholars use *imitatio Epicuri* as a technical term; however, I have not been able to find this exact phrase in any ancient source. (One of the anonymous readers of Oxford University Press has suggested to me that the expression is modern and built in analogy to *imitatio Christi*, a central concept of Christian spirituality (with rather striking similarities to its Epicurean counterpart), which was made famous especially by Thomas à Kempis's work of the same name—in my opinion, an attractive scenario. My thanks go to Greta Austin for clarification on this matter.) On the idea itself, and on the ethical and pedagogical practice of Epicurean communities in general, see esp. D. Clay 1983*a* and Nussbaum 1986 (esp. 46–7); cf. also DeWitt 1936*a* and 1936*b*; Frischer 1982: 124–5; and Erler 1993, and 1994: 154.

imagery' (D. West 1994), but that has not hitherto been seriously studied in Lucretian scholarship (cf. n. 68, above). By this method, Epicurus can be said to be both 'light' and 'dark' (see my discussion in Sect. 3.2) and Venus can appear as a Muse, the personification of *uoluptas*, the principle of life and creation, base sexuality (see 4. 1058 and its context), and a number of other things. However, she is never explicitly identified with any of these, and after all, Epicurean natural philosophy allows neither for the existence of Muses, nor indeed for that of a force of creation, given that the coming into being and disintegration of its cosmos is wholly a matter of chance. Likewise, Epicurus is never explicitly called a poet—a designation that would be wholly absurd—but it is only through the connotations of the words and images associated with him that we get the impression that the speaker regards him as anything but a philosopher.

Lucretius' use of language and his technique of changing the reference of a term from one occurrence to the next is fascinating and would be a fruitful subject for further study. Note, however, one thing: it is thoroughly un-Epicurean (cf. Gale 1997). Epicurus was especially concerned that words should be used according to their primary meaning, which he considered the only way to ensure meaningful philosophical discourse:

πρῶτον μὲν οὖν τὰ ὑποτεταγμένα τοῖς φθόγγοις, ὦ Ἡρόδοτε, δεῖ εἰληφέναι, ὅπως ἂν τὰ δοξαζόμενα ἢ ζητούμενα ἢ ἀπορούμενα εἰς ταῦτα ἀναγαγόντες ἐπικρίνειν, καὶ μὴ ἄκριτα πάντα ἡμῖν εἰς ἄπειρον ἀποδεικνύουσιν ἢ κενοὺς φθόγγους ἔχωμεν. ἀνάγκη γὰρ τὸ πρῶτον ἐννόημα καθ' ἕκαστον φθόγγον βλέπεσθαι καὶ μηθὲν ἀποδείξεως προσδεῖσθαι, εἴπερ ἕξομεν τὸ ζητούμενον ἢ ἀπορούμενον καὶ δοξαζόμενον ἐφ' ὃ ἀνάξομεν. (*Ep. Hdt.* 37–8)

(First, Herodotus, we must understand the meanings of words in order that by expressing our opinions, investigations, and problems in exact terms, we may reach judgments and not use empty phrases, leaving matters undecided although we argue endlessly. We must accept without further explanation the first mental image brought up by each word if we are to have any standard to which to refer a particular inquiry, problem, or opinion.) (trans. Geer 1964)[129]

It would seem that Lucretius did not share this principle, and indeed, this may be one of the main differences between poetry and

---

[129] See the discussion in Long and Sedley 1987: 1. 88–90 and 100–1.

philosophy. As I have argued, it is not necessary, or even useful, to assume that because the *De rerum natura* treats Epicurean philosophy, the poem and its poet, too, have to behave according to Epicurean principles. Rather than concluding, with Schrijvers 1970: 140, that Lucretius' work is 'un poème qui expose les doctrines d'Epicure d'une manière épicurienne', I believe that it is more appropriate to describe it as a poem that expounds the doctrines of Epicurus in a uniquely *Lucretian* way.

4

The Poet's Choice: Vergil's *Georgics*

> cetera, quae uacuas tenuissent carmine mentes,
> omnia iam uulgata.
>
> Vergil, *Georgics*

> Vergilius noster, qui non quid uerissime sed quid decentissime diceretur aspexit, nec agricolas docere uoluit sed legentes delectare.
>
> Seneca, *Epistulae*

At the beginning of his film *Milou en Mai* (1990), the French director Louis Malle makes use of Vergil's *Georgics* to paint an idyllic, as well as ironic, vignette of old-fashioned country life. We see an old man, who is 'standing under a swarm of bees, which envelops the crown of his head. Hundreds of bees cluster on his face'. His friend Milou, the title character, stands next to him, a book in hand, reading aloud the following lines:

> his quidam signis atque haec exempla secuti
> esse apibus partem diuinae mentis et haustus
> aerios dixere.
>
> (Verg. *G.* 4. 219–21)

(Because of these signs and on account of these instances, some people have said that bees possess a share of divine reason and draughts of ether.)

Milou explains what he is doing with reference to 'Uncle Albert', who 'used to say "the only way to calm bees down is a bit of Virgil" '. The other man agrees, adding, 'but dialect works as well . . . with bees from round here, anyway'. That Milou's method is successful becomes clear when after a short cut to another location, the camera returns to the two men: the swarm has now gathered on a branch and is ultimately induced by Milou to return peacefully to its hive.[1]

---

[1] All quotations are from the English version of the script, Malle and Carrière 1990: 1 and 3.

The attitude of Malle's character toward the *Georgics* is interestingly similar to that of many modern Latinists. For what is striking about Milou's Vergilian approach to bee-keeping is that he does not in fact endeavour to follow any of the instructions given in *Georgics* 4;[2] rather, he uses the text as though it were a spell and attempts to charm the bees simply by reciting it (tellingly, he chooses the passage that deals with the animals' presumed divine nature). Likewise, critics believe that the poem does not work as a farmer's manual, but that it somehow conveys its meaning on a higher, symbolic, level. While the *Georgics* continues to be labelled didactic poetry, it is now the *communis opinio* that the poem's explicit claim to teaching agriculture, viticulture, animal husbandry, and bee-keeping (see *G.* 1. 1–5) is nothing but a pretext and that its technical instructions to the farmers are but the packaging of a more universal message.[3] Vergil's work is thus a typical example of Effe's 'transparenter Typus' of didactic poetry (1977: 80–97), a poem that pretends to be teaching one thing but is really about something else.

There has been considerably less agreement as to what this 'something else'—the real meaning of the *Georgics*—actually is.[4] Generally speaking, scholars regarding the work as characterized in the first place by poetic playfulness and the love of description[5]

---

[2] The *Georgics* does not treat the exact situation that Milou encounters; still, he might have attempted to follow *G.* 4. 62–6 and tried to lure the swarm to its hive by means of aromatic plants (*huc tu iussos asperge sapores, | trita melisphylla et cerinthae ignobile gramen*, 4. 62–3) and percussion instruments (*tinnitusque cie et Matris quate cymbala circum*, 4. 64). That bees are susceptible to rhythmic noise is a widespread belief, in both antiquity and modern times (see Mynors 1990 *ad loc.*); I wonder whether the idea of Milou and his friend that the swarm would react to a marked form of human speech (Vergilian hexameters or dialect) reflects a related concept.

[3] Already in 1929, Erich Burck wrote, 'wir wissen heute, daß die Georgika dieser Gattung [*didactic poetry*] überhaupt nur der Form nach zugerechnet werden können, da ihr lehrhafter Charakter rein fiktiv ist' (1929: 279); the same view is expressed in Klingner 1963: 15; Otis 1963: 144; Cox 1969: 146–7; Wilkinson 1969: 3; Thomas 1988: 1. 4 and 7; Perkell 1989: 8 and 17–18; Mynors 1990: pp. v–vi; and Dalzell 1996: 108. For a more positive view of the *Georgics* as an agricultural handbook, see Christmann 1982 and esp. Spurr 1986.

[4] Short surveys of modern critical positions are found in Perkell 1989: 13–16 and Batstone 1997: 143–4.

[5] See Kroll 1924: 189–97 (Vergil and his readers were interested in 'die rein poetischen Werte'; unfortunately, 'ein Rest von Erdenschwere' could not be wholly avoided, 197) and Wilkinson 1969: 3–15 (note his exasperated question, 'Why should everything have to be *interpreted?*', 7); cf. also Dalzell 1996: 118–24, who examines the role of humour in the *Georgics*, an undertaking that, as he himself points out, may 'appear to some as a sort of heresy' (124). Seneca, whose claim that Vergil wished to 'delight his readers' I have quoted as an epigraph to this chapter, might have been rather more sympathetic to this kind of now-unfashionable reading.

have been greatly outnumbered by those critics who hold that the *Georgics* is a serious poem concerned with issues of paramount importance to humanity. Most scholars of the latter stripe—whose studies are indeed often marked by what Dalzell 1996: 121 calls 'that dreadful solemnity which seems to descend on modern Latinists when they open a text of the *Georgics*'—would probably concur with the assessment of Adam Parry that Vergil's poem 'is ultimately about the life of man in this world' (1972: 36), while at the same time differing greatly about the poet's take on this universal question. In a development that mirrors the scholarship on the *Aeneid*, recent critical studies of the *Georgics* have tended to fall into one of two camps, optimistic and pessimistic. While the optimists hold that Vergil's poem is about the virtues of country life, the dignity of labour, and the impending return of the Golden Age as a result of the efforts of Augustus (see, e.g., Buchheit 1972 and now Cramer 1998 and Morgan 1999), the pessimists believe that the work is expressive of the never-ending toils of the farmer's existence and the fact that the Golden Age is irretrievably lost to mankind (see esp. Thomas 1988). The stern contrast between these two schools has led a number of scholars to conclude that there is some truth to both approaches and that it is the *Georgics* itself that is characterized by a deep ambivalence (thus esp. Perkell 1989 and now Gale 2000; see also Nelson 1998: 82–8); this view is taken to an extreme in the recent deconstructionist reading of William Batstone (1997; note that this essay is part of the *Cambridge Companion to Virgil*, a volume intended as a general introduction), who finds in the *Georgics* an overall 'failure of message' but reassures us that, nevertheless, the poem 'can enrich our lives even as it exceeds our grasp' (1997: 129). While thirty years ago, L. P. Wilkinson could still begin his monograph with the promising observation 'The *Georgics* is a splendid poem' (1969: 1), Batstone now warns the reader in his very first sentence that the poem is 'one of the most fundamentally intractable works of ancient literature' (1997: 125).[6]

In what follows, I shall not propose a new interpretation of the *Georgics* or attempt to position myself in the scholarly debate. True to the goals of this book, I shall not deal with or try to understand all aspects of what I, too, regard as an extremely difficult and elusive

[6] Similarly Thomas 1988: 1. 16; Dalzell 1996: 105. When, by contrast, Jenkyns 1998: 297 now maintains that the *Georgics* 'is not essentially a difficult work', he is certainly being deliberately provocative.

text. Rather, I shall return to the question of genre, a topic that most critics, concerned with the 'deeper' meaning of the poem, tend to dispose of rather quickly. For, as has become clear from the previous chapters, the fact that the historical author Vergil may not have intended to instruct farmers in the art of ploughing and sowing (and, indeed, I do not believe that he did) does not have anything to do with the question of whether the *Georgics* is a didactic poem, in the sense of my definition in Chapter 2. Staying exclusively on the intra-textual level and taking a close look at the poem's self-referential passages, I shall examine the ways in which the first-person speaker presents himself as both a teacher and a poet, as well as the relationship he envisions between these two roles. Thus, I shall deal first with the persona's interactions with his main addressees (Sect. 4.1) and then turn to those parts where he is speaking more specifically about his activity as a poet (Sect. 4.2). By concentrating not on the presumed message of the *Georgics*, but on its poetics, I believe that I can throw light on certain hitherto baffling features of this controversial poem.[7]

4.1. THE FARMERS AND MAECENAS

Once one forsakes the quest for the author's intention and focuses on the formal elements of the text itself, the *Georgics* appears, at least at first glance, as a 'standard' didactic poem.[8] Such a generic affiliation is suggested already by the literary models that Vergil is following. Thus, at a central point in the text, the poet describes himself as singing an *Ascraeum carmen* (2. 176), and the influence of Hesiod is clear especially in Book 1; the title *Georgica* is taken from Nicander (cf. Quint. *Inst.* 10. 1. 56), even though the fragmentary character of the Greek poet's homonymous work does not allow us to ascertain the extent of Vergil's imitation; the discussion of weather signs in Book 1 is obviously modelled on Aratus; and the work of Lucretius, whose achievements the speaker praises in 2. 490–2, is used as a foil throughout the poem.[9]

---

[7] The text of Vergil used in this chapter and elsewhere is the *Oxford Classical Text* of R. A. B. Mynors (1969). The *vitae* are quoted from Bayer 1970.

[8] See also Kromer 1979: 7: 'Vergil explicitly identifies his work as a didactic poem'; I should note, though, that Kromer's idea of didactic poetry is rather different from mine.

[9] On the models of the *Georgics*, see esp. the monograph of Farrell 1991; note also Nelson 1998 specifically on the *Georgics*' relationship to Hesiod, as well as Schäfer 1996 and Gale 2000 on the influence of Lucretius.

Vergil's Georgics

Furthermore, the *Georgics* clearly qualifies as a didactic poem by all four criteria posited in Chapter 2. First, the speaker of the poem explicitly indicates his didactic intent, referring, at least on occasion, to his own speaking with such verbs as *praecepta referre* (1. 176), *edicere* (3. 295), *iubere* (3. 300, 329; 4. 62), *docere* (3. 440), and *suadere* (4. 264). He announces his agricultural subject matter in the very first lines of Book 1 (1–4), a passage that outlines the orderly structure of the *Georgics*, which devotes one book to each of its four principal topics (1: agriculture, *quid faciat laetas segetes, quo sidere terram | uertere . . . | conueniat*; 2: viticulture and trees, *quo sidere . . . | . . . ulmis . . . adiungere uitis | conueniat*; 3: animal husbandry, *quae cura boum, qui cultus habendo | sit pecori*; and 4: bee-keeping, *apibus quanta experientia parcis*). Each book opens with a reference to the new subject matter about to be treated (2. 1–3; 3. 1–2 and 286–8; 4. 1–5), and at the end of the poem, the persona recapitulates the topics of his teaching in the *sphragis* (4. 559–60; here *pecora* must be understood as including the bees).

Second, the *Georgics* exhibits the teacher–student constellation typical of didactic poetry. It becomes clear in 1. 41 that the beneficiaries of the persona's teaching are to be the farmers, and indeed, the larger part of the poem consists of instructions directed at them; they are addressed repeatedly, with such vocatives as *agricolae* (1. 101; 2. 36), *uiri* (1. 210), *coloni* (3. 288), and *pastor* (3. 420).[10] Since the *Georgics* belongs to the kind of didactic poetry that the *Tractatus Coislinianus* calls ὑφηγητική, 'instructional', it concentrates on its student figures in a different way from and more extensively than, say, the *De rerum natura*. Instead of conveying theoretical knowledge, the Vergilian teacher dispenses practical advice; as a result, his speech is not a descriptive scholarly discourse, but a series of orders addressed directly to the farmers. Critics have often remarked on the syntactic *variatio* of the speaker's instructions: while heavily relying on imperatives, both singular and plural (e.g., *umida solstitia atque hiemes orate serenas*, 1. 100), the teacher makes extensive use also of jussive subjunctives, often in the third-person singular or plural (e.g., *depresso incipiat iam tum mihi taurus aratro | ingemere*, 1. 45–6), and of gerunds and gerundives (e.g., *praeterea tam sunt Arcturi sidera nobis | Haedorumque dies seruandi et lucidus Anguis*, 1. 204–5); he also frequently couches his advice in descriptions in the

---

[10] See Rutherford 1995: 20; his entire paper is important for the understanding of the didactic addressees in the *Georgics*.

indicative (e.g., the instructions on how to build a plough, 1. 169–75).[11]

As for the third criterion, poetic self-consciousness, the persona of the *Georgics* clearly presents his teaching speech as poetry. He repeatedly uses *canere* to describe his own activity (1. 5, 12; 2. 2, 176; 3. 1; 4. 119, 559; cf. also *sonandum*, 3. 294) and refers to his words as *carmen* (2. 45, 95, 176; 3. 3) and *uersus* (2. 42; 3. 339). This choice of vocabulary is enough for the moment to establish that the speaker thinks of himself as not merely a teacher, but also a poet; later in this chapter, I shall discuss in greater detail some of the passages where the persona reflects more explicitly on his poetic career.

Fourth and finally, the *Georgics* presents what might be called a textbook case of poetic simultaneity. Creating the vivid impression that the composition of his poem is going on 'now', the poet starts his work with the announcement, *hinc canere incipiam* (1. 5), and ends with the observation, *haec super aruorum cultu pecorumque canebam | et super arboribus* (4. 559–60). As Thomas 1988 *ad loc.* points out, *canebam* is an example of the 'epistolary' imperfect used at the end of letters. Its implication is that the action described is not yet quite completed at the moment of utterance; thus, the correct translation of *canebam* is 'I have been singing' (note, by contrast, the perfect *cecini* in 4. 566, which refers to a past, long-finished work, the *Eclogues*).

Throughout the poem, the speaker keeps up the illusion of simultaneity, referring to the process of his ongoing poem and to its changing topics with such announcements as *hactenus aruorum cultus et sidera caeli; | nunc te, Bacche, canam* (2. 1–2); *te quoque, magna Pales, et te memorande canemus | pastor ab Amphryso, uos, siluae amnesque Lycaei* (3. 1–2); *nunc, ueneranda Pales, magno nunc ore sonandum* (3. 294); and *protinus aerii mellis caelestia dona | exsequar* (4. 1–2). Again and again, he gives the impression of making up his song only as he goes along, as in his tour de force about the different types of vines (2. 89–108), where he tries to do justice to all species (raising the stylistic level considerably, he even addresses some of them in an almost hymnic tone: *quo te carmine dicam, | Rhaetica*, 2. 95–6 and *non ego te, dis et mensis accepta secundis, | transierim, Rhodia, et tumidis, bumaste, racemis*, 2. 101–2), but in the end has to admit defeat, overwhelmed by their sheer number (2. 103–8). Similarly, in Book 3, the poet has to call himself

---

[11] On the instructional passages of the *Georgics*, see the classic discussion in Burck 1926: esp. 87–101 (Burck stresses the formal influence of Hesiod), as well as now Schiesaro 1993: 137; Horsfall 1995: 66–7; and Rutherford 1995: 21–4; cf. also Gibson 1997.

to order and back to his topic, after having been carried away by his description of the mares' sexual fury:

> sed fugit interea, fugit inreparabile tempus
> singula dum capti circumuectamur amore.
>
> (3. 284–5)

(But meanwhile time is flying, irrevocable time, while I, captivated by love, dwell on every detail.)

In 4. 116–48, the speaker likewise refers to restraints of time that prevent him from treating the topic of horticulture—even though he shows himself to be very tempted indeed.

Having thus come to the positive result that the *Georgics* is indeed a didactic poem and that its speaker presents himself as both a teacher and a poet, I have to add the—from the point of view of this book—unfortunate observation that, unlike the Lucretian persona in the *De rerum natura*, the Vergilian 'I' does not offer any explicit reflection on the relationship of didactic subject matter and poetic form. There is no equivalent of the honeyed-cup simile and no explanation of why instructions on ploughing are best presented in verse, or even why the speaker has undertaken to treat this particular topic (though see below on 3. 41). However, one has to keep in mind that, within the history of didactic poetry, Lucretius is rather unusual in discussing his choice of medium and that his 'apology' for poetry may be motivated at least in part by Epicurus' hostility to it; if one looks at the works of Aratus or Nicander, for example, one does not find any explicit reflections on their poets' attitude toward their own activities.

What separates the teacher-poet of the *Georgics* from his Hellenistic predecessors and brings him rather closer to the Lucretian persona is that he exhibits a certain degree of personal involvement in his agricultural subject matter, as well as quite a bit of enthusiasm for his own composing poetry about it. Just as the speaker of the *De rerum natura* expressed ecstatic pleasure in roaming through the untouched realm of the Muses (1. 921–30), the Vergilian persona, too, shows himself in a kind of rapture:

> sed me Parnasi deserta per ardua dulcis
> raptat amor; iuuat ire iugis, qua nulla priorum
> Castaliam molli deuertitur orbita cliuo.
>
> (3. 291–3)

(But sweet love drives me through the steep loneliness of Parnassus: it is pleasing to go on mountain ridges where no forerunners' track runs down on gentle slope toward Castalia.)

The allusion to Lucretius is clear: in both passages, the speaker claims that he is motivated by *amor* (cf. Lucr. 1. 924–5), uses the Callimachean image of the untrodden path, and expresses his joy at his own undertaking (the *iuuat* of *G*. 3. 292 harks back to the repetition of the same word in Lucr. 1. 927–8; cf. also *G*. 2. 37).

The Vergilian persona does not dispense advice in an impersonal manner, but rather finds ways to signal his own involvement in what he teaches (see Rutherford 1995: 21–4, cf. Perkell 1989: 30–1). He thus on occasion uses the first-person plural to align himself with the farmers, as in 2. 393–6, where he imagines himself as part of a rural celebration of Bacchus, or in 1. 204–5 (quoted above), where he employs the dative of agent *nobis* to express that 'we' have to watch out for the rising and setting of the constellations. This practice is reminiscent of that of the speaker of the *De rerum natura*, who, as discussed in Chapter 3, likewise uses the first-person plural to create a strong connection between himself and his addressee. However, in the *Georgics*, the same method is used to achieve what is in a sense the opposite effect: while the Lucretian teacher strives to involve Memmius in his own Epicurean discourse, the Vergilian persona aims at making himself part of the life of the farmers. I have pointed out in my examination of the teaching speech of the *De rerum natura* that its speaker repeatedly uses the ethical dative *tibi* to give Memmius the impression that the subject matter being treated is of immediate relevance to him. Interestingly, in the *Georgics*, the teacher employs, in his very first set of instructions, the ethical dative *mihi* to show his own interest in the activity of the farmers:

> uere nouo, gelidus canis dum montibus umor
> liquitur et Zephyro putris se glaeba resoluit,
> depresso incipiat iam tum *mihi* taurus aratro
> ingemere et sulco attritus splendescere uomer.
>
> (1. 43–6)

(At the beginning of spring, when icy water runs down from the snowy mountains and the crumbling soil is loosened by Zephyrus, at that time already (as far as I am concerned) let the bull begin to groan and the plough be pressed down, and the ploughshare sparkle, grinding against the furrow.)

As another way of expressing his own involvement in his subject matter, the speaker of the *Georgics* a number of times employs the figure that Godo Lieberg has called *poeta creator* (see Lieberg 1982 and Sect. 3.1, above), that is, he presents himself as doing what he is really only describing. Thus, for example, in the internal proem of Book 3, when he switches from the topic of cattle and horses to that of sheep and goats, he states:

> hoc satis armentis: superat pars altera curae,
> lanigeros agitare greges hirtasque capellas.
>
> (3. 286–7)

(So much for cattle. The second part of my task remains, to herd woolly flocks and hairy goats.)[12]

Such expressions have the effect of blurring the boundary between signifier and signified, *carmen* and *res*, since instead of staying outside his song, the poet gives the impression of being part of it, in this case, of being a shepherd himself. A similar involvement with his topic is evident in the two lines immediately preceding the passage just quoted, where, as mentioned above, the speaker reproaches himself for losing too much time, *singula dum capti circumuectamur amore* (3. 285). As Thomas 1988 *ad loc.* points out, this is a 'brilliantly ambiguous phrase', with *amor* referring both to the poet's love of his subject matter *and* to the subject matter itself (the sex drive of animals).

So far, so good. Having reached the conclusion that the *Georgics* formally qualifies as a didactic poem and that its speaker is a teacher enthusiastic about his topic and intent on aligning his poetry and his subject matter, I might have closed the chapter right here—were it not for the fact that I have hitherto taken a deliberately limited and narrow approach to the poem, tacitly passing over those aspects that would have disturbed my simple picture. For, as many critics have pointed out, there are a number of facts about the *Georgics* that would appear to speak against labelling the work as unequivocally didactic. It will be useful to survey briefly the arguments that have been advanced against such a generic designation; a consideration of these disruptive factors will ultimately yield a more complex view of the *Georgics* as a whole.

---

[12] See Lieberg 1982: 14–15; other instances of the *poeta creator* figure in the *Georgics* include 2. 7–8, 37–8 (on this passage, see also below in the text); and 3. 46.

First, it is usually said that the material presented in the *Georgics* is extremely selective; furthermore, the view of farming conveyed in the poem is unrealistic and, from the perspective of the first century BC, old-fashioned (thus, for example, it is typically pointed out that Vergil does not mention slaves).[13] Scholars have therefore concluded that it would be virtually impossible to use the *Georgics* as a textbook on agriculture; also, it is unclear why anyone interested in farming would have turned to a didactic poem anyway, given that more comprehensive prose treatises, like that of Varro, were readily available. However, as mentioned above, none of these observations prevents the *Georgics* from being a didactic poem in the purely literary sense in which I have defined the term, and it may be noted also that other, more generally accepted, examples of the didactic genre likewise fail to be either comprehensive (not even the six books of the *De rerum natura* treat all of Epicurean physics) or of practical use (attempting to follow Nicander's advice against poisonous snakes might be positively pernicious).

The second argument against regarding the *Georgics* as a predominantly didactic poem is rather more serious. Even a cursory reading of the poem reveals that a large part of it does not consist of instructions to the farmers at all, but of so-called digressions, which, as Nicholas Horsfall has calculated, account for about 30 percent of the work as a whole (Horsfall 1995: 75, based on the list of della Corte 1985). Now, digressions are in fact a typical feature of didactic poetry, witness, for example, Aratus' Myth of Dike (*Phaen.* 96–136) or Lucretius' treatment of the Great Mother (2. 600–60). However, while not always strictly necessary, they tend to play a subordinate role and to arise out of their argumentative contexts, often serving to illustrate the point at hand. By contrast, the digressions in the *Georgics* very frequently do not appear to be integral parts of the argument: to choose the most notorious example, the Aristaeus story, which takes up nearly half of Book 4, is hardly relevant to the practical exigencies of bee-keeping. The existence of such extensive 'purple passages', seemingly disjunct from the poem's overtly instructional parts, does make the didactic intent of the speaker appear rather less prominent.[14] Still, I do not believe

---

[13] In striking contrast to the *communis opinio*, Spurr 1986 argues that in the *Georgics*, Vergil paints a realistic picture of contemporary agriculture and that he is no more selective than other agricultural writers.

[14] Since Burck 1929, most scholars have tended to stress the unity of the *Georgics*, arguing that the poem's instructional passages and digressions form an organic whole. This view

that this is enough to disqualify the work as a didactic poem: after all, the persona does explicitly present himself as a teacher, and thus fulfils our first criterion. There is nothing in our definition that prevents him from being the kind of teacher who tends to stray from his declared topic of instruction.

A third argument against viewing the *Georgics* as straightforwardly didactic does, I believe, pose a real problem. The neat teacher–student constellation that I have been describing is made rather more complicated by the fact that the *agricolae* are not the only people that the speaker addresses.[15] Some of the additional addressees are, of course, far from being a serious competition to the farmers: thus, for example, the speaker invokes the Muses (4. 315) and other deities whom he asks for assistance with his poem (gods of agriculture: 1. 5–23; Bacchus: 2. 2–8); the extended 'prayer' to Octavian (*Caesar*) in 1. 24–42 falls under the same category.[16] By contrast, the second address to Octavian, in the *laudes Italiae* (2. 170), is one of a large number of instances where the speaker, in elevated poetic style, addresses directly the current object of his song, such as, for example, the river Clitumnus in 2. 146, Mantua in 3. 12, or, as already mentioned, various types of vines in 2. 95–6 and 101–2. The solemn apostrophe of Italy (*salue, magna parens frugum, Saturnia tellus,* | *magna uirum,* 2. 173–4) presents a similar case. Note, though, that in this last passage, the country is actually treated as though it were itself the dedicatee of the *Georgics*: tibi *res antiquae laudis et artem* | *ingredior* (2. 174–5; see Wilkinson 1969: 153). Of course, this single elevated address does not displace the farmers from their position as the main addressees and student figures of the *Georgics*, especially given that the *agricolae* and the *Saturnia tellus* are not in fact two separate entities: in a sense, singing a song for Italy is a metonymy for singing a song for the Italian farmers.

typically goes hand in hand with the devaluation of the didactic parts as mere pretence: they now appear as covert ways of expressing the message that is conveyed more explicitly in the non-didactic passages, which are no longer regarded as 'digressions', but as the central parts of the poem.

[15] On the multiplicity of addressees in the *Georgics*, see Schiesaro 1993: 133–5 and *passim*, as well as Rutherford 1995: 19–20.

[16] Octavian is invoked as an inspiring figure; *pace* Rutherford 1995: 19–20 and Gale 2000: 25–7, he is not a dedicatee of the poem. In this regard, his role in the *Georgics* is quite different from that of Germanicus in Ovid's *Fasti*, who in the proem to Book 1 (a passage that otherwise owes much to the beginning of *G.* 1) is addressed as both the poet's patron and, as it were, his Muse—a double responsibility that does indeed lead to certain confusions within the text (see Volk 1997: 291–2).

This leaves one character who seriously challenges the view that the *Georgics* is addressed primarily to the *agricolae*: Maecenas. The persona speaks directly to him four times in the course of the poem, once in each book, and these addresses are spaced so symmetrically (1. 2; 2. 41; 3. 41; and 4. 2) that it is clear that they are of central importance.[17] Given that he is the very first person to be addressed in the *Georgics*, one can easily get the impression that the poem is in fact directed at him, and this impression is maintained for quite some time, since the *agricolae* are explicitly addressed only at 1. 101. When they are first mentioned, in 1. 41, they appear in the third person, as the object of Octavian's and the speaker's pity (*ignarosque uiae mecum miseratus agrestis*), not as the poem's addressees, and even when the teacher begins his practical instructions in 1. 43, he still does not speak to the farmers directly, but dispenses his advice for seasonal ploughing in the impersonal third-person singular: *incipiat iam tum mihi taurus aratro* | *ingemere* (1. 45–6), etc. The first second-person address occurs in 1. 56, but, tellingly, it is in the Lucretian formula *nonne uides*, which gives no clue as to whom it is directed; as Servius remarks, *NONNE VIDES aut Maecenati dicit aut rustico* (*Serv. Dan. ad* 1. 56). In 1. 71, the speaker begins to use the second-person singular to describe the farmer's activity (*patiere*, 1. 72; *seres*, 1. 73; etc.), and one can infer from the contents that he is no longer speaking to Maecenas; however, the shift of addressee becomes 'official' only with the vocative *agricolae* in 1. 101.[18]

This long and skilful transition glosses over the problematic fact that the *Georgics* has indeed two distinct addressees, the farmers and Maecenas. Of the two, only the first group plays the role of students in the poem's didactic constellation of characters since, *pace* Schiesaro 1993: 138, Maecenas never explicitly appears as the recipient of the speaker's instructions on agriculture, and there is no indication that he somehow acts as a representative of the farmers (Octavian is asked to take pity on them, Maecenas is not). Servius

---

[17] On the role of Maecenas, I cannot agree with Thomas 1988, who remarks that he seems to 'have little to do with the poem' (*ad* 1. 2) and belittles the four addresses to him as his 'mandatory appearance[s]' (*ad* 3. 41).

[18] Note that in the *Works and Days* and in the *De rerum natura*, too, the students Perses and Memmius are first simply mentioned as recipients of the poet's teaching (thus, their names first appear in the dative, see Hes. *Op.* 10; Lucr. 1. 26) and only later explicitly addressed (Hes. *Op.* 27; Lucr. 1. 50). By contrast to the *agricolae* in the *Georgics*, however, once they have been established as addressees, they encounter no serious competition (the occasional addresses to the kings in the *Works and Days* are a different matter).

(*Praef. ad Georg.* 129. 11–12 Thilo) is thus quite wrong to claim that in the *Georgics*, Maecenas plays the *persona discipuli* in the same way in which this role is taken on by Perses in the *Works and Days* and by Memmius in the *De rerum natura*. In fact, the comparison with Lucretius is especially enlightening: both Memmius and Maecenas are educated Roman noblemen, the friends and patrons of the poets who address them, but while Memmius is both the dedicatee and student figure of the *De rerum natura*, Maecenas in the *Georgics* acts only as the dedicatee, while leaving the student role to the *agricolae*.[19] One fairly obvious reason for this is that a man of Memmius' and Maecenas' status could realistically be depicted as showing some interest in philosophy, whereas it would be absurd to portray him as actively engaged in building a plough or tying vines to elm trees.[20] It is therefore unnecessary for Memmius ever to 'fade' out of the *De rerum natura*, well suited as he is to be both the poem's dedicatee and its student; by contrast, in the *Georgics*, Maecenas must again and again step into the background and hand over the stage to the farmers.

To arrive at a more satisfying understanding of what Maecenas is doing in the poem, we must take a close look at the four passages in which he is addressed directly. Strikingly, each of them is characterized by a high degree of poetic self-consciousness. At the beginning of Book 1, as we have seen, the speaker announces to Maecenas that he is about to begin his song (*hinc canere incipiam*, 1. 5) and enumerates his topics (1. 1–4). The next and far more substantial address occurs in Book 2, in a passage where the persona first speaks to the *agricolae* (explicitly addressed as such in 2. 36), exhorting them to learn about and practise arboriculture (2. 35–7), and only then turns to Maecenas:

---

[19] As discussed in Sect. 3.1, Lucretius provides little information on Memmius, and Vergil is no more forthcoming on Maecenas; still, by naming their addressees, the poets invite readers to identify the intra-textual 'Memmius' and 'Maecenas' with their extra-textual namesakes and to supply at least some of the missing characteristics. It is thus impossible to read the *Georgics* and assume that the 'Maecenas' addressed is, say, an old veteran who has just been allotted a farm and is now in need of agricultural instruction.

[20] This is not to say that wealthy and educated Romans did not own farms and did not take an either purely theoretical or economically motivated interest in agriculture. However, most scholars agree that the students of the *Georgics* are not rich landowners whose *latifundia* are managed by a *uilicus* and worked by slaves, but rather small farmers cultivating their own soil. Spurr 1986: 171–5 presents the unorthodox view that Vergil is indeed describing the running of a villa estate; if this is true, it must be observed that the poet has filtered out the more 'unromantic' aspects of life on a large farm (e.g., the employment of slaves).

> tuque ades inceptumque una decurre laborem,
> o decus, o famae merito pars maxima nostrae,
> Maecenas, pelagoque uolans da uela patenti.
> non ego cuncta meis amplecti uersibus opto,
> non, mihi si linguae centum sint oraque centum,
> ferrea uox. ades et primi lege litoris oram;
> in manibus terrae. non hic te carmine ficto
> atque per ambages et longa exorsa tenebo.
>
> (2. 39–46)

(You, too, my glory, deservedly the greatest part of my fame, Maecenas, be present and traverse with me the task begun, and speedily set sail for the open sea. I do not wish to encompass everything with my verses—not if I had a hundred tongues and a hundred mouths and a voice of iron. Be present and steer along close to the shore: the land is right here. I shall not detain you here with made-up song, detours, and long introductions.)

The way in which Maecenas is introduced shows clearly that the speaker treats him and the farmers as two different and distinct audiences: *tuque ades* (2. 39) signals that he is addressing a new person, one not part of the group to whom he was speaking earlier, and the vocatives *agricolae* (2. 36) and *Maecenas* (2. 41), both placed prominently at the beginning of the hexameter, nicely underline this contrast. Also obvious is that the change of addressee entails a change of topic. To the farmers, the poet speaks about the growing of trees and orders them to 'learn' (*discite*, 2. 35), as befits their role as students and addressees of his teaching speech. To Maecenas, by contrast, he talks about poetry, specifically about the very poem that, in the familiar illusion of poetic simultaneity, he is composing right now. The one and a-half lines that link the address to the farmers with that to Maecenas already hint at the shift in the speaker's topic:

> iuuat Ismara Baccho
> conserere et olea magnum uestire Taburnum.
>
> (2. 37–8)

(It is pleasing to cover Ismaros with vines and to dress great Taburnus with olive trees.)

The impersonal *iuuat* leaves open who it is who feels joy at the planting of vine and olive tree. While the immediate choice would appear to be the farmers, it is also possible to take the sentence as another example of the *poeta creator* figure mentioned above and to understand that it is the poet who enjoys singing about these topics (cf. Gale 2000: 185; this latter interpretation is strengthened by the similar use of *iuuat* in the likewise metapoetic passage 3. 292–3, discussed above). The very ambiguity of the lines thus reflects the speaker's transition from teaching arboriculture to talking about poetry.

In the following lines, the poet not only tells Maecenas about his poem, but also alludes to his addressee's own role in its composition: while in 2. 45–6, Maecenas simply appears as the speaker's audience (a part he played already in 1. 2), the earlier string of imperatives (2. 39, 41, and 44) implies that he is supposed also to act as an inspiring figure, much like Octavian in 1. 40–2.[21] The two invocations are similar also in that they both employ journey metaphors: the poet asks Octavian, *da facilem cursum* (1. 40) and *mecum . . . | ingredere* (1. 41–2[22]); likewise, he implores Maecenas, *inceptumque una decurre laborem* (2. 39). In the case of Maecenas, he additionally uses seafaring imagery,[23] in a way that has struck commentators as singularly self-contradictory; indeed, despite R. A. B. Mynors' attempts to reconcile the two concepts (1990 *ad* 2. 41; see also Lieberg 1969: 230–3), it is hard not to see a contrast between the poet's exhortation to 'set sail for the open sea' (2. 41) and his subsequent advice to hug the shore (2. 44). While I am not necessarily convinced that the images are meant to convey that (as argued by Thomas 1985: esp. 69–70, and 1988: 1. 2–3) in the *Georgics*, Vergil is, as it were, torn between his Callimachean predilection for the small and unambitious (staying close to the coast) and the temptations of 'grand', epic, poetry (venturing onto the open sea),[24] I do think that the passage reflects the poet's coming

---

[21] See Buchheit 1972: 27–8. That Maecenas is to a certain extent taking over Octavian's role as 'Muse' is underscored by the fact that the poet's appeal to him in Book 2 occurs in the same position (around l. 40) as his final prayer to Octavian in Book 1; note also that *tuque ades* (2. 39), the words with which the speaker turns to Maecenas, echo the likewise verse-initial *tuque adeo* (1. 24), with which he first addressed Octavian. On the practice of poets' addressing their patrons as sources of inspiration, see White 1993: 20.

[22] I take *mecum* with both *miseratus* (1. 41) and *ingredere*.

[23] As both Thomas 1988 and Mynors 1990 *ad loc.* point out, already *decurre* (2. 39) can be understood in a specifically nautical sense; cf. Lieberg 1969: 231.

[24] The great importance of 'Callimachean' poetics (by which I mean a certain rhetoric, employed by Latin poets and derived from the *Aetia* prologue and similar passages, which may have very little to do with any literary 'programme' that Callimachus himself may or may not have professed; cf. now Asper 1997) for the *Georgics* has been examined by Richard F. Thomas in a number of publications (now conveniently collected in Thomas 1999), esp.

to a decision on what kind of poem he actually wishes to compose. It is interesting that he presents himself as making a deliberate choice (note the verb *opto*, 2. 42) in favour of being selective with his subject matter; as Thomas 1988 *ad loc.* points out (see also Thomas 1985: 73 n. 28), the poet strikingly reinterprets the Homeric topos of the multiple mouths, claiming that even if he had *linguae centum . . . oraque centum,* | *ferrea uox* (2. 43-4), he still would not wish to treat 'everything' in his verse (there is no hint that he would not be able to—which is the sense in which the figure is used by Homer and others, including Vergil himself at *Aen.* 6. 625-7). This insistence on the poet's ability to make conscious choices is evident elsewhere in the *Georgics* and will be discussed in greater detail in Section 4.2.

The third address to Maecenas occurs at the beginning of Book 3. The poet has been describing at some length a project that he intends to undertake in the future (see below), but now announces that, for the time being, he is sticking with the poem at hand:

> interea Dryadum siluas saltusque sequamur
> intactos, tua, Maecenas, haud mollia iussa:
> te sine nil altum mens incohat.
>
> (3. 40-2)

(In the meantime, I shall head for the Dryads' woods and untouched glades—your not so easy orders, Maecenas. Without you, the mind does not undertake anything grand.)

Here the role of Maecenas has been even more extended: simply a listener in Book 1, but invoked for assistance in Book 2, he is now

---

Thomas 1985. However, Thomas's view is too rigid for my taste: by his description, Vergil is a sort of card-carrying Callimachean who, whenever he diverges from the ideal of *tenuis*, feels the need to apologize (thus, in the case of our passage in *G.* 2, his daring wish to set sail for the open sea is followed by the retraction that, of course, he will stay close to the shore). In my opinion, Vergil uses 'Callimachean' imagery in a rather more playful manner, often defying the readers' expectations. Thus, for example, in 4. 6, the phrase *in tenui labor* would appear to be a good Callimachean axiom, were it not immediately subverted by *at tenuis non gloria*, a sentiment at odds with the lack of ambition typically associated with the poetry of the 'small' and 'refined' and in strong contrast with the speaker's professed decision to forego glory and stick to the countryside as one who is *inglorius* (2. 486, in a passage discussed in greater detail in Sect. 4.2). At the end of Book 4, the poet is again dedicated to *ignobile otium* (4. 564) and leaves fame to Octavian, who is in the process of making his way to Olympus (4. 562); his wish for *gloria* was only an interlude, and I cannot help feeling that Vergil enjoys keeping his readers on their toes with such surprising self-contradictions (cf. also Jenkyns 1998: 317-20 on the poet's 'characteristic fluctuation' between the 'ample' and the 'slender' and Gale 2000 generally on the persona's refusal throughout the poem to commit himself to one particular point of view).

said to be the very reason why the poet is involved in this particular work in the first place. The force of *haud mollia iussa* (3. 41) is hard to determine, but it is unlikely that it implies a complaint about the 'harshness' of Maecenas' 'orders'. As Peter White has shown, '[t]he word *iussa* is conventional language in literary requests' (1993: 136; see 266–8 for a list of passages in Latin literature where *iubere* is used in this sense), and most critics agree that *haud mollia* means something like 'difficult to carry out' (see also *altum* in 3. 42). Note also that in 3. 40–5, the poet's and Maecenas' joint enterprise is described as the roaming through untouched countryside, specifically as hunting (see the barking dogs of 3. 43–6 and Mynors 1990 *ad loc.*), an activity that is definitely *haud mollis*.

At the opening of Book 4, the Vergilian persona addresses Maecenas for the last time:

> protinus aerii mellis caelestia dona
> exsequar: hanc etiam, Maecenas, aspice partem.
> admiranda tibi leuium spectacula rerum
> magnanimosque duces totiusque ordine gentis
> mores et studia et populos et proelia dicam.
> in tenui labor; at tenuis non gloria, si quem
> numina laeua sinunt auditque uocatus Apollo.
>
> (4. 1–7)

(Presently, I shall treat the heavenly gifts of airy honey: pay attention to this part also, Maecenas. I shall speak to you of the admirable spectacles of light things, of great-hearted leaders, and, in due order, of the entire species' character, pursuits, peoples, and battles. I labour in small things; but the glory is not small if favourable gods allow it and Apollo heeds my prayer.)

The speaker implies that Maecenas has been closely following the entire poem: asking that his patron pay attention to this part, just as he took interest in the others (this is the force of *etiam* in 4. 2), the poet for a moment treats Maecenas as though he were in fact his only audience (*tibi . . . dicam*, 4. 2–5[25]). And indeed, if by some chance of textual transmission the *Georgics* had come down to us in fragments and we possessed only the four passages that I have been examining, we would unquestioningly assume that Maecenas was in fact the one addressee of the poem to whom, we would imagine, the poet was speaking all the time.

---

[25] In my view, *tibi* goes with both *admiranda* and *dicam*.

The doubling of addressees in the *Georgics* is unparalleled in earlier didactic poetry and thus a real issue that calls for an explanation. Unless we want to assume that the Vergilian persona is simply a scatterbrain who jumps from one addressee to the next without rhyme or reason, we must try to comprehend how it is that the farmers and Maecenas can exist side by side and both act as audience for the same text. The solution of this problem will be crucial to our understanding of the poem as a whole and of its (often questioned) status as didactic poetry.

As I have endeavoured to demonstrate, the persona's interaction with the farmers constitutes a teaching speech comparable to that of other didactic poems and is thus unremarkable; it is the addresses to Maecenas that disrupt the uniformity of the speaker's discourse. I suggest that a way to reconcile the two is to conceive of what one might call the speaking situation of the *Georgics* as follows: throughout the poem, the poet/persona is in the process of instructing the farmers, that is, of composing a didactic poem; while he is doing this, he is, as it were, at the same time talking to Maecenas, telling him, in a very self-conscious way, about what he is in the process of doing, that is, about his ongoing poem. His addresses to Maecenas are thus, in a sense, spoken *a parte*. Put another way, the speaker's conversation with Maecenas is like a self-referential frame drawn around the teaching speech; as we have seen, whenever Vergil's patron is explicitly addressed, it is in the context of a discussion of the poem itself. While the poet is speaking to the farmers, he says to Maecenas: 'Look at what I am doing: I am composing a didactic poem, *Ascraeumque cano Romana per oppida carmen*'.

It is often said that the *Georgics* has two audiences, the 'pretended' audience of the farmers and the 'real' audience of educated readers (see, e.g., Effe 1977: 87; Horsfall 1995: 65–6). What scholars have not hitherto realized is that the poem does indeed have these two audiences—but that both exist *inside the poem*. While, for example, Aratus' *Phaenomena* creates a marked contrast between the learned extra-textual readers of the poem and the unsophisticated intra-textual farmers and sailors addressed by the teacher (see Bing 1993), the *Georgics*, by making Maecenas an intra-textual character, brings the learned audience into the very poem itself.

The *Georgics* thus emerges as a work that takes poetic self-consciousness to an extreme level, drawing an extraordinary amount of attention to the artificiality of its discourse. As I have tried to show in Chapter 1, basically every poetic text can, by some token or other, be recognized as 'poetry', while those that also exhibit poetic self-consciousness explicitly highlight their status. In the *Georgics*, the teaching speech addressed by the speaker to the farmers, itself characterized by poetic self-consciousness, is additionally embedded in the same speaker's address to Maecenas; as a result, the persona himself is able to talk about his own poem, not just from 'inside', but also, at the same time, from a somewhat detached vantage point. To put it in an oversimplified way, the *Georgics* is not only clearly a poem, and not only explicitly says, 'I am a poem', but also has a character inside the text who looks at it as though from the outside and says, 'this is a poem'.

To this analysis of what might be called the *Georgics*' double discourse I would like to add two observations. First, the extra frame drawn around the teaching speech by means of the addresses to Maecenas has a distancing effect, which is, I believe, one of the reasons why readers of the *Georgics* often feel that they cannot take it seriously as a didactic poem. As Alexander Dalzell writes, one senses a certain 'lack of commitment' on the part of the poet,[26] and this impression becomes even stronger when one compares the *Georgics* to one of its most important models, Lucretius' *De rerum natura*. As I have shown in Chapter 3, the Lucretian persona is single-minded in his enterprise of teaching Epicurean philosophy to Memmius; regarding his didacticism and his poetry as an inseparable unity, he does not step back and talk to another character about what he is doing. By contrast, the Vergilian speaker shows himself to be quite detached from his undertaking, at least on occasion, and I return to his distanced attitude in Section 4.2, where I discuss the numerous instances in the *Georgics* where the poet considers practising kinds of poetry different from the one (didactic) in which he is involved right now—a thought that, needless to say, would never have crossed the mind of the Lucretian persona.

My second point is a caveat. Having argued that the *Georgics* consists of two different discourses—one addressed to the farmers and meant to teach agriculture, the other directed at Maecenas and to a great extent taken up with reflections about poetry—I would like to stress that it is ultimately not possible to wholly separate the

---

[26] Dalzell 1996: 123–4, at 124; see also Nelson 1998: 93–4, who notes that unlike the Hesiod of the *Works and Days*, the speaker of the *Georgics* is not himself a farmer, but merely a poet of farming, which distances him from the very material he teaches.

two. One might think that it would be desirable to divide up the *Georgics* into those passages addressed to the farmers and those geared to Maecenas: the first category would contain the technical instructions, while all the bothersome digressions could be attributed to the second one. To a certain extent, this will work: we have already seen how in 2. 39, the speaker pointedly turns from the *agricolae* to Maecenas, and one might reasonably argue that, for example, the long excursus at the end of Book 2 (2. 458–540; the praise of country life) is addressed not to the farmers, but to Maecenas. The passage does not contain any instructions, but the speaker' personal reflections, including on the subject of his own poetry (2. 475–94, discussed in Sect. 4.2, below), and it is striking that the *agricolae* are mentioned in the third person (2. 458–60)—the poet is speaking not to them, but about them. By contrast, however, at the beginning of Book 1, as I have shown, the persona carefully dissimulates his change of addressee and for a long time leaves open who he is talking to, even allowing for the humorous possibility that the second person, who comes into the picture in 1. 71, might for a moment be identified with Maecenas. I quoted above Servius *ad* 1. 56, who was undecided whether *nonne uides* was directed at Maecenas or the farmers. Likewise, *ad* 1. 176, *possum multa tibi ueterum praecepta referre*, he writes, '*tibi*' *autem, id est o Maecenas, inquit, uel o agricola* (*Serv. Dan.*). Indeed, while at this point the speaker is clearly engaged in instructing the farmers, the phrase, with its touch of antiquarianism (witness *ueterum praecepta*), sounds as though it might well be addressed to Maecenas, especially if we consider the clause that immediately follows, *ni refugis tenuisque piget cognoscere curas* (1. 177). While the farmers hardly have a choice to disdain *tenuis curas*, Maecenas might be the one uninterested in the subject's triviality.

In these passages, and many others throughout the poem, it is impossible to distinguish clearly whether the speaker is addressing the farmers or Maecenas. I would caution especially that, while the Maecenas discourse is clearly very much concerned with questions of poetics, it can by no means be claimed that poetic self-consciousness is restricted to those passages, or, vice versa, that any remark that has to do with poetry is addressed solely to Vergil's patron. Thus, for example, the proem to Book 2 clearly exhibits poetic self-consciousness (*canam*, 2. 2) and, with its invocation of Bacchus in high poetic diction, might be said to be geared more to Maecenas than to the *agricolae*. However, the proem serves as an announcement of topic and is thus clearly of interest to the speaker's students; furthermore, there is no indication that this passage is not 'meant' for them. If it is thus impossible to separate entirely the Maecenas and *agricolae* discourses, it is perhaps best to imagine the Vergilian persona as a character who is giving a speech/singing a song (making it up as he goes along) with two audiences listening, the farmers on the one side, Maecenas on the other. While from time to time, he explicitly and exclusively addresses one of the two (more often the farmers), for great stretches, he does not give any indication to whom he is speaking. We might add that while Maecenas is aware of the presence of the farmers (he watches his friend, the poet, as he instructs them), they do not know about him; from their point of view, the passages that are directed solely at Maecenas are spoken *a parte*, which is to say that they cannot hear them.

4.2. The Poet's Career

As discussed in Section 4.1, the speaker of the *Georgics* comments extensively on the poem that he is composing, notably in those passages where he addresses Maecenas. In addition to referring, again and again, to the ongoing process of his song ('now I shall sing of *x*', the kind of remark that helps keep up the illusion of poetic simultaneity), he reflects, as we have seen, on his patron's role in the creation of the poem, and presents himself as making conscious choices as to what kind of song it is that he wants to sing (see esp. 2. 41–6). If we look at a few additional passages, not hitherto considered, it turns out that throughout the poem, the speaker contrasts his present composition with different types of poetry that he practised in the past, intends to attempt in the future, or could have chosen, but rejected in favour of what he is doing right now. For the time being, the poet is engaged in an *Ascraeum carmen*, a didactic poem on agriculture; however, he makes it very clear that this is just one of the many options open to him. The *Georgics* thus exhibits to a great degree what Gian Biagio Conte has called 'the most characteristic, most constant element of Augustan poetry: the poet's insistence on letting us know that he could also be doing something else' (1994*a*: 123).

That the poet's career consists not only of giving instructions to farmers becomes clear in the *sphragis*, where the speaker mentions his earlier work:

> carmina qui lusi pastorum audaxque iuuenta,
> Tityre, te patulae cecini sub tegmine fagi.
>
> (4. 565–6)

(I who played shepherds' songs and, daring in my youth, sang of you, Tityrus, under the cover of the broad beech.)

Obviously, the reference to the *Eclogues* has the main function of identifying the speaker, just as the mention of his name does (*Vergilium me*, 4. 563). In addition, however, it serves to characterize the persona and throw light on his attitude toward his own poem. The speaker of the *Georgics* presents himself as what one might call a professional poet: he composed certain works in the past, is now finishing this one, and as we shall see, already has plans for the future. That this is remarkable becomes clear when we compare the persona of the *De rerum natura*: can we imagine that the Lucretian speaker would say something like, 'I am Lucretius, I am currently singing about Epicurean physics, I previously composed some love elegies, and will soon embark on an epic'? The difference in stance has nothing to do with the fact that Vergil did, after all, write both the *Eclogues* and the *Georgics*, not to mention the *Aeneid*, while the *De rerum natura* is, as far as we know, Lucretius' only work. My point is rather that the impression we have of the Lucretian poet's serious dedication to this one project would be badly disturbed if he presented it as being just one step in a larger poetic career.

From the point of view of the *Georgics*, the *Eclogues* lies in the past, and the poet is at present grappling with his ongoing work, which, even during the process of composition, calls for a number of decisions. We have already seen how he opts for selectivity (*non ego cuncta meis amplecti uersibus opto*, 2. 42), not because he *cannot* treat everything, but because he does not want to. Even when he claims to be actually overwhelmed by his material, as in 2. 103–8 (the many types of vines), there is a strong hint that, in fact, he simply sees no point in enumerating everything: *neque enim numero comprendere refert* (2. 104). The sentiment is similar to that of 2. 42–4: even if it were possible to be comprehensive, this poet would not be interested.

Similarly, when in the great *praeteritio* in Book 4, the speaker claims that he is unable to treat the subject of gardening because of constraints of time (*spatiis exclusus iniquis*, 4. 147) imposed by his being about to finish his work (*extremo ni iam sub fine laborum* | *uela traham et terris festinem aduertere proram*, 4. 116–17), it is obvious that the speaker chooses of his own volition not to engage in this particular topic. First of all, the figure of the *praeteritio* is easily recognized as a rhetorical conceit, as is the reference to lack of time; as Mynors 1990 writes *ad* 4. 147–8, 'Poets, who can to some extent at least lay down their own rules, reserve the right to complain, as though restrictions were imposed from without'. In the case of the *Georgics*, it is especially striking that the supposedly imminent end of the poem does not prevent the speaker from introducing the lengthy, and wholly extraneous, myth of Aristaeus. Also, the poet is by no means saying that if he only had the time, he would in fact sing about gardens; rather, he indicates that he would then *perhaps* (*forsitan*, 4. 118) take up this topic. Again, external constraints are presented as ultimately less important than the poet's own choice. The word *forsitan* adds to the teasing quality of the interlude: the speaker paints an appealing picture of gardens and of the charming world of the *Corycius senex*, the promising prospect of a poem that could be—only to then abruptly declare that he will *not* speak about these things and that he will leave the subject matter to someone else. Ultimately, gardening, though presented as an appealing and—as conveyed in the example of the old man—deeply meaningful activity, is just one poetic topic, and one that our poet eschews.

So far I have been discussing instances where the speaker makes choices about his own ongoing poem; however, there are a number of instances where he considers the possibility of composing a different type of a work altogether. These are clustered at the very centre of the *Georgics*, at the end of Book 2 and the beginning of Book 3, in a extended passage that stretches from 2. 458 to 3. 48 and that many critics regard as a unity.[27] It begins with a *makarismos* of the farmers, who are very fortunate indeed, or would be, if only they stopped to realize their own good fortune (*o fortunatos nimium, sua si bona norint,* | *agricolas!*, 2. 458–9), and continues with a description of the idyllic life in the country, which is contrasted with the evils of the city (2. 459–73). The speaker closes this section by noting that the country was the last place for *Iustitia* to leave when she abandoned earth (2. 473–4).

The poet then turns to himself, in a crucial passage that I quote in full:

---

[27] For the following, cf. esp. the discussions of Wimmel 1960: 167–87; Buchheit 1972: 45–159; P. R. Hardie 1986: 33–51; and Gale 2000: 11–15 and 42–4.

475 me uero primum dulces ante omnia Musae,
     quarum sacra fero ingenti percussus amore,
     accipiant caelique uias et sidera monstrent,
     defectus solis uarios lunaeque labores;
     unde tremor terris, qua ui maria alta tumescant
480 obicibus ruptis rursusque in se ipsa residant,
     quid tantum Oceano properent se tingere soles
     hiberni, uel quae tardis mora noctibus obstet.
     sin has ne possim naturae accedere partis
     frigidus obstiterit circum praecordia sanguis,
485 rura mihi et rigui placeant in uallibus amnes,
     flumina amem siluasque inglorius. o ubi campi
     Spercheosque et uirginibus bacchata Lacaenis
     Taygeta! o qui me gelidis conuallibus Haemi
     sistat, et ingenti ramorum protegat umbra!
490 felix qui potuit rerum cognoscere causas
     atque metus omnis et inexorabile fatum
     subiecit pedibus strepitumque Acherontis auari:
     fortunatus et ille deos qui nouit agrestis
     Panaque Siluanumque senem Nymphasque sorores.

(2. 475–94)

(First, indeed, may the Muses, sweet beyond everything, whose holy emblems I bear, struck by immense love, receive me and show me the paths and stars of heaven, the various solar eclipses and labours of the moon; where earthquakes come from; by which power the high seas swell, breaking dams, and then again subside into themselves; why in winter the suns hasten so much to dip into the Ocean, or what delay is in the way of slow nights. However, if cold blood around my heart should prevent me from being able to approach these realms of nature, may the countryside and swelling streams in valleys be pleasing to me, may I love rivers and woods, without glory. Oh, where are the fields, and Spercheos, and Taygetos, where the Laconian maidens revel! Oh, who places me in the icy glades of Haemus and covers me with the branches' broad shade! Blessed is he who was able to understand the causes of things and put his foot atop all fears, inexorable fate, and the din of greedy Acheron. Fortunate also is he who knows the country gods, Pan, old Silvanus, and the Nymphs, the sisters.)

These lines contrast two types of poetry, which, at the same time, appear as two different ways of life. The poet begins by expressing a preference: his first wish is to be 'received' by the Muses (see P. R. Hardie 1986: 38–42 on the use of initiatory language in this passage) and to be taught the explanations of natural phenomena (2. 475–82). This can only mean that he wishes to compose a poem on natural philosophy, and the choice of topics suggests that he is thinking of a work comparable to that of Lucretius; note also that he describes himself as *ingenti percussus amore* (2. 476), a phrase that evokes Lucretius 1. 922–5 (*acri | percussit thyrso laudis spes magna meum cor | et simul incussit suauem mi in pectus amorem | musarum*). However, if he proves incapable of achieving this goal (the phrase *frigidus . . . circum praecordia sanguis*, 2. 484, is taken from Empedoclean doctrine and implies a failure of intellect), he is happy to transfer his love (*amem*, 2. 486, surely harks back to *amore*, 2. 476) to the countryside, to streams and woods (2. 483–6); indeed, he immediately falls into a kind of rapture, expressing his wish to be placed in some romantic Greek landscape (2. 485–9). Obviously, 'loving the country' must be metaphorical for another kind of poetry, one that is viewed as an alternative to the Lucretian type, and it seems clear, especially given the praise of country life that preceded the passage, that the speaker is here referring to his own agricultural poem, that is, to the *Georgics* itself.[28] The two alternatives are recapitulated in 2. 490–4, where the poet praises both the man who understands the 'causes of things' (2. 490–2) and the one who 'knows the country gods' (2. 493–4). The first is clearly Lucretius (note especially his victory over *metus omnis et inexorabile fatum | . . . strepitumque Acherontis auari*, 2. 491–2);[29] the

---

[28] Thomas 1988 *ad* 2. 483–4 contends that '[t]hese lines hardly constitute reference to the *Georgics*, as some would wish; they rather suggest pastoral, and look specifically to the *Eclogues*', a claim in keeping with this scholar's reading of the entire passage, and one that is, in my view, misguided (see n. 29, below). While Thomas is correct to state that the idyllic Greek places, with their literary and mythological associations, have little to do with the toilsome life of the Italian farmer described elsewhere in the poem, there are two things to keep in mind. First, the lines form part of a larger context (2. 458–540) in which, as Thomas himself notes, country life is generally depicted in idealized and unrealistic terms. Second, the book about to begin treats animal husbandry and, as a result, country life as a whole begins to be seen in a more pastoral light, as does the poet's own activity; thus, in Book 3, the poet 'hears the call' of such Greek places as Cithaeron, Taygetus, and Epidaurus (3. 43–4) and describes himself as roaming through the deserted fields of Mount Parnassus (3. 291–2), both in passages where the reference is clearly to the ongoing poem.

[29] Thomas 1988 *ad* 2. 490 (and see his entire notes on 475–94) does not believe that the reference is first and foremost to Lucretius, but claims that '[i]t is "understanding" of nature that is the goal throughout the *Georgics*'. According to him, the alternative presented by the speaker is therefore not one of didactic poetry on natural philosophy (Lucretius) v. didactic poetry on agriculture (the *Georgics*), but of the *Georgics* (scientific understanding) v. the *Eclogues* (pastoral contentment)—a view that, in my opinion, constitutes a misunderstanding of Vergil's text.

second, one therefore concludes, is none other than the poet himself.

In this passage, the speaker once again makes a poetic choice: rejecting the type of song composed by Lucretius, he opts for agricultural poetry instead. The way in which he presents his decision has certain elements typical of the *recusatio*, the somewhat formalized 'staging' of the generic choice, with its Callimachean rhetoric, that is found in so many Augustan poets: there is the rejection of a more ambitious form of poetry with a grand subject matter (in this case, *rerum causae*) in favour of a more humble one; the implication that it is his own incapability that prevents the poet from attempting the more sublime genre (2. 483–4); and the renunciation, on the part of the poet, of the glory that the 'higher' kind of poetry could afford him (*inglorius*, 2. 486).[30] As in every *recusatio*, one has to wonder whether the speaker, in spite of his apologetic stance, does not in fact mean to imply that the supposedly inferior genre he has chosen is really superior. In the case of the Vergilian persona, scholars are divided: some take literally the poet's claim that his first choice of topic is natural philosophy and that the country is only a second-best (thus, e.g., J. S. Clay 1976: 239–40 and Mynors 1990 *ad* 2. 490); others have found that while praising Lucretius, the speaker is consistently undermining his model's Epicurean worldview (it is striking that immediately after 2. 491–2, lines that refer to Lucretius' fight against religion, the poet calls it a blessing to know the 'country gods') and thus hinting that his own poetry is preferable (see esp. Buchheit 1972: 55–77); still others believe that with *felix qui* . . . and *fortunatus et ille* . . . , the poet is presenting two different, but equally valid, ways of life and types of poetry (see, e.g., P. R. Hardie 1986: 43–7 and Schäfer 1996: 91).

What is odd about the passage is that it is not in fact a 'staging' of the poet's choice in keeping with poetic simultaneity: he does not make up his mind as we watch. As a matter of fact, since the speaker is already halfway through a poem on the country, he must have made his choice already earlier; however, his *recusatio* does not take the form of a report of past events (contrast, e.g., *Ecl.* 6. 3–5: *cum canerem reges et proelia* . . .). In fact, a close reading of the text reveals that the poet does not explicitly choose one of the two alternatives.

---

[30] Note that I am here using 'genre' in a much looser sense than in my discussion in Ch. 2; strictly speaking, at the end of *Georgics* 2, the decision is not between different genres, but between subgenres of didactic poetry.

His wish (expressed with two optative subjunctives, *accipiant* and *monstrent*, 2. 477) to become a poet of natural philosophy (2. 475–82) is followed in 2. 483–6 by a conditional construction whose protasis contains a potential subjunctive and thus expresses a possibility rather than a fact (see also Buchheit 1972: 66–7). It does not follow from *sin . . . obstiterit* that the poet is in fact prevented, by his intellectual deficiency, from reaching 'these parts of nature'; he simply states that this could potentially be the case. As in the other examples that we have seen, the persona appears extremely reluctant to admit to not being able to practise a certain type of poetry— as opposed to not wanting to. The subjunctives in the apodosis (*placeant*, 2. 485, and *amem*, 2. 486) can also be understood as potential ('then I might take pleasure in the countryside') or otherwise as optative ('then let me take pleasure in the countryside'); in either case, the sentence does not imply that this is what the speaker is in fact doing. Admittedly, the immediately following exclamations hint that he has actually chosen the inglorious poetry of the countryside (as has been obvious since the first line of Book 1). Note, however, that from 2. 490 onward, the persona no longer talks about the two alternatives in terms of his own choice (*felix qui . . .* and *fortunatus et ille . . .* are wholly impersonal statements), nor, in fact, in terms of poetry: the two fortunate men might simply be taken as representatives of two ways of life. This enables the speaker to return to his original topic, the praise of country life, without any apparent rupture: by 4. 495, 'he who knows the country gods', previously appearing to be the poet of agriculture, has turned into the farmer himself.[31]

The choice the poet makes is thus more hinted at than actually expressed in the passage just discussed. Still, the speaker makes it quite clear that his present subject, for all its appeal, is not the only one he could have chosen. He, as a poet, has alternatives and must make decisions, and this becomes an even greater concern in the famous proem to Book 3.[32]

The book opens with a straightforward announcement of its topic:

---

[31] See also Gale 2000: 43 n. 75, as well as J. S. Clay 1976 on the partial blending of the roles of farmer and poet at the end of Book 2 and on the text's subtle shifts from the one to the other.

[32] The literature on this central passage is enormous and cannot be discussed here in any detail; cf. esp. Fleischer 1960; Klingner 1963: 136–42; Wilkinson 1969: 165–72 and 323–4, and 1970; Buchheit 1972: 92–159; Thomas 1983: 92–101; Conte 1992: 150–2; Horsfall 1995: 96–8; and Balot 1998.

> te quoque, magna Pales, et te memorande canemus
> pastor ab Amphryso, uos, siluae amnesque Lycaei.
>
> (3. 1–2)

(Of you, too, I shall sing, great Pales, and of you, famous shepherd from Amphrysus, and of you, woods and streams of Lycaeus.)

Surprisingly, however, the poet goes on to state,

> cetera, quae uacuas tenuissent carmine mentes,
> omnia iam uulgata.
>
> (3. 3–4)

(All other topics that would have entertained unoccupied minds are already commonplace.)

He then enumerates some of these 'used' themes, mythological stories, all of which, as the commentators point out, were treated in Hellenistic poetry. Again, the poet has made a choice: he is singing of sheep and cattle, while drawing attention to the fact that he could also be talking about, say, the adventures of Heracles or the story of Pelops. In fact, the only reason, one has to infer, why he does what he does is because these other topics have been treated before.

Scholars have not always grasped the full implications of these lines, partly because they have often believed that the poet is criticizing and/or ridiculing the poetic subjects listed in 3. 4–9. This view is based on a misunderstanding of *quae uacuas tenuissent carmine mentes*, which I believe can only mean, 'which [like the topic I have chosen] would have entertained minds free of cares',[33] but which is often taken as 'which [unlike the topic I have chosen] would have entertained idle minds'. Thus, for example, Thomas 1988 *ad* 3. 3 writes, 'With *uacuas* V. makes a second point; not only are the "old" Alexandrian themes hackneyed, they are, unlike the new Virgilian themes, trivial'.[34] However, if the poet regards these mythological stories as trash fit only for 'empty' minds and something that he himself would not touch, why does he mention them? And especially, why does he mention the fact that they have already been treated too often, a point that ought to be of little interest to him if he regards them as trivial anyway?[35]

---

[33] Compare Servius' paraphrase (*ad* 3. 3): *hoc est fabulae, quae delectationi esse poterant, et occupare mentes curis solutas, iam descriptae a multis in omnium ore uersantur*.

[34] See also Perkell 1989: 12: 'The poet disdains idle minds (*vacuas mentes*) and the obvious and familiar (*omnia iam vulgata*)'.

[35] Thomas 1988 (see the quotation in the text) has the order of his two points wrong: the

There is in my eyes no doubt that the poet regards *uacuas tenere carmine mentes* as something positive and something that he wishes to achieve with his own work.[36] And he could, in theory, have achieved it with stories such as the one of the boy Hylas, were it not that these had already been used once too often. Again, the speaker appears as what I have called a professional poet: he knows what his goals are (in this case, entertainment of a carefree audience and originality as a poet) and is looking for the best way to achieve them. Any topic will do, as long as it is interesting to the audience and has not been treated before. Again, a comparison with Lucretius is instructive: could the speaker of the *De rerum natura* ever have said that he was composing poetry about Epicurean physics because all other topics had unfortunately already been taken up? The Vergilian persona, I believe, specifically marks this difference between himself and his model by alluding to Lucretius 1. 50–1, where the teacher addresses Memmius as follows:

> quod superest, uacuas auris ⟨animumque sagacem⟩
> semotum a curis adhibe ueram ad rationem.

(As for the rest, direct your unoccupied ears and sharp mind free from cares toward true reason.)

While the Lucretian speaker wishes to fill the *uacuas auris* of his addressee with *uera ratio*, the Vergilian speaker is happy to detain the *uacuas mentes* of his audience with anything—as long as it is new.[37] This attitude is deliberately outrageous, and I would add that I find 3. 3–9 generally quite humorous: after all, what the poet is saying is that he is about to sing of cattle and sheep because 'nice' topics like that of Heracles are no longer available. The sweeping generalization *cetera . . . omnia* underlines this point: the poor poet has to pick up the leftovers.

---

poet mentions first that these themes *uacuas tenuissent carmine mentes* and only then that they are *omnia iam uulgata*. If the first already disqualifies them, why even bring up the second?

[36] In this passage, the poet clearly envisages an educated and presumably urban audience: the minds of the farmers hardly ever seem to be *uacuae*, at least to judge from the speaker's own description, and as Horsfall 1995: 65–6 points out, *quis aut Eurysthea durum | et inlaudati nescit Busiridis aras?* (3. 4–5) implies a learned readership. It therefore makes sense to ascribe these lines and what follows to the Maecenas discourse (Maecenas himself is, of course, addressed in 3. 41).

[37] The Lucretian parallel provides a further reason to take the Vergilian *uacuas* in a positive, or at least neutral sense, contrary to the interpretation of Thomas and others; cf. also Mynors 1990 *ad* 3. 3.

This is not the whole story, however. Instead of starting on his treatment of animal husbandry, the speaker continues to reflect on his situation as a poet in search of suitable topics:

> temptanda uia est, qua me quoque possim
> tollere humo uictorque uirum uolitare per ora.
>
> (3. 8–9)

(I must try a path on which I, too, can lift myself from the ground and fly victorious through the mouths of men.)

His tone is much more serious now, and there certainly is a change of attitude: the speaker's wish for fame (*uictorque uirum uolitare per ora*) not only marks a departure from the immediately preceding lines, where the main objective of his poetry was to please the audience, but also presents a striking contrast to his rejection of glory at the end of Book 2 (*inglorius*, 2. 486).[38] What makes the sentence additionally difficult is that its referent is not at all clear: what is the poetic *uia* that will enable the poet to raise himself from the ground? Judging from the course of the argument so far, one has to conclude that it is the speaker's present poem or, more specifically, the book about to begin: 'I sing of farm animals—all other topics have been taken up—I must find another way to achieve poetic fame—which is why I sing of farm animals'. This nicely rounded argument is what one would expect, but it is not what the poet has provided. Already the language of 3. 8–9 militates against taking it as referring to the *Georgics*: the ambitiousness of the sentence is in strong contrast to the lack of ambition associated with agricultural poetry at the end of Book 2; the word *uictor* evokes such genres as epinician and epic, and even the poetry of Lucretius, who depicted Epicurus as a *uictor* (1. 75) who went 'flying' through the universe by means of his *ratio* (see esp. Buchheit 1972: 100–1); and, finally, the allusion to Ennius—*uirum uolitare per ora* recalls *uolito uiuu' per ora uirum*, part of

---

[38] P. R. Hardie 1986: 47–50 additionally points out that while at the end of Book 2, learning the 'paths of the sky' (2. 477) was an option not chosen by the poet, who settled for the 'low' countryside instead (cf. 2. 485–9), now, at the beginning of Book 2, he wishes to 'take flight'. In other words, the poet is now ready to attempt a more 'sublime' type of poetry (see the next para. in the text). Note, though, that shortly afterwards, the speaker subverts his clear-cut dichotomy of topographical metaphors: when returning to his ongoing project in 3. 40–5, he refers to his supposedly lowly poem as *altum* (3. 42) and claims to be following the call of Cithaeron and Taygetus, two mountain ranges. This is, in my view, another instance of the poet's playful and unexpected use of 'Callimachean' aesthetics and the rhetoric of the *recusatio* (see above, n. 24).

Vergil's Georgics

the archaic poet's funeral epigram (*Epigr.* 18 Vahlen)—also makes one think of epic poetry (see Suerbaum 1968: 172–6).

With the next lines it becomes clear that *temptanda uia est* refers to a future poem, and that lines 3. 4–8, as well as the deliberate ambiguity of 3. 8–9, have masked the poet's surreptitious transition from a discussion of his present poem to the announcement of a work to come.[39] What connects the two is the poet's consistent concern for originality, and this becomes even more obvious in the description of his future project:

> primus ego in patriam mecum, modo uita supersit,
> Aonio rediens deducam uertice Musas;
> primus Idumaeas referam tibi, Mantua, palmas,
> et uiridi in campo templum de marmore ponam
> propter aquam.
>
> (3. 10–14)

(If only my life should last, I shall be the first to lead the Muses with me to my fatherland, returning from the Aonian peak; I shall be the first, Mantua, to bring back to you Idumaean palms, and I shall build a marble temple on the green field next to the water.)

Here we find the *primus* motif, familar to us from Ennius and Lucretius; interestingly, it is applied not to the present poem, but to one planned for the future. Note, though, that already in 2. 174–6, the poet made the claim of bringing a Greek poetic genre to Rome:

> tibi res antiquae laudis et artem
> ingredior sanctos ausus recludere fontis,
> Ascraeumque cano Romana per oppida carmen.

(For you, I attempt a subject matter and art of ancient fame, daring to open up sacred springs, and sing an Ascraean song through Roman towns.)

There, when talking about his ongoing didactic poem on agriculture, the speaker does not explicitly call himself the 'first', though he hints at his originality with *sanctos ausus recludere fontis*, a phrase reminiscent of both Ennius' *nos ausi reserare* (*Ann.* 210 Skutsch), a fragment where the poet appears to stress his own achievement in

---

[39] Note that scholars are divided as to where exactly the speaker switches from discussing the *Georgics* to talking about his future poem. I believe that 3. 8–9 is pivotal (cf. also Mynors 1990 *ad loc.*), but others have located the switch as early as 3. 3. or as late as 3. 16. Obviously, this lack of clarity is part of the speaker's strategy; cf. Klingner on the 'bedeutsam raunende Unbestimmtheit' (1963: 136–42, at 139) of the passage.

relation to that of his inferior predecessors (see Waszink 1950: 225–6; Suerbaum 1968: 175 and 249–95), and Lucretius' *iuuat integros accedere fontis | atque haurire* (1. 927–8, in the context of the poet's roaming through the untouched realm of the Muses). In Book 3, when expounding on his future project, the Vergilian speaker is more self-confident, repeating *primus* in marked position at the beginning of the hexameter (3. 10 and 12). He also engages in a remarkable feat of one-upmanship vis-à-vis Ennius and Lucretius: while their ambition was simply to win a crown from the Muses (see Lucr. 1. 117–18 and 929–30), the poet of the *Georgics* intends to bring the goddesses themselves to Rome (see, e.g., Buchheit 1972: 101–2). His plan has clear imperialist undertones: as scholars have pointed out (see, e.g., Mynors 1990 *ad loc.*), *deducere* here means 'lead home in triumph', and the Muses thus appear as Greek captives led to Italy by a victorious Roman general (note the use of *uictor*, already in 3. 9 and again in 3. 17, where the imagery of triumph continues).[40]

This book is not the place to discuss in detail what kind of poem it is that the speaker is planning for the future and explicitly postpones for now, in order first to finish his present work (see 3. 40–5, discussed in Sect. 4.1). Its style and content have to be inferred mainly from the poet's description of the marble temple (3. 13) that he will build in honour of *Caesar* (3. 16) and specifically of its doors, which, he says, he will decorate with the military achievements of Octavian (3. 26–33). Later, he summarizes his project as *ardentis . . . dicere pugnas | Caesaris* (3. 46–7), but the exact content and even the genre of the poem (epinician or epic?) remain unclear.[41] Scholars

[40] Wimmel 1960: 171 notes how drastically the speaker's attitude toward the Muses has changed from the humble way in which he approached them at the end of Book 2. Pöhlmann 1973: 855–6 points out that while the poet of the *Georgics* treats Octavian and Maecenas as inspiring figures, he mentions the Muses only when talking about alternative poems in a higher style (Lucretian didactic at the end of Book 2 and the speaker's anticipated panegyric for *Caesar* at the beginning of Book 3) and when he invokes them at the outset of the Aristaeus myth in 4. 315–16, where, one might argue, he crosses over into a new genre (epic/epyllion); cf. also Rutherford 1995: 24.

[41] Thomas 1985: 68 claims that 'all agree' that the future poem is an epic; however, one has to wonder whether this belief is not merely an inference from the fact that Vergil did, after all, write an epic, the *Aeneid* (see immediately below in the text). Given the many epinician elements in 3. 10–39, which are usually attributed to the influence of Pindar (see Wilkinson 1969: 166–7, and 1970; Buchheit 1972: 148–59; and now Balot 1998—Thomas 1983: 92–101 believes instead that Callimachus' *Victoria Berenices* is the model; see also Thomas 1998: 103–8 and 1999: 9–10 n. 13), it seems just as likely that what the poet has in mind is a victory ode (cf. Hor. *Carm.* 4. 2); see Buchheit 1972: 158: 'Vergil kündigt damit ein pindarisches Siegeslied an'. Note also the unorthodox view of Morgan 1999: 50–101 that what is announced as a

have tended to identify this future work with the *Aeneid* (see, e.g., Thomas 1985: 68 and now Kraggerud 1998), but there are major problems with this equation. First, it is not the historical author Vergil, but his persona who announces the poem to come (beware the intentional fallacy!). Second, the work described bears very little similarity to the *Aeneid*, which, after all, does not in the first place deal with the 'battles of Caesar'. And third, the passage is perhaps best understood as a *recusatio* of the type where the mere description of a (panegyric, epic, etc.) work that the poet is not now composing (but will undertake in the future (as the poet claims in *G.* 3), or is unable to undertake for lack of talent) is intended to be a substitute for this work, which will never be. Thus, the description of the marble temple is not in fact an announcement of a *Caesareis*, it *is* already the entire *Caesareis* (see esp. Wimmel 1960: 182–3). Had Vergil never written an epic poem, far less attention would have been paid to the announcement in *Georgics* 3; now that we have the *Aeneid*, we are inclined to regard the passage as a sincere prediction, in spite of those details that do not quite fit. This tendency is, in my eyes, part of a general approach that many readers, ancient and modern, have taken to the *Georgics* as a whole and one that is, I believe, caused in large part by certain features of this poem that I have been discussing. I shall return to this point shortly.

I have endeavoured to show how the speaker of the *Georgics* presents himself as a poet somewhere in the middle of his career and how he draws attention to the poetic choices that he has already made and those that face him now. Especially in the addresses to Maecenas—as mentioned above, one might argue that more or less the entire extended, very self-conscious passage at the end of Book 2 and beginning of Book 3 is part of the Maecenas discourse—the poet discusses his work and looks at his present role as a didactic poet from the outside, as it were. This detachment has a distancing effect that is not overcome by the speaker's great enthusiasm for his subject matter or the pride in his achievement that he otherwise exhibits. How removed he really is from the life of the farmer, whose many toils and few rewards he so eloquently describes and which, in the opinion of many readers, he endeavours to imbue with deep meaning, becomes especially clear in the *sphragis*:

---

future (epic) poem is in fact the (highly epicized) Proteus episode in the Aristaeus story of Book 4.

> illo Vergilium me tempore dulcis alebat
> Parthenope studiis florentem ignobilis oti.
>
> (4. 563–4)

(At that time, sweet Parthenope nourished me, Vergil, when I flourished in the pursuits of inglorious leisure.)

The leisure (*otium*) of the poet is in strong contrast to not only the military campaigning of Octavian, described in the preceding lines (4. 560–2), but also the working life of the *agricolae*, whose *labor* (a keyword in the *Georgics*) has been the subject of the song about to finish.[42] Occupied not with manual labour, but with studies (*studia*), the poet has been dwelling in the refined, urban, Greek (i.e., un-Italian), and, as he says, pleasurable (*dulcis*) city of Naples, to which he refers with the poetic and learned name *Parthenope*. These lines and the two that follow provide us with our last glimpse of the *Georgics*' speaker and his attitude. He is, first and foremost, a poet, concerned with his poetry, and the poem that he is bringing to a close right now is just one step in his poetic career.

To conclude this chapter, I shall, as already hinted, briefly look at a specific trend in the reading of the *Georgics*—and indeed, of Vergil's entire work—that began already shortly after the poet's death and still continues today. In doing so, I not only wish to explain how this peculiar view of the *Georgics* arose, but also hope to vindicate my own reading as expounded in this section. What I intend to show is that certain of the poem's characteristics that I have been treating have in fact considerably influenced its reception—even though readers have by no means always been conscious of them.[43]

It is often said that the *Georgics* is a 'transitional' poem.[44] What this means is not just that the work happens to fall in the middle of Vergil's poetic output, between the *Eclogues* and the *Aeneid*, but also that it marks a transitional period in the poet's career (note that I am here talking about the real historical author), which can be conceived of in different ways. Thus, for example, Brooks Otis believes

---

[42] Earlier, the poet referred to his own work, too, as *labor* (2. 39; 4. 6, 116; cf. also 3. 288), as part of his strategy of aligning himself with the farmers (see Sect. 4.1, above). Generally on *labor* in the *Georgics*, see now the extensive treatment of Gale 2000: 143–95, who discusses the poet's *labor* on 185–95.

[43] For the following discussion of Vergil's 'career', compare—and contrast—Farrell (forthcoming).

[44] See, e.g., C. Hardie 1971; Thomas 1988: I. 1–3; and Horsfall 1995: 72–3.

that in the *Georgics*, Vergil is moving from non-narrative (*Eclogues*) to narrative poetry (*Aeneid*),[45] while Richard F. Thomas holds that the poem is indicative of a transition on the part of the poet 'from *recusatio* to commitment' (the title of Thomas 1985), that is from the Callimacheanism of his pastoral poetry to the national poetics of his epic.

Already in antiquity, Vergil's works were regarded as a triad, with the *Georgics* as the link that held together the *Eclogues* and the *Aeneid* (see Theodorakopoulos 1997: 155). This is clear from the funeral epigram transmitted in the *vitae*, where the poet sums up his achievement with the words *cecini pascua rura duces* (Donat. *Vit. Verg.* 36), as well as from the spurious proem to the *Aeneid*, which must have been composed already in the generation after Vergil's death:[46]

> ille ego, qui quondam gracili modulatus auena
> carmina et egressus siluis uicina coegi,
> ut quamuis auido parerent arua colono,
> gratum opus agricolis, at nunc horrentia Martis
> arma uirumque cano . . .
>
> (Donat. *Vit. Verg.* 42)

(I, the one who once played songs on the slender reed and, leaving behind the woods, forced— a work dear to country folk—the nearby fields to obey the farmer, however greedy, I now sing of the horrible arms of Mars and of the man . . .)

Also clear, however, is that already early on, the three poems were not considered equal and that the sequence *Eclogues–Georgics–Aeneid* was believed to reflect the poet's development. Thus, the *Donatus vita* suggests that the three works of Vergil trace the evolution of human civilization; men were first shepherds, then became farmers, and finally took to waging war:

quod uidetur Vergilius in ipso ordine operum suorum uoluisse monstrare, cum pastores primo, deinde agricolas canit et ad ultimum bellatores. (Donat. *Vit. Verg.* 57)

---

[45] See Otis 1963: 144–214, esp. 144–5; see also C. Hardie 1971: 8, who writes, 'The *Georgics* . . . from their conception were thought of as a means to epic, a preparatory stage, a transitional poem, an exploration of possibilities'.

[46] On the proem, see E. Brandt 1928; Austin 1968 (the classic refutation of its presumed authenticity); Lipking 1981: 69; La Penna 1985; and Theodorakopoulos 1997: 160–1.

(Vergil apparently wanted to demonstrate this in the very order of his works, singing first of shepherds, then of farmers, and finally of warriors.)

Shortly afterwards (58–9), the *vita* offers the alternative explanation that in his three poems, Vergil moved through three styles or *modi elocutionum*, from the *modus tenuis* (*Eclogues*) to the *modus moderatus* (*Georgics*) and finally to the *modus ualidus* (*Aeneid*). The final work, the *Aeneid*, thus appears as the pinnacle of Vergil's achievement, and indeed, the *Vita Bernensis I* contends that when Vergil wrote the *Eclogues* and *Georgics*, he was just practising:

in quibus [sc. Bucolicis] ingenium suum expertus est, fauoremque quoque Caesaris emeruit. ac deinde Georgica conscripsit, et in his corroborato ingenio [eius][47] Aeneida conscripsit.

(In the *Eclogues*, he practised his genius and also earned the favour of Augustus; then he composed the *Georgics* and, having strengthened his genius in this work, he composed the *Aeneid*.)

In the Middle Ages, the three Vergilian works came to be regarded as the representatives not just of three forms of life (shepherd, farmer, warrior) and three poetic styles (low, middle, high), but of a whole number of other hierarchies, for example, of tools or instruments (staff, plough, sword) or of animals (sheep, cow, horse). These equations could be expressed graphically, by means of concentric circles, in a schema called the 'wheel of Vergil', *rota Vergilii*.[48]

The teleological view of Vergil's career survives into modern times—Lawrence Lipking maintains that the poet 'spent his life preparing the *Aeneid*' (1981: 79)—and, as we have already seen, classical scholars have a strong tendency to regard the sequence *Eclogues–Georgics–Aeneid* as a unit, a kind of narrative of Vergil's progress. Thus, Friedrich Klingner, for example, argues at length for the 'Einheit des virgilischen Lebenswerkes' (1930), and the recent *Cambridge Companion to Virgil* includes in part 2 ('Genre and Poetic Career') not only three chapters on the great poems, but a fourth one (Theodorakopoulos 1997) on the 'Book of Virgil', that is, on the three works taken together and regarded as some sort of *Gesamtkunstwerk*.

[47] I do not think that *eius* can be correct here. It would have to refer to *Caesar*, which makes no sense, because it can hardly be claimed that in the *Georgics*, Vergil somehow 'strengthened' Octavian's *ingenium* and also because *ingenium*, when mentioned just one sentence earlier and there qualified by *suum*, clearly means the poet's genius.

[48] See, e.g., Curtius 1948: 236 and Stabile 1988; Bajoni 1997 interestingly suggests that the concept of the 'wheel of Vergil' may have arisen from the chariot metaphor for poetry.

It is obvious that there are certain problems with this view. Of course, Vergil wrote the *Eclogues*, the *Georgics*, and the *Aeneid*, in this order (though the beautiful symmetry suffers once one takes the poet's juvenilia into account), and one can trace certain developments from one poem to the next (as one can, in fact, with the individual works of any author) and even make out a generic progress from lower to higher. Still, it is unclear why this sequence of works would automatically warrant the designation 'the most perfect and complex literary career in this, and possibly in any, literature' (Thomas 1985: 71), or why it would make critics think that Vergil deliberately 'created' his career, as a kind of masterwork for posterity to emulate.[49] Even if we are not prepared to attribute the shape and order of Vergil's literary output wholly to chance, it is also obvious that it cannot in its entirety be the product of some conscious plan. What, for example, if the poet had not died prematurely in 19 BC and the *Aeneid* had not been his last work? If he had become a philosopher, as Donatus, *Vita Vergilii* 35 says he was planning (though this may well be an inference from *Georgics* 2. 475–82), how would we be looking at his 'perfect' career now?

To return to the *Georgics*, I suggest that this poem, and specifically the behaviour of its persona as discussed in this chapter, is one, and perhaps the main, reason for the ancient and modern idealization of Vergil's career. After all, as we have seen, the speaker of the *Georgics* is extremely forthcoming with information on his activity as a poet. He draws attention to his earlier work (4. 565–6), which is clearly identified with the *Eclogues* by means of the near-quotation of *Eclogues* 1. 1 (~ *G.* 4. 566), and he announces a future poem (3. 10–39) that can, with some special pleading, be taken to be the *Aeneid* or at least a kind of proto-*Aeneid*. Since the poet composed his *carmina pastorum* in his youth (*audax iuuenta*, 4. 565), is singing about agriculture now, and hints that his poem in honour of Octavian may take him close to his death (*modo uita supersit*, 3. 10), he appears to have mapped out his whole life's work: *Eclogues–Georgics–Aeneid*. It is thus in the *Georgics* that we find a poet who is plotting his career and it is, of course, easy to identify this character with the historical author and to extrapolate from his statements to the work of Vergil

---

[49] See Lipking 1981: 77: 'What he created, at last, was something larger than poems, larger even than the books within which those poems were arranged. His master creation was the sense of an inevitable destiny: his life as a poet' (see this author's whole discussion of Vergil's career, pp. 76–93). On the historical circumstances that gave rise to the idea of the poetic career in Rome, see Farrell (forthcoming).

himself. It is clear, for example, that whoever wrote the spurious *Aeneid* proem must have taken his cue from the *sphragis* of the *Georgics*: there, the speaker mentions the *Eclogues* as his past and the *Georgics* as his present work; in *ille ego qui quondam*, the poet has moved on and is now looking back on both the *Eclogues* and the *Georgics*, while about to embark on the *Aeneid* (see Mayer 1986).

The reason why the *Georgics* plays such a pivotal role in the shaping of our ideas about Vergil's career is not that it is in fact the middle one of the three poems. The real reason is that it is a didactic poem, and that didactic poetry is a genre that allows for extensive poetic self-consciousness and thus for the reflections of a persona who is at the same time a poet. It is not surprising that we hardly get a sense of Vergil's career from the poet's other works: the *Eclogues*, while rich in metapoetics, does not in fact exhibit poetic self-consciousness and does not have one voice that one could clearly identify with the poet (compare my brief discussion in Chapter 1); the *Aeneid* is poetically self-conscious, as all epic poems are, but, as in all epics, its speaker is bound by the convention of 'epic objectivity' and therefore does not have any possibility of reflecting at length on his own activity or his career beyond the poem.

If it is true that the idea of Vergil's straightforward development has to a large part been extrapolated from the speaker's poetically self-conscious statements in the *Georgics*, it is also the case that the Vergil who, in the opinion of so many critics through the centuries, moves straight from the *Eclogues* to the *Georgics* to the *Aeneid*, from low to middle to high, that this man with his perfect career is not in fact identical with the persona of the *Georgics*, but rather a simplified, idealized version of this rather more complex character. As I hope to have shown, the poet figure inside the *Georgics*, while actively plotting his career, is not in fact in the middle of a straight path from A to B, from the lowly *Eclogues* to the lofty *Aeneid*. He is a poet who considers many possibilities, from Lucretian didactic poetry to Hellenistic epyllion, and makes up his mind even as he goes along. In doing so, he does not follow some sort of necessity, but, as becomes clear again and again, makes his own poetic choices.

5

The Poem's Success: Ovid's *Ars amatoria* and *Remedia amoris*

> si quis in hoc artem populo non nouit amandi,
> hoc legat et lecto carmine doctus amet.
>
> Ovid, *Ars amatoria*
>
> Everybody understands anyway that he is only giving himself airs, and that consummate love amounts to something more than a bag of tricks.
>
> Hermann Fränkel, *Ovid: A Poet between Two Worlds*

If scholars are reluctant to classify Vergil's *Georgics* as a didactic poem because they feel that the work has a deeper and more serious meaning, they are often unwilling to regard Ovid's *Ars amatoria* and *Remedia amoris* as genuinely didactic for exactly the opposite reason, namely, that these poems are not serious enough. Thus, for example, Effe 1977 discusses Ovid's works not together with other didactic poetry, but in a special chapter entitled 'Sonderformen', claiming that 'nach antikem Verständnis', amatory behaviour as treated in the *Ars* and *Remedia* could not be an 'Objekt ernsthafter Lehre' (1977: 238).[1] However, it is by no means the case that didactic poetry as a genre restricts itself to subject matters of grave importance, eschewing the frivolous and unscientific. If we are to believe Ovid himself (*Tr.* 2. 471–92), poems that provided instruction on fashionable pastimes, such as playing board games or giving dinner parties, were a 'fad at the time' (Fränkel 1945: 55),[2] and the author puts his *Ars amatoria* explicitly in the same tradition (*Tr.* 2. 493–4). There is also no reason to believe that Ovid was the first to treat systematically the art of love. We know of prose handbooks that not

---

[1] Likewise, Downing 1993: 17 maintains that '[t]o the conventional Roman way of thinking, Ovid's application of this genre [*didactic poetry*] to erotic endeavours would be altogether startling'. For a useful (if biased) survey of modern scholarly views on the *Ars amatoria*, see Wildberger 1998: 381–414.

[2] Cf. Wilkinson 1955: 118; Dalzell 1996: 137.

only dealt with such technical matters as sexual positions, but also covered seduction and kissing; a papyrus fragment (*P Oxy.* 2891, published in 1972) offers a few scraps of one such manual, attributed to the infamous Philaenis, which shows astonishing parallels to the *Ars amatoria*.[3] Just as Lucretius used the writings of Epicurus, and Vergil got his technical information from various agricultural treatises, so too did Ovid the author probably consult some erotic *Fachschriftsteller* when writing his didactic poems—despite his persona's protestations that his expertise is solely based on *usus* (*Ars am.* 1. 29).[4]

Another argument against regarding the *Ars* and *Remedia* as seriously didactic is the observation, frequently found in the scholarly literature, that love cannot, after all, be learned or taught (unlike, say, agriculture or natural philosophy) and that a didactic poem on love is therefore a contradiction in terms. As I shall show in the course of this chapter, the question of what exactly the *Ars amatoria* endeavours to teach, and whether love can be an object of didacticism, is indeed of major importance for the understanding of the work. For the moment, however, I would like to point out that the presumed unteachability of love has, throughout the centuries, not deterred large numbers of people from seeking instruction in matters of the heart: from the ancient erotic manuals just mentioned to modern self-help books and magazine columns, the kind of advice found in the *Ars amatoria* and *Remedia amoris* has always had a captive audience.[5] It is obviously not my aim to vindicate the actual applicability of Ovid's teaching (though I would maintain that in terms of practical usefulness, the *Ars* easily surpasses a poem like the *Georgics*, not to mention the works of Nicander), which, just

---

[3] On ancient erotic handbooks, see Parker 1992, who mentions the Philaenis papyrus on p. 94. Cataudella 1973 and 1974 discusses the similarities between the fragment and certain passages in the *Ars amatoria*.

[4] See also Kleve 1983 and Dillon 1994 on Platonist ἐρωτικαὶ τέχναι and the possibility that Ovid used such treatises as sources for his *Ars amatoria*.

[5] To cite a rather striking example of the timelessness of amatory teaching, I own a reprint of a 1936 pamphlet (the sort of thing sold at news-stands) by one Hugh Morris entitled *How to Make Love: The Secret of Wooing and Winning the One You Love*, which exhibits remarkable similarities to the *Ars amatoria*. The frontispiece, for example, illustrates 'Different Ways of Meeting Your Mate', such as 'at the office', 'at a social', 'at a football game', and 'at the beach'; this reads like the American 1930s version of the first part of *Ars am.* 1 (*frequens quo sit disce puella loco*, 1. 50). In a later section, headed 'Gee! You're a Swell Kid', we are told that to prolong a love affair, one ought to show appreciation for one's partner's talents and praise his or her characteristics and achievements, the very same advice given in *Ars am.* 2. 295–314. It would seem that the author actually had a look at Ovid—and found him rather useful!

like authorial intention, belongs to the extra-textual aspects of didactic poetry not at issue in this book. My point is simply that there is nothing about the topic of the *Ars amatoria* and *Remedia amoris* that a priori prevents these two poems from qualifying as didactic.

Finally, the fact that Ovid's works are intrinsically funny and, as many scholars have observed, at points parody other didactic poems, including those of Lucretius and Vergil (see end of Sect. 5.2 with n. 49, below), does not mean that they do not themselves belong to the didactic genre as defined in Chapter 2, as I hope to demonstrate in what follows. I shall be concerned first with the poems' speaker and his triple role as teacher, poet, and lover (Sect. 5.1). I then examine the ways in which, especially in *Ars amatoria* 1 and 2, the process of the teacher's speech is presented as parallel to the students' learning process, with the effect that the *Ars* appears as what might be called a self-fulfilling didactic poem (Sect. 5.2). The last section (5.3) is dedicated to a more theoretical discussion of the Ovidian persona in these poems and to a number of methodological issues raised by certain recent interpretations of the *Ars amatoria*.[6]

5.1. THE *PRAECEPTOR AMORIS*

The didactic intent of the *Ars amatoria* is explicit in the poem's very first distich:

> si quis in hoc artem populo non nouit amandi,
> hoc legat et lecto carmine doctus amet.
>
> (1. 1–2)

(If anyone in this people does not know the art of love, let him read this and, having read the poem, love as an expert.)

Extremely self-confidently, the speaker advertises his book, which, he claims, will make the reader *doctus* without fail;[7] *docere* is thus, we may infer, the main purpose of the poem. Teaching the art of love

---

[6] The text of Ovid's amatory works quoted in this chapter and elsewhere is the *Oxford Classical Text* of E. J. Kenney (2nd edn. 1994).

[7] Wellmann-Bretzigheimer 1981: 1 stresses the originality of Ovid's self-advertisement (nothing like this is found in earlier didactic poetry; see also Verducci 1980: 32–3), which she compares to the texts on the dust jackets of today's books. On the reference to writing and reading in these two lines and elsewhere in the *Ars* and *Remedia*, see Sect. 5.2, below.

is the speaker's aim throughout the text, and he never once loses sight of his goal, which he pursues with a single-mindedness worthy of Lucretius (see Binnicker 1967: 1, as well as 52–8). Calling himself explicitly *praeceptor* (*Ars am.* 1. 17; 2. 161, 497) and *magister* (*Ars am.* 2. 173, 744; 3. 341, 812; *Rem. am.* 55), he repeatedly refers to his activity as *docere* (*Ars am.* 3. 43, 195, 251, 255, 320, 769; *Rem. am.* 9, 298) and *praecipere* (*Ars am.* 1. 264; 2. 273; 3. 28, 197; *Rem. am.* 803) and to his work as *praecepta* (*Ars am.* 2. 745; 3. 57, 257, 651; *Rem. am.* 41, 225, 349, 423, 489, 523). The *Ars amatoria* and *Remedia amoris* thus clearly meet our first criterion for didactic poetry.

The teacher–student constellation, too, is set up already in the first two lines, which amount to an invitation to all Romans, or at any rate those unskilled in the art of love, to take on the role of students in the didactic poem that follows. While in the *De rerum natura* and the *Georgics* the audience of the teaching speech is limited from the start to Memmius and the *agricolae* respectively, the Ovidian persona is happy to instruct anyone—and confident that his teaching will be successful. In what follows, it becomes clear that the instruction is addressed specifically to the *iuuenes*, who, one has to understand, are exactly that segment of the Roman people (*populus* understood as the body of male citizens) in need of the speaker's *ars amandi*. They are addressed throughout Books 1 and 2, while Book 3 (composed later, by popular demand—or so the speaker would have us believe, see *Ars am.* 2. 745–6) is in turn directed at the *puellae*.[8] The *Remedia amoris* is again geared primarily to the men, but the persona claims that his instructions are *mutatis mutandis* equally useful for the women (*Rem. am.* 49–52), whose presence in the audience is acknowledged again at 607–8 and 813–14.[9] Whether his student body is male, female, or co-educational, the teacher concentrates on his addressees throughout, continuously imparting knowledge to them and giving them detailed

---

[8] Scholars have usually taken seriously the persona's claim that Book 3 is secondary and assumed that the *Ars* did indeed originally consist of only Books 1 and 2. By contrast, Wellmann-Bretzigheimer 1981: 3–4 and n. 7, and 7 and Janka 1997: 502 suggest that the successive composition of the work is nothing but an amusing fiction and that the three books were planned and executed as a unity (see also Sharrock 1994: 18–20; Holzberg 1997: 112; and Wildberger 1998: 343–7), which is, in my view, certainly a possibility.

[9] As Wellmann-Bretzigheimer 1981: 4 points out (see also Wildberger 1998: 149–50 and 251), there are signs that in *Ars am.* 1 and 2, too, the *puellae* are part of the audience, though they are not the ones being taught (they are addressed in 1. 617, and 2. 745–6 presupposes that they know of the *praecepta* given to the men). Likewise, as 3. 6–8 shows, the men are well aware of (though not necessarily pleased with) what is going on in Book 3.

advice. His dedication to his students could easily win him a teaching prize, and the *Ars* and *Remedia* without doubt fulfil our second criterion.

The third criterion is poetic self-consciousness, and in both poems, the teacher explicitly presents himself as a poet, using the designations *poeta* (*Rem. am.* 398, 813) and *uates* (*Ars am.* 1. 29, 525; 2. 11, 165, 739; *Rem. am.* 3, 77, 767) and referring to his activity as *canere* (*Ars am.* 1. 30, 33, 297; 2. 493, 536; 3. 790; *Rem. am.* 703, 715) and to his work as *carmen* (*Ars am.* 1. 2, 34; 2. 3; 3. 342, 792; *Rem. am.* 252, 392, 766, 814). However, as he makes clear in the proem to *Ars amatoria* 1, he is an unusual kind of poet, and there is a crucial difference between his song and that of others:

> non ego, Phoebe, datas a te mihi mentiar artes,
> nec nos aeriae uoce monemur auis,
> nec mihi sunt uisae Clio Cliusque sorores
> seruanti pecudes uallibus, Ascra, tuis;
> usus opus mouet hoc: uati parete perito;
> uera canam.
>
> (1. 25–30)

(I will not pretend, Phoebus, that my art was given to me by you, nor am I advised by the voice of a bird in the air, nor did Clio and Clio's sisters appear to me when I was tending sheep in your valleys, Ascra. Experience inspires this work: obey the experienced poet. I shall sing of true things.)

The designation *uates peritus* is a deliberate oxymoron, given that in both of its meanings, 'prophet' and 'poet', *uates* would seem to imply the idea of divine inspiration, the very concept that is rejected by the poet of the *Ars amatoria*, who prefers to rely on his experience (*usus*) instead.[10] His disclaiming a divine source for his amatory knowledge, however, does not prevent him from citing the authority of Venus, who, he brags, appointed him teacher of her son Amor (*Ars am.* 1. 7),[11] and from appealing to the same goddess for

---

[10] See the discussion of Ahern 1990. Detailed treatments of the passage (and esp. discussions of the identity of the mysterious *aeria auis* in v. 26) are also found in Lenz 1961: 135–9; Suerbaum 1965; Lefèvre 1967; Hollis 1977 *ad loc.*; La Penna 1979; Miller 1983: 27–32, and 1986 (with a discussion of passages in Propertius and Persius where divine inspiration is likewise eschewed); and Wildberger 1998: 4–6.

[11] The scene of Venus' employing a teacher for her son, with its humorous introduction of bourgeois elements into the sphere of the divine, is typically Hellenistic. Hollis 1977 *ad* 7 ff. compares Bion fr. 10 Gow, but I feel reminded specifically of the beginning of the third book of Apollonius, where Aphrodite complains about the unruliness of Eros and her own inability to deal with the boy (esp. 3. 90–9).

assistance immediately after having denounced inspiration: *coeptis, mater Amoris, ades* (*Ars am.* 1. 30). As Miller 1983: 31–2 notes, the invocation to Venus right after the speaker's stressing his own independence certainly does have a funny effect; however, Suerbaum 1965: 493–4 and 494 n. 1 is in my view correct that there is not in fact a logical contradiction and that the Ovidian persona is simply distinguishing between divine inspiration (rejected) and divine assistance (desired).[12] Also, the contrast between *usus* on the one hand and Venus on the other appears less pronounced once we remember that *uenus*, after all, means '(physical) love', which is, of course, the exact area of the poet's *usus*. Thus, there is perhaps not too great a difference between being inspired by *usus* and being inspired by Venus. Note that at the beginning of Book 2, the poet appeals again to Amor, Venus, and Erato (2. 15–16); when setting out on the *Remedia*, he prays to Apollo, whom he fittingly invokes as the god of both poetry and medicine (*Rem. am.* 75–8).[13]

The poet's claim to being a *uates peritus* and the stress he lays on his *usus* are part of the proem's strategy of aggressive self-promotion, which begins with the teacher's claim that reading his book will make anyone a *doctus amator* (1–2), continues with his comparing himself to such masters of their respective *artes* as Automedon and Tiphys (5–8) and with the mention of his appointment as *praeceptor Amoris* by Venus (7–18), and culminates in his boast that he will definitely conquer Amor/*amor* (19–24). In addition, the reference to the poet's amatory experience puts the work about to begin into a context that is both autobiographical and literary. It implies that the speaker has been active as a lover, and this in turn invites his identification with the persona of Ovid's earlier work, the *Amores*, which is mentioned by title in *Ars amatoria* 3. 343–4 as one of the

[12] In the *De rerum natura* and *Georgics*, too, appeals to (near-)divine figures, such as Venus and Calliope in Lucretius and Octavian and Maecenas in Vergil, are usually for assistance, not actual inspiration in the sense of transference of knowledge. This is not surprising: unlike in epic, where the Muses are invoked as repositories of knowledge about a past that is otherwise inaccessible to the poet (see esp. *Il.* 2. 485–6), in didactic poetry, the necessary expertise can normally be acquired in a purely human way.

[13] In addition, there are a number of divine epiphanies (Apollo, *Ars am.* 2. 493–510; Venus, *Ars am.* 3. 43–56; Amor, *Rem. am.* 1–40 and 555–76), in which a god, without having been invoked, appears to the poet and offers either amatory advice (Apollo and Amor in his second epiphany) or comments and orders concerning the poem (Venus and Amor in his first epiphany). These conversations with divine interlocutors are clearly modelled on the practice of Callimachus in the *Aetia*, both on the famous epiphany of Lycian Apollo in the prologue and on the many 'speaking deities' found throughout the work; see Miller 1983: 32–4.

books recommended to the *puellae*.[14] That the *Ars amatoria* is a continuation of the *Amores* is suggested also by the use of the elegiac metre instead of the hexameter traditionally employed in didactic poetry;[15] note that in the programmatic passage *Remedia amoris* 361–98 (the poet's reply to Envy), the speaker explicitly classifies his didactic poem as *Elegia* (379–88), advocating a generic division of poetry according to metre (*ad numeros exige quidque suos*, 372).

One of the constituting features of Latin love elegy is that the persona of the lover is at the same time a poet.[16] His love and his poetry are closely connected: it is the girl that inspires him to compose elegy, and his poems, in turn, are intended to win his beloved for him. This double role of the speaker survives into the *Ars amatoria*, even though his situation has changed in a crucial way. No longer primarily motivated by his own amatory interests (though see below), the persona now draws on his vast experience to instruct others in the art of love; however, his utterances still take the same poetic form, that of elegy, which, as he maintains, is simply dictated by the subject matter (*Rem. am.* 379–88; see n. 15). The question of *carmen* v. *res* therefore does not pose itself to the speaker: just as in love elegy, being a lover and being a poet are two sides of the same coin, in Ovid's amatory didactic, too, being a teacher of love means at the same time being an elegiac poet.

The persona of the *Ars amatoria* is thus not only, like all other didactic speakers, both a teacher and a poet, but at the same time also a lover, that is, a practitioner of the art he teaches.[17] As a result, he shows extreme personal involvement with his subject matter, in

---

[14] As we have already seen in the case of Vergil, readers have a tendency to think of the personae of a poet's consecutive works as one and the same character (and ultimately, of course, to identify this character with the actual author), a tendency that is additionally enforced if a later text makes explicit reference to a former one.

[15] As mentioned in Sect. 2.3, we know of Greek didactic poems in non-hexametric metres; in the Roman tradition, note Porcius Licinus and Volcacius Sedigitus, who wrote in trochaic septenarii and iambic senarii. Their choice of metre may have been inspired by their subject matter (both treated literary history, esp. that of comedy), and the Ovidian speaker, too, argues (in his defence against criticism in the *Remedia*) that elegiacs are simply the metre appropriate for treating amatory topics: *blanda pharetratos Elegia cantet Amores* (379).

[16] I briefly mentioned in Ch. 1 that, despite this fact, love elegy does not typically exhibit poetic self-consciousness: the speaker has much to say about poetry, but usually does not refer to his ongoing utterance as a poem.

[17] In *Ars am.* 2. 738, he calls himself an *amator*, which in this context (a comparison of himself with other masters of their crafts) means that he is, as it were, the representative of a profession ('Vertreter einer "Berufsgruppe"', Wellmann-Bretzigheimer 1981: 4).

a way quite unparalleled in other didactic poetry.[18] For example, his earlier amatory exploits enable him to illustrate his teachings with examples from his own experience. Thus, for instance, he cautions the women not to trust their girlfriends and maidservants, claiming that he himself repeatedly (*non semel*; *saepe*) availed himself of the services of such supposed confidantes of his girl (*Ars am.* 3. 659–66)—a behaviour that he deems rather too risky to be wholeheartedly recommended to the young men (*Ars am.* 1. 375–98). The speaker's reference to his own earlier practice is, at the same time, a reference to his earlier poetry: in a pair of poems in the *Amores* (2. 7 and 8), the lover first addresses Corinna, denying that he had sex with her slave-girl Cypassis; in the second poem, he chides Cypassis for having let the mistress find out and blackmails her into spending another night with him.

Often, the teacher uses his own experience as a negative example, to illustrate how his students should *not* act. A poor lover, he cautions, ought to be careful not to attack his mistress physically (a standard elegiac behaviour):

> me memini iratum dominae turbasse capillos;
>   haec mihi quam multos abstulit ira dies!
> nec puto nec sensi tunicam laniasse, sed ipsa
>   dixerat, et pretio est illa redempta meo.
> at uos, si sapitis, uestri peccata magistri
>   effugite et culpae damna timete meae.
>
>   (*Ars am.* 2. 169–74)

(I remember how in anger I ruffled my mistress's hair: how many days did that anger take away from me! I do not think, and I did not notice, that I ripped her tunic; but she herself said so, and a new one was bought at my expense. But you, if you have sense, avoid the mistakes of your teacher and beware the losses caused through my fault.)[19]

This and similar passages have been taken as an indication that despite the speaker's boisterous self-confidence, he himself is a failure in love, or at least the kind of love taught by his own *Ars amatoria*. He himself admits, apropos of his advice to be tolerant if the girl has a second lover at the same time,

---

[18] The closest parallel is the Hesiodic speaker of the *Works and Days*, who is not only himself a farmer, but also has his own agenda in addressing a poem on agriculture to his brother Perses.

[19] The poet is probably alluding specifically to *Am.* 1. 7. On *memini* (*Ars am.* 2. 169) as a marker of intertextuality, see Conte 1986: 60–2 and Hinds 1998: 3–4.

> hac ego, confiteor, non sum perfectus in arte;[20]
> quid faciam? monitis sum minor ipse meis.
>
> (*Ars am.* 2. 547–8)

(In this art, I admit, I am not perfect. What can I do? I fall short of my own teachings.)

Some scholars have drawn from this the further conclusion that the speaker's art of love is either ridiculously unrealistic (since people, even the teacher, are emotionally unable to adhere to its precepts) or sinister and threatening (since it forces its practitioners to suppress their spontaneous and natural reactions). I return to this sort of reading (for which see especially the references in n. 53, below) in Section 5.3; for the moment, I note simply that, in my view, the occasional admission of failure on the part of the speaker is primarily a source of humour and ultimately strengthens, rather than diminishes, his control and authority. Also (and this is a related point), for a teacher to admit his own fallibility is in fact a useful didactic strategy, as long as he maintains the general impression of competence.[21] Rather than creating a strict dichotomy of knowledge (teacher) and ignorance (student) as, for example, the speaker of the *De rerum natura* does, the *praeceptor amoris* to a certain extent puts himself on the same level with his students, both admitting his own errors and acknowledging that his addressees possess some competence even without him (see, e.g., *Ars am.* 3. 193–8, where the speaker realizes that there is no need for him to instruct the girls in basic hygiene).

The fact that the teacher is a lover himself makes his teaching not only more personal, but to a certain extent also less objective. Far from being a detached observer, the persona is still, we have to understand, an active participant in the game of love, and some of his advice, especially in Book 3, is clearly self-serving.[22] One suspects, for example, that the teacher is not wholly disinterested when he advises the women to follow the maxim *carpe diem* and make themselves available to men while they are young and beautiful (*Ars am.* 3. 59–98); in the same vein, his instruction to them to

---

[20] Strictly speaking, the 'art' referred to here is that of putting up calmly with the *riualis*, but the use of the word *ars* makes one think of the speaker's entire *ars amandi*.

[21] See Durling 1958: 164: 'The mistakes of the *persona qua* lover, of course, simply make it possible for him to be all the more effective as *magister*—and all the more amusing'.

[22] See Verducci 1980: 36; Wellmann-Bretzigheimer 1981: 4–5; E. F. Wright 1984: 5; and Holzberg 1997: 111–15.

favour the poets among their suitors and to demand no gifts from them other than poems (3. 533–51) is obviously intended to benefit the speaker (who expressly uses the first-person plural: *carmina qui facimus*, 3. 533)—even though he himself knows well enough that this particular advice will go unheeded (3. 552).

Some scholars have argued that Book 3 in its entirety, despite its professed purpose of arming the *puellae* against the *iuuenes* (3. 1–6), really serves the interests only of the teacher and his fellow men and endeavours to create the 'perfect passive mistress, equipped only to gratify her lover'.[23] This claim is, in my view, greatly exaggerated. First, not all the advice in *Ars amatoria* 3 is intended to make life easy for the men. Even if it ultimately increases their desire, few men welcome the opportunity to spend frequent nights on the doorstep of their beloved (3. 581–2) or rejoice at the news that their girl has a second lover (3. 593–4). Even more strikingly, the advice to the *puellae* to dissimulate their wish for costly presents until their 'prey' has gone into the trap (3. 553–4) constitutes nothing but a disadvantage to the men. Second, despite the frequent war metaphors and the stress on mutual deceit, love, as described in the *Ars amatoria*, is ideally a game in which both sides win. Ultimately, what is good for the men is good for the women, too, an idea expressed most clearly in what appears as the *telos* of the *ars amandi*, the simultaneous orgasm of man and woman (*Ars am.* 2. 725–30). Thus, in Book 3, the *puellae* are indeed told to make themselves pleasant and desirable to men, but then again, this is to their own advantage, and in Books 1 and 2, the men were told to do the same for the women, even to the extent of adopting slave-like behaviour. While the teacher exhibits a male bias and, not surprisingly, typically argues along the lines of his culture's gender roles (e.g., women do not proposition, but are propositioned; see especially *Ars am.* 1. 707–14), he certainly is not the self-serving sexist some modern scholars have made him out to be.

To return to the implications of the persona's triple role as teacher, poet, and lover, it appears that his earlier amatory experience, as represented, at least in part, in the *Amores*, not only qualifies the speaker to be a teacher of love, but in fact constitutes

---

[23] E. F. Wright 1984: 5. Somewhat differently, Wildberger (1998: 343–80) claims not so much that the *praeceptor amoris* is selfishly pursuing his own interests as that he is working on behalf of his male students, whom he wants to prevent from falling in with a woman who is a harsh elegiac *domina*.

his primary motivation for composing the *Ars amatoria*. As we have seen, the poet begins with the speaker's appointment as *praeceptor Amoris*, the teacher of a *saeuus puer* (*Ars am.* 1. 18), whom the poet will nevertheless subdue:

> et mihi cedet Amor, quamuis mea uulneret arcu
>   pectora, iactatas excutiatque faces;
> quo me fixit Amor, quo me uiolentius ussit,
>   hoc melior facti uulneris ultor ero.
>
> (1. 21–4)

(And Love will yield to me, however much he wounds my chest with his bow and arrows and shakes his brandished torches; the more Love pierced me, the more violently he burned me, the better avenger I shall be of the inflicted wound.)

These lines hark back to the very first encounter of the poet with the god of love, in the first poem of the *Amores*, where the same *saeuus puer* (*Am.* 1. 1. 5) not only changed the speaker's poetry from epic to elegy by stealing a foot from every second hexameter (3–4), but also transfixed his chest with an arrow (21–5) and thus caused him to burn (*uror*, 25) with love. Through this act of violence on the part of the god, the Ovidian persona became an elegiac lover-poet and composed the *Amores*. Now, however, it is time for the speaker to turn the tables and avenge the wound inflicted on him.[24] Once he yielded to Amor: *cedimus, an subitum luctando accendimus ignem? | cedamus . . .* (*Am.* 1. 2. 9–10); now the god will yield to him: *et mihi cedet Amor* (*Ars am.* 1. 21; see Wellmann-Bretzigheimer 1981: 18–19). As commentators have noted (McKeown 1989 *ad Am.* 1. 2. 9–10; Hollis 1977 *ad Ars am.* 1. 21), in both of the passages just cited the poet is alluding to Vergil's famous line *omnia uincit Amor: et nos cedamus Amori* (*Ecl.* 10. 69). Given that in *Eclogues* 10, this line is spoken by Gallus, the founder of Roman love elegy, it is attractive to assume that the verse is in fact a quotation from one of Gallus' own poems[25] and that

---

[24] While it is possible to take *Ars am.* 1. 23–4 as referring solely to the speaker's punishment for those wounds that Amor will inflict on him in the struggle about to begin (1. 21–2), it is more attractive to see an allusion to the old injuries of *Am.* 1. 1, an interpretation made easy through the use of the perfects *fixit* and *ussit* and the perfect participle *facti*, which make it possible to understand that the speaker is talking of past wounds. On the *Ars* as a revenge against Amor, see also McLaughlin 1979 and Wildberger 1998: 19–21.

[25] Servius *ad Ecl.* 10. 46 states, *hi autem omnes uersus Galli sunt, de ipsius translati carminibus*, but it is impossible to determine the extent of the quotation/adaptation; see Ross 1975: 85–106 and Wildberger 1998: 21 and n. 52, with further references.

it was known as something like the 'motto' of love elegy, a most concise expression of the genre's spirit. With his decision to yield to Amor in *Amores* 1. 2. 9–10, the poet thus signals his conscious embarking on a career as love elegist.[26] In the *Ars amatoria*, by contrast, the daring claim *et mihi cedet Amor* initiates the poet's revenge against Amor and his reversal of the *Amores* and of love elegy in general.

Before we return to the relationship of the *Ars amatoria* to the genre of elegy, it will be useful to consider briefly the exact meaning of the word *amor*, given that *amare* is the very skill the poet purports to teach (see *Ars am.* 1. 1–2). When he describes himself as *praeceptor Amoris* (*Ars am.* 1. 17), the primary reference is, of course, to the boyish god of love, whom Venus has handed over to the speaker as a pupil; *Amoris* thus functions as a possessive genitive.[27] At the same time, it is possible to read *amoris* (of course, the distinction between upper- and lower-case letters was unknown to Ovid) and take the genitive as objective: *praeceptor amoris* is thus the equivalent of *praeceptor amandi* (*Ars am.* 2. 161), and this is how the phrase is reused in *Tristia* 1. 1. 67, where Ovid's book from exile reassures potential readers, *non sum praeceptor amoris*. The ambivalence of Amor/*amor* persists in the following lines: the speaker claims that he will subdue the god, but at the same time implies that he will conquer love. The play with the word's double meaning returns at the beginning of Book 2, where the poet announces instructions on how to 'keep love', that is, both how to keep a relationship going and how to detain Amor, the elusive, winged god (*Ars am.* 2. 17–20 and 97–8), and again in the very first distich of the *Remedia amoris*, where the god interprets the title of the book as an attack against his own person.

Even apart from the references to the god Amor, what does the speaker mean when he claims to be teaching 'love'? The answer to this question is not as easy as it would appear, for what the *praeceptor amoris* teaches is by no means what we call 'love', which the *American Heritage Dictionary* defines as either a 'deep, tender, ineffable feeling of affection and solicitude toward a person' or otherwise a 'feeling

---

[26] The use of the first-person plural for the singular in these two lines enables the poet to achieve, with *cedamus*, an exact verbal echo of the Gallan/Vergilian line. Note that by hinting at the possibility of his *not* yielding to love (see the question of *Am.* 1. 2. 9), the Ovidian persona already somewhat undermines the elegiac topos of love's irresistible force.

[27] For the following discussion of Amor v. *amor*, cf. Heldmann 1981.

of intense desire and attraction toward a person'. Emotions of this kind do not usually enter into the picture of the *Ars amatoria*, though they are sometimes glimpsed at the margins, as in 1. 255–62, when the speaker mentions the 'wounds' one can acquire in fashionable out-of-town places like Baiae and Nemi, or in 1. 615–16, when he discusses the likelihood that someone who pretends to be in love will ultimately fall in love for real. This last example shows that the emotion of love is only a by-product of the speaker's art, whose conception of *amor* is quite different. What the poet treats is the *practice* of love in a specific cultural and social milieu, a kind of teachable behaviour that can be glossed as 'courtship', 'conducting a love affair', or 'making love' (in the old-fashioned sense of 'wooing', not the modern meaning of 'having sex'). If *amor* is taken in this sense, then it is not surprising that there would be an 'art' of love, a systematic *techne* that can be learned and taught.[28] From the instructions on where to find a mate to the advice on how to act during intercourse, the *Ars amatoria* teaches its students to master a string of types of behaviour, which, if performed correctly, will enable them to achieve their goal, a long-term male–female relationship based primarily on mutual sexual fruition.

If 'love' as taught by the *Ars amatoria* is thus a particular kind of social behaviour, which can be viewed and executed in a systematic, rational manner, it is also true that for the Romans, the words *amor* and *amare* largely had the same meaning the word 'love' has for us and that the speaker's claim to teach *amor* was, and is, therefore prone to be misunderstood. Throughout the *Ars amatoria* and *Remedia amoris*, there is a continuous play with the double meaning of *amor* and *amare*: while the speaker is really concerned with the practical aspects of courtship, he likes to toy with the idea that his teaching amounts to a mastery of the powerful force of love as an emotion, which, of course, is not in fact anything that can be taught or learned. This play begins in the very first distich, which introduces the teasing notion that there is something like an 'art of love', which can be acquired by reading a book. The tentative wording 'if anyone does not know . . .' already implies that in the opinion of most people, *ars amandi* is an oxymoron, love cannot be taught, and everyone already knows what it is to feel love and needs no

---

[28] Note that the title *Ars amatoria* alludes to *Ars oratoria*, the traditional title for handbooks of rhetoric, another art that can be studied in a systematic way; see Stroh 1979*b*: 118 (and cf. the entire article for parallels between Ovid's art of love and the art of rhetoric).

teacher.²⁹ The speaker then proceeds to claim that *amor* can and should indeed be the subject of an *ars* (*arte regendus Amor*, 1. 4), that he himself is the teacher of *amor* (*ego sum praeceptor Amoris*, 1. 17), and that he will indeed master *amor* (*et mihi cedet Amor*, 1. 21). Throughout this argument, however, the poet does not indicate what he means by *amor*, and especially the mention of the violent nature of the god Amor, who hurts people with arrows and torches (1. 21–4), helps keep up the erroneous impression that the speaker is actually concerned with *amor* in its usual sense, that of strong emotion. Only from 1. 31 onward does it become clear that what the teacher's *ars amandi* covers is simply the business of conducting love affairs with freedwomen,³⁰ a practical skill which can be mastered in three easy steps (see the *divisio*, 1. 35–40) and whose potential connection to *amor* in the sense of 'love' is never made explicit.³¹

The play with the meanings of *amor* and *amare* continues throughout the poem. For example, the first task of the young man is to find the right girl: *quod amare uelis, reperire labora* (1. 35). Hollis 1977 *ad loc.* glosses *quod amare uelis* with 'an appropriate object for your love', noting the 'dry and unemotional tone' and comparing 1. 49, *materiam . . . amori*. Here as elsewhere, *amare* appears as a wholly rational activity that can be planned according to the teacher's systematic instructions: the student simply has to search the various urban 'hunting grounds' to catch the appropriate *puella*. At the same time, *amare* still has the connotation of uncontrollable emotion, and at points, the speaker allows this original meaning to surface, hinting at the possibility that the *iuuenis* might actually 'catch fire' or be 'wounded', that is, really fall in love (see esp. 1. 79–88, 165–70, 255–62).³² However, as mentioned above, this

---

²⁹ Cf. *Tr.* 1. 1. 112, where the poet says of his *Ars amatoria*, *hi* [sc. *libri*] . . . , *quod nemo nescit, amare docent*.

³⁰ In *Ars am.* 1. 31–4, the poet explicitly excludes matrons from participation in the kind of *amor* he is teaching (see also 2. 599–600; 3. 27, 57–8, 483; *Rem. am.* 385–6); *Ars am.* 3. 613–16 shows that the *puellae* he has in mind are specifically freedwomen. The background of these explicit restrictions is Augustus' *lex Iulia de adulteriis* of 18 BC; on Ovid's (partly extremely daring) allusions to this law in the *Amores* and *Ars amatoria*, see Stroh 1979a.

³¹ See Verducci 1980: 33, who remarks on the 'happy oblivion which the *praeceptor* exhibits from the very first in a matter of no small moment: the questionable decorum of treating love exclusively as an *activity*: isn't love first, if not equally, a *condition*?'

³² See Hollis 1977: p. xviii, who comments on the 'constant ambiguity as to whether Ovid's young men and women are really "in love", or playing a game according to set rules'. Wildberger 1998: 45–9, 77–82, and 332–42 discusses in detail the relationship of 'real' love (usually presented as something that happens to others) and the craft the teacher wishes to impart to his students.

potential aspect of the young man's amatory pursuits is kept out of consideration.

A striking example for the speaker's reinterpretation of *amor* occurs at the beginning of Book 3. There the poet makes the paradoxical claim that the problem of such unhappy heroines as Medea, Ariadne, Phyllis, and Dido was simply that they did not know how to love: *quid uos perdiderit, dicam: nescistis amare* (3. 41). One might maintain that, on the contrary, these jilted wives and girlfriends are typical women who 'love too much' (*amor* as strong emotion)—but not, of course, in the sense in which the word is used by the *praeceptor amoris* (*amor* as social practice).

It is only in the *Remedia amoris* that the teacher is concerned with *amor* in its primary sense, that is, with the overwhelming and potentially self-destructive emotion that both we and the Romans call 'love' (see Henderson 1979: p. xiii). In this poem, of course, *amor* is viewed as something painful and dangerous, a disease that the afflicted needs to get rid of—and will get rid off with the help of the advice dispensed by the speaker. The *Remedia* is therefore not, strictly speaking, a reversal of the *Ars* (cf. Stroh 1979*b*: 126): both deal with *amor*; however, the 'good' love of the *Ars* is a rational sequence of behaviour, while the 'bad' love of the *Remedia* is the irrational force typically associated with the word.[33] Again, the speaker glosses over this crucial difference, maintaining that his second work is simply undoing the effects of the first:

> discite sanari per quem didicistis amare;
> una manus uobis uulnus opemque feret.
>
> (*Rem. am.* 43–4)

(Learn to be healed from the one from whom you learned to love; one hand will bring you both wound and remedy.)

The ambivalent use of the word *amor* in both poems is part of a larger strategy discernible in the two works. As already mentioned, Ovid's amatory didactic poems develop out of his love elegy; the *Amores*, on the one hand, and the *Ars* and *Remedia*, on the other, are connected not only by means of the elegiac metre, but also through their topic. Both take as their subject the love affairs of freeborn

---

[33] Note that therefore the *Remedia* works rather differently as a didactic poem: it does not teach an art, but stands in the tradition of so-called cure-poems (e.g., the works of Nicander) and other, medical or philosophical, works of a therapeutic character; see Henderson 1979: pp. xii–xvii on the poem's nature and sources.

young men with freedwomen, a topic they treat by means of a whole number of stock themes and situations, such as the banquet, the writing of love letters, the *exclusus amator*, the avarice of women, the use and abuse of cosmetics, and so on. The world of the *Amores* and that of the *Ars* and *Remedia* are thus the same. However, as scholars have frequently observed, there is a sense in which Ovid's didactic poems can be understood as actively subverting love elegy or even as dealing the deathblow to the very genre.[34] By definition, love elegy is concerned with love, *amor*, which is typically viewed as an overpowering emotion, a disease, a wound, a burning fire. In the elegiac world, love conquers all (see Gallus in Verg. *Ecl.* 10. 69), and the afflicted cannot do anything but yield to love (just as the Ovidian speaker does at the beginning of *Amores* 1. 2), even though this entails leading a life given over to *nequitia* and self-humiliation in the form of *seruitium amoris*. The *Ars amatoria* also deals with *amor*, but with an *amor* that has been tacitly redefined: what used to be an affliction has become a social skill, what used to be wholly irrational can be taught and learned. The life-shattering experience of the elegiac lover has been replaced by the calculated behaviour of the *doctus amator*. Now, from a strictly logical point of view, the two characters are not comparable since the first is defined by his being 'in love', while the second is not, and since, as Hermann Fränkel put it, 'Everybody understands that . . . consummate love amounts to something more than a bag of tricks' (1945: 61–2, quoted as an epigraph to this chapter). However, it is the very ambivalence of the word *amor* that enables the *praeceptor amoris* to give the impression that what he is teaching is the same love as that treated in elegy and thus to suggest that, yes, love is a bag of tricks, and if you read this book you will know how to perform them. And if even after the teacher's course, someone is still suffering from *amor*, he can read the *Remedia*, which will finally rid him of the disease.

Gian Biagio Conte ends his study of the relationship of the *Remedia amoris* to love elegy with the well-phrased conclusion 'The *Remedies against Love* present themselves as a cure for those in love, but in fact they function as a remedy against a form of literature' (1994*a*: 65). I would suggest that it is really a two-part cure and that the *Ars amatoria* and *Remedia amoris* constitute two different attempts to conquer the wild god Amor, that is, to overcome the destructive

---

[34] See esp. Conte 1994*a*: 35–65, as well as Hollis 1973: 94–6; Holzberg 1981; Wellmann-Bretzigheimer 1981: 18–19; and now the monograph by Wildberger 1998.

force of *amor*.[35] While the *Ars* undertakes to tame Amor by suggesting that *amor* is nothing but an easily mastered way of behaviour, the *Remedia* cures the lover of any possible remnant of the destructive *amor* so well known to the elegists. As the poet assures Amor at the beginning of the *Remedia*, his book is not intended as an attack against the god—as long as he remains the good boy he has become through the teacher's *Ars amatoria*. Once *amor* has thus been partly reinterpreted, partly eradicated, love elegy has lost its *raison d'être*.

5.2. Simultaneity

Both the *Ars amatoria* and the *Remedia amoris* exhibit poetic simultaneity, our fourth criterion for didactic poetry. In the proem to *Ars amatoria* 1, the poet uses the future to indicate that he is just about to sing (*canam*, 1. 30; *canemus*, 1. 33) and asks Venus to assist his *coepta* (1. 30). He then lays out the structure of Books 1 and 2, his amatory course for the men, which consists of finding the girl, winning the girl, and keeping the girl (1. 35–40), three steps that the teacher treats in order. He clearly indicates when he is moving from one topic to the next; thus, for example, in *Ars amatoria* 1. 263–6, he announces,

> hactenus, unde legas quod ames, ubi retia ponas,
>   praecipit imparibus uecta Thalea rotis.
> nunc tibi quae placuit, quas sit capienda per artes,
>   dicere praecipuae molior artis opus.

(Up to this point, Thalia, driving on uneven wheels, teaches where to gather an object for love, where to spread your nets. Now, I begin to tell you by which arts to capture the one pleasing to you—a work of special skill.)

Likewise, he signals a break at the end of Book 1,

> pars superat coepti, pars est exhausta, laboris;
>   hic teneat nostras ancora iacta rates.
>
>   (1. 771–2)

(Part of the undertaken task remains, part is over. Let the thrown anchor detain our ships here.)

---

[35] See Verducci 1980: 36: '[T]he *Ars amatoria* is really a disguised *Remedia amoris*, with the significant difference that it offers an inoculation which dispenses with the need for a cure'.

At the end of Book 2, he clearly states that his work is finished, *finis adest operi* (2. 733). Book 3 and the *Remedia*, too, operate according to the principle of poetic simultaneity; in both, the poet makes it clear at the beginning that he is now embarking on a new project (in the case of *Ars amatoria* 3, this is already announced in *Ars amatoria* 2. 745–6, where the teacher promises a book for the *puellae*) and explicitly marks his having come to the end of his work (*lusus habet finem, Ars am.* 3. 809; *hoc opus exegi, Rem. am.* 811).

Like other didactic personae, the speaker of the *Ars* and *Remedia* continuously reflects on the progress of his teaching speech. What sets him apart is the extreme 'spontaneity' with which he comments on his making up his song, something that gives his teaching a vividness unparalleled in other didactic poetry. There is an intensely dramatic quality to his composition: we watch him as he deliberates what to include in his poem and what to leave out and witness how he arrives at his (sometimes unexpected) decisions. In addition to statements indicative of a choice made by the speaker, such as *fert animus propius consistere* (*Ars am.* 3. 467) and *et pudet, et dicam* (*Rem. am.* 407),[36] the poems abound in self-referential questions, for example, *quid tibi femineos coetus uenatibus aptos | enumerem?* (*Ars am.* 1. 253–4) and *quid moror in paruis?* (*Ars am.* 2. 535), which likewise serve to indicate his poetic decisions.[37] There are also several instances where, before our eyes, as it were, the speaker suddenly changes his mind, either calling himself back from a topic that he realizes does not need treatment (e.g., *quam paene admonui, ne trux caper iret in alas | neue forent duris aspera crura pilis!, Ars am.* 3. 193–4), or, on the contrary, deciding to treat what he would otherwise have left unmentioned (e.g., *finiturus eram, sed sunt diuersa puellis | pectora; mille animos excipe mille modis, Ars am.* 1. 755–6).[38]

Obviously, in many cases, such references to the persona's poetic decision-making are conventional and employ well known rhetorical formulas, for example, *quid referam?* or *praeteriturus eram*.

[36] See also *Ars am.* 2. 511 (*ad propiora uocor*); 3. 353 (*parua monere pudet*), 499 (*si licet a paruis animum ad maiora referre*), 747 (*sed repetamus opus*); *Rem. am.* 109 (*maius opus superest*), 397–8 (*hactenus inuidiae respondimus: attrahe lora | fortius et gyro curre, poeta, tuo*), 757 (*eloquar inuitus*).

[37] See also *Ars am.* 1. 255 (*quid referam Baias . . . ?*), 283 (*Byblida quid referam . . . ?*), 739 (*conquerar an moneam mixtum fas omne nefasque?*); 2. 273 (*quid tibi praecipiam . . . ?*), 425 (*docta, quid ad magicas, Erato, deuerteris artes?*); 3. 651 (*quid iuuat ambages praeceptaque parua mouere?*); *Rem. am.* 461 (*quid moror exemplis . . . ?*), 577 (*quid faciam?*).

[38] See also *Ars am.* 3. 611–12 (*qua uafer eludi possit ratione maritus | quaque uigil custos, praeteriturus eram*), 769–70 (*ulteriora pudet docuisse, sed alma Dione | 'praecipue nostrum est, quod pudet', inquit, 'opus'*); *Rem. am.* 439 (*di melius, quam nos moneamus talia quemquam*).

However, there are a number of more dramatic moments, as in *Ars amatoria* 3. 667–72, where the poet finds himself in a conflict between his own interests as a male lover and his duty as the women's teacher of love:

> quo feror insanus? quid aperto pectore in hostem
>   mittor et indicio prodor ab ipse meo?
> non auis aucupibus monstrat, qua parte petatur,
>   non docet infestos currere cerua canes.
> uiderit utilitas; ego coepta fideliter edam:
>   Lemniasin gladios in mea fata dabo.

(What am I doing in my insanity? Why do I meet the enemy with unprotected chest and let myself be betrayed by my own evidence? The bird does not tell the birdcatchers where it can be caught, and the doe does not teach the hostile dogs to run. Forget about expedience. I shall faithfully deliver my promises: I shall give the Lemnian women swords, to my ruin.)

The passage is reminiscent of the kind of tragic monologue in which the protagonist deliberates which of two possible courses of action to take: in his brilliant parody, the Ovidian persona dutifully chooses heroic 'death' (possible disadvantages in future amatory relationships) at the hand of the 'enemy' (the *puellae*).[39] A similarly lively effect in the 'staging' of the poet's composition is achieved also by the divine epiphanies, such as that of Apollo in *Ars amatoria* 2, who appears while the poet is speaking, and by his very appearance influences the course of the poem:

> haec ego cum canerem, subito manifestus Apollo
>   mouit inauratae pollice fila lyrae.
>
>   (2. 493–4)

(While I was singing this, Apollo suddenly appeared, moving with his finger the strings of his golden lyre.)

What Apollo tells the poet immediately enters into the teaching speech (2. 497–508); again, we have witnessed the poem in its very making.[40]

---

[39] A further funny effect is produced by the pompous phrase *quo feror insanus?* (3. 667), which might first be taken to refer to the speaker's getting 'carried away' with poetic *enthousiasmos* (cf., e.g., Hor. *Carm.* 3. 25. 1–3; Ov. *Met.* 15. 176–7), but turns out to mean simply 'Am I crazy? What am I doing?'

[40] The fact that the epiphany of Apollo (like those of Venus, *Ars am.* 3. 43–56, and Amor, *Rem. am.* 1–40 and 555–76) is told in the perfect does not mean that it is not taking place 'now', as the speaker is speaking. In the *Fasti*, too, conversations with divine informants are narrated

If the *Ars amatoria* and *Remedia amoris* thus present a particularly lively case of poetic simultaneity, it should also be pointed out that there are elements in the poems that would appear to disrupt the illusion that the speaker's words are being uttered only right 'now'. As I mentioned in Chapter 1, a text that exhibits poetic simultaneity typically creates the impression of coming into being in an oral composition-cum-performance; by contrast, the mention of writing usually occurs in references to an already finished work.[41] It is therefore striking that the *praeceptor amoris* repeatedly refers to his work as a book, stressing that his art of love can be acquired through reading. This is obvious already in the very first distich of *Ars amatoria* 1, which implies that the book the Romans are told to read already exists (note the deictic *hoc*, *Ars am.* 1. 2), even though later in the proem, the poet is only just starting to sing (30, 33). At the end of Book 2, the *magister amoris* promises the women, *uos eritis chartae proxima cura meae* (2. 746), thus clearly presenting himself as a writer. In Book 3, the previous two books are referred to as *gemini . . . libelli* (3. 47; see also 341–2), just as other earlier works of the poet are naturally imagined as books to be read (see 3. 205–8 and 339–46). From the point of view of the *Remedia*, the *Ars* as a whole is viewed as a written work, which the teacher recommends for reading (*artes tu perlege nostras*, 487) and which has been the subject of some readers' criticism (*nuper enim nostros quidam carpsere libellos*, 361). However, the *Remedia* itself, too, appears as a book (Amor is disturbed when he reads its title, 1–2), a book directed at the same readership as the *Ars*:

> Naso legendus erat tum cum didicistis amare;
> idem nunc uobis Naso legendus erit.
>
> (71–2)

(Naso was the one to read when you learned to love; now the same Naso will be the one for you to read.)

Presenting himself as both a singer and a writer, the Ovidian persona seems to want to have his cake and eat it too. Of course, as

---

in the past tense, even though they are clearly happening simultaneously to the poem's composition, and I have argued (Volk 1997: 296–8, esp. 297 n. 26) that in these cases, Ovid uses different tenses to distinguish not between different levels of time, but between different types of event.

[41] As we have seen, Lucr. 1. 24–6 is an exception in that the persona speaks of the verses he is 'about to write'.

briefly mentioned in Chapter 1, poetic simultaneity, understood as the illusion of composition-cum-performance, is never wholly realistic, and conflations of (pretended) orality and (actual) literacy are found in other poems as well (see also Volk 1997: 291–2). It is also the case that the references to reading and writing in the *Ars* and *Remedia* are placed in such a way as to only minimally disturb the impression of poetic simultaneity. They typically occur in the proems (or, in the case of 2. 746, at the very end of the book) and thus can be understood, to a certain extent, as standing outside the 'song' proper (Wellmann-Bretzigheimer's comparison of *Ars am.* 1. 1–2 with the advertisement on a book's dust jacket is instructive; see n. 7, above). Otherwise, what is referred to as a book is typically a work already finished, including *Ars amatoria* 1 and 2 from the point of view of Book 3 and the entire *Ars* from the point of view of the *Remedia*.[42]

Still, the poet could have avoided references to writing altogether (the Vergilian persona in the *Georgics*, for example, never appears as anything but a singer), and if he insists on the fact that his *Ars amatoria* is a book, there must be a reason for this. I have suggested that the speaker of the *De rerum natura* occasionally refers to his poem as something written both because he wishes to place himself in the tradition of Epicurus, who is a writer, not a singer, and because doing so enables him to use the atoms–letters analogy. In the case of the *praeceptor amoris*, I believe that the mention of writing serves to underline the teacher's claim that *amor* can be learned and taught in a rational way—a claim that is unremarkable if *amor* is just a social behaviour, but one that appears counterintuitive and outrageous if *amor* is taken in its regular sense of overpowering emotion. What the speaker is saying, and what he makes clear at the very beginning of his poem, is not only that *amor* can be learned, but that it can be learned *by reading a book* (cf. the use of *ars* to mean 'handbook'). This blunt mention of what was, in Ovid's time, a modern mass medium is deliberately anti-romantic and disperses right from the beginning all cosy notions one might conceivably associate with erotodidaxis: this is not the one-on-one instruction of an inexperienced lover by an older friend, not the personal sharing of erotic secrets. The

---

[42] A notable exception is 3. 341–2, where the entire *Ars amatoria* (the finished Books 1 and 2 and the ongoing Book 3) is referred to as a written work: *atque aliquis dicet 'nostri lege culta magistri | carmina, quis partes instruit ille duas'*. Note, though, that it is not the speaker who describes his poems in this way, but a hypothetical *aliquis* whose utterance will take place only in the future.

speaker's *Ars amatoria* is for everybody—everybody who does not yet know the art of love and, one has to infer, everybody who is willing to buy the book. This unsentimental approach is, of course, especially funny when viewed before the background of love elegy: all the suffering and failure experienced by the elegiac lovers could easily have been avoided if they had simply got themselves the right handbook.

I would therefore maintain that the mention of reading and writing in the *Ars amatoria* and *Remedia amoris* serves an important purpose while not particularly disturbing the impression of poetic simultaneity. As demonstrated above, the poems reflect extensively on the purported progress of the poet's composition and thus, like all texts that exhibit poetic simultaneity, tell the story of their own coming into being. Interestingly, though, this is not the only story they have to tell, and at least in the case of *Ars amatoria* 1 and 2 (I shall return to Book 3 and the *Remedia* below), one might claim that a second plot is evolving at the same time.

As already mentioned, the teacher's art of love for the *iuuenes* is divided into three parts. Moving in Book 1 from advice on how to find a girl to instructions on how to woo and win her, the teacher in Book 2 turns to the treatment of how to make a relationship last. This third section is itself split up somewhat more loosely into tips for a new *amor* and advice for an already firm relationship (see the transitional passage *Ars am.* 2. 337–44). In his teachings, the poet thus traces the more or less ideal development of a love affair, which fittingly culminates in the *concubitus* (*Ars am.* 2. 703–32). However, as scholars have pointed out, the speaker does not simply provide a theoretical treatment for his passively listening students. Rather, as he is speaking, the young men—or so the poem would have us believe—are already following the teacher's advice, and the love affair the persona is describing is at the same time actually taking place.[43]

At the beginning of the poem, the students are still inexperienced in the art of love (*Ars am.* 1. 1), as can be seen in the speaker's description, *qui noua nunc primum miles in arma uenis* (*Ars am.* 1. 36).[44] Within the

---

[43] For the following discussion, cf. esp. Küppers 1981: 2530–41 and Myerowitz 1985: 73–103; see also Durling 1958: 159 and n. 13; Stroh 1976: 563–4; Wellmann-Bretzigheimer 1981: 8 and 15; E. F. Wright 1984: 9–10; Downing 1993: 12; and Holzberg 1997: 106.

[44] Like the Vergilian speaker in the *Georgics*, the *praeceptor amoris* sometimes addresses his students as a group in the plural and sometimes speaks to 'the young man' in the singular.

fictional world of the poem, *nunc* functions as a real temporal marker: 'now', at the time of the utterance, the addressee is still a recruit in the *militia amoris*. At the outset of Book 2, however, we find that the situation has changed completely:

> dicite 'io Paean' et 'io' bis dicite 'Paean':
>   decidit in casses praeda petita meos.
> laetus amans donat uiridi mea carmina palma
>   praelata Ascraeo Maeonioque seni.
> talis ab armiferis Priameius hospes Amyclis
>   candida cum rapta coniuge uela dedit;
> talis erat qui te curru uictore ferebat,
>   uecta peregrinis Hippodamia rotis.
> quid properas, iuuenis? mediis tua pinus in undis
>   nauigat, et longe quem peto portus abest.
> non satis est uenisse tibi me uate puellam;
>   arte mea capta est, arte tenenda mea est.
>
> (2. 1–12)

(Say 'io Paean' and, again, say 'io Paean': the desired prey has gone into my nets. The happy lover presents the green victory palm to my song, which he prefers to the Ascraean and Maeonian old men. In this mood, the guest-friend, the son of Priam, set off with white sails from arms-bearing Amyclae, abducting a wife; he was in this mood, he who was carrying you in his victorious chariot, Hippodamia, driven along on a stranger's wheels. Why are you hurrying, young man? Your ship is sailing in the middle of the waves, and the port to which I am steering is far away. It is not enough that the girl has come to you according to my song: she was captured by my art, she must be kept by my art.)

Halfway through the teacher's course, the students have succeeded in 'catching their prey', that is, in finding and winning their girls. The perfects *decidit* (2) and *uenisse* (11) present the capture of the *puellae* as a fact, and we are invited to think that it took place, as it were, simultaneously to the teacher's voicing his instructions on how to bring it about. The claim *arte mea capta est, arte tenenda mea est* (12) indicates not only that it was the *ars* or technique imparted by the teacher that made possible the students' success, but also that it was his *Ars*, that is, the first book of his *Ars amatoria*; just as the students won their loves by means of and, so to speak, during *Ars amatoria* 1, so too will they manage to retain them with the help and in the course of *Ars amatoria* 2. Indeed, at the very end of Book 2, the young men have succeeded in securing satisfying relationships, and their proud teacher invites them to celebrate him for his help (*Ars am.* 2. 733–44).

The programmatic passage at the beginning of Book 2 just cited shows how closely the speaker's amatory teaching and the students' amatory practice are intertwined. The girl was won *tibi*, for the student, but *me uate*, with the help of the poet/persona (11)—in fact, by means of *his* art (12). The prey is that of the addressee, but it has fallen into the speaker's nets (*in casses . . . meos*, 2). It is the student whose metaphorical ship is in the middle of the sea (*mediis tua pinus in undis | nauigat*, 9–10), but it is the speaker who steers it toward the faraway harbour (*longe quem peto portus abest*, 10); see Janka 1997 *ad* 9–10.

Specifically the image of the ship and the related one of the chariot are used throughout the poem to align the speaker's poem with the students' amatory adventures (compare the literature cited in n. 43, as well as Binnicker 1967: 65–84). These familiar journey metaphors, which we have seen at work in the *De rerum natura* and the *Georgics* as well, serve their usual purpose of self-referentially underlining the poem's progress. Thus, for example, the speaker concludes his 'table of contents' (1. 35–8),

> hic modus, haec nostro signabitur area curru;
> haec erit admissa meta premenda rota.
>
> (1. 39–40)

(This is the method, this field will be covered by my chariot, this turning-post must be grazed by my speeding wheel.)

As we have already seen, he closes Book 1 with a ship metaphor: *hic teneat nostras ancora iacta rates* (1. 772). However, this second example hints that the poet is not the only metaphorical sailor of the *Ars amatoria*: while the plural *nostras . . . rates* can, of course, be taken as merely poetic, it is more likely that the speaker wishes to give the impression that he and his students really are 'in the same boat' (compare the similar inclusive use of the first-person plural by Lucretius and Vergil, discussed above); this impression is confirmed a few lines later by 2. 9–10, already quoted.

Both teacher and students are on a journey, and the shared metaphors serve to indicate how their progress is intimately connected. Seafaring and chariot-riding thus function as leitmotifs in the *Ars amatoria*; they appear all over the text, and the poet is fond of playing with them, mixing metaphorical and literal usage. For example, in the passage at the beginning of Book 2 quoted above, the successful student (and, implicitly, the teacher himself) is compared to Paris, who sailed from Sparta to Troy in the company of the conquered Helen (5–6), and to Pelops, who carried Hippodamia off on his chariot (7–8). Of course, the ship and chariot of Paris and Pelops are real rather than figurative, but the two examples are clearly chosen with the metaphorical use in mind. Note also that both images can be used in a sexual sense (especially on nautical erotic metaphors, see Janka 1997 *ad* 9–10); this is particularly obvious in the description of ideal intercourse (2. 725–7):

> sed neque tu dominam uelis maioribus usus
> desere, nec cursus anteat illa tuos;
> ad metam properate simul.

(But do not leave behind the mistress, using larger sails, and do not let her overtake your course: hasten to the goal together.)

The object is simultaneous orgasm. However, if the situation is less than ideal, the *praeceptor amoris* advises the following:

> cum mora non tuta est, totis incumbere remis
> utile et admisso subdere calcar equo.
>
> (2. 731–2)

(If delay is not safe, it makes sense to press on with all oars and give the spur to the dashing horse.)

Finally, the art of the charioteer and that of the helmsman appear as early as *Ars amatoria* 1. 3–4 as parallels to the art of love:

> arte citae ueloque rates remoque mouentur,
> arte leues currus: arte regendus Amor.

(By art ships with sail and oar are steered, by art light chariots are steered: by art must Love be directed.)[45]

Automedon and Tiphys are cited as masters of the two arts (1. 5–6); what they were for ships and chariots, the poet is for love: *Tiphys et Automedon dicar Amoris ego* (1. 8; cf. 2. 738).

We have seen that the *De rerum natura*, too, uses journey metaphors to associate the speaker, the student, and Epicurus,

---

[45] On these two lines, see Citroni 1986, who points to *Il.* 23. 315–18 as a model and shows the topical nature of the use of seafaring and charioteering as paradigms for arts or skills.

implying that the three are travelling along the same path (Sect. 3. 2, above). However, their connection is purely conceptual since there is no indication that the wholly passive figure of Memmius is actually making progress or even has any intention of moving toward Epicurean *ratio*. In the *Ars amatoria*, by contrast, the students learn their lessons and immediately put them into practice. The speaker's teaching speech causes them to act, and their actions in turn influence the teaching speech in that the speaker reacts to what the students are doing. He not only, as other didactic personae do, immediately answers the questions raised by his instructions (see, e.g., *quaeris an hanc ipsam prosit uiolare ministram?*, 1. 375; also 2. 455; *Rem. am.* 487, 803), but adjusts his advice to fit the exact situations in which the students find themselves as he speaks. Thus, *colloquii iam tempus adest* (1. 607) indicates that the young man is 'now' going on his first date; likewise, in 2. 703, *conscius, ecce, duos accepit lectus amantes*, we are to understand that the lovers have gone to bed *hic et nunc* (witness the vivid *ecce*). In both cases, the teacher's speech and the students' action are closely intertwined: *colloquii iam tempus adest* can also be understood as 'it is now time for me to treat the topic of conversation', and the statement about the bed that has received the lovers is followed immediately by the self-referential *ad thalami clausas, Musa, resiste fores* (2. 704), a verse that mixes signifier and signified by putting the Muse (who belongs to the realm of the poem) literally in front of the bedroom doors (which belong to the realm of the poem's subject matter).

In *Ars amatoria* 1 and 2, the evolving of the poem is thus presented as simultaneous not only to its own composition (poetic simultaneity), but also to an 'external' chain of events (the development of the love affairs of the young men), another ongoing process on which the poem keeps commenting. This second phenomenon is one that I have elsewhere described as *mimetic simultaneity*, a term I coined specifically to account for the fact that in Ovid's *Fasti*, the progress of the poem is presented as simultaneous to the passing of the year, the *Fasti*'s subject matter (Volk 1997: 292–4). There, I defined mimetic simultaneity as the 'narrator's continuous description of what is allegedly happening at the same time as he is speaking' (Volk 1997: 294), a definition that also applies to the situation in the *Ars amatoria*. However, there is one crucial difference: in the *Fasti*, the passing of the year is a given, and the poet can only react to it; in *Ars amatoria* 1 and 2, by contrast, the amatory adventures of the students referred to by the speaker are themselves caused by the same speaker's words.

To a certain extent, the *Ars amatoria* and *Fasti* can be compared with so-called 'mimetic poems', such as Hymns 2, 5, and 6 of Callimachus, where the persona is placed in a specific situation (in the case of Callimachus, a religious festival) and comments on events that take place as he is speaking (see Volk 1997: 293). Winfried Albert has dedicated a monograph to this type of poetry (Albert 1988);[46] however, his treatment does not include the *Ars amatoria* and *Fasti*, and there is, I believe, an important way in which these texts are different. Mimetic poems are typically short, they are often not poetically self-conscious, and their being 'mimetic' implies an attempt at realism. For example, a *paraklausithyron* typically purports to be the real lament of an *exclusus amator*, who reacts hopefully to any possible indication that the door might be opened for him after all (see Albert 1988: 234–5). By contrast, the two Ovidian works characterized by mimetic simultaneity are long, exhibit poetic self-consciousness, and are wholly unrealistic. Just as it is an obvious fiction that a poem like the *Ars amatoria* is created 'while we watch' in an oral composition-cum-performance, it is equally clearly not true that right at the moment when the poet is talking about it, certain young men and women are getting into bed. Both types of simultaneity are highly artificial, and by insisting on them, the *Ars amatoria* flaunts their artificiality. The most extreme case is found in Book 2, where the speaker stresses that an unfaithful lover must hide his infidelity at all costs (2. 389–414), but then changes his mind and advises the young man to make his betrayal apparent in order to incite his mistress's love:

> qui modo celabas monitu tua crimina nostro,
> flecte iter et monitu detege furta meo.
>
> (2. 427–8)

(You who were just now covering up your crimes, following my advice: turn around and, following my advice, lay open your thefts.)

The humour of this sudden reversal lies not only in the fact that the

---

[46] Albert 1988: 24 defines the mimetic poem as follows: 'Ein mimetisches Gedicht besteht in einer poetisch gestalteten zusammenhängenden Rede, die eine als Sprecher auftretende Person in einer Szenerie äußert und in der sie auf Vorgänge oder Geschehnisse Bezug nimmt, die sich während des Sprechens in der Szenerie ereignen und eine Szenerieveränderung bewirken'.

teacher now regards as desirable what he previously described as something to be absolutely avoided (compare his *makarismos* of the man, *de quo laesa puella dolet*, 2. 447–54, with the earlier terrifying description of a cheated woman's anger, 2. 373–86), but also in the deployment of mimetic simultaneity. The formulation *qui modo celabas monitu tua crimina nostro* implies that the student has indeed so far been covering up his unfaithfulness, presumably following the detailed advice of the teacher up to the final instruction that he is not to 'spare his manhood' and to appease the suspicious girlfriend in bed (2. 413–14). Now it turns out that all his efforts have been in vain and that he is instead supposed to tell her the whole truth! What has brought the fictional lover into this absurd situation is the poem's strict adherence to mimetic simultaneity, according to which teaching and execution take place at exactly the same time.

Before investigating further the implications of mimetic simultaneity for the interpretation of *Ars amatoria* 1 and 2, let us quickly consider Book 3 and the *Remedia amoris*. The course for the women also to a certain extent follows the development of the love affair, beginning with the notion that the *puellae* are as yet 'unarmed' (3. 1–6) and ending, like *Ars amatoria* 2, with a treatment of the *concubitus*. However, the book is structured much more loosely, and much of the advice given—for example the long treatment of *cultus*, which takes up nearly the entire first half of *Ars amatoria* 3—is such as to be useful at all stages of a relationship. Also, there are hardly any indications that the women are actually imagined as simultaneously putting into practice what the speaker is teaching them. The only striking instance of a close connection between teacher's speech and students' action is 3. 749, *sollicite expectas, dum te in conuiuia ducam*, where, in an erotic use of the *poeta creator* figure (see Chs. 3 and 4, above), the poet himself appears as the man who at this very moment is about to take the girl out to dinner. On the whole, however, *Ars amatoria* 3 does not exhibit mimetic simultaneity. One of the reasons for this is certainly that in the kind of love affair taught by the *praeceptor amoris*, women play a rather more—though not wholly—passive role; their experience therefore does not lend itself as easily as that of the men to being made into a progressing narrative (see Myerowitz 1985: 97).

The *Remedia amoris*, finally, does not operate according to the principle of mimetic simultaneity (differently Küppers 1981: 2539–40), but rather, like a medical textbook, presents its 'remedies against love' by means of a number of 'if-then' scenarios. The first piece of advice is introduced as follows:

> dum licet et modici tangunt praecordia motus,
> si piget, in primo limine siste pedem.
>
> (79–80)

(While it is possible, and only faint impulses move your heart, if you do not like it, stop your foot right on the threshold.)

However, the teacher knows that early resistance does not work for everyone:

> si tamen auxilii perierunt tempora primi
> et uetus in capto pectore sedit amor,
> maius opus superest; sed non, quia serior aegro
> aduocor, ille mihi destituendus erit.
>
> (107–10)

(If, however, the time of first aid has passed and an old love is sitting in your captured heart, the task is more difficult; but because I am called to the patient later, I will not therefore give him up.)

The patient of the first scenario, who is only beginning to love, and the long-time sufferer of the second are not one and the same person; rather they present different hypothetical cases, each of which the teacher knows how to treat. While it is true that the teacher moves from advice on how to rid oneself of love in the first place to instructions for avoiding a relapse (609–10 functions as a transition between the two parts),[47] there is no sign that the students are literally being healed of their love while the persona is speaking. Again, it is probably the topic itself that prevents the *Remedia amoris* from exhibiting mimetic simultaneity: unlike winning and keeping a girl (the social behaviour taught in the *Ars*), freeing oneself from a painful emotion is not necessarily a straightforward process. Note also that strict mimetic simultaneity would in a sense defeat the purpose of the poem; if, for example, the student were to follow the teacher's very first instruction, *principiis obsta* (91), the rest of the *Remedia* would be superfluous.

To return to *Ars amatoria* 1 and 2, the conceit of mimetic simultaneity, by integrating into the poem itself the imagined audience's reception of and reaction to the poem (see Wellmann-

---

[47] See the synopsis in Henderson 1979: pp. xx–xxii, as well as Küppers 1981: 2539.

Bretzigheimer 1981: 7), produces a kind of text that is quite unparalleled: the speaker's art of love for young men is what we might call a self-fulfilling didactic poem. Thus, the boastful claim of the first couplet turns out to be wholly warranted, for, indeed, the *iuuenis* needs to read (or 'listen to') the speaker's instructions only once to be transformed into a *doctus amator* (see Durling 1958: 158; Myerowitz 1985: 101). The possibility of failure does not come into the picture; both teacher and students of the *Ars amatoria* are unequivocally successful, and at the end of Book 2, they celebrate their victory together (2. 733–44). The young man who entered his military service at the beginning of Book 1 is now a veritable Achilles (741–2), while the poet proclaims himself the greatest craftsman of love (*amator*) of all times (735–8).

The way in which the *Ars amatoria* treats not only the art of love, but also the successful application of this art, has a number of important implications for the interpretation of the work. First, we have seen how the *Ars* reacts to the genre of love elegy and, specifically, how the persona presents his present stance as a teacher of love as both a continuation and a reversal of his earlier role as an elegiac lover. His *ars amandi* is intended as a revenge for his earlier injury at the hands of the god of love: now, he claims, he is going to conquer Amor, a feat that, if accomplished, would mean the complete reversal of the situation that is the very constituent of the genre of love elegy. And, indeed, as we have seen, it is accomplished: at the end of the work, a *grata iuuentus* (2. 733) has mastered the art of love and rejoices in triumph (2. 733–44, see also 2. 1–4). The triumph is that over the captive girl (2. 2) or defeated Amazon (2. 743); however, to a certain extent it is also a triumph over Amor/*amor*. In *Amores* 1. 2, immediately after giving in to Amor (9–10), the poet was led as *praeda* (19) in the god's triumphal procession, together with *capti iuuenes* (27). Now, by contrast, the speaker himself is the *triumphator*, and the young men are captors, not captives.[48] Love has been conquered; the poet's revenge is perfect.

Mimetic simultaneity thus greatly helps the persona's defeat of elegiac *amor*, since it enables him not only to describe love as a

[48] As just mentioned, the captives in the young men's triumph are really the girls, not Amor, but note that the god of love and the beloved person are conflated elsewhere in the *Ars amatoria* (*amor*, of course, can also mean the object of love). Most strikingly, at the beginning of Book 2, the art of keeping, *tenere*, the girl (*arte tenenda mea est*, 12) is at the same time the art of keeping, *detinere*, Amor (*ipse deum uolucrem detinuisse paro*, 98).

rational and teachable social skill, but also to present this new kind of *amor* as a fait accompli. If the young men are already successfully executing the teacher's instructions, there can be no doubt that it is possible to be a *doctus amator* and to dispense with the dangerous emotion otherwise associated with love. What deals the deathblow to the genre of love elegy is not so much that there is such a thing as an *ars amandi* (after all, people have tried to rationalize love before and failed), but that it is so successful.

If the *Ars amatoria*'s relationship to the genre of love elegy is thus clearly and dangerously subversive, the poem's treatment of the didactic tradition is rather more playful. As I have tried to show, the *Ars* is formally a 'regular' didactic poem; this, however, does not prevent it from poking fun at its own genre. Scholars have studied in some depth Ovid's parodies of earlier didactic poetry, especially of Lucretius and Vergil, and there is no need for me to provide yet another discussion of parallels that are well known.[49] On the whole, it is certainly true that the very idea of a didactic poem about love is funny in itself, not even so much because love (in its usual sense, not in the restricted one used by the *praeceptor amoris*) cannot be taught as because the kind of love that can be taught is a frivolous subject rather unlike at least some of those treated in other didactic poems. As I pointed out at the beginning of the chapter, the lack of dignity of a topic like *amor* does not prevent it from being treated in didactic form—but then, on the other hand, nothing prevents a didactic poem from being funny and from exploiting the incongruity between a less-than-serious subject and certain formal elements originally developed for and associated with rather less frivolous topics.

As discussed above, the idea of teaching and teachability is crucial to the *Ars amatoria*'s approach to *amor* and to its deconstruction of the genre of love elegy. To achieve his revenge against Amor/*amor*, the poet employs the genre of didactic poetry and, in doing so, humorously develops it beyond its boundaries. With the help of mimetic simultaneity, the *Ars amatoria* reaches what might be viewed as the perfection of the didactic genre: it is the first and, as

---

[49] On the *Ars amatoria*'s (parodic) relationship to earlier didactic poetry in general, see Kenney 1958; Krókowski 1963; Viansino 1969; and esp. Steudel 1992 (with detailed discussion of the parallels to Hesiod, Lucretius, and Vergil); specifically on the relationship to Lucretius, see Sommariva 1980 and Shulman 1981; on the imitation of the *Georgics*, see Leach 1964; Döpp 1968: 94–103; and Baldo 1989. In contrast to these scholars, Wildberger 1998 argues against viewing the *Ars* as a parody of didactic poetry (see esp. 382–93).

far as I know, only didactic poem that actually and verifiably 'works'. The reader of the book 'really' does become a *doctus amator*, the teacher's advice is automatically put into practice and has its desired effect. This is simply not something that can be said for other didactic poems. We may recall Memmius, the eternally unresponsive addressee of the *De rerum natura*: did he ever understand anything his exasperated teacher told him, did he ever come any closer to the true *ratio* of Epicureanism? We shall never know. By contrast, the Ovidian *iuuenes* learn their lesson, apparently without any effort. It may be that they are better students, but the implication certainly is that their teacher is the better teacher. The *praeceptor amoris*, preferred by his students to Homer and Hesiod (2. 3–4), has shown himself to be the ideal didactic poet.

5.3. Poet and Persona

I have argued in the preceding section that the *Ars amatoria*'s purported success as a didactic poem is a feature crucial to the understanding of the work. I would also maintain that this conceit is one of the major sources of humour in Ovid's text: watching the *praeceptor amoris* as he effortlessly orchestrates the love affairs of boys and girls is a lot of fun, just as it is fun to observe how he mercilessly demolishes the ideals of love elegy, mocks the pomposity of didacticism, provides satirical descriptions of human behaviour, and generally produces fireworks of wit. In control of his poem and in control of *amor*, the persona is central to the working of the *Ars amatoria* in a way that very few first-person speakers ever are, at least in ancient literature.[50]

However, it should be pointed out that in recent years, a number of scholars have put forward a rather different view of the *praeceptor amoris*, arguing that he is by no means the text's all-powerful agent. In their opinion, rather than depicting the persona's success, the poem is aimed at exposing his fundamental failure. Since this kind of interpretation is part of a growing trend in Ovidian scholarship and since it raises a number of methodological issues of importance for this book, I shall use the rest of this chapter to examine, and combat, these critics' claims.

In my first chapter, I argued in favour of ascribing the utterances of a literary text's first-person speaker not to the actual author, but

---

[50] Cf. esp. Durling 1958, the classic article on the persona of the *Ars amatoria*.

to an intra-textual persona, so as to avoid the intentional fallacy. This practice is, of course, now quite common among classicists, but one has to keep in mind that this is in fact a rather recent development. Interestingly, however, in the case of Ovid, scholars have been aware for a much longer time that the speaker of such works as the *Ars amatoria* cannot be identical with their author and have thus been happy to speak of a persona instead.[51] The reason for this is not hard to understand: given that the content of Ovid's amatory poems was long perceived as scandalous (and sometimes still is), a critic had the choice of either believing that, to quote Lord Byron, 'Ovid's a rake, as half his verses show him' (*Don Juan*, canto 1. 42) or accepting a disjunction of poet and work, as suggested by Ovid himself:

> crede mihi, distant mores a carmine nostro
>   (uita uerecunda est, Musa iocosa mea)
> magnaque pars mendax operum est et ficta meorum:
>   plus sibi permisit compositore suo.
>
>   (*Tr.* 2. 353–6)

(Believe me, my character is different from my song (my life is reverent, my Muse a jokester), and a great part of my work is made up and fictitious: it allowed itself more than its author.)

Readers who are reluctant to believe that Ovid, for example, frequently betrayed his mistress with her maidservant (because they find it either offensive or improbable), will be rather happier to ascribe this feat to the persona instead.

There are, however, two different ways of conceiving of such an intra-textual character. The first is to use 'persona' exactly as earlier critics used 'author', that is, to regard the first-person speaker as the repository of all intentions that we no longer wish to ascribe to the actual author. The persona is the source of his or her own speech, with all its implications, while the author with his or her interests and motives is no longer a subject of consideration. This approach, which entails complete agnosticism about authorial intention and shifts all functions of the author to the intra-textual speaker, is the one I have been taking in this book.

---

[51] Note again the seminal article of Durling 1958. Already P. Brandt 1902: p. xvi observes, 'Wenn je, so muss man bei der Beurteilung dieses Gedichtes [*the* Ars amatoria] beachten, dass Theorie und Praxis himmelweit von einander verschieden ist, und dass es sehr wohl denkbar ist, dass man Verse macht, die bei moralisch-ängstlichen Gemütern Anstoss erregen, und dass man dabei doch ein ganz ehrenwerter Mann sein kann'.

The second way of understanding the workings of a text's persona, by contrast, posits a sort of split between author and persona. While it is the persona who is speaking, he or she is not in control of all the implications of his or her speech, which are in turn controlled by the real source of the speech, the author or, to use a construct that avoids the intentional fallacy, the 'implied author' (the force controlling the text, not identified with any speaker).[52] This kind of disjunction is exploited to great effect in, for example, Ovid's *Heroides*, where the speakers (or, rather, letter writers) have themselves an extremely limited perspective on the events their own words describe and where their lack of knowledge makes for funny and pathetic effects. This is clear, for example, in *Heroides* 16, where Paris reassures Helen that it is unlikely that their elopement will cause a war:

> nec tu rapta time, ne nos fera bella sequantur,
> concitet et uires Graecia magna suas.
> tot prius abductis ecqua est repetita per arma?
> crede mihi, uanos res habet ista metus.
>
> (341–4)

(And once abducted, do not be afraid that fierce wars will follow us and that great Greece will rouse its strength. Out of so many women who eloped, which one was demanded back by arms? Believe me, this matter causes you unfounded fears.)

Every reader familiar with the story of the Trojan War will perceive the irony of this passage; however, this irony is not a feature that can be ascribed to the intention of the speaker (Paris, after all, cannot know whether there will be a war or not), but rather an effect engineered by an agent above and in control of the speaker, that is, the (implied) author. In other words, there is, as it were, a communication between author and reader that both bypasses the persona and, at the same time, exposes the persona's imperfection. In the case of the *Heroides* passage quoted, the joke is not only not made by Paris, it is in fact enjoyed, by both author and reader, *at the expense* of Paris.

In the opinion of a number of scholars, the persona of the *Ars amatoria* functions in a similar way.[53] According to Ellen F. Wright,

---

[52] On the concept of the implied author, see, e.g., O'Neill 1994: 66–71.
[53] See esp. Fyler 1971; Blodgett 1973; Verducci 1980; E. F. Wright 1984; Myerowitz 1985: 37 and 150–74; and Downing 1993: 6–74. Cf. also the survey of scholarly opinions in Wildberger 1998: 384 n. 8 and 394–8.

for example, Ovid the author makes the readers 'gradually grow suspicious of' and ultimately 'question' (1984: 1, 7) the persona, who, we come to understand, is intent only on deceiving his audience in order to serve his own purposes: 'He is a charlatan, writing some parts of the *Ars* and *Remedia* to smooth the way for his future amatory adventures, and writing the work as a whole, not to help others, as he claims, but to achieve, what would surely be a most undeserved, fame and fortune' (1987: 11). Similarly, a number of other scholars believe that in the *Ars amatoria*, Ovid is making the point that the persona's art of love, which privileges rationality over emotion, is highly questionable, if not positively sinister. Thus, such critics as John F. Fyler, E. D. Blodgett, Florence Verducci, and Molly Myerowitz hold that the poem exposes its own ineffectiveness: as especially the mythological exempla show, art cannot prevail over passion, and the ambitious enterprise of the *praeceptor amoris* is ultimately condemned to failure.[54] By contrast, Eric Downing believes that it is the very success of the speaker's *ars* that points to 'our need to distance ourselves from its designs' (1993: 39) and that Ovid wishes to demonstrate by means of the negative example of the persona that the 'lifeless and mechanical is not *supposed* to be preferred to the natural and spontaneous' (ibid.).

Obviously, these views are extremist in that they introduce a strong moral component into the discussion of Ovid's poems. Wright clearly feels personally offended by the *praeceptor amoris*, who does not meet her expectations of a didactic poet ('He is not in fact writing these verses to help other people at all', 1984: 9), and Downing and others are horrified at the idea that a spontaneous emotion such as love could be suppressed through artifice (a process that Downing 1993: 15 describes as 'dehumanizing violence').[55] Scholars such as these stand in the time-honoured tradition of the moral criticism and condemnation of Ovid's works, a trend that

[54] On this reading, e.g., the story of Daedalus and Icarus (*Ars am.* 2. 21–96), explicitly introduced by the speaker as a parallel to his undertaking to retain the flighty god Amor, really (but, as it were, unbeknownst to the persona) points to the failure of art: Icarus dies despite his father's superior craftsmanship.

[55] Downing is one of many critics who believe that in the *Ars amatoria*, Ovid is seriously concerned with propagating the ideal of *ars* or culture (v. nature); Wellmann-Bretzigheimer 1981: 14–24 even regards the work as *transparentes Lehrgedicht* in the sense of Effe 1977 ('... bildet der Kultivierungsgedanke den transparenten Horizont und die eigentliche Botschaft der Liebeslehre', 14). See also, e.g., Fyler 1971; Blodgett 1973; Solodow 1977; Myerowitz 1985; and the discussion of Wildberger 1998: 401–3. In all these works, whether *ars* is something positive or negative appears to depend to a large part on the individual critic's personal preference.

began in the poet's own time (see *Rem. am.* 361–2: *nuper enim nostros quidam carpsere libellos, | quorum censura Musa proterua mea est*[56]) and one that may have contributed to his banishment.[57] The difference is that modern scholars are wary of blaming the author for whatever they perceive as offensive in his work; instead, they simply blame the persona. This way, the author can be on the side of the good guys: after all, he has created the persona only as a negative exemplum.[58]

Despite their narrow moralistic approach, which, fortunately, is not shared by most Ovidian scholars today, such critics as Wright and Downing raise an issue of major importance for the understanding of both the *Ars amatoria* and the working of literary personae in general. Which parts and implications of a persona's speech do we ascribe to the intention of the persona him- or herself and which, if any, to the (implied) author? To take an example from the *Ars amatoria*, and one that E. F. Wright 1984: 1–2 believes is most likely to make us suspicious of the persona, what if a speaker contradicts him- or herself? In *Ars amatoria* 1. 283–342, when encouraging the young men, the *praeceptor amoris* makes the argument that women are basically nymphomaniacs; in *Ars amatoria* 3. 9–22, by contrast, when justifying his book for the *puellae*, the speaker maintains that women are typically chaste. E. F. Wright 1984: 2 calls this a 'questionable procedure'; most readers would probably rather call it funny, but the question is, Where exactly is the joke? Does the (implied) author mean us to smile at his persona's inconsistency (or, otherwise, be wary of his deviousness)? Or is it the speaker himself who knowingly flaunts his own self-contradiction?

To take another example, critics have often felt that specifically in Book 3, the *praeceptor amoris* is less than completely in control of his teaching, given that, in the battle of the sexes, he is both the enemy and the ally of the women (see esp. Miller 1993). We have already seen in Section 5.2 how at a particular dramatic moment, he

[56] E. F. Wright 1984: 7 even uses the persona's mention of his critics in the *Remedia* as one of her arguments for his untrustworthiness: if he is being criticized, it must be for a reason (cf. also 11)!

[57] Ovid famously mentions both a *carmen*, i.e., the *Ars amatoria*, and a mysterious *error* as reasons for his exile (*Tr.* 2. 207). The latter was probably the real cause, but the notoriety of the *Ars* certainly provided Augustus with a welcome pretext; cf. White 1993: 152–4.

[58] According to E. F. Wright 1984: 11, however, even the real author of the *Ars amatoria* is not wholly blameless: 'He too is something of a charlatan; he has in essence written a trivial poem about nothing, and has attempted to get away with it by attributing the poem to his discredited poet-narrator'.

addresses himself, *quo feror insanus?* (3. 667), first expressing shock at his betrayal of his own side and then heroically deciding to give himself up to the attack of the 'Lemnian women' (3. 667–72). Again, the scene is hilarious, but does its humour lie in the fact that the (implied) author has made us see his persona in a state of genuine confusion and loss of control or in the fact that the speaker has deliberately brought himself into this funny situation, which he is then able to exploit with all the wit at his command?

In my opinion, in both examples, and in the *Ars amatoria* and *Remedia amoris* in general, the persona controls his own speech with all its implications. He himself introduces his self-contradictions, failures, and moments of confusion for funny and unexpected effects. I thus agree with Robert M. Durling, who writes about the persona of the *Ars amatoria* that his 'posture of lack of control— whether over the process of writing or over the course of a love affair—is . . . one of the important subsidiary devices by which the absolute technical control of the poem is suggested' (1958: 164).[59] There is no point in the poem where the persona is not absolutely in charge.

The question is whether this interpretation is simply my own reading, which may be influenced by personal preference (unlike, say, Wright, I happen to like the *praeceptor amoris*), or whether there is an objective criterion that would settle the question. I believe that there is. Let us return briefly to the *Heroides*, a work where there is an obvious split between author and persona. A crucial way in which, for example, the letter of Paris to Helen (*Her.* 16) is different from the *Ars amatoria* is that the former does not exhibit poetic self-consciousness: while the fictional character Paris is writing the letter, he is not writing it *as poetry*; by contrast, the equally fictional *praeceptor amoris* explicitly composes a didactic *poem*. As a result, there are a number of features of Paris' letter that we cannot trace back to Paris and of which Paris himself is, so to speak, unaware, such as the elegiac metre or the fact that the letter happens to contain a number of allusions to the *Ars amatoria*. In the *Ars amatoria*, by contrast, the persona consciously fashions his teaching in elegiacs (see esp. 1.

---

[59] Proponents of a split in agency between the persona and the (implied) author, and thus of a 'weak' persona, typically cite Durling as one of their predecessors (e.g., Myerowitz 1985: 37 and n. 79). In my understanding, however, Durling is simply a good anti-intentionalist who completely excludes the author from consideration and instead concentrates on the wholly artificial world of the persona, whose stance of control he stresses over and over again (see the quotation in the text).

263–4) and, we are to understand, knowingly and intentionally alludes, for example, to the *Amores*. Unlike Paris, he is both the speaker and the poet, that is, he is creating his speech as a literary text and must therefore be regarded as responsible for all its effects, including, for example, irony and jokes at his own expense.[60]

While this question certainly warrants further investigation, I tentatively conclude that within the text of the *Ars amatoria*, there is no agent above the speaker and that he, qua poet, is responsible for everything that is going on in the text.[61] In other words, no one is making fun of the *praeceptor amoris* except the *praececptor amoris* himself, and if we happen to find him pathetic, annoying, or evil, this is the result of our own opinions and moral standards, and not of any cue provided by the poem itself.

If there is thus, in my opinion, only one poet in the *Ars amatoria*, a final question imposes itself: How many audiences are there? Obviously, there are the intra-textual addressees and there is the actual, extra-textual, readership; the question is only, Which aspects of the persona's speech are geared to which? In other words, Is the persona's virtuoso performance, with all its funny self-contradictions and sly reversals, appreciated only by the real readers, such as ourselves, while the intra-textual students innocently follow the teacher's instructions, without noticing his ironies? This is the opinion of Durling 1958: 166, who distinguishes between the 'fictitious audience' of the poem, that is, the 'appliers of the art', and the 'actual audience', which 'observes and appreciates the sophist's manipulations'. Somewhat differently, Miller 1993: 238–41 believes that in *Ars amatoria* 3, many of the speaker's comments, especially those in which he voices his misgivings about betraying male interests, are directed not at his female students, but

---

[60] I would like to point out, though, that the *Heroides*, which I have chosen as a foil simply because it is another work by Ovid, does not in fact provide quite so clear-cut a contrast to the *Ars amatoria*: through its stress on writing the *Heroides* does raise the question of authorship, and it is sometimes difficult to decide whether the writers themselves are aware of certain aspects of their letters or not. In the case of the letter of Sappho (*Her.* 15), the persona, who is, of course, a poet herself, even explicitly presents her letter as an elegiac poem (5–8), which does, however, not prevent her from having as limited a perspective on her own situation as the other heroes and heroines.

[61] As pointed out above, there has been a general trend in recent scholarship on Ovid to regard the personae of his various works (not just the *Ars amatoria*) as 'failures' who have lost control of both their poetry and their subject matter. Thus, e.g., Williams 1996 has argued that in the *Ibis*, the speaker loses himself in a manic fit, and according to Newlands 1995, the persona of the *Fasti* becomes more and more frustrated with the Roman calendar, with the result that he finally falls silent.

at an audience of males who, as it were, observe him as he teaches the women.[62]

In my view, the question of how much the internal audience knows and understands cannot be answered with certainty and is to some extent misguided from the beginning. However much the teacher–student constellation makes didactic poetry resemble drama, the student figure is never an independent character with genuine reactions, but always a creation of the teacher's speech (see also my remarks in Sect. 3.1, above). Everything we know about him or her, we know from the speaker, and everything the speaker does not tell us must remain unclear. We therefore cannot know, and had better not ask, whether the young men also noticed that the speaker first claimed that all women were libidinous and later said that they were all chaste (and whether they also thought that this was funny)—or whether, by contrast, they were so enchanted by their teacher's rhetoric that they never noticed the contradiction. There is, however, a small indication that the *praeceptor amoris* ultimately does not aim at deceiving his pupils: as mentioned briefly above (n. 9), he seems to envisage that the women will read the books for the men and vice versa, just as the *Remedia* is intended for both sexes. In the end, there will be no more secrets; everybody will know all the tricks. It would thus appear that the Ovidian persona expects his fictional students, the young Romans, to be as sophisticated as Ovid the author envisages his actual readers.

---

[62] To a certain extent, the scenario envisaged by Miller for *Ars amatoria* 3 is similar to what I have suggested for the *Georgics*, where, as I believe, Maecenas is imagined as witnessing the poet's instructing the *agricolae* (see Sect. 4.1, above). Note, though, that in *Ars amatoria* 3, unlike in the *Georgics*, the presence of a second audience is not made explicit and that many of Miller's so-called asides need not be taken as such. In my opinion, there is no reason to believe that, e.g., 3. 667–72 (discussed above) is not addressed to the women.

6

The Song of the Stars: Manilius' *Astronomica*

> iuuat ire per ipsum
> aera et immenso spatiantem uiuere caelo
> signaque et aduersos stellarum noscere cursus.
>
> Manilius, *Astronomica*
>
> Froh, wie seine Sonnen fliegen,
> durch des Himmels prächtgen Plan,
> laufet, Brüder, eure Bahn,
> freudig wie ein Held zum Siegen.
>
> Friedrich Schiller, *An die Freude*

To finish my investigation of didactic poetry with a discussion of Manilius' *Astronomica* after chapters on such classics of Latin literature as Lucretius, Vergil, and Ovid may well appear anticlimactic. Especially among English-speaking scholars, Manilius continues to be regarded as a second-rate poet, and this reputation, together with the many difficulties that beset his text and the extremely technical nature of his subject matter, has prevented widespread study of the author's work.[1] The only thing that most classicists know about Manilius (whom the *New York Times* recently introduced to its readers as 'one of the most boring writers that Rome produced'[2]) is that his poem on astrology was edited by A. E. Housman. Tellingly, it is not Housman who is remembered for Manilius, but vice versa, and it has not helped the Roman's reputation that Housman himself did not think much of the object of his study either, but scoffed at Manilius as a 'facile and frivolous poet, the brightest facet of whose genius was an eminent aptitude for doing sums in verse' (quoted by Gow 1936: 13).

---

[1] An obvious exception is George P. Goold, who in his *Loeb* edn. (1977; 2nd rev. edn. 1992 = Goold 1992) has done everything to make Manilius accessible to the English-speaking reader; the same author's *Teubner* (1985; 2nd rev. edn. 1998) is now the standard text. Wilson 1985 and Neuburg 1993 are two recent noteworthy articles in English.

[2] Benedict Nightingale in a review of Tom Stoppard's *Invention of Love*, a play about A. E. Housman (19 Oct. 1997, *Arts & Leisure*, p. 5); Manilius is—of course (see immediately below in the text)—mentioned only apropos of his famous editor.

The neglect of Manilius in Anglo-American scholarship is in strong contrast to the interest that German and especially Italian Latinists have taken in this author, particularly in the poetic qualities of his work. As for Germany, the dissertations of Lühr 1969 and Reeh 1973 continue to be important since they are more or less the only monographs available on Manilius (another one is Salemme 1983); Effe 1977: 106–26 provides a useful chapter on the *Astronomica* (which he classifies as belonging to the type of didactic poetry that is 'sachbezogen'); and the work of Wolfgang Hübner—who unlike other, more purely literary-minded Manilius scholars, actively engages with the astrological content of the poem—is the most significant recent German contribution to Manilian studies (see esp. Hübner 1984, his magisterial *ANRW* article with extensive bibliography). Italy seems to be the only country where Manilius is read and studied widely. This is apparent from the flood of articles on the poet, many of which will be quoted in this chapter, as well as from the fact that the last decade has seen the publication of two separate editions with commentary by Italian scholars, that of Dora Liuzzi (1991–7[3]) and the Mondadori edition with a text by Enrico Flores (Feraboli, Flores, and Scarcia 1996–2001).

For the student of poetics, Manilius is a grateful subject. Owing, perhaps, to a certain post-classical 'inferiority complex' on the part of the poet who feels he has to prove that he can compose original poetry even after Lucretius and Vergil, the *Astronomica*—to an even greater extent than any of the other extremely self-conscious didactic poems treated so far—abounds in explicit self-referential reflections on the poet's activity and the principles of his work. Scholars have not failed to pick up on this fact, and as a result (and perhaps also because the self-referential passages are the more easily accessible parts of the poem), the poetic programme of Manilius has been rather well studied. Thus, many of my observations in this chapter have already been made. However, since we lack a comprehensive treatment of the poetics of the *Astronomica* and since the insights of individual scholars are scattered over numerous publications that are not always easily accessible to scholars in the English-speaking world, I see myself justified in providing here what is to a certain extent a synthesis of previous Manilian scholarship. At the same time, I hope to show how my and other readers'

---

[3] Liuzzi had published a number of editions of Manilius; I quote the most recent one published by Congedo (Book 1: 1995; Book 2: 1991; Book 3: 1992; Book 4: 1994; Book 5: 1997).

observations on Manilius fit into the larger picture of didactic poetics that I have been painting.

In the *Astronomica*, Manilius describes a world in which everything is connected to everything else, according to the Stoic principle of *sympatheia*. The same principle holds for Manilius' poetics: the persona's statements about his activity as a poet are all to a certain extent interconnected, and I have therefore found it less easy than in the other chapters to divide my treatment of the speaker's self-representation into sections and have taken recourse to frequent cross-references. Roughly speaking, I shall be concerned first with the persona in his role as a teacher, that is, with the first two criteria of my definition for didactic poetry (Sect. 6.1). I then move on to the ways in which the speaker portrays himself as an original poet and to the central tenet of his poetics, his claim to be inspired by his subject matter, the divine *mundus* itself (Sect. 6.2). After this, I treat Manilius' use of the journey metaphor (Sect. 6.3) and finish the chapter with a look at how the poet constructs the relationship between his song and his subject matter, *carmen et res* (Sect. 6.4).[4]

6.1. THE TEACHER OF ASTROLOGY

Manilius' *Astronomica* without a doubt exhibits my first two criteria for didactic poetry, didactic intent and the teacher–student constellation. However, the speaker does nothing to set himself up specifically as a teacher figure or to introduce explicitly an individualized student or students. He does not mention either his didactic intent or his addressee in the proem to Book 1 (on the address to *Caesar* in 1. 7–10, see below); by contrast, he dwells extensively on the poetic nature of the work about to begin (see esp. *carmine*, 1. 1, the very first word of the poem). Didacticism does not play a role in the proems to the later books either (though note 2. 136–49 and 3. 36–42, both discussed below), which are likewise, with the exception of the one to Book 4, dedicated to reflections on the speaker's role as poet.

Still, the persona of the *Astronomica* does refer to his own speech as *docere*, if only rarely[5] (the passages are 2. 751; 3. 39, 447, 560; 4.

---

[4] The text of Manilius used in this chapter and elsewhere is the *Teubner* edition by George P. Goold (2nd edn. 1998). I have also made frequent use of the concordance of Manzino and Manzino (1991–2).

[5] Interestingly, the poet more often ascribes *docere* to the specific phenomenon he is talking

119⁶), and beginning with 1. 194, where *tibi* indicates for the first time the presence of an addressee, he continually addresses a student figure in the second-person singular.⁷ The teacher–student constellation typical of didactic poetry is thus clearly a central constituent of Manilius' poem as well, despite the casual and belated way in which it is brought to the reader's attention. The failure of the Manilian persona to make his role as a teacher and the existence of a student explicit at the beginning of the poem is reminiscent of Aratus' *Phaenomena*, where, as mentioned in Section 2.3, above, the anonymous addressee is introduced only late (*Phaen.* 75) and without an explanation on the part of the speaker. This comparison is instructive also because Manilius is obviously indebted to Aratus for the content of his poem as well, especially for that of the first book, which, like the first and larger part of the *Phaenomena*, consists mainly of a description of the fixed stars. Now, we have seen (in Sect. 2.2, above) that in Aratus, once the poet leaves the theoretical *Phaenomena* proper and turns to the so-called *Diosemiae*, the instructional part of his poem dedicated to the art of the weather forecast, his second-person addresses increase.⁸ The *Astronomica*, too, combines theoretical and instructional teaching, the astronomical description of the cosmos and the astrological advice on how to make predictions concerning fate; not surprisingly, the teacher addresses his student more frequently when giving him advice on practical matters, such as the calculation of the Lot of Fortune and the *horoscopus* in Book 3.⁹

about (1. 702; 4. 759, 848) or to the divine *mundus* in general (2. 262; 4. 918) or to *ratio* (1. 541; 2. 699). This is in keeping with his idea (discussed in detail in Sect. 6.2) that the cosmos voluntarily reveals itself to those who undertake to investigate it and that the teacher-poet is but a medium of this revelation.

⁶ After the example of Bentley and Housman, Goold deletes the verse 4. 119 and the two that follow; these scholars feel that *quod quoniam docui* in 4. 119 provides an inadequate ending to the proem of Book 4 since, to quote Housman 1903–30 *ad loc.*, 'in toto hoc prooemio nihil sane poeta docuit'. The argument that the poet has not been 'teaching' about the omnipotence of fate, but only 'talking' about it appears overly pedantic, though: after all, as Liuzzi 1991–7 *ad loc.* points out, 'in un'opera didascalica il "parlare" di qualcosa possa essere anche "insegnare"', and *quoniam docui* is a Lucretian formula that Manilius employs also at 3. 560; see also Lühr 1969: 136–7.

⁷ See Reeh 1973: 48–51 for a list and discussion of all instances of the second-person singular in the *Astronomica*. On the student figure in Manilius in general, see esp. Neuburg 1993: 257–82, as well as Romano 1978.

⁸ On the difference between theoretical and instructional didactic poetry, a distinction I have taken over from the *Tractatus Coislinianus*, see Sect. 2.2, above.

⁹ As can be seen from the list in Reeh 1973: 48–9, Book 3, though being the shortest book of the *Astronomica*, contains the most examples of the second-person singular, the majority of

Despite these parallels, the student figure in the *Astronomica* plays a more prominent role than the more or less generic addressees of Aratus, and it is worth investigating this shadowy figure a little further. First, it must be pointed out that he is not identical with the very first person addressed in the poem, *Caesar*, a character who is himself somewhat mysterious:

> hunc mihi tu, Caesar, patriae princepsque paterque,
> qui regis augustis parentem legibus orbem
> concessumque patri mundum deus ipse mereris,
> das animum uiresque facis ad tanta canenda.
>
> (1. 7–10)

(Caesar, leader and father of the fatherland, you who rule an earth obedient to your august laws and, yourself a god, merit the heavens granted to your father, you give me this spirit and provide me with strength to sing of such great things.)

The identity of *Caesar* here and in the other places where he is mentioned or alluded to (1. 7–10, 384–6, 925–6; 2. 507–10; 4. 547–52, 763–6, 773–7) has exercised students of Manilius for centuries and is obviously of interest in determining the date of the author, about whose life we otherwise know nothing. Unfortunately, the passages in question admit of differing interpretations, and individual scholars have used the same lines to argue for one of three possibilities: either the emperor addressed in 1. 7–10 and referred to repeatedly later is Augustus; or he is Tiberius; or Books 1 and 2 were written under and dedicated to Augustus, whereas Books 4 and 5 belong to the reign of Tiberius (Book 3 does not contain any datable material; neither does Book 5, but it is generally assumed that it was written after Book 4).[10]

While inclining toward this last solution, a compromise espoused, among others, by Housman and Goold and the one scenario of the three that is in my opinion the least open to objections (though see Neuburg 1993: 245–51), I feel unable to reach a conclusion on this matter; however, I also agree with Effe 1977: 107

which occur in the section about the calculation of the Lot of Fortune and the *horoscopus* (3. 169–509), the most 'practical' part of Manilius' poem.

[10] On the individual arguments, see the survey in Liuzzi 1991–7: 1. 13–16, with references, as well as Neuburg 1993: 243–57. Neuburg himself concludes that Tiberius is most likely the dedicatee of the entire poem, but argues that the vagueness of Manilius' references to the emperor may be intentional and indicative of the poet's belief that the individual living emperor's power is trivial by comparison to the influence of fate.

n. 1 that '[d]ie Frage ist von verhältnismäßig geringer Bedeutung', at least in the present context. For whoever *Caesar* is, it is quite clear that in the *Astronomica* he plays the role of a dedicatee, not that of a student.[11] He thus functions similarly to Maecenas in the *Georgics*, while obviously also resembling Vergil's *Caesar*, whom the poet invokes as a 'god' and asks to assist his poetic enterprise (*G.* 1. 24–42, esp. 40–2). Vergil was the first Latin author to cast a member of the imperial family in the role of an inspiring deity; he was followed by Ovid (*Fast.* 1. 1–26), Germanicus (*Arat.* 1–16), and Manilius, all writing at about the same time (see Pöhlmann 1973: 863–5).[12] It seems that the motif quickly turned into a topos and that every poet felt that he had to lay it on thicker than his predecessors: the modest Vergilian appeal to Octavian, *da facilem cursum atque audacibus adnue coeptis* (*G.* 1. 40), is greatly extended in Ovid's dedication to Germanicus, which contains a whole series of entreating imperatives, and while these poets simply ask for assistance with their work, Germanicus mentions Tiberius (?) as not only the source of his poem, but as a near-cosmic force who has taken over the role of Aratus' Zeus, and Manilius presents it as a fact that he owes his *animus . . . uiresque . . . ad tanta canenda* (Man. 1. 10) to *Caesar*. By the time we get to Lucan, the emperor (in this case Nero), has become a source of inspiration preferable to Apollo and Dionysus:

> nec, si te pectore uates
> accipio, Cirrhaea uelim secreta mouentem
> sollicitare deum Bacchumque auertere Nysa:
> tu satis ad uires Romana in carmina dandas.
>
> (Luc. 1. 63–6)

---

[11] This appears intuitively obvious to me, though I suppose that someone bent on identifying *Caesar* with the student could argue that there is nothing in the text that actively precludes such an identification, while the fact that both characters are addressed in the second-person singular speaks in favour of it. Still, the appeal to *Caesar* in 1. 7–10 contains no hint that he is supposed to act as the recipient of the speaker's teaching, and none of the numerous addresses to the student implies that he is the emperor. Given that more than 150 lines lie between the address to *Caesar* and the first one to the student and that, as the example of the *Georgics* shows, it is not impossible for a Latin didactic poem to have a dedicatee/patron other than the student (see also immediately below in the text), there is, in my opinion, no good reason why the two characters should be regarded as one and the same (though see below on Augustus' and Tiberius' interest in astrology).

[12] The respective chronology of the three works is unclear. Fantham 1985: 254–6 argues that Germanicus preceded Ovid, but admits (255 and 277 n. 37) that the situation is complicated by the fact that Germanicus might in turn be imitating Manilius (whose poem can, of course, itself not be dated exactly).

(And if I, the singer, receive you in my heart, I would not wish to trouble the god in charge of Delphic mysteries or to summon Bacchus from Nysa: you are enough to give me strength for a Roman song.)

In invoking *Caesar* at the beginning of the *Astronomica*, the poet is thus following what by his time had become a poetic convention. Since the emperor is never addressed again, he does not cause any of the problems the continued presence of the dedicatee Maecenas does in the *Georgics* (see Sect. 4.1, above). As already mentioned, there is no reason to identify him with the anonymous student who suddenly surfaces at 1. 194; however, it should be pointed out that—unlike in the *Georgics*, where it is clear that Maecenas, who is not a farmer, cannot play the role of the student—in Manilius' poem, the emperor could be imagined at least potentially as the recipient of the poet's teaching and instructions. Both Augustus and especially Tiberius were interested in astrology, a discipline whose rise to prominence in Rome was closely connected with the political change from republic to principate, as Tamsyn Barton has argued.[13] The brief appearance of *Caesar* in the *Astronomica* is thus wholly unproblematic (apart from the question of his identity), and Manilius does not present us with any of the difficulties caused by the doubling of addressees in the *Georgics*.

To return to the actual student, it is clear that the poet does not imagine his addressee as one individual person, even though he consistently addresses him in the second-person singular, never plural. Unlike Lucretius' Memmius, the student of the *Astronomica* is not given any particular character traits and does not stand in a personal relationship to the speaker. There are, however, two passages in which the poet is somewhat more explicit as to the identity of his audience. The first is an appeal to the addressee that occurs at the end of the proem to Book 3, immediately after the persona has stressed the difficulty of treating in verse his unwieldy subject matter (on this topic, see Sect. 6.4, below):

> huc ades, o quicumque meis aduertere coeptis
> aurem oculosque potes, ueras et percipe uoces.
>
> (3. 36–7)

(Come here, whoever is able to direct ear and eyes to my undertaking, and hear true utterances.)

---

[13] See Barton 1994*a*: 38–44 and 1994*b*: 33–62; cf. also Domenicucci 1996 generally on the role of astronomy/astrology under Caesar and the early emperors.

The address starts off sounding like an invocation to an assisting deity or patron,[14] but turns out to be an exhortation to the student to pay attention and be rewarded with the truth, of the kind often found in didactic poetry.[15] In the relative clause, the poet defines the student body he is talking to: while the indefinite pronoun *quicumque* appears at first sight to invite everybody to join the speaker's audience (cf. *si quis* in the first line of Ovid's *Ars amatoria*; cf. also the repeated generalizing *quisque* in Man. 3. 393 and 395), the rest of the clause shows that the persona does not believe that everybody is able to do so. The ability to 'direct ear and eyes' to the poet's undertaking is the condition for becoming a student of the Manilian teacher; who, we may ask, are the people that qualify for this role?

The answer, it turns out, has been given already, at the end of the proem to Book 2, where the poet declares:

> haec ego diuino cupiam cum ad sidera flatu
> ferre, *nec in turba nec turbae carmina condam*
> sed solus, uacuo ueluti uectatus in orbe,
> liber agam currus non occursantibus ullis
> nec per iter socios commune regentibus actus,
> *sed caelo noscenda canam*, mirantibus astris
> et gaudente sui mundo per carmina uatis,
> *uel quibus illa sacros non inuidere meatus*
> *notitiamque sui, minima est quae turba per orbem.*
>
> . . . .
> *hoc quoque fatorum est, legem perdiscere fati.*
>
> (2. 136–44 and 149)

(Since I desire to carry these things to the stars with inspired breath, I shall compose my songs neither in the crowd nor for the crowd; but alone—carried, as it were, in an empty orbit[16]—I shall freely drive my chariot with

---

[14] The verse-initial *huc ades* recalls *tuque ades* in Verg. *G.* 2. 39, the poet's appeal to Maecenas for help (the address of the student with *o* is likewise reminiscent of the Vergilian double use of *o* when speaking to Maecenas in the same passage, Verg. *G.* 2. 40); *coepta* is also typically used in the context of asking for assistance with a poetic enterprise (see Verg. *G.* 1. 40, *audacibus adnue coeptis*; Ov. *Met.* 1. 2–3, . . . *di, coeptis* . . . | *adspirate meis* . . .).

[15] Note, though, that in this case, *ueras* . . . *uoces* (3. 37) is not simply the teacher's conventional claim to truth, but makes a contrast to *dulcia carmina* in the next line: the poet can offer truth, but not sweetness (on this passage, see further Sect. 6.4, below).

[16] Unlike Housman 1903–30, who is followed by Goold, I take *ueluti* solely with the participial phrase *uacuo . . . uectatus in orbe* (138), not with the entire clause *liber agam* . . . . Thus, *agam* (an emendation by Scaliger, which must be correct; cf. Goold's apparatus for the corrupt state of the text at this point) is in my opinion a future not a present subjunctive, as

no one meeting me or steering a friendly course along the same route; and I shall sing for the sky to hear, with the stars marvelling and heaven taking joy in the songs of its poet, or for those whom they have not begrudged knowledge of the sacred motions and of themselves, which is the smallest crowd on earth.... This too is fated: to learn the law of fate.)

I shall return to other aspects of this central passage, while for the moment concentrating on those parts that I have highlighted here. The poet states that he is composing his songs 'neither in the crowd nor for the crowd' (2. 137); instead, he is singing for the sky itself, to the approval of the stars and the entire cosmos (2. 141–2), as well as for 'those whom they (*illa*, sc. *astra et mundus*) have not begrudged knowledge of the sacred motions[17] and of themselves', a group that is described as a *minima turba*. The speaker's audience is thus rather exclusive, restricted to the happy few able to follow the teacher's exposition of the truth, a small group that has this ability because it has been favoured by the cosmos, that is, by fate itself. As the poet puts it pithily at the very end of our passage, *hoc quoque fatorum est, legem perdiscere fati*.

The restrictive elitism expressed by the teacher makes perfect sense in its context, fitting in with the poet's solitary Callimachean chariot ride on the untrodden paths of heaven (2. 138–40; on the use of the chariot metaphor in the *Astronomica*, see Sect. 6.3, below), as well as with the language of religious initiation he uses (the speaker is the *uates* of the cosmos, 2. 142; only a small group is allowed knowledge of the divine, 2. 143–4).[18] However, it must be noted that it is strangely contradictory to what the speaker says elsewhere. On numerous occasions, the poet of the *Astronomica* stresses that according to the divine order of the universe, man (and we have to understand: every man) is given the ability to understand the workings of the cosmos and that god—and that is, in Manilius' Stoic world, the *mundus* (see 1. 483–5)—reveals himself to the human mind in general. This is the central thought of the grand finale of Book 4

Housman would have it: it seems to me highly unlikely that Manilius, who elsewehere presents himself as actually traversing the sky (see Sect. 6.3, below), would here use the image of the chariot ride as a mere comparison.

[17] On the meaning of *sacros . . . meatus* (2. 143), see n. 74, below.

[18] Baldini Moscadi 1986: 15 fittingly describes the relationship between the poet and his audience envisioned here as that 'fra l'operatore del sacro, ispirato dalla divinità, e la *minima turba* degli iniziati al mistero del dio'. Note incidentally that, as Asper 1997: 72–94 has shown, the metaphor of the untrodden path in Callimachus is itself influenced by the imagery of the mysteries.

(866–935), where the poet argues that man is a microcosm and thus born to understand the macrocosm:

> quid mirum, noscere mundum
> si possunt homines, quibus est et mundus in ipsis
> exemplumque dei quisque est in imagine parua?
> an cuiquam genitos, nisi caelo, credere fas est
> esse homines?
>
> (4. 893–7)

(What wonder if men are able to understand the cosmos since they have a cosmos in themselves and each is a miniature likeness of the god? Or is it right to believe that men come from anywhere other than heaven?)

However, we find the same idea already in the proem to Book 2:

> quis dubitet post haec hominem coniungere caelo
> ⟨cui, cupiens terras ad sidera surgere, munus⟩[19]
> eximium natura dedit linguamque capaxque
> ingenium uolucremque animum, quem denique in unum
> descendit deus atque habitat seque ipse requirit?
>
> (2. 105–8)

(After this, who would hesitate to connect man with the heavens, man, to whom nature, desiring that earth rise to the stars, has given outstanding gifts, speech and an understanding intelligence and a swift mind, and, finally, into whom alone god descends and makes his dwelling place and searches for himself?)

This optimistic belief that man, by virtue of being human, is *meant* to enquire into and ultimately understand the divine laws of the universe (on which see also Sect. 6.2, below) jars with the claim, voiced less than forty lines later, that it is only a *minima turba* that is chosen to gain *notitia* of the *mundus*.[20]

---

[19] This supplement nicely exemplifies Goold's creative approach to the many textual problems in Manilius. Housman 1903–30 simply states that a line containing *cui* must have been lost. More conservative editors try to avoid a lacuna by changing *eximium* in 106, e.g., Garrod 1911 (*consilium*), Liuzzi 1991–7, following earlier scholars (*eximiam* [sc. *linguam*]), and Flores in Feraboli, Flores, and Scarcia 1996–2001 (*cui uires*). I personally like Bentley's fanciful *cui xenium*, which, however, has not found favour with modern editors.

[20] As Vallauri 1954: 147–51 points out, this same contradiction is found in the Hermetic Corpus, a body of philosophical treatises whose main tenets, as Vallauri and others have argued, are extremely close to the world-view of Manilius. However, at least some Hermetic thinkers recognized the problem and attempted to deal with it; thus, e.g., the author of *CH* 4 maintains that 'God shared reason [λόγος] among all people . . . but not mind [νοῦς]' (*CH* 4. 3; trans. Copenhaver 1992), which enables him to claim that only those few people gifted with 'mind' are actually capable of attaining the highest form of knowledge.

This self-contradiction (which one might attempt to explain away one way or another) is part of a general tension in the *Astronomica* between the speaker's rigid determinism and his role as a teacher, as Matt Neuburg has demonstrated. Neuburg 1993: 257–76 examines in detail the persona's addresses to the student and concludes that 'He goes out of his way to encourage and foster his student's mental agility, observational powers, and deliberate application, through the manner in which he addresses and maintains contact with the student' (1993: 258). It should be pointed out that Neuburg, who looks only at Manilius, has a tendency to regard the teacher's interaction with the student in the *Astronomica* as though it were unique; in fact, the kinds of addresses we find in Manilius (Neuburg mentions commands, exhortations not to be surprised, exhortations to mental alertness, appeals to observation, and transitions to a new topic) are typical of didactic poetry in general and similar especially to the addresses in Lucretius, Manilius' main literary model.[21] However, Neuburg is right to stress that the speaker of the *Astronomica* is a very encouraging teacher, who keeps telling his student that with the necessary effort, he will succeed—quite unlike the Lucretian speaker, who, as we have seen, continually anticipates Memmius' failure. Twice, he answers an objection of the student reported in direct speech (4. 387–9 and 869–72[22]); interestingly, unlike the reported objections in Lucretius (1. 803–8, 897–900), these are not contradictions on individual points, but general expressions of discouragement and scepticism. In both cases, the speaker encourages his addressee to persevere, in the first with a brief *exhortatio*, in the second with the extended microcosm–macrocosm argument mentioned above. His concern for the student's progress is apparent also from the reflection on his didactic method in 2. 750–87, where the teacher

[21] I cannot believe Neuburg's hypothesis that the Manilian persona's method of teaching is informed by Stoic pedagogy. The stress on mental alertness on the one hand and sense perception on the other cannot be regarded as exclusively Stoic and can be paralleled, e.g., in the wholly un-Stoic *De rerum natura*. Neuburg's wish to see Manilius as a specifically Stoic teacher is comparable to the claim of Schrijvers 1970 that the didactic method of Lucretius is intrinsically Epicurean, a view I argue against in Sect. 3.1. On Manilius' agonistic relationship to Lucretius, see more below, esp. Sect. 6.4.

[22] In the second passage, the speech is introduced by third-person *inquit* (or rather, this is Bentley's convincing reconstruction; the transmitted text is corrupt at this point); this use of an anonymous objector (who must, however, have been part of the poet's audience so far, i.e., must be [one of] his student[s]) is paralleled, e.g., in Horace's *Satires* (cf. Housman 1903–30 *ad loc.*).

explains—and illustrates with two similes, that of the children who learn to read and write (2. 755–64) and that of the building of a city (2. 772–83)—why he is first supplying the student with raw facts, whose meaning and connection will become clear only later.

As Neuburg 1993: 276–82 notes, this pedagogic optimism on the part of the speaker is not wholly reconcilable with his belief, expressed especially in the proem to Book 4, that everything is determined by fate. As we have already seen, the speaker to a certain extent contradicts himself when he claims both that every human being has been given the ability to understand the *mundus* and that it is only a *minima turba* that has been granted such knowledge. In addition, we may wonder what role didacticism can play if learning is already predestined. In other words, does the student learn because he is taught by the Manilian teacher or does he learn because he is fated to learn? And finally, what is the point of finding out about the workings of fate if the whole point is that fate is altogether unchangeable?

These problems, which boil down to the contrast between determinism and free will, are to a certain extent inherent in Manilius' subject matter[23] and philosophical bent, as Neuburg 1993: 280–1 points out. However, both astrology and Stoicism could in fact have furnished the poet with arguments to smooth over these contradictions. Thus, he might have taken the point of view that not every detail of human life is predestined by the stars and that there remains some leeway for individual intervention.[24] Or if he wished to retain his 'strong' form of determinism (as expressed in the proem to Book 4), he might at least have contended that knowledge of fate, unalterable though it may be, gives us the peace of mind necessary to accept it.[25] The Manilian persona, however, does not do anything of the kind, allowing his text to be, at least implicitly, self-contradictory.

Neuburg 1993: 281–2 believes that Manilius' failure or refusal to engage with the implications of the determinism he proposes can be explained by the fact that his aim is, not to present a philosophical system, but to reveal what amounts to a kind of religion: 'He does

---

[23] See Barton 1994*a*: 52–7 on how astrology was typically criticized for the fatalism it entailed.

[24] An attitude espoused, among others, by Ptolemy; see the quote in Neuburg 1993: 280 n. 71, as well as Long 1982: 178–83.

[25] As examples for this view Neuburg 1993: 281 quotes Seneca's famous *ducunt uolentem fata, nolentem trahunt* (*Ep.* 107. 11) and Cicero's *ut uideret interitum, non ut caueret* (*Div.* 1. 119).

not want to raise details, metaphysical or ethical, about the nature of inevitability, because this might detract from the impression he wants to give, of the stars' absolute power, on which (for him) the reality and importance of astrology is based; he wants his reader, not to question or mitigate the absolute control of everything by the stars, but to worship it' (1993: 281). I think this is a fair assessment; however, it cannot quite explain the contradiction between the teacher's elitism (*minima turba* of students), on the one hand, and his claim to universal appeal (man as such is meant to understand the universe), on the other. It seems to me rather that Manilius is here (and, as I shall show, also elsewhere) operating according to a kind of have-one's-cake-and-eat-it-too principle. Put differently, the poet behaves not like a philosopher, who wishes to present a coherent explanation of the universe, but like a student of rhetoric, who is happy to draw arguments from different backgrounds, with an eye not to internal coherence, but to the maximal effect at each individual moment. He finds a number of different discourses ready for him to use (Callimachean elitism and claim to novelty; the restrictive rhetoric of mystical initiation; the belief that fate rules the world; the microcosm–macrocosm argument; and the optimism and encouraging attitude of the pedagogue), and he wants to use them all, exploit the potential of every single one of them, without regard to the contradictions that might arise from such a procedure. Thus, when the poet in 2. 138–42 rejoices in his solitary heavenly chariot ride and extends this elitist sentiment to his students with the help of the language of initiation (2. 143–4), we have to understand that while working on this motif, he has temporarily suspended his earlier theme of man's intrinsic ability to understand the universe, which, however, he will take up again to great effect later.

To view the poet as a kind of composer who works with a number of often traditional themes and motifs, not all of equal importance and not all strictly logically compatible, which he introduces at different points in his work, repeats, combines, and sometimes simply juxtaposes without an explanation—this analogy is, I believe, useful in understanding the rhetoric of the Manilian persona. In the following, I shall explore a few more of the themes of the *Astronomica*; I shall, however, close this section with the brief mention of one motif that the poet does not employ. Unlike his Lucretian model, the speaker of Manilius' poem never offers any explicit reflection on why he uses poetry as a medium for his teaching. There is no equivalent of the honeyed-cup simile, and scholars (e.g., Reeh 1973: 18–19, 169 and n. 1, 213; differently and correctly Dams 1970: 33) who claim that in Manilius, too, poetry has the function to sweeten and embellish the difficult subject matter, simply interpolate such an interpretation from Lucretius.[26] As a matter of fact, while, as we shall see, the speaker of the *Astronomica* clearly presents himself as a poet and dwells extensively on his status, the question of the relationship between *carmen* and *res* in Manilius turns out to be anything but simple.

6.2. *VATES MUNDI*

If the speaker of the *Astronomica* is comparatively sparing with comments on his role as a teacher, he makes up for it with extensive reflections on his activity as a poet. The poem clearly exhibits poetic self-consciousness, my third criterion for didactic poetry; as mentioned above, the self-reflexive *carmine* is the very first word of the work, and *carmen* is used repeatedly throughout the poem for the poet's own song (1. 1, 12, 22, 114, 118, 810; 2. 137, 142, 754, 765, 928; 3. 4, 35, 38, 270; 4. 430, 436). The persona refers to his own activity with *canere* (1. 10, 22, 120, 256; 2. 767, 965; 3. 93, 164, 586; 5. 27) and calls himself a *uates* (1. 23; 2. 142; 3. 41; 4. 121).

Poetic simultaneity, the fourth criterion for didactic poetry, likewise plays a major role in the *Astronomica*. In 1. 4, the speaker uses the verb *aggredior* to indicate that he is 'approaching' his subject matter 'now', and at the end of the proem to Book 1, the sense of a beginning is especially strong:

> hoc mihi surgit opus non ullis ante sacratum
> carminibus. faueat magno fortuna labori,
> annosa et molli contingat uita senecta,
> ut possim rerum tantas emergere moles
> magnaque cum paruis simili percurrere cura.
>
> (1. 113–17)

(This task rises before me, never before hallowed by songs. May fortune favour my great labour and may a long life with gentle old age be granted

---

[26] The fact that the poet on occasion worries about not being able to present his difficult subject matter in a 'sweet' or pleasing form (the relevant passages are discussed in Sect. 6.4, below) merely shows that aesthetic appeal is important to him, not that it has a pedagogic function.

to me, in order that I be able to surmount the great mass of my subject matter and run through topics large and small with similar care.)

The speaker's wish to 'run through' (*percurrere*, 1. 117) everything is, of course, an instance of the journey motif typically associated with poetic simultaneity.[27] In Manilius, this metaphor, especially the idea that the poet is literally travelling through the universe he describes, plays such a large role that I shall treat it separately in the next section; however, I shall already now take a look at one passage that offers a particularly lively case of poetic simultaneity, the opening of Book 5:

> hic alius finisset iter signisque relatis
> quis aduersa meant stellarum numina quinque
> quadriiugis et Phoebus equis et Delia bigis
> non ultra struxisset opus, caeloque rediret
> 5   ac per descensum medios percurreret ignes
> Saturni, Iouis et Martis Solisque, sub illis
> post Venerem et Maia natum te, Luna, uagantem.
> me properare etiam mundus iubet omnia circum
> sidera uectatum toto decurrere caelo,
> 10   cum semel aetherios ausus conscendere currus
> summum contigerim sua per fastigia culmen.
>
> (5. 1–11)

(At this point, another one would have ended his journey and—having treated the signs contrary to which move the five stellar deities and Phoebus with his team of four and Delia with her team of two—he would not have constructed his work further, but would return from the sky, and, on the way down, move through the fires in the middle: Saturn, Jupiter, Mars, and the Sun, and below them, after Venus and the son of Maia, you, wandering Moon. Me the cosmos additionally orders hurriedly to drive around all the stars and make my descent via the entire firmament—since, having once dared to mount the heavenly chariot, I have reached the highest point of the sphere.)

The speaker declares that 'at this point' (*hic*, 5. 1), another poet would have stopped and descended from the heavens via the seven planets (5. 4–7). In other words, it would have been possible and not unreasonable to bring the poem to an end here, or at least after first

---

[27] The idea of the poet's movement in space is implicit already in *emergere* (1. 116), which must mean something like 'surmount, get clear of, emerge from' (for the unusual transitive use, see *OLD* s.v. 'emergo' 5a). Lines 116–17 present thus, strictly speaking, a ὕστερον πρότερον: the speaker must first *percurrere* his material before he can *emergere* from it.

having treated the planets 'on the way down' (*per descensum*, 5. 5). However, this option is not open to the poet since the universe 'orders' him (*iubet*, 5. 8) instead 'hurriedly to drive around all the stars and make [his] descent via the entire firmament', that is, as it turns out, to treat the so-called *paranatellonta*, the risings of extra-zodiacal constellations and their influence. I believe that we are supposed to imagine the order of the *mundus* as being issued 'right now', in the typical illusion of poetic simultaneity: the poet is, as it were, about to descend from the heavens and finish his song, as an *alius* would do, but then he receives the command to go on and sing more about the fixed stars.[28] The scene becomes even more vivid in the lines that follow (5. 12–26), where the southern constellations 'call' the poet from the one side (*hinc uocat Orion* . . . , 5. 12) and the northern ones from the other (*illinc per geminas Anguis qui labitur Arctos*, 5. 19) and he heeds their call.[29]

In those passages where the speaker reflects most extensively on his poetics (especially the proems to Books 1–3), one theme emerges that appears to be of special importance to him: his originality as a poet. Drawing heavily on Lucretius' and Vergil's use of the *primus* motif (Liuzzi 1991–7 lists many parallels; cf. also Lühr 1969: 31–43), the Manilian persona again and again stresses the novelty of his enterprise, beginning with the very first sentence of the poem:

> aggredior primusque nouis Helicona mouere
> cantibus et uiridi nutantis uertice siluas
> hospita sacra ferens nulli memorata priorum.
>
> (1. 4–6)

(And I undertake to be the first to move with new songs Helicon and the woods that nod with green treetops, bringing sacred offerings from a foreign land, unmentioned by any predecessor.)

At the end of the first proem, as we have already seen, he describes the work about to begin as *opus non ullis ante sacratum* | *carminibus* (1. 113–14).

Since, as we have had occasion to observe in the previous chapters, it is standard practice in Latin poetry to claim originality for one's work, it is not remarkable that Manilius would use the

---

[28] See Romano 1979: 66–8, who compares the Ovidian persona of the *Ars amatoria*, who, at the end of Book 2/beginning of Book 3, is about to finish his poem but receives the order to continue with a book for the *puellae*.

[29] Cf. Verg. *G*. 3. 43, *uocat ingenti clamore Cithaeron* (see Hübner 1984: 246–7).

same topos, given also that the *Astronomica* is indeed (as far as we know) the first Latin didactic poem on astrology.[30] However, this poet is not content with having announced the novelty of his enterprise once and for all; the topic is of special concern to him, and one reason for this is obviously that he feels like a latecomer in the field of poetry (see Lühr 1969: 40), a theme that he develops at great length in the proems to Books 2 and 3.[31] Book 2 starts with an extended history of hexameter poetry, beginning with Homer. The Greek poet's genius is compared to a mighty river, which was divided into channels by his later emulators:

> ... cuiusque ex ore profusos
> omnis posteritas latices in carmina duxit
> amnemque in tenuis ausa est deducere riuos
> unius fecunda bonis.
>
> (2. 8–11)

(... from whose mouth all posterity drew ample water for their songs and dared to channel the river into slender streams, fertile because of one man's bounty.)[32]

After a survey of this 'derivative' poetry (2. 11–24: Hesiod; 25–38: astronomical poems (Aratus and *Aratea*?); 39–42: bucolic poetry (Theocritus?); 43–5: poetry on birds, animals, poisonous snakes, and potent herbs (Hellenistic didactic poetry, e.g., Nicander?); 46–8: *katabaseis* (?)), the poet concludes pessimistically:

> omne genus rerum doctae cecinere sorores,
> omnis ad accessus Heliconos semita trita est,
> et iam confusi manant de fontibus amnes
> nec capiunt haustum turbamque ad nota ruentem.
>
> (2. 49–52)

---

[30] The Latin versions of Aratus by Cicero, Varro of Atax, Ovid, and Germanicus are concerned with astronomy rather than astrology. Note that since Manilius does not have a Greek poetic model either, he cannot present himself in the familiar role of the Latin poet who imitates a supreme Greek predecessor, as Vergil and (as I have argued) Lucretius had done; the poet mentions, though, that his sources are foreign, i.e., Greek when he describes himself as *hospita sacra ferens* (1. 6; cf. also 2. 693–4, 829–30, and 3. 40–2, where the speaker apologizes for using Greek terminology).

[31] For the following discussion, cf. esp. Baldini Moscadi 1986.

[32] The image—though not in this form attested in Callimachus (see Asper 1997: 123–5, with rich bibliography)—is 'Callimachean' (for my use of this term, see Ch. 4 n. 24); note also Manilius' use of such buzzwords as *tenuis* and *deducere* (on *deducere* in the *Astronomica*, see also n. 49, below). Dams 1970: 15–37 provides a useful, though somewhat one-sided, discussion of the Callimachean aspects of Manilius' poetics (see esp. 20–9 on the proem to Book 2).

(Every kind of theme the learned sisters have sung, every path that leads to Helicon has been trodden, and the streams flow muddied from the springs and cannot sustain the drinkers and the crowd that rushes toward the well known.)

The scene described is a Callimachean's nightmare (trodden paths, dirty rivers, crowds), and given the generalizing diction of the passage (*omne... omnis...*, 2. 49–50), one might well think that a poet who arrives at this stage of the game simply has no chance of producing anything original. However, the Manilian persona is not one to give up easily, and like his predecessors, he goes in search of some still untouched meadow:

> integra quaeramus rorantis prata per herbas
> undamque occultis meditantem murmur in antris,
> quam neque durato gustarint ore uolucres,
> ipse nec aetherio Phoebus libauerit igni.
>
> (2. 53–6)

(Let us seek untouched meadows with dewy grass and water intent on murmuring in hidden caves, which neither birds have tasted with hard beak nor Phoebus drunk with heavenly fire.)

And apparently he finds what he is looking for, witness his immediately following proud claim:

> nostra loquar, nulli uatum debebimus ora[33],
> nec furtum sed opus ueniet, soloque uolamus
> in caelum curru, propria rate pellimus undas.
>
> (2. 57–9)

(I shall speak my own words, I shall owe my utterances to none of the poets; not a theft is coming but my own work; and I fly into heaven alone in my chariot and push through the waves with my own ship.)

The poet's absolute originality, as expressed in these lines, stands out by contrast to the preceding depressing description of all the epigones and their unsuccessful efforts, and, of course, the speaker has cleverly constructed the entire proem so far as to culminate in this effective declaration. Still, the proem is not even half over at this point, and the poet has more and different things to say about the novelty of his work. However, before we come to this, the most

---

[33] Goold and Housman print *orsa*, an emendation by Dulcinius, which seems unnecessary to me (see Feraboli, Flores, and Scarcia 1996–2001 *ad loc.*).

important, aspect of Manilian poetics, let us briefly look at the proem to Book 3, another passage where the speaker reflects on the poetic tradition that has preceded him.

The book opens with the *Astronomica*'s only invocation to the Muses:

> in noua surgentem maioraque uiribus ausum
> nec per inaccessos metuentem uadere saltus
> ducite, Pierides. uestros extendere fines
> conor et ignotos in carmina ducere census.
>
> (3. 1–4)[34]

(Muses, lead me who rise to new themes and dare more than I have strength for and fear not to walk through inaccessible glades. I am trying to extend your territory and to make unknown riches a topic for my song.)

These lines, replete with allusions to Lucretius, Vergil, and Ovid (see Liuzzi 1991–7 *ad loc.* and note in addition the parallel to Lucr. 1. 926–7), stress again the novelty of the poet's work, and it seems to follow logically that the speaker then launches into an extended *recusatio*, listing numerous well-known poetic subjects, from the gigantomachy to the 'origin of the Roman people', that he is not going to treat. The reader's first assumption is that this is just another instance of the *omnia iam uulgata* motif employed to such lengths in the proem to Book 2 and, indeed, the topics enumerated appear hackneyed enough.[35] However, the poet has a surprise in store for us. As he explains in 3. 26–30, the reason why he is not dealing with these traditional subjects is not because they are too *common*, but because they are too *easy*:

> facile est uentis dare uela secundis
> fecundumque solum uarias agitare per artes

---

[34] It should be pointed out that the last line (which I have taken over without changes from Goold's text) is heavily reconstructed, with Housman's *ignotos* for *(in)dignos* and Unger's *census* for *cantus*.

[35] There is another aspect that many of the subjects listed have in common and that puts them in strong contrast to the poet's own topic. From the gigantomachy (3. 5–6) to Medea and her magic (9–13) to the Theban stories (15–16, Seven against Thebes; 17, Oedipus) to Thyestes (18–19) to Xerxes' bridging the Hellespont and sailing through Mount Athos (19–21), the stories mentioned involve perverse and nefarious reversals of the order of nature (even those that do not are presented in a paradoxical manner, e.g., the deeds of Alexander: *non regis magni spatio maiore canenda,* | *quam sunt acta loquar,* 22–3). By contrast, the poet of the *Astronomica* treats the harmonious and orderly working of the universe (see also Sect. 6.4, below, on Manilius' use of such words as *ordo*), and his work is thus preferable from a philosophical point of view as well.

> auroque atque ebori decus addere, cum rudis ipsa
> materies niteat. speciosis condere rebus
> carmina uulgatum est, opus et componere simplex.

(It is easy to set sail in favourable winds, to work fertile soil with various arts, and to add splendour to gold and ivory, where the raw material itself is shining. It is trite to compose a song about an attractive topic and create a straightforward work.)

This statement leads to a *captatio benevolentiae* (3. 31–42) in which the speaker stresses the difficulty of putting into verse his own unwieldy subject matter and warns the addressee, *nec dulcia carmina quaeras* (3. 38). I shall come back to this passage in Section 6.4; for the moment let us return to where we left the poet in the proem to Book 2.

As we have seen, at the beginning of Book 2, the speaker presents a survey of literary history (2. 1–48), followed by the statement that all topics have already been treated (2. 49–52), which then leads to the poet's own declaration of absolute originality (2. 53–9). So far, the discourse is solely about poetry and about the possibility of creating something new and unheard of. The topic is, by the time Manilius is writing, wholly conventional, and so is the language with its many Callimachean metaphors. Thus, when the poet goes on his quest for *integra . . . prata* and then duly announces that his work is indeed entirely his own (*nostra loquar*, 2. 57), lending sublimity to his claim with the traditional chariot and ship metaphors (2. 58–9), we may well feel that he is simply following a script and that the excessive stress on his originality is really due to the inferiority complex of the latecomer, who has to compete against all of literary history. However, if we think that the Manilian persona is just the *n*th poet going over possible poetic subjects, *omnia iam uulgata*, and finally carving out a little niche for himself in some previously neglected corner, we are wrong. As it turns out, there is something about this poet that makes him different from everybody else.

In the proem to Book 2, the speaker's claim to originality is followed by an explanation, *namque canam . . .* (2. 60). This might appear completely straightforward, as though the poet were now proving that his topic is indeed new. However, the Manilian persona's description of the Stoic cosmos (2. 60–135) goes well beyond such a purpose.[36] The poet begins by describing how the

[36] For the Stoic nature of Manilius' description of the universe here and elsewhere, see Lapidge 1989: 1393–7; the same author provides a useful summary of Stoic cosmology on 1381–5.

universe is permeated and governed by divine *ratio* (2. 60–81) and how life on earth is influenced by the heavenly bodies (2. 82–104). He then proceeds to argue, in a passage whose beginning (2. 105–8) I discussed already in Section 6.1, that man by his nature is pre-destined to gain knowledge of the *mundus*, that god himself wishes to enter into a relationship with the human mind, as seen in these lines:

115   quis caelum posset nisi caeli munere nosse,
      et reperire deum, nisi qui pars ipse deorum est?
      quisue hanc conuexi molem sine fine patentis
      signorumque choros ac mundi flammea tecta,
      aeternum et stellis aduersus sidera bellum
120   [ac terras caeloque fretum subiecta utrisque]
      cernere et angusto sub pectore claudere posset,
      ni sanctos animis oculos natura dedisset
      cognatamque sibi mentem uertisset ad ipsam
      et tantum dictasset opus, caeloque ueniret
125   quod uocat in caelum sacra ad commercia rerum?

(2. 115–25)

(Who would be able to understand the cosmos unless through the gift of the cosmos or to find god unless he had a place among the gods himself? Or who could see and encompass in his narrow chest the mass of the infinitely vaulted sphere, the dances of the stars, the flaming roofs of the universe, and the eternal war of planets against constellations, [and the land and sea beneath the sky and what is beneath both,] unless nature had given sacred eyes to the soul and turned the cognate mind toward herself and dictated such a great work, and unless there came from heaven something to call us into heaven for a sacred exchange of things?)

The poet is speaking about the ability and vocation of mankind in general. However, it is clear that he is also to a certain extent speaking about himself: he is composing a work about the universe because the universe itself invites him to understand its workings, nature turns his 'mind toward herself' (2. 123), the sky calls him into the sky for a 'sacred exchange' (125) and 'dictates such a great work' (124). While the phrase *tantum dictasset opus* can be taken in a number of senses,[37] one way of understanding it is that the universe—the

---

[37] Garrod 1911 translates '[nature] unfolding to him [man] all her mighty works', while Goold 1992 understands the phrase as a reference to the establishment of the science of astrology ('had prescribed so great a science'). The two Italian editions are rather ambiguous in their translations, 'l'avesse indirizzata verso una sì grande opera' (Liuzzi 1991–7) and

'all' that the poet refers to interchangeably with *natura, deus, caelum, mundus,* and *ratio*—itself wishes the persona to compose ('dictates' to him) his cosmological poem. It is not that the poet has chosen his topic out of many and for the sole, purely literary, reason that it has not been treated before. On the contrary, it is the topic that has literally chosen the poet: he sings about the cosmos because it is the wish of the cosmos or, put differently, of fate, that he should do so.

The sense that the speaker has been elected, as it were, poet of the universe becomes even clearer at the end of the proem, where, in a passage quoted in Section 6.1 (2. 136–44), the speaker describes himself as inspired by *diuino . . . flatu* (2. 136) and as singing to an audience that consists of the heavens themselves:

> sed caelo noscenda canam, mirantibus astris
> et gaudente sui mundo per carmina uatis.
>
> (2. 141–2)

(I shall sing for the sky to hear, with the stars marvelling and heaven taking joy in the songs of its poet.)

However, the idea that the poet is acting as *uates mundi* recurs throughout the poem, being expressed as early as 1. 11–12:

> iam propiusque fauet mundus scrutantibus ipsum
> et cupit aetherios per carmina pandere census.

(Now the universe is more favourably inclined to those researching it and desires to reveal its heavenly riches by means of song.)

Here, too, we find both the motif that the divine cosmos is generally favourably disposed toward those who strive to understand it and the notion that the *mundus* is interested specifically in revealing itself to the poet and thus to become song.[38]

'avesse dettato una così gran costruzione' (Feraboli, Flores, and Scarcia 1996–2001). On the different meanings of *opus* in the *Astronomica*, see also n. 86, below.

[38] The word *iam* (1. 11) adds a special vividness to the scene and helps constitute poetic simultaneity: 'now', at this very moment as the poet starts out on his song, the *mundus* favours his enterprise. There is a political dimension to this sense of καιρός: the poet can realize his project 'now' only because this is a time of peace (*hoc sub pace uacat tantum*, 1. 13; the sentiment is similar to that of Lucr. 1. 29–43), a situation for which, one assumes, the speaker implicitly gives credit to the emperor just mentioned (1. 7–10; cf. Germ. *Arat.* 5–16, where the peace established by the emperor is explicitly said to enable the poet's work). At the same time, the propitious moment described by the poet surely has to be taken in an astrological sense: the *mundus* is favourable 'now' in the sense that the present alignment of the stars bodes well for the poet's undertaking.

The speaker thus presents himself as a *uates*, both a poet and a prophet, who receives his inspiration from god, that is, from his subject matter, the universe itself.[39] His calling is to act as a medium for the cosmos, which wishes to reveal itself to mankind in the medium of verse; as the poet avows, in composing his poem, he is simply following the 'commands' of the *mundus*.[40] Being chosen for this task, which has never been attempted before, puts the poet in an outstanding position and guarantees the absolute novelty of his work, a work that is not only an original piece of poetry, but a fulfilment of man's highest faculties and, as a revelation of fate, obviously of crucial importance to everyone.[41]

To come back to the *primus* motif, we may now conclude that the Manilian speaker employs this topos only in order ultimately to transcend it. As it turns out, he is not really a poet who has arrived too late and is now desperately trying to come up with an original topic; rather, his divine mission places him on a level radically different from that of all other poets, puts him, as it were, outside the competition.[42] By tacitly altering the rules, he has beaten his predecessors at their own game: it is one thing to compose a poem that is new; to compose one that is fated is quite another. We may compare the wholly different approach to the question of poetic novelty exhibited by the speaker of the *Georgics*, who at the beginning of Book 3 casually goes through a series of 'used' topics while

---

[39] See Reeh 1973: 11–12, 14–15, 213; Effe 1977: 108–9; Flores 1982: 121–3; Schrijvers 1983: 144–5; and Neuburg 1993: 267–8. On Manilius as a *uates* (a designation used four times for the speaker; note that he never calls himself *poeta*), see Newman 1967: 115–22.

[40] See 4. 436–7 (*sed mihi per carmen fatalia iura ferenti | et sacros caeli motus ad iussa loquendum est*) and 5. 8 (*mundus iubet*). Note that in these instances, the Manilian speaker presents the *mundus* the way earlier poets had presented their patrons, whose 'orders' they claimed to be following (see Sect. 4.1, above, on Maecenas' *haud mollia iussa* in the *Georgics*). On the way in which the poet of the *Astronomica* on occasion uses the 'orders' of the cosmos as a kind of excuse for his artistic shortcomings, see Sect. 6.4, below.

[41] The poet's 'fatalistic' view of his own activity might be summarized neatly with his own sententious line 4. 118, *hoc quoque fatale est, sic ipsum expendere fatum*, which Goold 1992 translates, 'This, too, is sanctioned by fate, that I should thus expound the rule of fate'. Goold here follows the interpretation of Housman 1903–30 *ad loc.* (as does Liuzzi 1991–7), which makes the verse into a nice counterpart to 2. 149, *hoc quoque fatorum est, legem perdiscere fati*. However, I wonder with Neuburg 1993: 268 n. 50 whether in its context (a discussion not of poetics, but of determinism, specifically of why we ought to hate criminals despite the fact that their evil deeds are due to fate) the line is not more naturally understood as 'It is part of fate that one must thus pay for [a crime which is] fate itself' (thus Neuburg).

[42] See Baldini Moscadi 1986: 5, who writes, 'Manilio è cosciente di accingersi ad un'opera che non vuol essere, nel suo proposito, solo creazione poetica, ma assume i caratteri di una vera rivelazione nel senso religioso del termine'.

searching for an original subject, a 'path' to 'lift himself from the ground', and who, as we have seen in Section 4.2, throughout the poem reflects on possible other works that he might undertake. This insistence on the poet's freedom of choice is in stark contrast to the deterministic poetics of the *Astronomica*; it is also, as I pointed out in Chapter 4, wholly different from the attitude of the Lucretian speaker, whose dedication to his subject matter is such that he could never claim to have chosen it out of many just because of its novelty. Note, though, that the persona of the *De rerum natura*—who never reflects on his choice of topic—could not possibly cast himself in the sublime role of the prophet of the divine universe the way the Manilian speaker does: the Epicurean world, governed by blind chance, does not afford its poet similar possibilities for self-aggrandizement. I shall discuss below other instances in the *Astronomica* where his Stoic beliefs enable the Manilian persona to develop further certain ideas found in rudimentary form already in Lucretius, who, however, because of his Epicurean world-view is unable to exploit them to maximum effect.

The repeated claim of the persona that it is his fate to sing about the fateful workings of the universe provides another example of the way in which the speaker of the *Astronomica* manipulates the themes and motifs of his work. For, as we have seen, the idea of the poet's 'being chosen' is but one variation, albeit a crucially important one, of the more general notion of the cosmos's voluntary self-revelation.[43] This central theme is used throughout the poem in a number of different ways: depending on his argumentative strategy at the individual moment, the poet either maintains that everybody is by nature capable of gaining knowledge about the divine universe (the macrocosm–microcosm argument, see esp. 2. 105–25; 4. 866–935, both discussed above) or—a position not necessarily wholly reconcilable with the first—he claims that it is specifically certain people who are granted such a privilege. These include, at various points in the text, the poet himself (who in addition to learning the workings of the cosmos is also called upon to make them into song) and the *minima turba* of his students, as well as the oriental kings (1. 40–5) and priests (1. 46–50) to whom nature first 'unlocked herself' (*natura . . . seque ipsa reclusit*, 1. 40). In more general terms, whether a person is meant to become knowledgeable in astronomy/astrology

---

[43] This theme is one that Manilius clearly shares with the *Corpus Hermeticum*; see Vallauri 1954: 142–51.

may simply depend on his or her sign of the zodiac. In particular, those born under Gemini have a strong tendency toward both the study of the skies and ... poetry:

>   mollius e Geminis studium est et mitior aetas
>   per uarios cantus modulataque uocibus ora
>   et gracilis calamos et neruis insita uerba
> 155   ingenitumque sonum: labor est etiam ipse uoluptas.
>   arma procul lituosque uolunt tristemque senectam,
>   otia et aeternam peragunt in amore iuuentam.
>   inueniunt et in astra uias numerisque modisque
>   consummant orbem postque ipsos sidera linquunt:
> 160   natura ingenio minor est perque omnia seruit.
>   in tot fecundi Gemini commenta feruntur.
>
>   (4. 152–61)

(From Gemini comes a more pleasant pursuit and a sweeter life, by means of various songs and voices tuned to melodies and slender reed pipes and words fitted to strings and their inherent sound: even work itself is a pleasure to them. They want arms and the trumpets of war and sad old age to be far away and to spend leisure and eternal youth in love. They find paths to the stars even, sum up the heavens with rhythm and melody, and leave the constellations behind themselves. Nature yields to their genius and serves them in everything. To such designs are the blessed Gemini carried.)

While this description of the influences of Gemini is to a certain extent traditional (see the commentary of Hübner 1982: 543–5), it is very tempting to view it as a self-portrait of the speaker, the poet-astrologer equally dedicated to *carmen* and *res* (see esp. 1. 20–2 and Sect. 6.4, below) who finds 'paths to the stars' (4. 158; see Sect. 6.3, below, on the journey metaphor).[44] I think we can be certain that Manilius, or at least his persona, was born under Gemini, and it is therefore not surprising—indeed, from the astrologer's point of view, altogether predictable—that the *mundus* should reveal itself to him and choose him as its poet.

To conclude this brief survey of the various ways in which the

---

[44] Hübner 1984: 127–8 points out that the sign of Gemini is associated particularly with two gods/planets, namely Phoebus/Apollo (cf. Man. 2. 440) and Mercury. The former is obviously responsible for the poetic talents the sign imparts, the latter, as the inventor of astronomy (as which he is to be identified with the Egyptian Hermes Trismegistos; see esp. Valvo 1978), for the interest in the stars exhibited by those born under Gemini. On Apollo and Mercury as the possible dedicatees of the two altars mentioned in Man. 1. 20–2, see n. 76, below.

Manilian speaker employs the theme of the cosmos's self-revelation, it should be pointed out that in spite of the generally friendly attitude of the *mundus* toward those who wish to investigate it, there is also a wrong way to approach the universe and one that will not yield the desired results.[45] In the proem to Book 2, after stressing, in a passage discussed above, that man (and, as I have argued, specifically the poet) is called into heaven *sacra ad commercia rerum* (2. 125), the speaker adds,

> quis neget esse nefas inuitum prendere mundum
> et uelut in semet captum deducere in orbem?
>
> (2. 127–8)

(Who would deny that it is a sacrilege to take hold of an unwilling heaven and lead it as a captive down to earth as if onto oneself?)

The poet here creates a contrast between the 'sacred exchange' of the universe with those who, like the speaker himself, are invited to gain knowledge of its secrets and the nefarious attempt to take the *mundus* by force and 'lead it as a captive down to earth'. In other words, instead of rising to the skies themselves, those with the wrong attitude try to pull heaven down, thus reducing it to human dimensions (this must be the force of *uelut in semet*[46], 2. 128). The verb *deducere* unfailingly makes us think of poetry,[47] and indeed, as we learn from another passage, the *nefas* described is one that has been perpetrated by poets. Earlier in the proem to Book 2, in the course of his survey of hexameter poetry, the speaker mentions poets who in their works dealt with the constellations (2. 25–7) and goes on to list a number of catasterisms treated by the authors to whom he is alluding (2. 28–36). While the persona's description is neutral in tone, his two concluding lines are damning:

---

[45] For a more detailed discussion of the following, see Volk 2001.

[46] I take *semet* as accusative and as referring to the implicit subject of the AcI (those people who attempt the *prendere* and *deducere*). By contrast, to interpret it as an ablative that refers to the *mundus* and thus to understand *in semet* as 'in mundo siue caelo' (Housman 1903–30 *ad loc.*) or 'in its own domain' (the translation of Goold 1992) does not make much sense. Garrod 1911 sees *semet* as an accusative but also thinks that it refers to the *mundus*: his translation of *uelut in semet . . . in orbem* as 'unto that earth which itself is' (i.e., the *mundus* is drawn down *in semet*, that is, onto itself) is in my opinion absurd.

[47] We may be reminded also of the Vergilian persona of *G.* 3. 10–11, who, as we have seen in Ch. 4, prepares to bring the Greek Muses to Mantua. The verb used there is likewise *deducere*, and the image conjured up is clearly that of leading captives in a triumph.

> quorum carminibus nihil est nisi fabula caelum
> terraque composuit mundum quae pendet ab illo.
>
> (2. 37–8)

(In their songs, heaven is just a story, and the earth made up the sky from which it depends.)

Scholars (e.g., Effe 1977: 123–5) have accused Manilius of inconsistency since, after all, the *Astronomica* itself contains numerous catasterisms, not to mention the extended narrative of Perseus and Andromeda in Book 5 (538–618), a *fabula* if ever there was one. In my view, this is just another instance of the have-one's-cake-and-eat-it-too principle: the poet has nothing against catasterisms as such and uses them himself whenever he sees fit (though, to be fair, the *Astronomica* does go well beyond the kind of simple description of the constellations and their origins that we find, for example, in Aratus and his Latin imitators, who would appear to be major targets of the criticism of 2. 25–38).[48] However, this does not prevent him from jumping at the opportunity to criticize his predecessors in the field of astronomical poetry for exhibiting the kind of wrong attitude toward their subject matter that he condemns in 2. 127–8: to regard the constellations merely as catasterized humans and animals is to think of the heavens in purely terrestrial terms and thus presents a paradoxical case of the earth's 'making up the cosmos' (*terraque composuit mundum*, 2. 38). In reality, of course, it is the other way around: the earth depends on the *mundus* (*pendet ab illo*, 2. 38).

The tension between the poet's own pious approach to the divine cosmos and the violent kind of attack he criticizes in 2. 127–8 and (obliquely) in 2. 37–8 underlies already the very opening of the poem, where the poet cleverly plays with the connotations of his words and the expectations of his audience. I have already had occasion to comment on part of the first sentence of the *Astronomica* (1. 1–6), a passage that is extremely dense and one to which I shall return again in the course of this chapter. At this moment, I am interested in one specific aspect of its first half:

> carmine diuinas artes et conscia fati
> sidera diuersos hominum uariantia casus,

---

[48] Note also the observation of Romano 1979: 51–3 and 61–4 that catasterisms play a role only in Books 1 and 5 of the *Astronomica* and do not make an appearance in the much more technical central books.

> caelestis rationis opus, deducere mundo
> aggredior . . .
>
> (1. 1–4)

(By song I undertake to draw down from heaven the divine arts and the stars, privy to fate, which govern the various fortunes of men, a work of divine reason . . .)

Given that *deducere* is frequently used in the meaning 'to treat (in poetry)', Manilius' *carmine . . . deducere* might, at first glance, appear to mean simply 'to sing of'. However, the ablative of separation *mundo* (1. 3), somewhat slyly placed only after the infinitive, indicates that we have to do with quite a different kind of *deducere*. As noted by many scholars (see Lühr 1969: 17 n. 2; Dams 1970: 16; Flores 1982: 109–10; Schrijvers 1983: 146; and Wilson 1985: 290), the collocation *carmine . . . deducere mundo* is clearly evocative of magical practices: the speaker is, as it were, getting ready to draw the stars from the sky by means of an incantation.[49] The belief that heavenly bodies, in particular the moon, can be removed from the heavens through spells (a practice ascribed specifically to Thessalian witches) is a commonplace in antiquity,[50] and Manilius' formulation appears to be indebted especially to Vergil, *Eclogues* 8. 69, *carmina uel caelo possunt deducere lunam*.[51] Since in magical practice the magician is often imagined as 'capturing' or 'binding' gods or spirits and putting them to work for his own purposes (see Graf 1997: 222–9) and since from the point of view of the *Astronomica*, the stars may be regarded as divine, the poet in this first sentence of his work appears in the role of a sorcerer about to exert his power to make the forces of nature do his bidding. His attitude is aggressive (witness *aggredior*,

---

[49] As we have seen throughout this section, Manilius likes to play with the verb *deducere* and its different connotations. From the early Augustan period onward, the word can be used poetically to mean 'compose (a work of literature)', in what is originally a spinning metaphor (*deducere* = 'draw out a thread in spinning'; see *OLD* s.v. 'deduco' 4). However, each of the three times *deducere* shows up in the *Astronomica* in the context of poetry, the underlying, non-metaphoric meaning of the verb is different: in 1. 3 it refers to the magic removal of heavenly bodies from the sky; in 2. 10 it means 'derive (channels from a stream)'; and in 2. 128 the connotation is that of 'leading down (captives in triumph)'.

[50] The attestations are collected and discussed by Hill 1973.

[51] Cf. Wilson 1985: 289–90, who also makes the attractive suggestion that the immediately following lines Man. 1. 4–5 still continue the magic theme: *nouis Helicona mouere* | *cantibus et uiridi nutantis uertice siluas* can be taken as referring to the literal setting into motion of mountain and trees through the magic of music, a feat traditionally ascribed to the likes of Orpheus (the same idea in Schrijvers 1983: 146–7).

1. 4), and given the magnitude of his enterprise, he is badly in need of *animus* and *uires*, provided to him by *Caesar* (1. 7–10).

The poet's use of the well-known ambiguity of *carmen* ('poem' v. 'spell') to cast himself in the role of a magician and the way in which he employs the topos of the manipulation of heavenly bodies by means of *carmina* to indicate his astrological subject matter makes for a powerful and highly original opening of the poem. What is startling, however, is that the approach of the speaker in this passage is surprisingly similar to the one condemned as *nefas* in 2. 127–8. For what the poet-magician is planning to do in 1. 1–4 might well be described as *inuitum prendere mundum | et uelut in semet captum deducere in orbem*.[52] Now, at the beginning of the poem the audience is obviously still unaware of the speaker's later verdict. However, it is quite clear that the manipulation of heavenly bodies by magical means constitutes a disquieting and impious disruption of the order of nature and that the persona's enterprise, as he so grandly presents it at the outset of his song, is not only extremely daring, but very possibly downright nefarious.

I suggest that the poet has deliberately devised the opening of the *Astronomica* so as to achieve a kind of shock effect: for a moment, he takes on the titillatingly outrageous role of the sorcerer about to work his magic over the stars and to overpower what is, after all, *caelestis rationis opus* (1. 3; on this expression see further Sect. 6.4, below). The tension created by his grand declaration is resolved only in 11–12, where we learn, to our relief, that the *mundus*, instead of being *inuitus* (2. 127), actually favours the speaker's enterprise (*fauet*, 1. 11) and actively wishes to reveal itself in the medium of song (*cupit aetherios per carmina pandere census*, 1. 12). Thus, after first having misleadingly taken on an attitude antagonistic to nature, the persona ultimately affirms and stresses that he is acting in concord with nature, indeed, at the behest of the cosmos itself. Far from engaging in the *nefas* of subjecting the *mundus* to force, he is piously acting according to the order of fate.[53]

---

[52] Note that in this passage, the poet uses *mundus* in a slightly different sense from 1. 3: there *mundus* must mean 'firmament', i.e., the natural locus of the stars from which the speaker threatens to remove them; in 2. 127, by contrast, *mundus* includes the stars, meaning 'heaven' in a more general sense.

[53] There are numerous other places in the *Astronomica* where the pursuit of astronomy/astrology (whether on part of the teacher or his students) is paradoxically presented in terms evocative of impiety, a phenomenon I discuss in detail in Volk 2001.

6.3. THE HEAVENLY JOURNEY

As we have seen in Chapter 3, the persona of Lucretius' *De rerum natura*, struck by 'great hope of fame' (1. 923) and 'sweet love for the Muses' (1. 924-5), rejoices in roaming the untrodden paths of the *Musenlandschaft*:

> auia Pieridum peragro loca nullius ante
> trita solo. *iuuat* integros accedere fontis
> atque haurire, *iuuat*que nouos decerpere flores
> insignemque meo capiti petere inde coronam
> unde prius nulli uelarint tempora Musae.
>
> (1. 926–30)

(I roam through the pathless realm of the Pierides, never before trodden by any foot. It is pleasing to approach untouched fountains and drink there; it is pleasing to gather new flowers and win for my head a crown of fame from a spot from which the Muses have wreathed the brow of no one.)

Similarly, in the *Georgics*, the Vergilian speaker enjoys his meta-poetic hike (or is it a chariot ride?; cf. *orbita* in 293) on Mount Parnassus:

> sed me Parnasi deserta per ardua dulcis
> raptat amor; *iuuat* ire iugis, qua nulla priorum
> Castaliam molli deuertitur orbita cliuo.
>
> (3. 291–3)

(But sweet love drives me through the steep loneliness of Parnassus: it is pleasing to go on mountain ridges where no forerunners' track runs down on gentle slope toward Castalia.)

In the *Astronomica*, too, the poet expresses joy at going on a poetic journey. However, his route is somewhat more ambitious:

> *iuuat*[54] ire per ipsum
> aera et immenso spatiantem uiuere caelo
> signaque et aduersos stellarum noscere cursus.
>
> (1. 13–15)

---

[54] Like Lucretius, Manilius repeats *iuuat*, though not immediately: after first having stated that it is not in fact enough to know about the constellations and the movement of the planets (i.e., to have a knowledge of astronomy), he expresses the wish to learn and sing about the influence of the zodiac (i.e., to practise astrology): *impensius ipsa | scire* iuuat *magni penitus praecordia mundi, | quaque regat generetque suis animalia signis | cernere et in numerum Phoebo modulante referre* (1. 16–19).

(It is pleasing to walk through the air itself and live strolling in the immense sky and get to know the constellations and the contrary movements of the planets.)[55]

The idea that the poet is travelling through the skies returns again and again in the *Astronomica*. While in some instances, his means of transportation is not made explicit (in the passage just quoted, *spatiantem* would appear to indicate that the poet is walking), he most often presents himself as riding a chariot, for example, as we have seen, in the proem to Book 2 (*solus, uacuo ueluti uectatus in orbe, | liber agam currus*, 2. 138–9) and at the beginning of Book 5:

> me properare etiam mundus iubet omnia circum
> sidera uectatum toto decurrere caelo,
> cum semel aetherios ausus conscendere currus[56]
> summum contigerim sua per fastigia culmen.
>
> (5. 8–11)

(Me the cosmos additionally orders hurriedly to drive around all the stars and to make my descent via the entire firmament—since, having once dared to mount the heavenly chariot, I have reached the highest point of the sphere.)

The ship, a conveyance favoured by many poets, but one presumably less useful for journeys in space, makes an appearance only once and even then in connection with the chariot:

> nec furtum sed opus ueniet, soloque uolamus
> in caelum curru, propria rate pellimus undas.
>
> (2. 58–9)

(Not a theft is coming but my own work; and I fly into heaven alone in my chariot and push through the waves with my own ship.)

The motif of the heavenly journey as employed by Manilius is a sophisticated amalgam of many sets of imagery, worthy of our eclectic poet.[57] First, of course, it is to be regarded as an instance of

---

[55] Landolfi 1999: 158–9 points out a close parallel in the Ovidian Pythagoras speech: *iuuat ire per alta / astra, iuuat terris et inerti sede relicta | nube uehi* (*Met.* 15. 147–9).

[56] Line 10 is an allusion to the *De rerum natura*, where the poet likewise at the beginning of his last book describes himself as a charioteer: *quandoquidem semel insignem conscendere currum* (Lucr. 6. 47; as mentioned in Sect. 3.2, this Lucretian verse is unfortunately followed by a lacuna, but gains context through 6. 92–5, where the speaker makes clear that he is on the last lap of a chariot race); cf. Rösch 1911: 56–7 and 68–9.

[57] On various aspects of the motif, see now Landolfi 1999, as well as Lühr 1969: 19–23, 43–52, and 73–82; Salemme 1983: 38–9; and Scarsi 1987: 101–14.

the poetic journey metaphor, familiar to us from the previous chapters, which depicts the poet's composition as his travelling along a certain path. The poet of the *Astronomica* is only one of many authors who have adapted this traditional image to their particular purposes: just as in Pindar, the motif of the poet's chariot is especially fitting because he is, after all, concerned with actual chariot racing (a connection he himself exploits), and just as the speaker of Vergil's *Georgics*, the poet of the countryside, presents himself as roaming through romantic landscapes (e.g., *G.* 2. 485–9; 3. 42–5, 291–3), the Manilian persona, who is singing about the stars, is logically described as driving his poetic chariot in the heavens. By thus transferring the route of his journey from the earth to the sky, the poet is able to add a special twist to one aspect of the motif especially popular with Manilius' predecessors in the field of Latin poetry. Ever since Lycian Apollo advised the poet of the *Aetia* to avoid roads frequented by carts and to choose untrodden paths instead (Callim. *Aet.* fr. 1. 25–8 Pfeiffer), the poetic journey motif had often been connected with a Callimachean search for novelty, for the route not yet travelled (cf., e.g., Lucretius' *auia Pieridum*-passage quoted above). And as we have seen, in the proem to Book 2, the poet of the *Astronomica*, too, goes on a Callimachean quest for the 'untouched', a quest that is made extremely difficult by the fact that at this point in literary history, *omnis ad accessus Heliconos semita trita est* (2. 50). However, the Manilian persona finds an original solution: leaving behind the traditional paths of poetry, he drives his chariot into a wholly unexplored territory, the heavens. There, for obvious reasons, the traffic is considerably less dense:

> sed solus, uacuo ueluti uectatus in orbe,
> liber agam currus non occursantibus ullis
> nec per iter socios commune regentibus actus.
>
> (2. 138–40)

(But alone—carried, as it were, in an empty orbit—I shall freely drive my chariot with no one meeting me or steering a friendly course along the same route.)

As discussed in Section 6.2, the poet is able to beat his predecessors in the competitive Callimachean search for an original topic by introducing a wholly new aspect, that of the 'fatedness' of his work. In his modification of the journey metaphor, too, he literally transcends the rules of the game by moving his poetic chariot into a realm not previously covered in song. In doing so, he extends the territory of poetry, as he himself proudly proclaims at the beginning of Book 3:

> in noua surgentem maioraque uiribus ausum
> nec per inaccessos metuentem uadere saltus
> ducite, Pierides. uestros extendere fines
> conor et ignotos in carmina ducere census.
>
> (3. 1–4)

(Muses, lead me who rise to new themes and dare more than I have strength for and fear not to walk through inaccessible glades. I am trying to extend your territory and to make unknown riches a topic for my song.)

What starts out as a humble appeal to the Muses to lead him through their realm (*inaccessos . . . saltus* conjures up a typical *Musenlandschaft*) quickly turns into the self-confident announcement of the poet that he will in fact assist the Muses by extending the boundaries of their sphere of influence.

If his poetic chariot ride through the skies enables the speaker of the *Astronomica* to claim with right that he is travelling on untrodden paths, it must also be noted that the concept of the heavenly journey is not original to Manilius. In presenting himself as moving through the heavens, the poet is drawing on a discourse that has nothing a priori to do with poetry, but rather with both intellectual and spiritual activities and achievements. Thus, people who are thinking about or researching celestial phenomena, such as astronomers and philosophers, can be metaphorically described as travelling the skies in their mind (see Delatte 1935: 327–32), as, for example, in this passage from Horace's *Archytas* ode (*Odes* 1. 28. 4–6):

> . . . nec quicquam tibi prodest
> aerias temptasse domos animoque rotundum
> percurrisse polum morituro.

(. . . and it is of no use to you to have touched the heavenly dwellings and to have traversed the sphere of heaven in your mind—since you had to die.)

While the speaker of the ode sarcastically points out the futility of any such enterprise (despite his astronomical studies, Archytas, being human, had to die), the persona of *Anthologia Palatina* 9. 577, an epigram ascribed to the astrologer Ptolemy, maintains that his occupation with the heavens makes him transcend his own mortality:

οἶδ' ὅτι θνητὸς ἔφυν καὶ ἐφάμερος· ἀλλ' ὅταν ἄστρων
ἰχνεύω κατὰ νοῦν ἀμφιδρόμους ἕλικας,
οὐκέτ' ἐπιψαύω γαίης ποσίν, ἀλλὰ παρ' αὐτῷ
Ζηνὶ θεοτρεφέος πίμπλαμαι ἀμβροσίης.

(I know that I am mortal, a creature of one day; but when I follow in my mind the circular movements of the stars, I no longer touch the earth with my feet, but at the side of Zeus himself I partake of god-nourishing ambrosia.)[58]

The idea that the astrologer's intellectual occupation with the stars resembles an actual journey through the universe is itself part of a larger motif, that of the 'flight of the mind'. This 'utter commonplace'[59] occurs in two manifestations, the 'figurative ascent' and the 'supernatural and eschatological ascent', which are not always easy to keep apart (see Jones 1926: 99). In the first, the movement through space ascribed to a person or his or her mind is purely metaphorical. Thus, neither Archytas nor Ptolemy 'really' travelled in the heavens, nor did Epicurus (to use an example that has nothing to do with astrology) 'really' move beyond the boundaries of the universe, as described by Lucretius:

> ergo uiuida uis animi peruicit, et extra
> processit longe flammantia moenia mundi
> atque omne immensum peragrauit mente animoque.
>
> (1. 72–4)

(Thus the lively force of his mind prevailed, and he marched far beyond the flaming ramparts of the world and travelled through the immeasurable universe in thought and mind.)[60]

However, this metaphorical use is not always easily distinguishable from the religious or mystical belief that the human soul can literally 'go to heaven', either by means of spiritual practices during life or, more commonly, after death. This idea is, of course, familiar from the Judaeo-Christian tradition, but it occurs in Classical antiquity as well, for example, in Plato's myth of Er (*Resp.* 10. 614b2–

---

[58] On this epigram and on the metaphor of the astrologer's heavenly journey in general, see Boll 1921, whose text I quote.

[59] Thus Jones 1926: 98 in his comprehensive treatment of the topos; see also Delatte 1935: 325–35; Kerényi 1930: 393–4; and Nisbet and Hubbard 1970 *ad* Hor. *Odes* 1. 28. 5 (quoted above in the text).

[60] Manilius, too, describes the ability of the human mind in general to travel through the entire universe (4. 877–81; this interpretation of the passage is admittedly helped by the additional line supplied by Goold in the supposed lacuna before v. 877).

621b7) or in the notion that the Milky Way is the home of dead heroes and statesmen (found in Cic. *Somn.* 16 and in Man. 1. 758–804).[61]

In the *Astronomica*, the poet's celestial journey is mostly to be understood figuratively—obviously, the speaker is not in fact driving a chariot through the constellations. Still, there is a spiritual side to his use of the motif as well. Apart from his general belief that 'souls come from heaven and return to heaven',[62] the poet maintains that he (and man in general) is explicitly being called into heaven *sacra ad commercia rerum* (2. 125) and claims that the ultimate goal of astronomical/astrological study is a quasi-mystical union with god: *impendendus homo est, deus esse ut possit in ipso* (4. 407). In ecstatic moments like these, the poet comes very close to the mysticism of the Hermetic tradition (which itself draws on a number of sources); compare, for example, *Corpus Hermeticum* 1. 24–6, which describes the 'way up' (ἄνοδος) of the good soul. This spiritual journey culminates in the soul's becoming identical with god since, as the treatise points out, 'This is the final good for those who have received knowledge: to be made god' (26; trans. Copenhaver 1992).

If rising into the heavens is the ultimate goal of the human soul, it is also—to come to yet another aspect of the heavenly journey motif in Manilius—a typical wish of ambitious poets. In the proem to *Georgics* 3, for example, the Vergilian persona is searching for a *uia . . . qua me quoque possim | tollere humo* (*G.* 3. 8–9), and at the end of Horace's *Odes* 1. 1, the speaker tells Maecenas, *quodsi me lyricis uatibus inseres, | sublimi feriam sidera uertice* (35–6).[63] As Baldini Moscadi 1986: 14 phrases it, the poet of the *Astronomica* 'resemanticizes' what had become a topos ('risemantizzazione di una formula poetica ormai canonizzata'): for him, the stars are not just a metaphor (reaching them means to attain poetic fame) but the actual object of his interest.[64] One passage that exploits this ambiguity and that might

---

[61] There is an extensive literature on the concept of the soul's ascent in antiquity; for an introduction, see Courcelle 1972; Colpe and Habermehl 1996; and Colpe et al. 1996, all with copious references.

[62] Man. 4. 886–7: *an dubitum est . . . | in caelumque redire animas caeloque uenire?*

[63] See Nisbet and Hubbard 1970 *ad loc.*, who describe *feriam sidera* as a 'proverbial phrase', providing numerous parallels.

[64] Cf. Reeh 1973: 123–4 on Man. 5. 11 (*summum contigerim sua per fastigia culmen*): 'Das Berühren des himmlischen Gipfels ist sicherlich in zweifacher Weise zu verstehen: Einmal meint es ganz konkret, daß Manilius mit seiner Himmelsbeschreibung bis in die äußerste Spitze des Himmelsgewölbes vordringt, zum andern aber liegt darin auch eine Anspielung auf das Verdienst des Dichters, der sich mit seinem Werk höchsten Ruhm verschafft hat'.

be influenced specifically by the two Horatian lines just quoted (note the use of *uates* and *sidera*), is the following:

> quod quoniam docui, superest nunc ordine certo
> caelestis fabricare gradus, qui ducere flexo
> tramite pendentem ualeant ad sidera uatem.
>
> (4. 119–21)

(Since I have taught this, it now remains for me to build heavenly steps in a certain order, which can lead the suspended poet to the stars on a curved path.)[65]

To conclude this survey of the various aspects of Manilius' use of the journey metaphor, it remains to be pointed out that the poet applies this image not just to himself, but to others as well, most notably to his student. In doing so, he follows the practice of Lucretius: as we have seen, in the *De rerum natura*, both teacher and student are described as travelling on what one assumes is the same path, the one from ignorance to knowledge, with the teacher leading the way. The same is true in the *Astronomica*, where the speaker, before embarking on detailed advice on how to calculate the rising times of individual signs of the zodiac, announces,

> a me sumat iter positum, sibi quisque sequatur
> perque suos tendat gressus, mihi debeat artem.
>
> (3. 393–4)

(Let everyone take the path laid down by me, follow it himself and pursue it with his own steps, and let him owe his art to me.)

More specifically, the student is likewise imagined as travelling in the sky, in a passage where the speaker predicts his addressee's future success as an astrologer:

> hinc quoque magna tibi uenient momenta futuri,
> cum ratio tua per stellas et sidera curret
> argumenta petens omni de parte uiasque
> artis.
>
> (2. 448–51)

(This, too, will provide you with crucial information about the future, when your mind will run through the planets and constellations, everywhere seeking proofs and the paths of the art.)[66]

---

[65] As mentioned in n. 6, above, these lines are rejected by Bentley, Housman, and Goold, for reasons that are not, in my opinion, conclusive.

[66] Cf. also *conaris scandere caelum*, 4. 390.

As the discussed examples show, the heavenly journey is an extremely versatile image, which in its numerous variations serves as a kind of leitmotif in Manilius' *Astronomica*. At the end of our examination, we may ask one more question: is it possible, as it were, to chart the poet's route across the sky, that is, are we supposed to imagine him as taking an actual trip through space with a fixed starting point and well-defined end, or can we at least tell in which direction he is travelling? Hübner 1984: 242–68, taking his cue from Manilius 1. 118 (*caelo descendit carmen ab alto*) has argued that the poet's, and the poem's, movement is a *descensus*: 'Das Gedicht steigt vom Himmel auf die Erde herunter' (1984: 245). Thus, Books 1–3 are concerned with the constellations, specifically the signs of the zodiac (heaven), while Books 4 and 5 mostly deal with human beings, their (astrologically determined) characters and occupations (earth).[67] This, however, is only the macrostructure of the work; looking at the *Astronomica* in greater detail, Hübner 1984: 248 discerns three separate *descensus*, thematic movements from heaven to earth (Book 1; Books 2–4; and Book 5).

While Hübner's observations are certainly interesting, it seems to me that if the *descensus* is really the 'philosophisch-poetisches Konzept' (Hübner 1984: 242) that underlies the *Astronomica*, this is not made explicit. As a matter of fact, *descendere* and *descensus* are used of poetry only twice in the work, at 1. 118 (*caelo descendit carmen ab alto*) and at 5. 5. The latter occurrence is part of the description of the hypothetical *alius* who would have finished the poem at this point and treated only the planets *per descensum* (presumably, 'on the way down', i.e., from the heavens to earth). It therefore cannot be regarded as representative of anything our poet is doing. Generally speaking, while it is certainly true that the speaker repeatedly proceeds from talking about celestial phenomena to dealing with their influence on human beings (a movement that perhaps can be termed a *descensus*), we do not really get any sense of an actual downward movement on the part of the poet.[68]

In fact, it seems that more often than going down, the speaker and his poem are actually rising. In a section entitled 'Ratio und

---

[67] Hübner 1984: 244 sees a parallel to the structure of Aratus' poem, which likewise first describes the stars (*Phaenomena*) and then deals with the weather-signs, which occur closer to earth and are relevant to humans (*Diosemiae*).

[68] The only exception is the description of the fixed stars in 1. 275–442, where the speaker starts from the North Pole and spirals downward, through the northern constellations to the southern ones.

Ascensus', Lühr 1969: 73–82 examines Manilius' combination of the purely metapoetic journey metaphor with the notion—touched upon already numerous times in this chapter—that the human mind can lift itself up to the sky, that is, gain an understanding of the workings of the universe. Thus, the human intellect, the poet, and his work all move upward: *caelum ascendit ratio* (1. 97)—*soloque uolamus | in caelum curru* (2. 58–9)—*hoc mihi surgit opus* (1. 113). Many of the passages quoted earlier likewise show how the poet conceives of his journey as an *ascensus*.[69] What is especially noteworthy is that man's/the speaker's ascending movement is complemented by a descending one on the part of the divine universe itself: not only do humans lift themselves up to god, but god is coming down to meet them (*quem* [sc. *hominem*] *denique in unum | descendit deus atque habitat seque ipse requirit*, 2. 107–8), inviting them into heaven (*caeloque ueniret | quod uocat in caelum sacra ad commercia rerum*, 2. 124–5).[70]

If the poet's journey is thus perhaps better imagined as an *ascensus* than a *descensus*, it must ultimately be pointed out that the poet's descriptions of his own and his poem's movement are self-contradictory. Within less than ten lines, for example, he presents his work, which is just about to begin, as both 'going up' (*hoc mihi surgit opus non ullis ante sacratum | carminibus*, 1. 113–14) and as 'going down' (*et quoniam caelo descendit carmen ab alto | et uenit in terras fatorum conditus ordo*, 1. 118–19). We might say that this collision of images is due to a rather ruthless application by the poet of the have-one's-cake-and-eat-it-too principle: he wants both to employ *surgit opus*, a classical *iunctura* used by Propertius and Ovid,[71] and to construct a clever metonymy (*caelo descendit carmen* must mean 'the subject matter of my song comes from the heavens'[72]), notwithstanding the fact that the literal meanings of *surgere* and *descendere*—both ascribed to the poem—are opposites. However, there is, I believe, yet another reason why the poet again and again, and not in a strictly logical manner, speaks of both himself and his poem as both moving upward and moving downward. Words like *descendere* and

---

[69] See also, apart from the passages mentioned in this para., 2. 136–7; 4. 119–21; 5. 11.

[70] As discussed in Sect. 6.2, the opposite of this 'sacred exchange' between descending god and ascending human mind is the impious attempt on the part of humans to 'draw down' the *mundus* (2. 127–8; cf. 1. 1–4) and, perversely, make it depend on the earth (2. 38).

[71] See Prop. 4. 1. 67; Ov. *Fast.* 4. 830; 5. 111; and *OLD* s.v. 'surgo' 6c. The Manilian persona uses *surgere* of poetry also at 2. 760 and of himself as a poet at 3. 1.

[72] I will come back in greater detail to this reading—which is wholly different from that of Hübner 1984, mentioned above—in Sect. 6.4.

especially *surgere* are extremely common in the *Astronomica*, but most often they have nothing to do with poetry, but rather describe the rising and setting of stars. By employing the same vocabulary to refer to his poem and to the poem's subject matter, the poet manages subtly to align the two. The constellations *surgunt* and *descendunt*; so does the poem; so does the poet himself on his journey through the heavens.[73] And of course, these movements up and down are not fortuitous, but governed, as the Manilian persona maintains, by unalterable fate.[74] The poet's heavenly journey, just as the rising and setting of stars, is part of the orderly working of the divine universe.[75] This parallel between song and subject matter will occupy us further in the following section.

6.4. *Carmen et Res*

In the proem to Book 1, just before embarking on his work, the Manilian persona stresses his dual allegiance to both his song and his subject matter:

> bina mihi positis lucent altaria flammis,
> ad duo templa precor duplici circumdatus aestu
> carminis et rerum.
>
> (1. 20–2)

(Twin altars burn for me with lit flames; I pray at two temples, inspired by a double passion, for my song and for my subject matter.)

---

[73] Cf. Schindler 2000: 271–2. The ambiguity of *surgere* is fully exploited in 2. 690, *quae mihi mox certo digesta sub ordine surgent*, where *quae* presumably refers to the *partes* (2. 687) or *dodecatemoria* (2. 695) of the single signs of the zodiac (each sign is subdivided into twelve parts, each of which is in turn governed by one zodiacal sign), which the poet treats from 2. 693 onward. Goold 1992 translates, 'These matters will be treated by me next and follow in due order'; at the same time, however, we are welcome to understand, 'they will rise in their due order'.

[74] The addressee, too, participates in this motion, as becomes clear in 2. 143, where the *minima turba* of students is described as *quibus illa* [the heavenly bodies] *sacros non inuidere meatus* (cf. my discussion in Sect. 6.1, above). While *sacros meatus* can certainly be understood as a metonymy, short for 'the knowledge of their sacred wanderings' (see *notitiamque suam* in the next line), it also refers to the imagined journey through the heavens that the universe grants to the small privileged group that includes the poet (whose heavenly chariot ride has just been described, 2. 138–42) and his students. Learning about the movement of the stars means mystically being part of that movement. We may compare the idea found in Plato's *Timaeus* (47b5–e2; 90c7–d7) that human beings ought to imitate the revolutions of the heavens in the movements of their own souls.

[75] Cf. Flores 1982: 126, according to whom the poet 'parla di se stesso con un totale processo di immedesimazione nella materia trattata cosí da essere divenuto anch'egli parte della vita degli astri'.

This passage, in which the speaker appears in the elevated role of the *uates* officiating at two altars,[76] is as clear a statement as we could have hoped for from a didactic poet about his equal commitment to both teaching and poetry. However, we may ask ourselves why it is that the poet of the *Astronomica* feels near-religious enthusiasm not only for his subject matter (which is, after all, the divine *mundus* and the workings of fate), but also for its poetic form. Since to him, as we have seen in Section 6.1, poetry does not seem to have a pedagogic function (there is no equivalent of the Lucretian honeyed-cup simile), we may even wonder why he has chosen to treat his extremely technical topic in verse at all.

The Manilian persona never reflects explicitly on his choice of medium; however, already the very first word of his poem, *carmine*, shows that the fact that the speaker will treat his topic specifically 'in song' is anything but unimportant. Since he avowedly acts on the order of the universe itself, we may surmise that the choice of medium, too, is due to the *mundus*. And indeed, it is said of the cosmos, *cupit aetherios per carmina pandere census* (1. 12). Why the universe is not only eager to disclose its workings, but also especially sympathetic to the medium of song may find an explanation in the one and a half lines that follow immediately on the poet's description of the two altars:

> certa cum lege canentem
> mundus et immenso uatem circumstrepit orbe.
>
> (1. 22–3)

(The universe resounds with its immense sphere around the poet who sings to a fixed measure.)

Scholars have taken this description as a reference to the music of the spheres, a phenomenon mentioned, for example, in Plato's myth of Er (*Resp.* 10. 617b4–7) and Cicero's *Somnium Scipionis* (18–19):[77] as the poet prays at the two altars, the *mundus* surrounds him with its sound (*circumstrepit*).[78] If the movements of the cosmos are

---

[76] The suggestion of Hübner 1984: 127–8 (cf. also Flores 1982: 121 and Feraboli, Flores, and Scarcia 1996–2001 *ad loc.*) that we are to imagine the two altars and temples as dedicated to Apollo (*carmen*) and Mercury (*res*), respectively (see also n. 44, above, on the sign of Gemini), is attractive.

[77] See van Wageningen 1921 *ad loc.*; Schrijvers 1983: 148–50; Wilson 1985: 293–4; and Liuzzi 1991–7 *ad loc.*

[78] See also *duplici circumdatus aestu* (21), which, as Wilson 1985: 293 points out, refers not only to the poet's enthusiasm for both his song and his subject matter, but also, when taken with *rerum*, to the 'whirling motions of the heavenly bodies'.

thus themselves music, it is obviously fitting that they be treated in the kindred medium of song.[79] The relationship of *carmen* and *res* is not arbitrary, but reflects an existential connection: just as the poem about the universe is itself part of the universe it describes (being, like everything, a product of fate), it is also, in a sense, a microcosm of the macrocosm, sharing the same (musical) structure.[80] The analogy between the two becomes clear through the ambivalent diction and syntax of our passage. Scholars are divided as to whether *certa cum lege* (1. 22) belongs with *canentem . . . uatem* (where it would refer to the metre of his song)[81] or with *mundus . . . circumstrepit* (where it would mean the regular motions of the heavenly bodies),[82] but surely the point is that it is to be taken (or, at least, can be taken) with both: both poem and universe follow a *certa lex*, and, the poet implies, this defining order is ultimately the same for both.[83]

Such instances of linguistic ambivalence that hint at the structural similarity of poem and subject matter and thus blur the boundary between signifier and signified abound throughout the poem. I have already commented on the use of verbs like *surgere* and *descendere* to refer to the movement of both the poem and the heavenly bodies it describes. Two other keywords used for both the orderly structure of the universe and the related one of the poet's song are *lex* (as seen already in 1. 22) and especially *ordo*. Witness, for example, the teacher's address to the student in 1. 255–6:

> nunc tibi signorum lucentis undique flammas
> ordinibus certis referam.

(Now I will tell you about the flames of stars that shine everywhere in a fixed order.)

---

[79] Both Schrijvers 1983: 149 and n. 24 and Wilson 1985: 293–4 compare *Somnium Scipionis* 18, where it is claimed that human poetry and music is an imitation of the music of the spheres. Schrijvers 1983: 150 and n. 32 additionally points out that the Stoic philosopher Cleanthes held that metre, melody, and rhythm were uniquely able to convey a vision of the divine (*SVF* 1. 486). Note that Plato, too, maintains that the purpose of music is to bring us 'in sync' with the revolutions of the heavenly bodies (*Ti.* 47d1–e2).

[80] Cf. Schrijvers 1983: 150 ('La musique du monde et le monde de la musique s'accompagnent mutuellement') and Wilson 1985: 293 ('Manilius . . . is drawing a parallel between his song about the stars and their movements and the actual movements of the stars which produce their own music').

[81] Thus van Wageningen 1921 *ad loc.*; Liuzzi 1991–7 *ad loc.*; Goold 1992 (trans.); and Feraboli, Flores, and Scarcia 1996–2001 (trans.).

[82] Thus Wilson 1985: 294.

[83] See Schrijvers 1983: 150.

Here, *ordinibus certis* is best taken with both *lucentis . . . flammas* and *referam*: the fixed order in which the constellations shine in the sky is, of course, the same order in which the poet will describe them.[84]

The word *ordo* is, of course, also used throughout the *Astronomica* to refer to the unalterable order of fate, which, by means of the orderly motions of the stars, governs everything that goes on in the universe. This meaning is clear in the following passage, part of which I have already discussed:

> et quoniam caelo descendit carmen ab alto
> et uenit in terras fatorum conditus ordo,
> ipsa mihi primum naturae forma canenda est
> ponendusque sua totus sub imagine mundus.
>
> (1. 118–21)

(And since the song descends from high heaven and the fixed order of fate comes to earth, I first must sing of the shape of nature and fashion an image of the entire universe.)

The order of fate moves from heaven to earth since—according to astrology—the stars are the medium through which god administers the destiny of human beings (see, e.g., Man. 2. 82–6). However, as we have already seen, not only the *fatorum ordo* describes such a downward movement, but the *carmen* itself behaves in the same way. In order to make sense of *caelo descendit carmen ab alto*, I suggested above that we understand it as a somewhat forced metonymy: 'the subject matter of my song descends from the high heaven'. On this reading, the next line is simply a paraphrase of the preceding one since *fatorum conditus ordo* is the topic of the speaker's song. Through what might be described as a semantic zeugma, the poet has created the impression that his *carmen* and the fateful order of the universe are in fact the same thing, both coming from high and both influencing him—after all, the two sentences are part of a causal clause with *quoniam* and serve to explain why the poet begins his song with a description of the cosmos as a whole.[85]

---

[84] Similar uses of *ordo* are found in 2. 690 (discussed in Sect. 6.3 in connection with *surgere*), 750; 3. 93, 157; 4. 119, 123; for ambivalent uses of *lex*, see 2. 204; 3. 390; 4. 408. Note that in these passages, the poet frequently describes his activity as *reddere* (see also *referre* in 1. 256), a choice of verb that indicates that in his poem, the poet is merely 'reflecting', 'reproducing' the order of the phenomena he treats.

[85] The poet's reasoning here is anything but clear. Does he feel called upon to describe the *mundus* because this is the wish of the *fatorum conditus ordo* that governs his activity as a poet (i.e., can 118–21 be paraphrased as 'Since in my poem I follow the command of fate, I will [follow

The same technique of tying together elements that, strictly speaking, belong to different spheres is employed by the poet elsewhere. Already in the first sentence of the poem, the speaker makes both *diuinas artes* and *conscia fati | sidera diuersos hominum uariantia casus* the object of *deducere*, despite the fact that the first refers to the science of astrology and the second to the actual phenomena that are the object of this science. This combination is unobjectionable as long as we translate *carmine . . . deducere* merely as 'treat in verse'; however, once we see the magical association of *carmine . . . deducere mundo*, the juxtaposition of the two accusative objects becomes a problem. While it is possible to 'draw the stars from heaven by means of a spell', one cannot do the same thing with the 'divine arts', and the sentence becomes an actual zeugma that cannot be properly translated (see also Lühr 1969: 17 n. 2). Again, by putting together two objects that do not belong in the same category, the poet suggests that they are in fact intrinsically connected. After all, astrology is a 'divine' art, given to man by the gods (see 1. 25–39), while the stars can be regarded either as gods themselves or as the means by which god/fate rules the universe. Both can thus fittingly be described as *caelestis rationis opus* (1. 3), an apposition that can, again, be taken with both objects of *deducere*. However, this is not the only syntactic possibility: alternatively, we might understand the phrase *caelestis rationis opus* as the object, not of *deducere*, but of *aggredior*, and thus as an apposition to the entire infinitival clause. The poet would then be saying that he is beginning a 'work informed by divine *ratio*' or 'task of divine *ratio*' (since human *ratio* is ultimately part of divine *ratio*), namely the treatment (*deducere*) of astrology and the stars.[86] Again, the syntactic ambiguity is deliberate, created by the poet to hint, already at the very beginning of his work, that his

its order, that is, I will] begin with a description of the universe'?), or is he saying, 'Since my song deals with the heavens, it is necessary for me first to give you a description of what the universe actually looks like'? Of course, the claim of a poetic persona that he 'must' sing about a certain topic (often expressed, as here, with the passive periphrastic) is a common topos; since the reasons given (if any) are hardly ever compelling, the trope ultimately rather serves to underline the poet's free command of his own material (cf. Sect. 4.2, above, on the *praeteritio* in *G.* 4, as well as Volk 1997: 301 and n. 32).

[86] On the different uses of *ratio* in the *Astronomica*, see Lühr 1969: 73–111. As for *opus*, this is one of the poet's favourite designations for his own work (1. 113; 2. 58; 3. 41) and for poetry in general (2. 24; 3. 30; 5. 4). Tellingly, he also repeatedly uses *opus* to refer to the orderly structure of the *mundus* (see, e.g., *hoc opus immensi constructum corpore mundi*, 1. 247). Cf. my discussion in Sect. 6.2 and n. 36, above, of 2. 124 (*tantum dictasset opus*) and of the various ways scholars have understood this phrase.

song and his subject matter are ontologically connected, both works of fate that share the same structure.[87]

The idea that the poem is a microcosm of the macrocosm it describes, that it works, *en miniature*, according to the same rules—we have already seen this notion at work in another didactic poem. As discussed in Chapter 3, the repeated comparison of the atoms to the letters of the poem in Lucretius' *De rerum natura* serves to create the impression that the poem functions according to the same principle—unlimited combination of a fixed number of types of smallest parts—that governs the natural world. However, as I pointed out there, the analogy is only this, an analogy, and there is, in my opinion, no actual connection between letters and atoms (in other words, we are not invited to view the poem as a physical object). Now, Manilius is often regarded as a deliberate 'Anti-Lucretius', and it is clear that the *De rerum natura*, the first major Latin poem to expound a system of natural philosophy, is his most important poetic model, which he is striving to emulate.[88] At the same time, the Stoic poet cannot but vehemently oppose the Epicurean world-view of Lucretius, whom he attacks most explicitly in 1. 483–7:

> ac mihi tam praesens ratio non ulla uidetur,
> qua pateat mundum diuino numine uerti
> atque ipsum esse deum, nec forte coire magistra,
> ut uoluit credi, qui primus moenia mundi
> seminibus struxit minimis inque illa resoluit.

(No other reason [other than the argument just mentioned] seems equally compelling to me as a proof that the universe is ruled by a divine being and is a god itself and has not come together at random, as he wanted it to be believed who first built the ramparts of the world out of smallest parts and again resolved them into these.)[89]

---

[87] Compare in this context also Hübner 1984: 214–27, who maintains that Manilius' language frequently mirrors, in various ways, the astrological phenomena it describes.

[88] See Rösch 1911: 63 and *passim*; Lühr 1969: 7 and *passim*; Pöhlmann 1973: 894; Wilson 1985: 286–9; and Toohey 1996: 181 (who points to the extraordinary length of the *Astronomica* as an indication of its rivalry with the *De rerum natura*, the only didactic poem that is longer).

[89] See also the next four lines. Whether the *primus* of 486 is Lucretius or Epicurus or even Democritus, it is clear from the diction that the poet intends to attack Lucretius; see Lühr 1969: 90–2, who on p. 91 n. 2 lists the many verbal allusions to Lucretius in this passage. Note esp. the poet's pointed use of one of Lucretius' favourite tropes (see Sect. 3.1, above), the *creator* motif (*struxit, resoluit*, 487, continued by *fabricantem* in 489; the Manilian persona occasionally uses the *creator* motif elsewhere, e.g., 4. 119–20).

The competition between the poet of the *Astronomica* and Lucretius thus works on two levels, that of poetry and that of philosophy. I have already suggested that in claiming to be inspired by his subject matter, the divine *mundus* itself, the Manilian persona manages to get the better of his Lucretian antagonist, who is undoubtedly equally dedicated to his topic but has no opportunity to capitalize on this fact the way the Stoic poet does. I believe that the situation is similar in regard to the relationship of *carmen* and *res* in the *De rerum natura* and the *Astronomica*, respectively. When the Lucretian poet stresses the similarity between the letters of his poem and the atoms, he is engaging in clever rhetoric, using an analogy. By contrast, when the Manilian speaker presents his work as a microcosm, on the one hand, and as an intrinsic part of the universe it describes, on the other, he has a real ontological point. In the *De rerum natura*, signifier and signified are separate: the poem talks about the world, the impersonal world of material objects, governed by chance. In the *Astronomica*, the boundary between poem and universe is blurred: in a divine cosmos ruled by fate, in which everything is linked to everything else by universal *sympatheia*, the poem not only talks about the world, but actually resembles the world, while at the same time being part of the world itself. And at least from the point of view of the enthusiastic Manilian poet, this situation is highly preferable.

However, the speaker's presentation of the relationship between *carmen* and *res* is not without its internal contradictions (a state of affairs we have come to expect from our poet). If from the passages discussed so far it appears that the poetic form is especially appropriate to the treatment of the persona's subject matter, to the extent that it seems as 'fated' as his topic, there are other points in the *Astronomica* where the poet's choice of medium is presented as rather more problematic. Already in the proem to Book 1, the description (1. 22–3) of the *mundus* that surrounds the poet with sound (presumably the music of the spheres) continues with the rather cryptic line, *uixque soluta suis immittit uerba figuris* (1. 24). Scholars are not agreed on the force of this statement. Goold 1992 translates, 'scarce allowing even words of prose to be fitted to their proper phrasing', following Housman 1903–30 in understanding the *figurae* as σχήματα τῆς λέξεως. However, I believe that such editors as Bentley, van Wageningen, and Liuzzi must be right that *figurae* here refers to the constellations (on this point, cf. the discussion of Waszink 1956:

589-90), even though it is, of course, interesting and wholly in keeping with our earlier observations that the poet, in talking about the structure of the *mundus*, uses an expression that can otherwise also refer to the structure of a speech or poem. Still, what does it mean that the cosmos 'hardly allows prose to be fitted (*immittit = immitti sinit*, see Housman 1903-30 *ad loc.*) to its figures/constellations'? The poet seems to be saying that the topic of the *Astronomica* is such that it is difficult enough to treat in prose—which would imply that it is next to impossible to do so in poetry.[90] Now, in itself this statement would not be remarkable and would make perfect sense as a *captatio benevolentiae* at the beginning of the poem. However, the *mundus* that *uix soluta suis immittit uerba figuris* is in strange contrast to the *mundus* that *cupit aetherios per carmina pandere census* (1. 12), as well as to the poet's subtle attempts to align through his diction the structure of the universe and that of his poem.

The theme of the difficulty of treating in verse the poet's astronomical/astrological subject matter returns, in greatly extended form, in the proem to Book 3. There, as mentioned in Section 6.2, the speaker rejects a number of well-worn poetic topics, giving the surprising reason that they are too simple. The same cannot be said for the persona's own poem:

>   at mihi per numeros ignotaque nomina rerum
>   temporaque et uarios casus momentaque mundi
>   signorumque uices partesque in partibus ipsis
>   luctandum est. quae nosse nimis, quid, dicere quantum est?
> 35 carmine quid proprio? pedibus quid iungere certis?
>   huc ades, o quicumque meis aduertere coeptis
>   aurem oculosque potes, ueras et percipe uoces,
>   impendas animum; nec dulcia carmina quaeras:
>   ornari res ipsa negat contenta doceri.
> 40 et, siqua externa referentur nomina lingua,
>   hoc operis, non uatis erit: non omnia flecti
>   possunt, et propria melius sub uoce notantur.
>
> (3. 31-42)

(But I must struggle with unknown numbers and names of things, with times, changing fortunes, and the movements of the heavens, with the changes of the signs and the divisions within their divisions themselves.

---

[90] The interpretation of Lühr 1969: 24 (taken over by Effe 1977: 114 and n. 22) that the *mundus* does not admit prose, but only poetry ('Der Kosmos läßt nur den Dichter zu'), is in my opinion impossible, disregarding, as it does, the crucial *uix* at the beginning of 1. 24.

How difficult is it to express what is already too difficult to understand? And in a fitting song? And to join it with the right metre? Come here, whoever is able to direct ear and eyes to my undertaking, and hear true utterances. Concentrate your mind; do not ask for sweet songs: the subject matter itself, happy to be taught, refuses to be adorned. And if some words in a foreign language are mentioned, this will be the fault of the song, not the singer: not everything can be bent, and things are better called by their proper names.)

Instead of the universe that favours the poet's enterprise and meets him halfway, what we have here is a subject that is extremely recalcitrant (note the violence of the speaker's attempt to deal with it: he is struggling, *luctandum*, 3. 34, and tries in vain to bend it, *flectere*, 3. 41). It is so resistant, in fact, that the poet has to settle for a compromise: with effort, he can understand his topic, talk about it, even make it into verse (3. 34–5); what he cannot do is add 'sweetness' (*nec dulcia carmina quaeras*, 38) or 'adornment' (*ornari res ipsa negat*, 39). This claim to failure can, of course, be understood as an example of the modesty topos and need thus not be taken too seriously (see Lühr 1969: 38). At the same time, it is another attempt to outdo Lucretius: the poet of the *De rerum natura* remarked, rather more soberly, on the difficulty of 'illustrating' the *Graiorum obscura reperta* by means of Latin verse (Lucr. 1. 136–9), but nevertheless undertook to make his song 'sweet' in order to better teach Memmius (cf. the honeyed-cup simile); the Manilian persona now has the chance to claim, with great pathos, that his topic is even more difficult, so difficult, in fact, that sweetness is out of the question and that, unlike with Lucretius, the student need not even expect *dulcia carmina*. The opportunity to imitate, and surpass, his great predecessor is too good to pass up, and according to the have-one's-cake-and-eat-it-too principle, the poet is not worried about the fact that the subject matter (*res*) that is just about 'happy to be taught' (*contenta doceri*, 3. 39) is a far cry from the *mundus* eager to reveal its riches through song of the proem to Book 1 (1. 12).

In 4. 431–42, a passage that is, unfortunately, beset by a number of textual problems, the poet provides a last variation on the theme of his difficult subject matter. As printed by Goold, the lines read,

> sed quis tot numeros totiens sub lege referre,
> tot partes iterare queat, tot dicere summas,
> perque paris causas faciem mutare loquendi?
> ⟨dum canimus uerum, non aspera ponere, ut illis⟩

incidimus, sic uerba piget; sed gratia derit,
435   in uanumque labor cedit quem despicit auris.
sed mihi per carmen fatalia iura ferenti
et sacros caeli motus ad iussa loquendum est,
nec fingenda datur, tantum monstranda figura.
ostendisse deum nimis est: dabit ipse sibimet
440   pondera. nec fas est uerbis splendescere mundum:
rebus erit maior. nec parua est gratia nostri
oris, si tantum poterit signare canenda.

(But who could relate so many numbers so often in metre, repeat so many divisions, mention so many sums, and change the appearance of his speech during so many similar themes? While singing the truth, I do not mind putting down inelegant words as I chance on them; however, there will be no charm, and the labour which the ear despises is in vain. But I, who express the laws of fate and the sacred motions of the stars in song, must speak as ordered and am not allowed to invent, but only show, the pattern. It is already all too much to reveal the god: he will lend weight to himself. It is not right to polish the universe with words: it will be grander just the way it is. And the charm of my utterance will not be small if it can only signify what ought to be sung.)

Indeed, many a reader who struggles through the following exposition of the *partes damnandae*, the part of the *Astronomica* that best exemplifies Manilius' 'eminent aptitude for doing sums in verse' (Housman), may feel that certain topics are perhaps best not treated in Latin hexameters and that the apologetic stance of the poet is therefore entirely appropriate. However, we have to ask ourselves how the speaker's words fit in with his poetics as expounded elsewhere in the poem. By contrast to the passage from the proem to Book 3 just discussed, the poet now does not so much complain about his own difficulties in treating his subject as deplore the loss of pleasure his audience will experience (4. 434–5); his attitude toward the *res* is no longer antagonistic, but piously resigned. After all, he is only following the orders of the divine *mundus*, which does not allow any *fingere* (438) and *splendescere* (440)[91] on the part of its *uates*, but only

[91] A number of scholars (e.g., van Wageningen 1921; Lühr 1969: 39 n. 3; Effe 1977: 115 n. 25; Hübner 1984: 128 and n. 4; and Liuzzi 1991–7) prefer the manuscript reading *suspendere* over *splendescere*, which is a conjecture by Bentley. Indeed, *suspendere* makes for a very nice parallel to 2. 38 (*terraque composuit mundum quae pendet ab illo*), discussed in Sect. 6.2, above; however, this reading rather destroys the necessary parallelism between *uerbis* and *rebus*, and I would therefore adopt, with Housman and Goold, the admittedly somewhat anaemic *splendescere*.

monstrare (438) and *signare* (442).[92] This argument is, of course, in keeping with the idea, so central in the *Astronomica*, that the poet is acting according to the will of fate/god/the cosmos. At the same time, as in the other two passages just examined (1. 24 and 3. 31–42), it jars with the notion that the universe, which itself produces the music of the spheres, wishes to reveal itself specifically *per carmina* (1. 12), an art form in which it is elsewhere described as taking pleasure (2. 142). Once again, the poet has it both ways.

To conclude, the relationship between *carmen* and *res* is depicted in the *Astronomica* in a number of different, not always wholly compatible, ways. While the poet explicitly declares that he is equally dedicated to both, he does not provide a reason why he is treating his topic specifically in poetic form; unlike Lucretius, he apparently does not conceive of poetry as a didactic tool, even though he is aware of the appeal (*gratia*) it can, and ideally should, have (see 4. 434–5). Hinting again and again at the structural similarity between his poem and the universe (the movements of the latter can likewise be understood as musical), the poet implies that poetry is especially apt for the description of the cosmos; in addition, his claim that the *mundus* wishes to reveal itself through *carmina* makes his choice of medium appear to be equally 'fated' as his choice of topic. However, this impression is muted by the speaker's insistence on the difficulty of treating his subject matter in verse and, following this realization on his part, his rejection—an odd move in a poet—of 'sweetness', *gratia*, and *ornatus*.

---

[92] The last word of line 442 poses a severe problem in this context. Goold, following Bühler 1959: 484–5, prints *canenda*, which he translates, in Goold 1992, as 'what ideally should be sung'. This reading, however, threatens to destroy the logic of the passage: for according to which principle should that which the poet can only 'signify' (*signare*) ideally be sung? Certainly not according to his divine subject matter, which, as we have just been told, allows itself only to be 'pointed out' (cf. *monstrare*, *ostendere*) by the speaker. If the persona were to introduce with *canenda*, as it were, a different authority to put him under obligation (for this is the force of the gerundive; I doubt that *canenda* can simply mean 'der Gegenstand meines Gedichts', as Bühler 1959: 485 suggests), there would be an unbearable conflict between two equal ideals that the poet cannot follow at the same time. After his stressing how he is following the commands of the divinity that is his inspiration and how it is simply neither right nor possible for his subject matter to be poetically adorned, it is hardly believable that, in the very last word of his apology, he would effectively say, 'but these things should really be treated in proper poetry after all'. I would therefore follow Housman 1903–37 and Liuzzi 1991–7 and accept *cauenda* ('the places to beware of', i.e., the *partes damnandae*), the *varia lectio*. This is, however, not wholly satisfying either, and Goold 1992: 256 is certainly right that 'infants about to be born can hardly "beware of" the injurious degrees', but if *canenda* were correct, I am afraid that not even the most generously applied have-one's-cake-and-eat-it-too principle could save the poet from appearing extremely muddle-headed.

As I hope to have shown in this chapter, Manilius' *Astronomica* clearly fits my description of didactic poetry as a genre with a high degree of poetic self-consciousness. In fact, the persona's reflection on his activity is so extensive that it might well appear excessive, and I have suggested, following earlier critics, that it is the 'inferiority complex' of the post-classical latecomer that is responsible for the large space allotted to questions of poetics in the poem. As especially the proem to Book 2 shows, the poet is aware that he is heir to a long tradition; however, he manages to escape not only the danger of being a mere epigone, but, as it were, the entire discourse of imitation versus originality by means of the ingenious conceit of having been chosen to treat his particular topic—that is, chosen by the divine universe, his subject matter itself.

The grand idea that the poet's song is 'fated' is the central concept of the poetics of the *Astronomica*, which the persona combines to great effect with other recurring motifs, such as the macrocosm–microcosm argument, the image of the heavenly journey, and the notion that the poem and its subject matter share the same structure. The effect envisaged (and—in my opinion—achieved) is one of sublimity: we watch the *uates mundi* on his glorious chariot ride through the constellations, whose music responds harmoniously to his song, and participate in his enthusiasm for the fateful workings of the cosmos. However, as I have pointed out again and again, in pursuing this effect, the speaker repeatedly jettisons logic in favour of exploring yet another beautiful metaphor or traditional motif, which may or may not be compatible with what he is saying elsewhere, a procedure that I have referred to as the have-one's-cake-and-eat-it-too principle. The resulting baroque quality of the poet's discourse, not to mention his occasional self-contradictions, may keep many readers from putting Manilius in the same league as Lucretius, Vergil, and Ovid. Still, his ambitious and original take on many of the themes employed by his great predecessors makes his poem an outstanding example of didactic poetry, the elusive genre that by this time had finally become wholly canonized.

Conclusion

> tu mihi supremae praescripta ad candida calcis
> currenti spatium praemonstra, callida musa
> Calliope.
>
> Lucretius, De rerum natura

> Kündige den Schluß deiner Rede lange vorher an, damit die Hörer vor Freude nicht einen Schlaganfall bekommen. . . . Kündige den Schluß an, und dann beginne deine Rede von vorn und rede noch eine halbe Stunde. Dies kann man mehrere Male wiederholen.
>
> Kurt Tucholsky, Ratschläge für einen schlechten Redner

In the preceding pages, I have approached the poetics of Latin didactic poetry on two different paths. First, I have been concerned with ancient didactic poetry in general and tried to arrive, through both theoretical considerations and the study of literary history, at an understanding of this oft-neglected genre. My second approach has consisted in the close reading of four major representatives of this type of literature, the didactic poems of Lucretius, Vergil, Ovid, and Manilius. Crucially, these ὁδοὶ διζήσιος have been complementary: the study of the individual authors has both confirmed and added to the picture of didactic poetry as a genre, and the knowledge of generic conventions has helped the interpretation of the single poems and thrown light on hitherto unnoticed or ill-understood features.

There are two main aspects to my definition of didactic poetry. First, I have argued that it is useful to regard the didactic nature of so-called didactic poems not as anything having to do with the historical author's actual intention of teaching his readers, but rather as a purely formal feature. Thus, a poem is didactic if, inside the text, a speaker is continuously speaking to an addressee explicitly in order to instruct him—in other words, if the poem exhibits *didactic intent* and the *teacher–student constellation*, my first two criteria for didactic poetry.

Second, didactic poetry is not only didactic in the sense just described, but it is also poetry and, crucially, explicitly presents itself as such. A didactic poem always shows *poetic self-consciousness* and *poetic simultaneity*, the other two criteria of my definition. A poem that is poetically self-conscious draws attention to its status as poetry; its first-person speaker is identified with the poet and refers to his words as poetry or song. Poetic simultaneity is usually concomitant with poetic self-consciousness, being the illusion, created by the speaker's self-referential statements, that the poem is coming into being 'right now', that its composition really is simultaneous to its evolving. While my first two criteria, didactic intent and the teacher–student constellation, are more or less generally recognized formal features of didactic poetry, the observation that didactic poems are poetically self-conscious and typically reflect at great length on their status as poetry is, I believe, original and the result of my investigations that I regard as most important.

In my interpretation of the poems of Lucretius, Vergil, Ovid, and Manilius I have concentrated especially on what these texts have to say about the relationship of the two aspects of didactic poetry just described: the poetry and the didactic, the *carmen* and the *res*. In Lucretius' *De rerum natura*, a text that has appeared to many as the ideal didactic poem, the speaker presents himself as both a dedicated teacher and a serious poet. Reacting, one assumes, to Epicurus' verdict against poetry, the Lucretian persona uses the honeyed-cup simile to show that in his teaching, poetry fulfills the important function of making Epicurean philosophy palatable to the student. By associating his verse with sweetness, light, and pleasure, the poet endeavours to 'Epicureanize' poetry; at same time, he is, I have argued, 'poeticizing' Epicurus by presenting the philosopher as though he were in fact a poet and by presenting his own relationship to his master as one of literary *imitatio*.

If the speaker of the *De rerum natura* is with heart and soul a didactic poet, the Vergilian persona in the *Georgics* makes it clear that being a singer and teacher of agriculture is nothing but a role that he has taken on for the moment. He is first and foremost a poet, who has chosen this particular project among many and who, even as he is talking about sowing and ploughing, keeps reflecting, especially in his addresses to Maecenas, on both his ongoing poem and his poetic career in general. I have argued further that the speaker's self-representation—which is made possible by the fact that, as a didactic poem, the *Georgics* encourages a high degree of poetic self-consciousness—has been crucial, from antiquity up to modern times, in shaping people's view of Vergil's development as a poet.

Ovid's *Ars amatoria* derives a large part of its humour from its subversion of love elegy and the claim on the part of the *praeceptor amoris* that *amor* is nothing but a type of behaviour that can be learned and taught. In order to prove his point, the poet playfully develops some of the potentials inherent in didactic poetry, notably the concept of poetic simultaneity. In *Ars amatoria* 1 and 2, the poem evolves simultaneously not only to its own composition, but also to the learning process of the young men whom the teacher addresses: while at the beginning of the poem, they are inexperienced in love, at the end, they have mastered the techniques taught by the poet and have succeeded in winning their girls. This further simultaneity, which I have labelled *mimetic*, makes Ovid's work a 'perfect' didactic poem, that is, one in which the teacher's teaching is immediately successful.

Finally, the persona of Manilius' *Astronomica* exploits to the full the metapoetic potential of didactic poetry, reflecting extensively on his role as the creator of a song about the cosmos. Realizing that he comes at the end of a long poetic tradition, he nevertheless claims absolute novelty for his work, on the grounds that it has, as it were, been commissioned by its subject matter, the divine universe itself. As a result, he presents his poem as a microcosm of the *mundus* and as being itself part of the very processes of fate that it describes. However, the speaker's enthusiastic celebration of a world governed by strict determinism is not easy to reconcile with his didactic optimism, and I have argued that this is but one of the many self-contradictions of a poet more intent on individual effects than on the internal coherence of his work.

Each of the four authors I have examined appropriates the didactic format in a unique and original way: Lucretius creates a treatise of Epicurean natural philosophy that is monumental in both size and style; Vergil combines down-to-earth instructions to farmers with high-flown metapoetic reflections (not to mention his meditations on human life, which I have chosen not to focus on in this book); Ovid wittily deconstructs the ideology of love elegy while painting an amusing picture of the amatory pursuits of the Roman *jeunesse dorée*; and, Manilius, while elaborating some of the more technical aspects of astrology, presents a sublime *hieros logos* about the fateful workings of the Stoic universe. In both subject matter and ethos, the four poems are all extremely different, and one might well argue that there is more that distinguishes the individual works than makes them alike. What does make them alike has been the focus of this book: a small number of distinct features, the observation of which in these and similar poems has led critics—beginning with the author of the *Tractatus Coislinianus* and the grammarian Diomedes—to posit a genre 'didactic poetry'. I hope to have shown that paying attention to such generic characteristics, while obviously not the key to all aspects of a given text, is nevertheless of major importance to its interpretation. As alien as the genre of ancient didactic poetry may appear to us, understanding its workings and conventions will afford us a greater appreciation of some of the greatest classics of Western literature.

BIBLIOGRAPHY

AHERN, JR., C. F. (1990). 'Ovid as *vates* in the Proem to the *Ars amatoria*'. *CPh*, 85: 44–8.

AHL, F. (1985). *Metaformations: Soundplay and Wordplay in Ovid and Other Classical Poets*. Ithaca, NY: Cornell University Press.

ALBERT, W. (1988). *Das mimetische Gedicht in der Antike: Geschichte und Typologie von den Anfängen bis in die augusteische Zeit*. Frankfurt: Athenäum.

ALBERTSEN, L. L. (1967). *Das Lehrgedicht: Eine Geschichte der antikisierenden Sachepik in der neueren deutschen Literatur mit einem unbekannten Gedicht Albrecht von Hallers*. Aarhus: Akademisk Boghandel.

ALBIS, R. V. (1996). *Poet and Audience in the* Argonautica *of Apollonius*. Lanham, Md.: Rowman and Littlefield.

ALGRA, K. A., KOENEN, M. H., and SCHRIJVERS, P. H. (eds.) (1997). *Lucretius and his Intellectual Background* (= *Verhandel. Nederl. Akad. van Wet. Afd. Letterk*. 172). Amsterdam: North-Holland.

AMORY, A. (1969). '*Obscura de re lucida carmina*: Science and Poetry in *De Rerum Natura*'. *YClS* 21: 143–68.

ANDERSON, W. S. (1960). 'Discontinuity in Lucretian Symbolism'. *TAPhA* 91: 1–29.

ARMSTRONG, D. (1995). 'The Impossibility of Metathesis: Philodemus and Lucretius on Form and Content in Poetry', in Obbink (ed.), 210–32.

ARRAGON, R. F. (1961). 'Poetic Art as a Philosophic Medium for Lucretius'. *Essays in Criticism*, 11: 371–89.

ARRIGHETTI, G. (1997). 'Lucrèce dans l'histoire de l'Épicurisme: Quelques réflexions', in Algra, Koenen, and Schrijvers (eds.), 21–33.

ASMIS, E. (1995). 'Epicurean Poetics', in Obbink (ed.), 15–34 (1st pub. in *Proceedings of the Boston Area Colloquium in Ancient Philosophy*, 7, 1991: 63–93 and 104–5).

ASPER, M. (1997). *Onomata allotria: Zur Genese, Struktur und Funktion poetologischer Metaphern bei Kallimachos*. Stuttgart: Steiner.

ATHERTON, C. (ed.) (1997). *Form and Content in Didactic Poetry* (= *Nottingham Classical Studies* 5). Bari: Levante.

AUSTIN, R. G. (1968). '*Ille ego qui quondam* . . .'. *CQ* 18: 107–15.

BAILEY, C. (1947). *Titi Lucreti Cari De Rerum Natura Libri Sex*, 3 vols. Oxford: Oxford University Press.

BAJONI, M. G. (1997). 'Da Ausonio a Giovanni di Garlandia: Un possibile percorso della *Rota Vergilii*'. *Emerita*, 65: 281–5.

BALDINI MOSCADI, L. (1986). 'Manilio e i poeti augustei: Considerazioni sul proemio del II and III libro degli *Astronomica*', in (no ed.), *Munus*

amicitiae: Scritti in memoria di Alessandro Ronconi, vol. 1. Florence: Le Monnier, 3–22.
BALDO, G. (1989) 'I mollia iussa di Ovidio (ars 2, 196)'. *MD* 22: 37–47.
BALOT, R. K. (1998). 'Pindar, Virgil, and the Proem to *Georgic* 3'. *Phoenix*, 52: 83–94.
BARCHIESI, A. (1989). 'Voci e istanze narrative nelle Metamorfosi di Ovidio'. *MD* 23: 55–97.
BARTON, T. S. (1994a). *Ancient Astrology*. London: Routledge.
—— (1994b). *Power and Knowledge: Astrology, Physiognomics, and Medicine under the Roman Empire*. Ann Arbor: University of Michigan Press.
BATSTONE, W. (1997). 'Virgilian Didaxis: Value and Meaning in the *Georgics*', in Martindale (ed.), 125–44.
BAYER, K. (1970). 'Vergil-Viten', in J. and M. Götte (eds.), *Vergil: Landleben*. Munich: Heimeran, 211–422 and 654–780.
BECKER, O. (1937). *Das Bild des Weges und verwandte Vorstellungen im frühgriechischen Denken*. Berlin: Weidmann.
BIGNONE, E. (1945–50). *Storia della letteratura latina*, 3 vols. Florence: Sansoni.
BING, P. (1990). 'A Pun on Aratus' Name in Verse 2 of the *Phainomena?*'. *HSPh*, 93: 281–5.
—— (1993). 'Aratus and his Audiences', in Schiesaro, Mitsis, and Clay (eds.), 99–109.
BINNICKER, JR., C. M. (1967). 'Didactic Qualities of Ovid's *Ars Amatoria*'. Diss. University of North Carolina, Chapel Hill.
BLODGETT, E. D. (1973). 'The Well Wrought Void: Reflections on the *Ars amatoria*'. *CJ* 68: 322–33.
BOLL, F. (1921). 'Das Epigramm des Claudius Ptolemaeus'. *Sokrates*, 9: 2–12 (repr. in *Kleine Schriften zur Sternkunde des Altertums*, ed. V. Stegemann. Leipzig: Köhler und Amelang, 1950, 143–55).
BOYANCÉ, P. (1947). 'Lucrèce et la poésie'. *REA* 49: 88–102.
—— (1950). 'Lucrèce et son disciple'. *REA* 52: 212–33.
—— (1960). 'Études lucrétiennes'. *REA* 62: 438–47.
—— (1962). 'Épicure, la poésie et la Vénus de Lucrèce'. *REA* 64: 404–10.
BRANDT, E. (1928). 'Zum Aeneis-Prooemium'. *Philologus*, 83: 331–5.
BRANDT, P. (1902). *P. Ovidi Nasonis de arte amatoria libri tres*. Leipzig: Dieterich.
BROGAN, T. V. F. (1993). 'Poetics I. Western', in Preminger and Brogan (eds.), 929–37.
BROWN, R. D. (1982). 'Lucretius and Callimachus'. *ICS* 7: 77–97.
BUCHHEIT, V. (1971). 'Epikurs Triumph des Geistes (Lucr. I, 62–79)'. *Hermes*, 99: 303–23.
—— (1972). *Der Anspruch des Dichters in Vergils Georgika: Dichtertum und Heilsweg*. Darmstadt: Wissenschaftliche Buchgesellschaft.
BÜHLER, W. (1959). 'Maniliana'. *Hermes*, 87: 475–94.

BURCK, E. (1926). *De Vergilii Georgicon partibus iussivis*. Lucka: Berger.
—— (1929). 'Die Komposition von Vergils Georgika'. *Hermes*, 64: 279–321.
CABISIUS, G. (1979). 'Lucretius' Statement of Poetic Intent', in C. Deroux (ed.), *Studies in Latin Literature and Roman History I* (= *Collection Latomus* 164). Brussels: Latomus, 239–48.
CAIRNS, F. (1972). *Generic Composition in Greek and Roman Poetry*. Edinburgh: Edinburgh University Press.
CAMERON, A. (1995). *Callimachus and his Critics*. Princeton: Princeton University Press.
CATAUDELLA, Q. (1973). 'Recupero di un'antica scrittrice greca'. *GIF* 4: 253–63.
—— (1974). 'Initiamenta Amoris'. *Latomus*, 33: 847–57.
CHANTRAINE, P. (1968–80). *Dictionnaire étymologique de la langue grecque: Histoire des mots*, 4 vols. Paris: Klinksieck.
CHATWIN, B. (1987). *The Songlines*. London: Cape.
CHRISTMANN, E. (1982). 'Zur antiken Georgica-Rezeption'. *WJA* 8: 57–67.
CITRONI, M. (1986). 'Ovidio, *Ars* 1, 3–4 e Omero, *Iliade* 23, 315–18: L'analogia tra le *artes* e la fondazione del discorso didascalico', in (no ed.), *Studi in onore di Adelmo Barigazzi*, vol. 1. Rome: Edizioni dell'Ateneo, 157–67.
CLASSEN, C. J. (1968a). 'Poetry and Rhetoric in Lucretius'. *TAPhA* 99: 77–118 (repr. in Classen (ed.) 1986b: 331–73).
—— (ed.) (1986b). *Probleme der Lukrezforschung*. Hildesheim: Olms.
CLAY, D. (1969). '*De rerum natura*: Greek Physis and Epicurean Physiologia (Lucretius 1.1–148)'. *TAPhA* 100: 31–47 (repr. in D. Clay 1998a: 121–37).
—— (1973). 'Epicurus' Last Will and Testament'. *AGPh*, 55: 252–80 (repr. in D. Clay 1998a: 3–31).
—— (1976). 'The Sources of Lucretius' Inspiration', in J. Bollack and A. Laks (eds.), *Études sur l'Épicurisme antique* (= *Cahiers de Philologie* 1). Lille: Publications de l'Université Lille III, 203–27 (repr. in D. Clay 1998a: 138–60).
—— (1983a). 'Individual and Community in the First Generation of the Epicurean School', in (no ed.), *ΣΥΖΗΤΗΣΙΣ: Studi sull'epicureismo greco e romano offerti a Marcello Gigante*, 3 vols. Naples: Macchiaroli, 1. 255–79 (repr. in D. Clay 1998a: 55–74).
—— (1983b). *Lucretius and Epicurus*. Ithaca, NY: Cornell University Press.
—— (1986). 'The Cults of Epicurus'. *CronErc*, 16: 11–28 (repr. in D. Clay 1998a: 75–102).
—— (1998a). *Paradosis and Survival: Three Chapters in the History of Epicurean Philosophy*. Ann Arbor: University of Michigan Press.
—— (1998b). 'The Theory of the Literary Persona in Antiquity'. *MD* 40: 9–40.

CLAY, J. S. (1976). 'The Argument of the End of Vergil's Second Georgic'. *Philologus*, 120: 232–45.
—— (1993). 'The Education of Perses: From "Mega Nepios" to "Dion Genos" and Back', in Schiesaro, Mitsis, and Clay (eds.), 23–33.
COLPE, C., and HABERMEHL, P. (1996). 'Jenseitsreise (Reise durch das Jenseits)'. *RLAC* 17: 490–543.
—— DASSMANN, E., ENGEMANN, J., and HABERMEHL, P. (1996). 'Jenseitsfahrt I (Himmelfahrt)'. *RLAC* 17: 407–66.
CONTE, G. B. (1986). *The Rhetoric of Imitation: Genre and Poetic Memory in Virgil and Other Latin Poets*. Ithaca, NY: Cornell University Press.
—— (1992). 'Proems in the Middle'. *YClS* 29: 147–59.
—— (1994a). *Genres and Readers: Lucretius, Love Elegy, Pliny's Encyclopedia*. Baltimore: Johns Hopkins University Press.
—— (1994b). *Latin Literature: A History*. Baltimore: Johns Hopkins University Press.
—— and MOST, G. W. (1996). 'Genre'. *OCD* (3rd edn.): 630–1.
COPENHAVER, B. P. (1992). *Hermetica: The Greek Corpus Hermeticum and the Latin Asclepius in a new English Translation, with Notes and Introduction*. Cambridge: Cambridge University Press.
COURCELLE, P. (1972). 'Flügel (Flug) der Seeele I'. *RLAC* 8: 29–65.
COURTNEY, E. (1993). *The Fragmentary Latin Poets*. Oxford: Oxford University Press.
COX, A. (1969). 'Didactic Poetry', in J. Higginbotham (ed.), *Greek and Latin Literature: A Comparative Study*. London: Methuen, 124–61.
CRAMER, R. (1998). *Vergils Weltsicht: Optimismus und Pessimismus in Vergils Georgica*. Berlin: de Gruyter.
CULLER, J. (1997). *Literary Theory: A Very Short Introduction*. Oxford: Oxford University Press.
CURTIUS, E. R. (1948). *Europäische Literatur und lateinisches Mittelalter*. Bern: Francke.
DAHLMANN, H. (1953). *Varros Schrift 'de poematis' und die hellenistisch-römische Poetik* (= *AAWM* 1953.3). Wiesbaden: Steiner.
DALY, L. W. (1943). 'The Entitulature of Pre-Ciceronian Writings', in (no ed.), *Classical Studies in Honor of William Abbott Oldfather*. Urbana, Ill.: University of Illinois Press, 20–38.
DALZELL, A. (1987). 'Language and Atomic Theory in Lucretius'. *Hermathena*, 143: 19–28.
—— (1996). *The Criticism of Didactic Poetry: Essays on Lucretius, Virgil, and Ovid*. Toronto: University of Toronto Press.
DAMS, P. (1970). *Dichtungskritik bei nachaugusteischen Dichtern*. Marburg: Symons.
DE JONG, I. J. F. (1987). *Narrators and Focalizers: The Presentation of the Story in the Iliad*. Amsterdam: Grüner.

DELATTE, L. (1935). '*Caelum ipsum petimus stultitia* . . . (Contribution à l'étude de l'ode I, 3 d'Horace)'. *AC* 4: 309–36.
DELLA CORTE, F. (1985). 'Georgiche: 4. Le digressioni'. *Enciclopedia Virgiliana*, 2: 678–86.
DEUFERT, M. (1996). *Pseudo-Lukrezisches im Lukrez: Die unechten Verse in Lukrezens 'De rerum natura'*. Berlin: de Gruyter.
DEWITT, B. (1936a). 'Epicurean Contubernium'. *TAPhA* 67: 55–63.
——(1936b). 'Organization and Procedure in Epicurean Groups'. *CPh*, 31: 205–11.
DILLON, J. (1994). 'A Platonist *Ars Amatoria*'. *CQ* 44: 387–92.
DIONIGI, I. (1988). *Lucrezio: Le parole e le cose*. Bologna: Pàtron.
DOMENICUCCI, P. (1996). *Astra Caesarum: Astronomia, astrologia e catasterismo da Cesare a Domiziano*. Pisa: Edizioni ETS.
DONOHUE, H. (1993). *The Song of the Swan: Lucretius and the Influence of Callimachus*. Lanham, Md.: University Press of America.
DÖPP, S. (1968). *Virgilischer Einfluß im Werk Ovids*. Munich: UNI-Druck.
DOVER, K. (1997). *The Evolution of Greek Prose Style*. Oxford: Oxford University Press.
DOWNING, E. (1993). *Artificial I's: The Self as Artwork in Ovid, Kierkegaard, and Thomas Mann*. Tübingen: Niemeyer.
DUBROW, H. (1982). *Genre*. London: Methuen.
DURANTE, M. (1958). 'Epea pteroenta. La parole come "cammino" in immagini greche e vediche'. *RAL* 13: 3–14 (repr. in modified form in *Sulla preistoria della tradizione poetica greca*, vol. 2. Rome: Edizioni dell'Ateneo, 1976, 167–84).
DURLING, R. M. (1958). 'Ovid as *Praeceptor Amoris*'. *CJ* 53: 157–67 (repr. in modified form in *The Figure of the Poet in Renaissance Epic*. Cambridge, Mass.: Harvard University Press, 1965, 26–43).
EFFE, B. (1977). *Dichtung und Lehre: Untersuchungen zur Typologie des antiken Lehrgedichts*. Munich: Beck.
ELLIOTT, R. C. (1982). *The Literary Persona*. Chicago: University of Chicago Press.
ERLER, M. (1993). '*Philologia Medicans*: Wie die Epikureer die Texte ihres Meisters lasen', in Kullman and Althoff (eds.), 281–303.
——(1994). 'Epikur. Die Schule Epikurs. Lukrez', in H. Flashar (ed.), *Die hellenistische Philosophie*. Basel: Schwabe, 29–490.
——(1997). 'Physics and Therapy: Meditative Elements in Lucretius' *De rerum natura*', in Algra, Koenen, and Schrijvers (eds.), 79–92.
ERREN, M. (1967). *Die Phainomena des Aratos von Soloi: Untersuchungen zum Sach- und Sinnverständnis*. Wiesbaden: Steiner.
——(1990). 'Die Anredestruktur im archaischen Lehrgedicht', in W. Kullmann and M. Reichel (eds.), *Der Übergang von der Mündlichkeit zur Literatur bei den Griechen*. Tübingen: Narr, 185–97.

FABIAN, B. (1968). 'Das Lehrgedicht als Problem der Poetik', in H. R. Jauß (ed.), *Die nicht mehr schönen Künste: Grenzphänomene des Ästhetischen*. Munich: Fink, 67–89.

FANTHAM, R. E. (1985). 'Ovid, Germanicus and the Composition of the *Fasti*'. *Papers of the Liverpool Latin Seminar*, 5: 243–81.

FANTUZZI, M. (1996). 'Aratos. [4]'. *Neuer Pauly*, 1: 957–62.

FARRELL, J. (1991). *Vergil's Georgics and the Traditions of Ancient Epic: The Art of Allusion in Literary History*. New York: Oxford University Press.

——(forthcoming). 'Greek Lives and Roman Careers in the Classical Vita Tradition'.

FERABOLI, S., FLORES, E., and SCARCIA, R. (1996–2001). *Manilio: Il poema degli astri (Astronomica)*, 2 vols. (n.p.) Mondadori.

FERGUSON, J. (1987). 'Epicurean Language-theory and Lucretian Practice'. *LCM* 12: 100–5.

FINNEGAN, R. (1992). *Oral Poetry: Its Nature, Significance and Social Context* (2nd edn.). Bloomington, Ind.: Indiana University Press.

FISH, S. E. (1974). 'How Ordinary Is Ordinary Language?', in W. Martin (ed.), *Language, Logic and Genre: Papers from the Poetics and Literary Theory Section, Modern Language Association*. Lewisburg, Pa.: Bucknell University Press, 13–27 (repr. in *Is there a Text in This Class?: The Authority of Interpretive Communities*. Cambridge, Mass.: Harvard University Press, 1980, 97–111).

FLEISCHER, U. (1960). 'Musentempel und Octavianehrung des Vergil im Proömium zum dritten Buche der Georgica'. *Hermes*, 88: 280–331.

FLORES, E. (1982). 'Dal fato alla storia: Manilio e la sacralità del potere augusteo fra poetica e ideologia'. *Vichiana*, 11: 109–30.

FÖGEN, T. (2000). '*Patrii sermonis egestas* und dichterisches Selbstbewußtsein bei Lukrez', in A. Haltenhoff and F.-H. Mutschler (eds.), *Hortus litterarum antiquarum: Festschrift für Hans Armin Gärtner zum 70. Geburtstag*. Heidelberg: Winter, 125–41.

FORD, A. (1992). *Homer: The Poetry of the Past*. Ithaca, NY: Cornell University Press.

FOWLER, A. (1982). *Kinds of Literature: An Introduction to the Theory of Genres and Modes*. Cambridge, Mass.: Harvard University Press.

FOWLER, D. (2000). 'The Didactic Plot', in M. Depew and D. Obbink (eds.), *Matrices of Genre: Authors, Canons, and Society*. Cambridge, Mass.: Harvard University Press, 205–19.

FOWLER, P. (1997). 'Lucretian Conclusions', in D. H. Roberts, F. M. Dunn, and D. Fowler (eds.), *Classical Closure: Reading the End in Greek and Latin Literature*. Princeton: Princeton University Press, 112–38.

FRÄNKEL, H. (1945). *Ovid: A Poet between Two Worlds*. Berkeley and Los Angeles: University of California Press.

FRIEDLÄNDER, P. (1941). 'Pattern of Sound and Atomistic Theory in

Lucretius'. *AJPh*, 62: 16–34 (repr. in *Studien zur antiken Literatur und Kunst*. Berlin: de Gruyter, 1969, 337–53 and in Classen (ed.) 1986*b*: 291–307).

FRISCHER, B. (1982). *The Sculpted Word: Epicureanism and Philosophical Recruitment in Ancient Greece*. Berkeley and Los Angeles: University of California Press.

FRISK, H. (1960–72). *Griechisches etymologisches Wörterbuch*, 3 vols. Heidelberg: Winter.

FUHRMANN, M. (1960). *Das systematische Lehrbuch: Ein Beitrag zur Geschichte der Wissenschaften in der Antike*. Göttingen: Vandenhoeck und Ruprecht.

FURLEY, D. (1970). 'Variations on Themes from Empedocles in Lucretius' Proem'. *BICS* 17: 55–64.

FYLER, J. M. (1971). '*Omnia uincit amor*: Incongruity and the Limitations of Structure in Ovid's Elegiac Poetry'. *CJ* 66: 196–203.

GALE, M. R. (1994*a*). 'Lucretius 4.1–25 and the Proems of *De Rerum Natura*'. *PCPhS* 40: 1–17.

—— (1994*b*). *Myth and Poetry in Lucretius*. Cambridge: Cambridge University Press.

—— (1997). 'The Rhetorical Programme of Lucretius I', in Atherton (ed.), 57–66.

—— (2000). *Virgil on the Nature of Things: The* Georgics, *Lucretius and the Didactic Tradition*. Cambridge: Cambridge University Press.

GARBER, F., ORSINI, G. N. G., and BROGAN, T. V. F. (1993). 'Genre', in Preminger and Brogan (eds.), 456–9.

GARROD, H. W. (1911). *Manili Astronomicon Liber II*. Oxford: Oxford University Press.

GEER, R. M. (1964). *Epicurus: Letters, Principal Doctrines, and Vatican Sayings*. New York: Macmillan.

GENETTE, G. (1977). 'Genres, "types", modes'. *Poétique*, 32: 389–421.

GIANCOTTI, F. (1959). *Il preludio di Lucrezio*. Messina: D'Anna.

—— (1960). 'La poetica epicurea in Lucrezio, Cicerone ed altri'. *Ciceroniana*, 2: 67–95.

GIANNISI, P. (1997). 'Chant et cheminement en Grèce archaïque'. *QS* 23.46: 133–41.

GIBSON, R. K. (1997). 'Didactic Poetry as "Popular" Form: A Study of Imperatival Expressions in Latin Didactic Verse and Prose', in Atherton (ed.), 67–98.

GIGON, O. (1978*a*). 'Lukrez und Ennius', in Gigon (ed.) 1978*b*: 167–96.

—— (ed.) (1978*b*). *Lucrèce* (= *Entretiens Hardt* 24). Geneva: Fondation Hardt.

GLEI, R. (1992). 'Erkenntnis als Aphrodisiakum: Poetische und philosophische *voluptas* bei Lukrez'. *A&A* 38: 82–94.

GOOLD, G. P. (1992). *Manilius:* Astronomica (2nd edn.). Cambridge, Mass.: Harvard University Press.

Gow, A. S. F. (1936). *A. E. Housman: A Sketch together with a List of his Writings and Indexes to his Classical Papers*. Cambridge: Cambridge University Press.
—— and SCHOLFIELD, A. F. (1953). *Nicander: The Poems and Poetical Fragments*. Cambridge: Cambridge University Press.
GRACA, C. (1989). *Da Epicuro a Lucrezio: Il maestro ed il poeta nei proemi del De rerum natura*. Amsterdam: Hakkert.
GRAF, F. (1997). *Magic in the Ancient World*. Cambridge, Mass.: Harvard University Press.
HARDIE, C. (1971). *The* Georgics: *A Transitional Poem*. Abingdon-on-Thames: The Abbey Press.
HARDIE, P. R. (1986). *Virgil's* Aeneid: *Cosmos and Imperium*. Oxford: Oxford University Press.
—— (1995). 'The Speech of Pythagoras in Ovid *Metamorphoses* 15: Empedoclean *Epos*'. *CQ* 45: 204–14.
HEINZE, R. (1897). *T. Lucretius Carus, De rerum natura, Buch III*. Leipzig: Teubner.
HELDMANN, K. (1981). 'Ovidius amoris artifex, Ovidius praeceptor Amoris (zu Ars am. 1, 1–24)'. *MH* 38: 162–6.
HENDERSON, A. A. R. (1970). '*Insignem conscendere currum* (Lucretius 6.47)'. *Latomus*, 29: 739–43.
—— (1979). *P. Ovidi Nasonis Remedia Amoris*. Edinburgh: Scottish Academic Press.
HERNADI, P. (ed.) (1978). *What is Literature?*. Bloomington, Ind.: Indiana University Press.
HILL, D. E. (1973). 'The Thessalian Trick'. *RhM* 116: 221–38.
HINDS, S. (1998). *Allusion and Intertext: Dynamics of Appropriation in Roman Poetry*. Cambridge: Cambridge University Press.
HOLLIS, A. S. (1973). 'The *Ars Amatoria* and *Remedia Amoris*', in J. W. Binns (ed.), *Ovid*. London: Routledge, 84–115.
—— (1977). *Ovid: Ars Amatoria, Book 1*. Oxford: Oxford University Press.
HOLZBERG, N. (1981). 'Ovids erotische Lehrgedichte und die römische Liebeselegie'. *WS* 15: 185–204.
—— (1997). *Ovid: Dichter und Werk*. Munich: Beck.
HORSFALL, N. M. (1995). '*Georgics*', in Horsfall (ed.), *A Companion to the Study of Virgil*. Leiden: Brill, 63–100.
HOUSMAN, A. E. (1903–30). *M. Manilii Astronomicon Libri*, 5 vols. London: Richards.
HÜBNER, W. (1982). *Die Eigenschaften der Tierkreiszeichen in der Antike: Ihre Darstellung und Verwendung unter besonderer Berücksichtigung des Manilius*. Wiesbaden: Steiner.
—— (1984). 'Manilius als Astrologe und Dichter'. *ANRW* 2.32.1: 126–320.
HUNTER, R. (1995). 'Written in the Stars: Poetry and Philosophy in the

Phaenomena of Aratus'. *Arachnion* 2 (on-line).
JAKOBSON, R. (1960). 'Linguistics and Poetics', in T. A. Sebeok (ed.), *Style in Language*. Cambridge, Mass.: MIT Press, 350–77 (repr. in *Selected Writings III: Poetry of Grammar and Grammar of Poetry*, ed. S. Rudy. The Hague: Mouton, 1981, 18–51).
JANKA, M. (1997). *Ovid*, Ars Amatoria, *Buch 2*. Heidelberg: Winter.
JANKO, R. (1984). *Aristotle on Comedy: Towards a Reconstruction of* Poetics *II*. Berkeley and Los Angeles: University of California Press.
JENKYNS, R. (1998). *Virgil's Experience: Nature and History, Times, Names, and Places*. Oxford: Oxford University Press.
JOBST, F. (1907). *Über das Verhältnis zwischen Lukretius und Empedokles*. Munich: Steinebach.
JOHNSON, W. R. (2000). *Lucretius and the Modern World*. London: Duckworth.
JONES, R. M. (1926). 'Posidonius and the Flight of the Mind through the Universe'. *CPh*, 21: 97–113.
KATZ, J. T. (1998). 'Topics in Indo-European Personal Pronouns'. Diss. Harvard.
KEEN, R. (1985). 'Lucretius and his Reader'. *Apeiron*, 19: 1–10.
KENNEY, E. J. (1958). 'Nequitiae Poeta', in N. I. Herescu (ed.), *Ovidiana: Recherches sur Ovide*. Paris: Les Belles Lettres, 201–9.
——(1970). 'Doctus Lucretius'. *Mnemosyne*, 23: 366–92 (repr. in Classen (ed.) 1986*b*: 237–65).
KERÉNYI, K. (1930). 'Religionsgeschichtliches zur Erklärung römischer Dichter'. *ARW* 28: 392–8.
KIDD, D. (1997). *Aratus: Phaenomena*. Cambridge: Cambridge University Press.
KLEVE, K. (1983). 'NASO MAGISTER ERAT—sed quis Nasonis magister?'. *SO* 58: 89–109.
——(1989). 'Lucretius in Herculaneum'. *CronErc*, 19: 5–27.
——(1997). 'Lucretius and Philodemus', in Algra, Koenen, and Schrijvers (eds.), 49–66.
KLINGNER, F. (1930). 'Die Einheit des virgilischen Lebenswerkes'. *MDAI(R)* 45: 43–58.
——(1963). *Virgils Georgica*. Zurich: Artemis.
KNOX, P. E. (1999). 'Lucretius on the Narrow Road'. *HSPh*, 99: 275–87.
KONSTAN, D., CLAY, D., GLAD, C. E., THOM, J. C., and WARE, J. (1998). *Philodemus,* On Frank Criticism: *Introduction, Translation and Notes*. Atlanta, Ga.: Scholars Press.
KOSTER, S. (1970). *Antike Epostheorien*. Wiesbaden: Steiner.
KRAGGERUD, E. (1998). 'Vergil Announcing the *Aeneid*: On *Georgics* 3.1–48', in H.-P. Stahl (ed.), *Vergil's* Aeneid: *Augustan Epic and Political Context*. London: Duckworth, 1–20.
KRANZ, W. (1944). 'Lukrez und Empedokles'. *Philologus*, 96: 68–107.

KRÓKOWSKI, J. (1963). '*Ars amatoria*—poème didactique'. *Eos*, 53: 143–56.
KROLL, W. (1924). *Studien zum Verständnis der römischen Literatur*. Stuttgart: Metzler.
——(1925). 'Lehrgedicht'. *Pauly-Wissowa*, 12.2: 1842–57.
KROMER, G. (1979). 'The Didactic Tradition in Vergil's Georgics'. *Ramus*, 8: 7–21.
KUHLMANN, G. (1906). *De poetae et poematis Graecorum appellationibus*. Diss. Marburg.
KÜHNER, R., and STEGMANN, C. (1955). *Ausführliche Grammatik der lateinischen Sprache: Satzlehre*, 2 vols. (3rd edn.). Leverkusen: Gottschalksche Verlagsbuchhandlung.
KULLMANN, W., and ALTHOFF, J. (eds.) (1993). *Vermittlung und Tradierung von Wissen in der griechischen Kultur*. Tübingen: Narr.
—— and ASPER, M. (eds.) (1998). *Gattungen wissenschaftlicher Literatur in der Antike*. Tübingen: Narr.
KÜPPERS, E. (1981). 'Ovids "Ars amatoria" und "Remedia amoris" als Lehrdichtungen'. *ANRW* 2.31.4: 2507–51.
LANDOLFI, L. (1999). '*OYPANOBATEIN*: Manilio, il volo e la poesia. Alcune precisazioni'. *Prometheus*, 25: 151–65.
LA PENNA, A. (1979). 'L'*usus* contro Apollo e le Muse: Nota a Ovidio, *Ars am.*, 1, 25–30'. *ASNP* 9: 985–97.
——(1985). 'Ille ego qui quondam e i raccordi editoriali nell'antichità'. *SIFC* 78: 76–91.
LAPIDGE, M. (1989). 'Stoic Cosmology and Roman Literature, First to Third Centuries A.D.'. *ANRW* 2.36.3: 1379–429.
LAUSBERG, M. (1990). 'Epos und Lehrgedicht: Ein Gattungsvergleich am Beispiel von Lucans Schlangenkatalog'. *WJA* 16: 173–203.
LEACH, E. W. (1964). 'Georgic Imagery in the *Ars amatoria*'. *TAPhA* 95: 142–54.
LEFÈVRE, E. (1967). 'Noch einmal: Ovid über seine Inspiration (Zur Ars amatoria I, 26)'. *Hermes*, 95: 126–8 and 256.
LEFKOWITZ, M. R. (1991). *First-Person Fictions: Pindar's Poetic 'I'*. Oxford: Oxford University Press.
——(1995). 'The First Person in Pindar Reconsidered—Again'. *BICS* 40: 139–50.
LENAGHAN, L. (1967). 'Lucretius 1.921–50'. *TAPhA* 98: 221–51.
LENZ, F. W. (1961). 'Das Proömium von Ovids Ars amatoria'. *Maia*, 13: 131–42.
LIEBERG, G. (1969). 'Seefahrt und Werk: Untersuchungen zu einer Metapher der antiken, besonders der lateinischen Literatur'. *GIF* 21: 209–40.
——(1982). *Poeta Creator: Studien zu einer Figur der antiken Dichtung*. Amsterdam: Gieben.

LIPKING, L. (1981). *The Life of the Poet: Beginning and Ending Poetic Careers*. Chicago: Chicago University Press.

LIUZZI, D. (1991-7). *M. Manilio: Astronomica*, 5 vols. Galatina: Congedo.

LONG, A. A. (1982). 'Astrology: Arguments pro and contra', in J. Barnes, J. Brunschwig, M. Burnyeat, and M. Schofield (eds.), *Science and Speculation: Studies in Hellenistic Theory and Practice*. Cambridge: Cambridge University Press, 165-92.

—— and SEDLEY, D. N. (1987). *The Hellenistic Philosophers*, 2 vols. Cambridge: Cambridge University Press.

LORD, A. B. (1960). *The Singer of Tales*. Cambridge, Mass.: Harvard University Press.

LOWRIE, M. (1997). *Horace's Narrative Odes*. Oxford: Oxford University Press.

LÜHR, F.-F. (1969). *Ratio und Fatum: Dichtung und Lehre bei Manilius*. Diss. Frankfurt.

McKEOWN, J. C. (1989). *Ovid: Amores, Text, Prolegomena and Commentary*, vol. 2. Leeds: Francis Cairns.

McLAUGHLIN, J. D. (1979). 'Vengeance with a Twist: Another Look at the *Prooemium* to Ovid's *Ars amatoria*'. *Maia*, 31: 269-71.

MALLE, L., and CARRIÈRE, J.-C. (1990). *Milou in May*. London: Faber and Faber.

MANZINO, M., and MANZINO, M. (1991-2). *Concordanze degli* Astronomica *di Manilio*, 2 vols. Genoa: D.AR.FI.CL.ET.

MARTIN, A., and PRIMAVESI, O. (1999). *L'Empédocle de Strasbourg (P. Strasb. gr. Inv. 1665-1666): Introduction, édition et commentaire*. Berlin: de Gruyter.

MARTIN, R. P. (1992). 'Hesiod's Metanastic Poetics'. *Ramus*, 21: 11-33.

MARTINDALE, C. (ed.) (1997). *The Cambridge Companion to Virgil*. Cambridge: Cambridge University Press.

MAYER, R. (1986). 'A Note on a "raccordo editoriale" of Virgil'. *Maia*, 38: 159.

—— (1990). 'The Epic of Lucretius'. *Papers of the Leeds International Latin Seminar*, 6: 35-43.

MEULI, K. (1935). 'Scythica'. *Hermes*, 70: 121-76 (repr. in *Gesammelte Schriften*, ed. T. Gelzer, 2 vols. Basel: Schwabe und Co., 1975: 2. 817-79).

MILANESE, G. (1989). *Lucida carmina: Comunicazione e scrittura da Epicuro a Lucrezio*. Milan: Vita e Pensiero.

MILLER, J. F. (1983). 'Callimachus and the *Ars Amatoria*'. *CPh*, 78: 26-34.

—— (1986). 'Disclaiming Divine Inspiration: A Programmatic Pattern'. *WS* 20: 151-64.

—— (1992). 'The *Fasti* and Hellenistic Didactic: Ovid's Variant Aetiologies'. *Arethusa*, 25: 11-31.

—— (1993). 'Apostrophe, Aside and the Didactic Addressee: Poetic Strategies in Ars Amatoria III', in Schiesaro, Mitsis, and Clay (eds.),

231–41.
MINADEO, R. (1969). *The Lyre of Science: Form and Meaning in Lucretius'* De Rerum Natura. Detroit: Wayne State University Press.
MITSIS, P. (1993). 'Committing Philosophy on the Reader: Didactic Coercion and Reader Autonomy in De Rerum Natura', in Schiesaro, Mitsis, and Clay (eds.), 111–28.
MORGAN, L. (1999). *Patterns of Redemption in Virgil's* Georgics. Cambridge: Cambridge University Press.
MOST, G. W. (1999). 'The Poetics of Early Greek Philosophy', in A. A. Long (ed.), *The Cambridge Companion to Early Greek Philosophy*. Cambridge: Cambridge University Press, 332–62.
MÜLLER, G. (1978). 'Die Finalia der sechs Bücher des Lucrez', in Gigon (ed.) 1978*b*: 197–231.
MÜNZER, F. (1931). 'Memmius 8'. *Pauly-Wissowa*, 15.1: 609–16.
MURLEY, C. (1947). 'Lucretius, *De Rerum Natura*, Viewed as Epic'. *TAPhA* 78: 336–46.
MUSSEHL, J. (1912). *De Lucretiani libri primi condicione ac retractatione*. Tempelhof: Schmidt.
MYEROWITZ, M. (1985). *Ovid's Games of Love*. Detroit: Wayne State University Press.
MYERS, K. S. (1994). *Ovid's Causes: Cosmogony and Aetiology in the* Metamorphoses. Ann Arbor: University of Michigan Press.
MYNORS, R. A. B. (1990). *Virgil: Georgics*. Oxford: Oxford University Press.
NAGY, G. (1990). *Greek Mythology and Poetics*. Ithaca: Cornell University Press.
——(1996). *Poetry as Performance: Homer and Beyond*. Cambridge: Cambridge University Press.
NELSON, S. A. (1998). *God and the Land: The Metaphysics of Farming in Hesiod and Vergil*. New York: Oxford University Press.
NEUBURG, M. (1993). 'Hitch Your Wagon to a Star: Manilius and his Two Adressees', in Schiesaro, Mitsis, and Clay (eds.), 243–82.
NEWLANDS, C. E. (1995). *Playing with Time: Ovid and the* Fasti. Ithaca, NY: Cornell University Press.
NEWMAN, J. K. (1967). *The Concept of Vates in Augustan Poetry* (= *Collection Latomus* 89). Brussels: Latomus.
NISBET, R. G. M., and HUBBARD, M. (1970). *A Commentary on Horace, Odes, Book 1*. Oxford: Oxford University Press.
NORDEN, E. (1891). *In Varronis Saturas Menippeas observationes selectae*. Leipzig: Teubner.
NÜNLIST, R. (1998). *Poetologische Bildersprache in der frühgriechischen Dichtung*. Stuttgart: Teubner.
NUSSBAUM, M. (1986). 'Therapeutic Arguments: Epicurus and Aristotle', in M. Schofield and G. Striker (eds.), *The Norms of Nature: Studies in*

Hellenistic Ethics. Cambridge: Cambridge University Press, 31–74.
OBBINK, D. (1993). 'The Adressees of Empedocles', in Schiesaro, Mitsis, and Clay (eds.), 51–98.
——(ed.) (1995). *Philodemus and Poetry: Poetic Theory and Practice in Lucretius, Philodemus, and Horace.* New York: Oxford University Press.
O'HARA, J. J. (1998). 'Venus or the Muse as "Ally" (Lucr. 1.24, Simon. Frag. Eleg. 11.20–22 W)'. *CPh*, 93: 69–74.
OLSON, S. D., and SENS, A. (2000). *Archestratos of Gela: Greek Culture and Cuisine in the Fourth Century BCE.* Oxford: Oxford University Press.
O'NEILL, P. (1994). *Fictions of Discourse: Reading Narrative Theory.* Toronto: University of Toronto Press.
OSBORNE, C. (1997). 'Was Verse the Default Form for Presocratic Philosophy?', in Atherton (ed.), 23–35 (= response to M. R. Wright 1997).
OTIS, B. (1963). *Virgil: A Study in Civilized Poetry.* Oxford: Oxford University Press.
PARKER, H. N. (1992). 'Love's Body Anatomized: The Ancient Erotic Handbooks and the Rhetoric of Sexuality', in A. Richlin (ed.), *Pornography and Representation in Greece and Rome.* New York: Oxford University Press, 90–111.
PARRY, A. (1972). 'The Idea of Art in Virgil's *Georgics*'. *Arethusa*, 5: 35–52 (repr. in *The Language of Achilles and Other Papers.* Oxford: Oxford University Press, 1989, 265–85).
PATIN, H. J. G. (1868–9). *Études sur la poésie latine*, 2 vols. Paris: Hachette.
PEASE, A. S. (1955). *M. Tulli Ciceronis De natura deorum*, vol. 1. Cambridge, Mass.: Harvard University Press.
PERKELL, C. G. (1989). *The Poet's Truth: A Study of the Poet in Virgil's* Georgics. Berkeley and Los Angeles: University of California Press.
PFEIJFFER, I. L. (1999). *First Person Futures in Pindar.* Stuttgart: Steiner.
PÖHLMANN, E. (1973). 'Charakteristika des römischen Lehrgedichts'. *ANRW* I. 3: 813–901.
PRATT, M. L. (1977). *Towards a Speech Act Theory of Literary Discourse.* Bloomington, Ind.: Indiana University Press.
PREMINGER, A., and BROGAN, T. V. F. (eds.) (1993). *The New Princeton Encyclopedia of Poetry and Poetics.* Princeton: Princeton University Press.
PRITCHARD, J. B. (1969). *Ancient Near Eastern Texts relating to the Old Testament* (3rd edn.). Princeton: Princeton University Press.
RAWSON, E. (1985). *Intellectual Life in the Late Roman Republic.* Baltimore: Johns Hopkins University Press.
REEH, A. (1973). *Interpretationen zu den Astronomica des Manilius mit besonderer Berücksichtigung der philosophischen Partien.* Marburg: Symons.
REGENBOGEN, O. (1932). 'Lukrez: Seine Gestalt in seinem Gedicht'. *Neue Wege zur Antike* 2.1 (repr. in *Kleine Schriften*, ed. F. Dirlmeier. Munich:

Beck, 1961, 296–386).
REIFF, A. (1959). Interpretatio, imitatio, aemulatio: *Begriff und Vorstellung literarischer Abhängigkeit bei den Römern*. Diss. Cologne.
REINSCH-WERNER, H. (1976). *Callimachus Hesiodicus: Die Rezeption der hesiodischen Dichtung durch Kallimachos von Kyrene*. Berlin: Mielke.
REITZENSTEIN, E. (1931). 'Zur Stiltheorie des Kallimachos', in E. Fraenkel, H. Fränkel, M. Pohlen, E. Reitzenstein, E. Schwartz, and J. Stroux (eds.), *Festschrift Richard Reitzenstein*. Leipzig: Teubner, 23–69.
ROMANO, E. (1978). 'Gli appelli al lettore negli *Astronomica* di Manilio'. *Pan*, 6: 115–25.
——(1979). *Struttura degli* Astronomica *di Manilio* (= Accad. di sc., lett. ed arti di Palermo cl. di sc. mor. e filol. Mem. 2). Palermo: Boccone del Povero.
RÖSCH, H. (1911). *Manilius und Lucrez*. Kiel: Fiencke.
ROSENMEYER, T. G. (1985). 'Ancient Literary Genres: A Mirage?'. *Yearbook of Comparative and General Literature*, 34: 74–84.
RÖSLER, W. (1973). 'Lukrez und die Vorsokratiker: Doxographische Probleme im 1. Buch von "De rerum natura" '. *Hermes*, 101: 48–64 (repr. in Classen (ed.) 1986*b*: 57–73).
——(1983). 'Über Deixis und einige Aspekte mündlichen und schriftlichen Stils in antiker Lyrik'. *WJA* 9: 7–28.
ROSS, D. O. (1975). *Backgrounds to Augustan Poetry: Gallus, Elegy, and Rome*. Cambridge: Cambridge University Press.
ROSSI, L. E. (1971). 'I generi letterari e le loro leggi scritte e non scritte nelle letterature classiche'. *BICS* 18: 69–94.
RUSSELL, D. A. (1981). *Criticism in Antiquity*. Berkeley and Los Angeles: University of California Press.
RUTHERFORD, R. (1995). 'Authorial Rhetoric in Virgil's *Georgics*', in D. Innes, H. Hine, and C. Pelling (eds.), *Ethics and Rhetoric: Classical Essays for Donald Russell on his Seventy-Fifth Birthday*. Oxford: Oxford University Press, 19–29.
SALEMME, C. (1983). *Introduzione agli* Astronomica *di Manilio*. Naples: Società Editrice Napoletana.
SCARSI, M. (1987). 'Metafora e ideologia negli *Astronomica* di Manilio'. *Analysis*, 1: 93–126.
SCHÄFER, S. (1996). *Das Weltbild der Vergilischen* Georgika *in seinem Verhältnis zu* De rerum natura *des Lukrez*. Frankfurt: Lang.
SCHIESARO, A. (1984). ' "Nonne vides" in Lucrezio'. *MD* 13: 143–57.
——(1987). 'Lucrezio, Cicerone, l'oratoria'. *MD* 19: 29–61.
——(1993). 'Il destinatario discreto: Funzioni didascaliche e progetto culturale nelle Georgiche', in Schiesaro, Mitsis, and Clay (eds.), 129–47.
——(1994). 'The Palingenesis of *De Rerum Natura*'. *PCPhS* 40: 81–107.
——MITSIS, P., and CLAY, J. S. (eds.) (1993). *Mega Nepios: Il destinatario*

nell'epos didascalico / *The Addressee in Didactic Epic* (=*MD* 31). Pisa: Giardini.

SCHINDLER, C. (2000). *Untersuchungen zu den Gleichnissen im römischen Lehrgedicht (Lucrez, Vergil, Manilius)*. Göttingen: Vandenhoeck und Ruprecht.

SCHMIDT, S. J. (1972). 'Ist "Fiktionalität" eine linguistische oder eine texttheoretische Kategorie?', in E. Gülich and W. Raible (eds.), *Textsorten*. Frankfurt: Athenäum, 59–71.

SCHRIJVERS, P. H. (1970). *Horror ac divina voluptas: Études sur la poétique et la poésie de Lucrèce*. Amsterdam: Hakkert.

—— (1983). 'Le Chant du monde: Remarques sur *Astronomica* I 1–24 de Manilius'. *Mnemosyne*, 36: 143–50.

SCHULER, R. M., and FITCH, J. G. (1983). 'Theory and Context of the Didactic Poem: Some Classical, Mediaeval, and Later Continuities'. *Florilegium*, 5: 1–43.

SEDLEY, D. (1989). 'The Proems of Empedocles and Lucretius'. *GRBS* 30: 269–96.

—— (1998). *Lucretius and the Transformation of Greek Wisdom*. Cambridge: Cambridge University Press.

SHACKLETON BAILEY, D. R. (1980). *Cicero: Epistulae ad Quintum fratrem et M. Brutum*. Cambridge: Cambridge University Press.

SHARROCK, A. (1994). *Seduction and Repetition in Ovid's* Ars Amatoria *2*. Oxford: Oxford University Press.

SHULMAN, J. (1981). '*Te quoque falle tamen*: Ovid's Anti-Lucretian Didactics'. *CJ* 76: 242–53.

SKUTSCH, O. (1985). *The* Annals *of Q. Ennius*. Oxford: Oxford University Press.

SNYDER, J. M. (1980). *Puns and Poetry in Lucretius'* De rerum natura. Amsterdam: Grüner.

SOLODOW, J. B. (1977). 'Ovid's Ars Amatoria: The Lover as Cultural Ideal'. *WS* 11: 106–27.

SOMMARIVA, G. (1980). 'La parodia di Lucrezio nell'*Ars* e nei *Remedia* ovidiani'. *A&R* 25: 123–48.

SPURR, M. S. (1986). 'Agriculture and the *Georgics*'. *G&R* 33: 164–87 (repr. in I. McAuslan and P. Walcot (eds.), *Virgil*. Oxford: Oxford University Press, 1990, 69–93).

STABILE, G. (1988). 'Rota Vergilii'. *Enciclopedia Virgiliana*, 4: 586–7.

STEINER, D. (1986). *The Crown of Song: Metaphor in Pindar*. London: Duckworth.

STEINMETZ, P. (1964). 'Gattungen und Epochen der griechischen Literatur in der Sicht Quintilians'. *Hermes*, 92: 454–66.

STEUDEL, M. (1992). *Die Literaturparodie in Ovids* Ars Amatoria. Hildesheim: Olms.

STOKES, M. C. (1975). 'A Lucretian Paragraph: III. 1–30', in G. M. Kirkwood (ed.), *Poetry and Poetics from Ancient Greece to the Renaissance: Studies in Honor of James Hutton*. Ithaca, NY: Cornell University Press, 91–104.

STROH, W. (1976). 'De crucibus quibusdam amatoriis', in N. Barbu, E. Dobroiu, and M. Nasta (eds.), *Acta Conventus Omnium Gentium Ovidianis Studiis Fovendis*. Bucharest: Tipografia Universităţii, 563–8 (repr. in *Apocrypha: Entlegene Schriften*, ed. J. Leonhardt and G. Ott. Stuttgart: Steiner, 2000, 175–9).

—— (1979*a*). 'Ovids Liebeskunst und die Ehegesetze des Augustus'. *Gymnasium*, 86: 323–52.

—— (1979*b*). 'Rhetorik und Erotik: Eine Studie zu Ovids liebesdidaktischen Gedichten'. *WJA* 5: 117–32.

SUERBAUM, W. (1965). 'Ovid über seine Inspiration (Zur Ars amatoria I, 26)'. *Hermes*, 93: 491–6.

—— (1968). *Untersuchungen zur Selbstdarstellung älterer römischer Dichter: Livius Andronicus, Naevius, Ennius*. Hildesheim: Olms.

TATUM, W. J. (1984). 'The Presocratics in Book One of Lucretius' *De rerum natura*'. *TAPhA* 114: 177–89.

THEODORAKOPOULOS, E. (1997). 'Closure: The Book of Virgil', in Martindale (ed.), 155–65.

THILL, A. (1979). *Alter ab illo: Recherches sur l'imitation dans la poésie personnelle à l'époque augustéenne*. Paris: Les Belles Lettres.

THOMAS, R. F. (1983). 'Callimachus, the *Victoria Berenices*, and Roman Poetry'. *CQ* 33: 92–113 (repr. in Thomas 1999: 68–100).

—— (1985). 'From *recusatio* to Commitment: The Evolution of the Vergilian Programme'. *Papers of the Liverpool Latin Seminar*, 5: 61–73 (repr. in Thomas 1999: 101–13).

—— (1988). *Virgil: Georgics*, 2 vols. Cambridge: Cambridge University Press.

—— (1998). 'Virgil's Pindar?', in P. Knox and C. Foss (eds.), *Style and Tradition: Studies in Honor of Wendell Clausen*. Stuttgart: Teubner, 99–120 (repr. in Thomas 1999: 267–87).

—— (1999). *Reading Virgil and His Texts: Studies in Intertextuality*. Ann Arbor: University of Michigan Press.

THURY, E. M. (1987). 'Lucretius' Poem as a *simulacrum* of the *rerum natura*'. *AJPh*, 108: 270–94.

TOMASCO, D. (1999), 'Su Lucrezio *De r. n.* III 1–30'. *Vichiana*, 1. 2: 17–37.

TOOHEY, P. (1996). *Epic Lessons: An Introduction to Ancient Didactic Poetry*. London: Routledge.

TOWNEND, G. B. (1978). 'The Fading of Memmius'. *CQ* 28: 267–83.

VALLAURI, G. (1954). 'Gli *Astronomica* di Manilio e le fonti ermetiche'. *RFIC* 32: 133–67.

VALVO, M. (1978). '*Tu princeps auctorque sacri, Cyllenie, tanti* . . . : La rivincita dell'uomo maniliano nel segno di Hermes'. *Sileno*, 4: 111–28.

VAN WAGENINGEN, J. (1921). *Commentarius in M. Manilii Astronomica* (= *Verhandel. Nederl. Akad. van Wet. Afd. Letterk.* 22.4). Amsterdam: Müller.
VERDENIUS, W. J. (1970). *Homer, the Educator of the Greeks* (= *Mededel. Nederl. Akad. van Wet. Afd. Letterk.* 33.5). Amsterdam: North-Holland.
VERDUCCI, F. (1980). 'The Contest of Rational Libertinism and Imaginative License in Ovid's *Ars amatoria*'. *Pacific Coast Philology*, 15.2: 29–39.
VIANSINO, G. (1969). 'La tecnica didascalica nell'ars amatoria di Ovidio'. *Rivista di Studi Salernitani*, 2: 487–502.
VOLK, K. (1997). '*Cum carmine crescit et annus*: Ovid's *Fasti* and the Poetics of Simultaneity'. *TAPhA* 127: 287–313.
—— (2001). 'Pious and Impious Approaches to Cosmology in Manilius'. *MD* 47, 85–117.
VON STADEN, H. (1998). 'Gattung und Gedächtnis: Galen über Wahrheit und Lehrdichtung', in Kullmann, Althoff, and Asper (eds.), 65–94.
WASZINK, J. H. (1950). 'The Proem of the *Annales* of Ennius'. *Mnemosyne*, 3: 215–40.
—— (1954). *Lucretius and Poetry* (= *Mededel. Nederl. Akad. van Wet. Afd. Letterk.* 17.8). Amsterdam: North-Holland.
—— (1956). 'Maniliana'. *SIFC* 27/28: 588–98.
—— (1974). *Biene und Honig als Symbol des Dichters und der Dichtung in der griechisch-römischen Antike* (= *Rheinisch-Westfälische Akademie der Wissenschaften: Vorträge G 196*). Opladen: Westdeutscher Verlag.
WATKINS, C. (1995). *How to Kill a Dragon: Aspects of Indo-European Poetics*. New York: Oxford University Press.
WELLMANN-BRETZIGHEIMER, G. (1981). 'Ovids *ars amatoria*', in H. G. Rötzer and H. Walz (eds.), *Europäische Lehrdichtung: Festschrift für Walter Naumann zum 70. Geburtstag*. Darmstadt: Wissenschaftliche Buchgesellschaft, 1–32.
WENDEL, C. (1914). *Scholia in Theocritum vetera*. Leipzig: Teubner.
WEST, D. (1994). *The Imagery and Poetry of Lucretius* (2nd edn.). Norman, Okla.: Oklahoma University Press.
WEST, M. L. (1978). *Hesiod: Works & Days*. Oxford: Oxford University Press.
WHEELER, S. M. (1999). *A Discourse of Wonders: Audience and Performance in Ovid's Metamorphoses*. Philadelphia: University of Pennsylvania Press.
WHITE, P. (1993). *Promised Verse: Poets in the Society of Augustan Rome*. Cambridge, Mass.: Harvard University Press.
WILDBERGER, J. (1998). *Ovids Schule der 'elegischen' Liebe: Erotodidaxe und Psychagogie in der Ars amatoria*. Frankfurt: Lang.
WILKINSON, L. P. (1955). *Ovid Recalled*. Cambridge: Cambridge University Press.
—— (1969). *The Georgics of Virgil: A Critical Survey*. Cambridge: Cambridge

University Press.
——(1970). 'Pindar and the Proem to the Third Georgic', in W. Wimmel (ed.), *Forschungen zur römischen Literatur: Festschrift zum 60. Geburtstag von Karl Büchner*. Wiesbaden: Steiner, 286–90.
WILLIAMS, G. D. (1996). *The Curse of Exile: A Study of Ovid's Ibis*. Cambridge: Cambridge University Press.
WILSON, A. M. (1985). 'The Prologue to Manilius 1'. *Papers of the Liverpool Latin Seminar*, 5: 283–98.
WILTSHIRE, S. F. (1974). 'Nunc Age: Lucretius as Teacher'. *CB* 50: 33–7.
WIMMEL, W. (1960). *Kallimachos in Rom: Die Nachfolge seines apologetischen Dichtens in der Augusteerzeit*. Wiesbaden: Steiner.
WIMSATT, JR., W. K., and BEARDSLEY, M. C. (1946). 'The Intentional Fallacy'. *Sewanee Review*, 54: 468–88.
WÖHRLE, G. (1991). 'Carmina divini pectoris oder *prodesse* und *delectare* bei Lukrez und Empedokles'. *WS* 104: 119–29.
——(1993). 'War Parmenides ein schlechter Dichter? Oder: Zur Form der Wissensvermittlung in der frühgriechischen Philosophie', in Kullmann and Althoff (eds.), 167–80.
——(1998). 'Bemerkungen zur lehrhaften Dichtung zwischen Empedokles und Arat', in Kullmann, Althoff, and Asper (eds.), 279–86.
WRIGHT, E. F. (1984). 'Profanum sunt Genus: The Poets of the *Ars Amatoria*'. *PQ* 63: 1–15.
WRIGHT, M. R. (1995). *Empedocles: The Extant Fragments* (2nd edn.). London: Bristol Classical Press.
——(1997). 'Philosopher Poets: Parmenides and Empedocles', in Atherton (ed.), 1–22.
YATES, F. A. (1966). *The Art of Memory*. Chicago: University of Chicago Press.
ZINTZEN, C. (1987). 'Das Zusammenwirken von Rezeption und Originalität am Beispiel römischer Autoren', in H. Lange and C. Zintzen, *Zum Problem der Rezeption in den Geisteswissenschaften* (= *AAWM* 1986.7). Stuttgart: Steiner, 15–36.

INDEX OF PASSAGES CITED

GREEK

Aesch. *Ag.* 1050–1: 110 n. 109

Antip. Sid. *Anth. Pal.* 7. 713. 7–8: 109–10

Ap. Rhod. *Argon.* 1. 1–4: 57 n. 65
  1. 22: 57 n. 65
  4. 1773–81: 13
  4. 1773–5: 13
  4. 1775–6: 13

Aratus, *Phaen.* 1–732: 41
  1–18: 56
  1: 56, 57
  15: 57
  16–18: 56, 57
  17: 57
  75: 199
  96–136: 128
  179–80: 56
  421–2: 83 n. 42
  460–1: 56
  607–8: 56
  733–1154: 41
  1036–7: 56

Archestratus 5. 2: 54
  18. 3: 54
  28. 1: 54
  36. 4: 54

Ar. *Ran.* 93: 110 n. 109

Arist.
Poet. 1447^a13–20: 2
  1447^a13–16: 7
  1447^b13–17: 29–30
  1447^b13–14: 7
  1447^b16–20: 33 n. 19, 53
  1447^b16–17: 33 n. 19
  1447^b16: 51, 53
  1447^b17–20: 70 n. 6
  1447^b17–18: 30 n. 13
  1447^b19–20: 30
  1448^a20–4: 11 n. 10, 28 n. 8
  1460^a5–11: 11 n. 10
fr. 70: 30 n. 13, 70 n. 6

Ath. 7. 278e: 54

Callim.
Aet. fr. 1. 13–16: 110 n. 108
  fr. 1. 21–2: 86 n. 49
  fr. 1. 25–8: 87, 227
  fr. 1. 27–8: 87
Epigr. 27: 55 n. 61
  27. 1: 57
  28. 1–2: 9 n. 5
Hymn 2: 183
  2. 110–12: 87–8
  5: 183
  6: 183

Cleanthes, *SVF* 1. 486: 236 n. 79

CH 1. 24–6: 230
  1. 26: 230

Diog. Laert. 8. 54: 51 n. 51
  10. 13: 93 n. 69
  10. 119: 86
  10. 121: 86 n. 48

Index of Passages Cited 269

Empedocles
B1: 51
  B2. 5: 52
  B3: 39
  B3. 2: 52
  B4: 39
  B4. 2: 51
  B8. 1: 51
  B17. 1: 51
  B17. 16: 51
  B23. 11: 39, 51, 53
  B35. 1–3: 39, 52 and n. 53
  B38. 1: 51
  B112: 51 n. 51
  B131: 39, 84 n. 44
  B131. 3–4: 52
  B139: 51 n. 50
P. Strasb. gr. Inv. 1665–6: 71 n. 6
  a (ii) 21–2: 51 n. 51
  a (ii) 29–30: 51 n. 51
  d 10–11: 51 n. 51

Epicurus
Ep. Hdt. 35–6: 76
  37–8: 117
fr. 20: 94 n. 72
fr. 54: 93 n. 69
fr. 117: 94
fr. 227: 94
fr. 228: 94
fr. 229: 94
fr. 230: 94
fr. 563: 86
fr. 568: 86 n. 48

Eur. *Or.* 1592: 80 n. 32

Gorg. *Hel.* 9: 5, 6

Hes.
Op. 1–10: 46, 47 and n. 46
  1–2: 39
  2: 46, 47 n. 46
  3–10: 47 n. 44
  10: 37, 45, 47 and n. 46, 130

    n. 18
  27: 130 n. 18
  106–7: 45–6
  107: 46 n. 43
  202: 46 n. 41
  274: 46 n. 43
  286: 46 and n. 43
  316: 46 n. 41
  367: 46 n. 41
  403: 46 n. 41
  536: 46 n. 41
  603: 46 n. 41
  623: 46 n. 41
  648: 46 n. 41
  654–62: 39
  654–9: 46
  654–7: 48 n. 47
  658–9: 48 and n. 47
  659: 20–1
  660: 48
  661–2: 46, 48
  661: 46 nn. 41 and 43, 48
  687–8: 46 n. 41
  826–8: 83 n. 42
Theog. 1–104: 47
  105–15: 47
  965–9: 45 n. 40
  1021–2: 45 n. 40
fr. 283: 49 n. 48

Hom.
Il. 1. 297: 46 n. 43
  2. 484–93: 12, 48
  2. 485–6: 12
  2. 761–2: 12
  4. 39: 46 n. 43
  5. 259: 46 n. 43
  9. 434–605: 46
  9. 611: 46 n. 43
  11. 218–20: 12
  12. 176: 12
  14. 508–10: 12
  16. 112–13: 12
  16. 444: 46 n. 43

Index of Passages Cited

Hom. *Il.* (cont.)
  16. 851: 46 n. 43
  21. 94: 46 n. 43
  23. 315–18: 181 n. 45
Od. 8. 74: 20
  8. 481: 20
  22. 347: 20

[Hom.] *Batrachomyomachia* 1:
    86 n. 49
  3: 86 n. 49

Hymn. Hom.
  2. 1: 13
  6. 2: 13
  10. 1: 13
  11. 1: 13
  13. 1: 13
  15. 1: 13
  16. 1: 13
  22. 1: 13
  23. 1: 13
  26. 1: 13
  28.1: 13
  30. 1: 13
Hymn. Hom. Merc. 451: 20 n. 30

Ibyc. fr. 287. 6–7: 111 n. 111

Leonidas of Tarentum, *Anth. Pal.*
  9. 24: 115 n. 124

Nic.
Alex. 5: 57
  629–30: 83 n. 42
  629: 11 n. 11, 39, 57
Ther. 4: 57
  957–8: 83 n. 42
  957: 11 n. 11, 39, 57

Parmenides B2: 50
  B2. 1: 50
  B2. 6: 50
  B4. 1: 50

B6: 50
B6. 2: 50
B6. 3: 50
B7: 50
B7. 2–8. 1: 50
B7. 5–8. 2: 50
B8. 50–2: 50
B8. 60–1: 50

Phld.
On Free Speech 45. 7–11: 115 n. 126
On Poems 5 col. 32. 17–19: 95 n. 74

Pind.
Nem. 3. 80–2: 109 n. 106
Ol. 2. 1–2: 14 n. 19
  2. 86–8: 109 n. 106
  6. 22–8: 19
  6. 23: 19
  6. 24–5: 19
  6. 27: 19
  6. 28: 19
Pyth. 4. 247–8: 21
Σ *ad* Pind. *Pyth.* 6. 22: 49 n. 48

Pl.
Ion 534a7–b3: 112
  540d1–541d7: 36
Resp. 3. 392c9–394c8: 7, 11 n. 10, 28 n. 8
  3. 393a6–7: 11 n. 10
  10. 614b2–621b7: 229–30
  10. 617b4–7: 235
Ti. 47b5–e2: 234 n. 74
  47d1–e2: 236 n. 79
  90c7–d7: 234 n. 74

Plato Com. fr. 189: 54

Plut.
Non posse 1095 C: 94 n. 72
Quomodo adul. 16 C: 30 n. 14

P Oxy. 2891: 158

Procl. *Prolegomena to Hesiod* (*Poetae Minores Graeci* 4. 4 Gaisford):
33 n. 20

Ptol. *Anth. Pal.* 9. 577: 228–9

Sext. Emp. *Math.* 7. 111: 50

Simon.
Anth. Pal. 6. 213. 4: 89 n. 58

fr. 11. 21: 85 n. 45

Suppl. Hell. 1001: 112

Theoc. *Id.* 5. 136–7: 109 n. 107
7. 39–41: 109
7. 47–8: 109

Thgn. 1. 943–4: 18 n. 24

Tractatus Coislinianus, *CGF* 50: 31

LATIN

Accius, *Didascalica*, fr. 13: 59

Bede, *De arte metrica*, *Gramm. Lat.* 7. 259. 14–260. 1: 33 n. 20

Catull. 10: 74
28: 74
68. 33–6: 112 n. 14

Cic.
De or. 1. 69: 61 n. 71
Div. 1. 119: 207 n. 25
Fin. 2. 4. 12: 94
Q Fr. 2. 10. 3: 60 and n. 70, 61 n. 71
Sen. 14: 111
Somn. 16: 230
18–19: 235
18: 236 n. 79

Diom. *Ars Grammatica*, *Gramm. Lat.*
1. 482. 14–25: 33 n. 20
1. 482. 14: 31
1. 482. 17–18: 31
1. 482. 20–1: 31
1. 482. 21: 39, 79
1. 482. 22: 40
1. 482. 23: 31
1. 482. 31–2: 31

1. 483. 1–3: 31–2

Donat. *Vit. Verg.* 35: 155
36: 153
42: 153
57: 153–4
58–9: 154

Dositheus, *Ars Grammatica*, *Gramm. Lat.* 7. 428. 6–14: 33 n. 20

Enn.
Ann. 34: 111 n. 112
206–10: 114 n. 120
210: 149
522–3: 111
Epigr. 18: 148–9
Hedyphagetica 4: 58
5: 58
6: 58
7: 58

German. *Arat.* 1–16: 201
5–16: 217 n. 38

Hor.
Ars P. 11: 42
24–5: 42

Hor. *Ars P. (cont.)*
  73–85: 27
  73–4: 27–8
  79: 28 n. 6
  301–8: 42
  306: 42, 48 n. 47
  333: 36
Carm. 1. 1. 35–6: 230
  1. 12: 14
  1. 12. 1–3: 14
  1. 12. 13–24: 14
  1. 12. 13: 14
  1. 12. 21: 14
  1. 12. 25–32: 14
  1. 12. 25: 14
  1. 12. 33–6: 14
  1. 28. 4–6: 228
  3. 25. 1–3: 175 n. 39
  3. 30: 15
  3. 30. 10–14: 114 n. 120
  4. 2: 150 n. 41
  4. 2. 25–32: 112 n. 115
Epist. 1. 19. 23–4: 114 n. 120
  2. 1. 50: 114 n. 121
Sat. 1. 4. 39–42: 42

Iunius Philargyrius *ad Verg. Buc.*
  Prooem. 1I,12–2I,8: 33 n. 20

Isid. *Etym.* 8. 7. 11: 33 n. 20

Jer. *Ab Abr.* 1923: 72 n. 10

Luc. 1. 63–6: 201–2
  2. 547: 78 n. 30

Lucr. 1. 1: 84 n. 44, 85 n. 46, 99
  1. 15–16: 98
  1. 21–3: 85
  1. 21: 85
  1. 22–3: 85
  1. 24–6: 16 n. 21, 84, 176 n. 41
  1. 24: 84, 85 and n. 45
  1. 25: 85, 105
  1. 26–8: 85
  1. 26: 74 n. 13, 130 n. 18
  1. 28: 87 n. 51, 98, 104
  1. 29–43: 217 n. 38
  1. 41–3: 74
  1. 41: 74
  1. 42: 74 n. 13
  1. 50–61: 80
  1. 50–1: 77, 80, 147
  1. 50: 130 n. 18
  1. 52–3: 80
  1. 62–79: 70
  1. 66: 90, 107 n. 101
  1. 71: 107 n. 101
  1. 72–4: 90, 229
  1. 75–9: 107 n. 101
  1. 75: 148
  1. 80–2: 89
  1. 117–18: 88, 114, 150
  1. 117: 107 n. 101, 114 n. 120
  1. 120–6: 63 n. 73
  1. 124–6: 88 n. 54, 105, 114
  1. 126: 106
  1. 127–8: 77
  1. 132–5: 77
  1. 136–9: 71, 242
  1. 136–7: 92
  1. 137: 84
  1. 140–5: 73
  1. 140–2: 99
  1. 140–1: 73
  1. 143–4: 113
  1. 143: 84
  1. 146–8: 76, 92
  1. 148: 75 n. 19
  1. 149: 75
  1. 156–7: 90
  1. 196–8: 85, 100 n. 84
  1. 215–64: 78
  1. 328: 92
  1. 329–97: 81 n. 36
  1. 332: 90
  1. 370–1: 90
  1. 398–417: 81

Index of Passages Cited

1. 402–3: 81
1. 410: 81 n. 36
1. 411–17: 81 n. 36
1. 411: 74 n. 13
1. 416: 84
1. 431–2: 78 n. 28
1. 499: 84
1. 539: 76
1. 638–44: 93 n. 67
1. 639: 93 n. 67
1. 673: 78
1. 731–3: 62–3, 106
1. 731: 106
1. 732: 106
1. 794: 76
1. 797: 78
1. 803–8: 40, 79, 206
1. 823–7: 85, 100 and n. 84
1. 823: 84, 100–1
1. 825: 84
1. 870–2: 102 n. 87
1. 897–900: 40, 79, 102 n. 87, 206
1. 901: 102 n. 87
1. 902–12: 102 n. 87
1. 907–14: 85, 100 n. 84, 102 n. 87
1. 911–12: 102 n. 87
1. 912–14: 102 n. 87
1. 916–20: 102 n. 87
1. 921–50: 86
1. 921–30: 125
1. 921–2: 92
1. 922–30: 97
1. 922–5: 143
1. 923: 87, 89, 225
1. 924–5: 87, 108, 126, 225
1. 924: 99
1. 926–50: 76 n. 25, 86
1. 926–30: 87, 107 n. 101, 225
1. 926–7: 87, 88, 115, 214
1. 926: 90
1. 927–30: 99
1. 927–8: 87, 126, 150
1. 927: 98 n. 80, 99
1. 928: 98 n. 80, 99
1. 929–30: 88, 89, 98 n. 80, 150
1. 930: 88
1. 931–4: 97
1. 933–4: 92, 112
1. 934: 84, 95, 98
1. 935: 95, 97 n. 79
1. 936–50: 96
1. 946: 84, 97 n. 79
1. 947: 96, 98
1. 948–9: 97
1. 948: 97 n. 79
1. 949: 84
1. 950: 105
1. 1052: 74 n. 13
1. 1115–17: 91
1. 1116: 91
2. 9–10: 91
2. 10: 91
2. 55–61: 76
2. 59–61: 92
2. 82: 90 n. 60
2. 143: 74 n. 13
2. 182: 74 n. 13, 76
2. 333–477: 102
2. 418–21: 79
2. 485–96: 79 n. 31
2. 529: 84
2. 600–60: 95 n. 75, 128
2. 677: 90
2. 688–99: 85, 100 n. 84
2. 688: 84, 101
2. 690: 84
2. 755: 79 n. 31
2. 756: 78
2. 834–6: 79 n. 31
2. 864: 78
2. 1013–22: 85, 100 n. 84
2. 1013: 84, 101
2. 1021: 101
2. 1040–1: 97
3. 1–2: 92
3. 3–8: 108, 111

Lucr. (*cont.*)
3. 3–6: 107 n. 99
3. 3–4: 115
3. 5–6: 108
3. 5: 108
3. 6–7: 110 and n. 108
3. 6: 108, 116
3. 7–8: 108, 110
3. 7: 111 n. 112
3. 8: 111
3. 9–13: 111
3. 9: 111
3. 10: 86, 111
3. 11: 112
3. 12–13: 112
3. 12: 86, 111, 113
3. 14–15: 106
3. 14: 106
3. 15: 106
3. 36: 84
3. 87–93: 76
3. 91–3: 92
3. 322: 80
3. 419: 113
3. 420: 84
3. 626: 79 n. 31
3. 1042–4: 107 n. 99, 115 n. 124
4. 1–25: 86
4. 9: 84
4. 11–25: 96
4. 21: 84
4. 24: 84
4. 26: 76
4. 30: 76
4. 33–45: 78
4. 33: 76
4. 180: 84, 110 n. 108
4. 181–2: 109
4. 453–68: 78
4. 802–15: 98
4. 909: 84, 110 n. 108
4. 910–11: 109
4. 969–70: 86, 105, 111 n. 113
4. 969: 111 n. 113
4. 970: 111 n. 113
4. 1058: 117
5. 1–2: 113, 116
5. 1: 84
5. 5: 113
5. 8: 74 n. 13, 116
5. 21: 113
5. 49–54: 113
5. 50: 113
5. 52–3: 113
5. 53: 113
5. 54: 106, 113
5. 55: 113
5. 56: 113
5. 93: 74 n. 13
5. 95: 104 n. 92
5. 164: 74 n. 13
5. 335–7: 111 n. 113
5. 509: 84
5. 867: 74 n. 13
5. 1000: 104 n. 92
5. 1091: 80
5. 1282: 74 n. 13
6. 7: 106
6. 26–8: 91
6. 35–41: 76
6. 39–41: 92
6. 46–7: 89
6. 46: 76 n. 21, 89
6. 47: 89 and n. 58, 110, 226 n. 56
6. 83: 84
6. 84: 84
6. 92–5: 76 n. 21, 89, 107 n. 101, 226 n. 56
6. 92–4: 110
6. 93–4: 84 n. 44, 102
6. 94: 84 n. 44
6. 95: 89
6. 673: 40, 80
6. 937: 84
6. 1247–51: 104 n. 90
6. 1283–5: 104 n. 90
6. 1250–51: 104 n. 90

6. 1251: 104 n. 90
6. 1286: 104 n. 90

Man. 1. 1–6: 222
1. 1–4: 222–4, 233 n. 70, 238–9
1. 1: 198, 209
1. 3: 223 and n. 49, 224 and n. 52, 238
1. 4–6: 211
1. 4–5: 223 n. 51
1. 4: 223–4
1. 6: 212 n. 30
1. 7–10: 198, 200, 201 n. 11, 217 n. 38, 224
1. 10: 201, 209
1. 11–12: 217, 224
1. 11: 217 n. 38, 224
1. 12: 209, 224, 235, 241, 242, 244
1. 13–15: 225–6
1. 13: 217 n. 38
1. 16–19: 225 n. 54
1. 20–2: 220 and n. 44, 234
1. 21: 235 n. 78
1. 22–3: 235–6, 240
1. 22: 209, 236
1. 23: 209
1. 24: 240–1 and n. 90, 244
1. 25–39: 238
1. 40–5: 219
1. 40: 219
1. 46–50: 219
1. 97: 233
1. 113–17: 209–10
1. 113–14: 211, 233
1. 113: 233, 238 n. 86
1. 114: 209
1. 116–17: 210 n. 27
1. 116: 210 n. 27
1. 117: 210
1. 118–21: 237–8 and n. 85
1. 118–19: 233
1. 118: 209, 232
1. 120: 209

1. 194: 199, 202
1. 247: 238 n. 86
1. 255–6: 236–7
1. 256: 209, 237 n. 84
1. 275–442: 232 n. 68
1. 384–6: 200
1. 483–5: 204
1. 483–7: 239
1. 486: 239 n. 89
1. 487: 239 n. 89
1. 488–91: 239 n. 89
1. 489: 239 n. 89
1. 541: 199 n. 5
1. 702: 199 n. 5
1. 758–804: 230
1. 810: 209
1. 925–6: 200
2. 1–48: 64 n. 74, 215
2. 8–11: 212
2. 10: 223 n. 49
2. 11–24: 212
2. 24: 238 n. 86
2. 25–38: 212, 222
2. 25–7: 221
2. 28–36: 221
2. 37–8: 222
2. 38: 222, 233 n. 70, 243 n. 91
2. 39–42: 212
2. 43–5: 212
2. 46–8: 212
2. 49–52: 212–13, 215
2. 49–50: 213
2. 50: 227
2. 53–9: 215
2. 53–6: 213
2. 57–9: 213
2. 57: 213 n. 33, 215
2. 58–9: 215, 226, 233
2. 58: 238 n. 86
2. 60–135: 215
2. 60–81: 216
2. 60: 215
2. 82–104: 216
2. 82–6: 237

Man. (*cont.*)
 2. 105–25: 219
 2. 105–8: 205 and n. 19, 216
 2. 106: 205 n. 19
 2. 107–8: 233
 2. 115–25: 216
 2. 123: 216
 2. 124–5: 233
 2. 124: 216–17 and n. 37, 238 n. 86
 2. 125: 216, 221, 230
 2. 127–8: 221, 222, 224, 233 n. 70
 2. 127: 224 and n. 52
 2. 128: 221, 223 n. 49
 2. 136–49: 198
 2. 136–44: 203–4 and n. 16
 2. 136–7: 233 n. 69
 2. 136: 217
 2. 137: 204, 209
 2. 138–42: 208, 234 n. 74
 2. 138–40: 204, 227
 2. 138–9: 226
 2. 141–2: 204, 217
 2. 142: 204, 209, 244
 2. 143–4: 204, 208
 2. 143: 204 n. 17, 234 n. 74
 2. 149: 203–4, 218 n. 41
 2. 204: 237 n. 84
 2. 262: 199 n. 5
 2. 440: 220 n. 44
 2. 448–51: 231
 2. 507–10: 200
 2. 687: 234 n. 73
 2. 690: 234 n. 73, 237 n. 84
 2. 693–4: 212 n. 30
 2. 693: 234 n. 73
 2. 695: 234 n. 73
 2. 699: 199 n. 5
 2. 722–83: 207
 2. 750–87: 206–7
 2. 750: 237 n. 84
 2. 751: 198
 2. 754: 209
 2. 755–64: 207
 2. 760: 233 n. 71
 2. 765: 209
 2. 767: 209
 2. 829–30: 212 n. 30
 2. 928: 209
 2. 965: 209
 3. 1–4: 214, 228
 3. 1: 233 n. 71
 3. 4: 209, 214 n. 34
 3. 5–6: 214 n. 35
 3. 9–13: 214 n. 35
 3. 15–16: 214 n. 35
 3. 17: 214 n. 35
 3. 18–19: 214 n. 35
 3. 19–21: 214 n. 35
 3. 22–3: 214 n. 35
 3. 26–30: 214–15
 3. 30: 238 n. 86
 3. 31–42: 215, 241–2, 244
 3. 34–5: 242
 3. 34: 242
 3. 35: 209
 3. 36–42: 198
 3. 36–7: 202
 3. 37: 203 n. 15
 3. 38: 209, 215, 242
 3. 39: 198, 242
 3. 40–2: 212 n. 30
 3. 41: 209, 238 n. 36, 242
 3. 93: 209, 237 n. 84
 3. 157: 237 n. 84
 3. 164: 209
 3. 169–509: 200 n. 9
 3. 270: 209
 3. 390: 237 n. 84
 3. 393–4: 231
 3. 393: 203
 3. 395: 203
 3. 447: 198
 3. 560: 198, 199 n. 6
 3. 586: 209
 4. 118: 218 n. 41
 4. 119–21: 199 n. 6, 231 and

Index of Passages Cited

n. 65, 233 n. 69
4. 119–20: 239 n. 89
4. 119: 198–9, 199 n. 6, 237 n. 84
4. 121: 209
4. 123: 237 n. 84
4. 152–61: 220
4. 158: 220
4. 387–9: 40, 206
4. 390: 231 n. 66
4. 407: 230
4. 408: 237 n. 84
4. 430: 209
4. 431–42: 242–4
4. 434–5: 243, 244
4. 436: 209
4. 436–7: 218 n. 40
4. 438: 243, 244
4. 440: 243 and n. 91
4. 442: 244 and n. 92
4. 547–52: 200
4. 763–6: 200
4. 759: 199 n. 5
4. 773–7: 200
4. 848: 199 n. 5
4. 866–935: 204–5, 219
4. 869–72: 40, 206 and n. 22
4. 877–81: 229 n. 60
4. 886–7: 230 n. 62
4. 893–7: 205
4. 918: 199 n. 5
5. 1–11: 210
5. 1: 210
5. 4–7: 210
5. 4: 238 n. 86
5. 5: 211, 232
5. 8–11: 226
5. 8: 211, 218 n. 40
5. 10: 226 n. 56
5. 11: 230 n. 64, 233 n. 69
5. 12–26: 211
5. 12: 211
5. 19: 211
5. 27: 209
5. 538–618: 222

Ov.
Am. 1.1: 167 n. 24
1. 1. 3–4: 167
1. 1. 5: 167
1. 1. 21–5: 167
1. 1. 25: 167
1. 2: 172, 186
1. 2. 9–10: 167, 168, 186
1. 2. 9: 168 n. 26
1. 2. 19: 186
1. 2. 27: 186
1. 7: 164 n. 19
1. 15. 23–4: 104 n. 92
2. 7: 164
2. 8: 164
Ars am. 1. 1–2: 37, 159, 162, 168, 176, 177
1. 1: 178, 203
1. 2: 161, 176
1. 3–4: 181 and n. 45
1. 4: 170
1. 5–8: 162
1. 5–6: 181
1. 7–18: 162
1. 7: 161 and n. 11
1. 8: 181
1. 17: 160, 168, 170
1. 18: 167
1. 19–24: 162
1. 21–4: 167, 170
1. 21–2: 167 n. 24
1. 21: 167, 170
1. 23–4: 167 n. 24
1. 25–30: 161
1. 29: 158, 161
1. 30: 161, 162, 173, 176
1. 31–4: 170 n. 30
1. 31: 170
1. 33: 161, 173, 176
1. 34: 161
1. 35–40: 170, 173
1. 35–8: 180

Ov. *Ars am.* (cont.)
  1. 35: 170
  1. 36: 178
  1. 39–40: 180
  1. 49: 170
  1. 50: 158 n. 5
  1. 79–88: 170
  1. 165–70: 170
  1. 253–4: 174
  1. 255–62: 169, 170
  1. 255: 174 n. 37
  1. 263–6: 173
  1. 263–4: 193–4
  1. 264: 160
  1. 283–342: 192
  1. 283: 174 n. 37
  1. 297: 161
  1. 375–98: 164
  1. 375: 182
  1. 525: 161
  1. 607: 182
  1. 615–16: 169
  1. 617: 160 n. 9
  1. 707–14: 166
  1. 739: 174 n. 37
  1. 755–6: 174
  1. 771–2: 22, 173
  1. 772: 180
  2. 1–12: 179–80
  2. 1–4: 186
  2. 2: 179, 180, 186
  2. 3–4: 188
  2. 3: 161
  2. 5–6: 181
  2. 7–8: 181
  2. 9–10: 22, 180
  2. 10: 180
  2. 11: 161, 179, 180
  2. 12: 179, 180, 186 n. 48
  2. 15–16: 162
  2. 17–20: 168
  2. 21–96: 191 n. 54
  2. 97–8: 168
  2. 98: 186 n. 48
  2. 161: 160, 168
  2. 165: 161
  2. 169–74: 164
  2. 169: 164 n. 19
  2. 173: 160
  2. 273: 160, 174 n. 37
  2. 295–314: 158 n. 5
  2. 337–44: 178
  2. 373–86: 184
  2. 389–414: 183
  2. 413–14: 184
  2. 425: 174 n. 37
  2. 427–8: 183–4
  2. 447–54: 184
  2. 455: 182
  2. 493–510: 162 n. 13
  2. 493–4: 175 and n. 40
  2. 493: 161
  2. 497–508: 175
  2. 497: 160
  2. 511: 174 n. 36
  2. 535: 174
  2. 536: 161
  2. 547–8: 165 and n. 20
  2. 599–600: 170 n. 30
  2. 703–32: 178
  2. 703: 182
  2. 704: 182
  2. 725–30: 166
  2. 725–7: 181
  2. 731–2: 181
  2. 733–44: 180, 186
  2. 733: 174, 186
  2. 735–8: 186
  2. 738: 163 n. 17, 181
  2. 739: 161
  2. 741–2: 186
  2. 743: 186
  2. 744: 11, 160
  2. 745–6: 160 and nn. 8 and 9, 174
  2. 745: 160
  2. 746: 176, 177
  3. 1–6: 166, 184

3. 6–8: 160 n. 9
3. 9–22: 192
3. 27: 170 n. 30
3. 28: 160
3. 41: 171
3. 43–56: 162 n. 13, 175 n. 40
3. 43: 160
3. 47: 176
3. 57–8: 170 n. 30
3. 57: 160
3. 59–98: 165
3. 193–8: 165
3. 193–4: 174
3. 195: 160
3. 197: 160
3. 205–8: 176
3. 251: 160
3. 255: 160
3. 257: 160
3. 320: 160
3. 339–46: 176
3. 341–2: 176, 177 n. 42
3. 341: 160
3. 342: 161
3. 343–4: 162–3
3. 353: 174 n. 36
3. 467: 174
3. 483: 170 n. 30
3. 499: 174 n. 36
3. 533–51: 166
3. 533: 166
3. 552: 166
3. 553–4: 166
3. 581–2: 166
3. 593–4: 166
3. 611–12: 174 n. 38
3. 613–16: 170 n. 30
3. 651: 160, 174 n. 37
3. 659–66: 164
3. 667–72: 175, 193, 195 n. 62
3. 667: 175 n. 39, 193
3. 747: 174 n. 36
3. 749: 184
3. 769–70: 174 n. 38
3. 769: 160
3. 790: 161
3. 792: 161
3. 809–12: 83 n. 42
3. 809: 174
3. 812: 11, 160
Fast. 1. 1–26: 201
1. 1–2: 13
1. 93: 16 n. 21
2. 119–26: 62
2. 119–20: 113 n. 116
2. 125–6: 62
4. 546: 112
4. 830: 233 n. 71
5. 111: 233 n. 71
Her. 15: 194 n. 60
15. 5–8: 194 n. 60
16: 190, 193
16. 341–4: 190
Met. 1. 1–4: 13
1. 1–2: 67 n. 78
1. 1: 13
1. 2–3: 203 n. 14
1. 2: 13, 67 n. 78
1. 5–31: 66 n. 76
1. 260–312: 66 n. 76
4. 285–388: 66 n. 76
4. 750–2: 66 n. 76
9. 530–63: 64
15. 75–478: 65
15. 75: 65
15. 76: 67 n. 78
15. 92: 65
15. 143–7: 65
15. 147–52: 65
15. 147–9: 226 n. 55
15. 156: 67 n. 78
15. 172: 65
15. 174: 65
15. 176–7: 66, 175 n. 39
15. 186: 65
15. 200: 65
15. 215: 67 n. 78
15. 237–51: 66 n. 76

Ov. Met. (cont.)
  15. 262–9: 66 n. 76
  15. 293–4: 65
  15. 308: 65
  15. 319–21: 66 n. 76
  15. 333: 65
  15. 362: 65
  15. 363: 67 n. 78
  15. 364: 65
  15. 382: 65
  15. 416–17: 66 n. 76
  15. 418–20: 66
  15. 419–20: 66 n. 78
  15. 453–4: 66
  15. 459: 67 n. 78
  15. 871–9: 13
  15. 878: 86 n. 49
Rem am. 1–40: 162 n. 13, 175 n. 40
  1–2: 176
  3: 161
  9: 160
  41: 160
  43–4: 171
  49–52: 160
  55: 160
  71–2: 11, 176
  75–8: 162
  77: 161
  79–80: 185
  91: 185
  107–10: 185
  109: 174 n. 36
  225: 160
  252: 161
  298: 160
  349: 160
  361–98: 63, 163
  361–2: 192
  361: 176
  372: 163
  379–88: 163
  379–80: 63
  379: 163 n. 15
  385–6: 170 n. 30
  392: 161
  397–8: 174 n. 36
  398: 161
  407: 174
  423: 160
  439: 174 n. 38
  461: 174 n. 37
  487: 176, 182
  489: 160
  523: 160
  555–76: 162 n. 13, 175 n. 40
  577: 174 n. 37
  607–8: 160
  609–10: 185
  703: 161
  715: 161
  757: 174 n. 36
  766: 161
  767: 161
  803: 160, 182
  811: 174
  813–14: 160
  813: 161
  814: 161
Tr. 1. 1. 67: 168
  1. 1. 112: 170 n. 29
  2. 207: 192 n. 57
  2. 353–6: 189
  2. 471–92: 157
  2. 493–4: 157
  3. 14. 37–8: 112 n. 114

Prop. 1. 1. 1: 9–10 and n. 6, 12
  3. 1. 3–4: 114 n. 20
  3. 3. 5–12: 88 n. 54
  4. 1. 64: 114 n. 121
  4. 1. 67: 233 n. 71

Quint. Inst. 10. 1. 46–72: 27 n. 5
  10. 1. 46–57: 29
  10. 1. 51: 29
  10. 1. 56: 29 n. 12, 122
  10. 1. 85–100: 27 n. 5
  10. 1. 85–6: 29

Index of Passages Cited

10. 1. 87: 29
10. 1. 88: 29
11. 2. 17–22: 23 n. 33

Sen. *Ep.* 11. 8–10: 115 n. 127
  25. 5: 115 n. 127
  52. 3: 115 n. 127
  86. 15: 120 n. 5
  107. 11: 207 n. 25

Serv. *Praef. ad Georg.* 1. 129. 9: 59 n. 68, 61
  1. 129. 9–12: 37–8, 80 n. 33
  1. 129. 11–12: 130–1
ad Ecl. 3. 1: 33 n. 20
ad Ecl. 10. 46: 167 n. 25
ad G. 1. 56: 130, 138
ad G. 1. 176: 138
ad G. 3. 3: 146 n. 33

Stat. *Theb.* 12. 810–19: 86 n. 49

Verg.
Aen. 1. 1: 9–10, 13, 16, 19
  5. 117–18: 85 n. 46
  6. 625–7: 134
  6. 713–892: 43
  6. 716–18: 43
  6. 722: 43
  6. 759: 43
  6. 760: 43 n. 36
  6. 771: 43 n. 36
  6. 779: 43 n. 36
  6. 788: 43 n. 36
  6. 817–18: 43 n. 36
  6. 825: 43 n. 36
  6. 855: 43 n. 36
  7. 37–45: 14
Ecl. 1. 1: 155
  4. 1: 15
  6. 3–5: 144
  6. 62–3: 79
  8. 69: 223
  9. 35–6: 109

10. 1: 15–16
10. 69: 167, 172
10. 70: 16
G. 1. 1–5: 120
1. 1–4: 123, 131
1. 2: 130, 133
1. 5–23: 129
1. 5: 124, 131
1. 12: 124
1. 24–42: 129, 201
1. 24: 133 n. 21
1. 40–2: 133, 201
1. 40: 133, 201, 203 n. 14
1. 41–2: 133
1. 41: 123, 130, 133 n. 22
1. 43–6: 126
1. 43: 130
1. 45–6: 123, 130
1. 56: 130
1. 71: 130, 138
1. 72: 130
1. 73: 130
1. 100: 123
1. 101: 123, 130
1. 169–75: 124
1. 176: 123, 138
1. 177: 63, 138
1. 204–5: 123, 126
1. 210: 123
2. 1–3: 123
2. 1–2: 124
2. 2–8: 129
2. 2: 124, 138
2. 7–8: 127 n. 12
2. 35–7: 131
2. 35: 132
2. 36: 123, 131, 132
2. 37–8: 127 n. 12, 132
2. 37: 126
2. 39–46: 132–4
2. 39: 132, 133 and nn. 21 and 23, 138, 152 n. 42, 203 n. 14
2. 40: 203 n. 14
2. 41–6: 139

Verg. G. (*cont.*)
2. 41: 130, 132, 133
2. 42–4: 140
2. 42: 124, 134, 140
2. 43–4: 134
2. 44: 133
2. 45–6: 133
2. 45: 124
2. 89–108: 124
2. 95–6: 124, 129
2. 95: 124
2. 101–2: 124, 129
2. 103–8: 124, 140
2. 104: 140
2. 146: 129
2. 170: 129
2. 173–4: 129
2. 174–6: 149
2. 174–5: 129
2. 176: 63, 122, 124, 136
2. 393–6: 126
2. 458–3. 48: 141
2. 458–540: 138, 143 n. 28
2. 458–60: 138
2. 458–9: 141
2. 459–73: 141
2. 473–4: 141
2. 475–94: 138, 142–5
2. 475–82: 143, 145, 155
2. 476: 143
2. 477: 145, 148 n. 38
2. 483–6: 143, 145
2. 483–4: 144
2. 484: 143
2. 485–9: 143, 148 n. 38, 227
2. 485: 145
2. 486: 143, 144, 145, 148, 134 n. 24
2. 490–4: 143
2. 490–2: 122, 143
2. 490: 145
2. 491–2: 143, 144
2. 493–4: 143
2. 495: 145

3. 1–2: 123, 124, 146
3. 1: 124
3. 3–4: 146
3. 3: 124, 149 n. 39
3. 3–9: 147
3. 4–9: 146
3. 4–8: 149
3. 4–5: 147 n. 36
3. 8–9: 148, 149 and n. 39, 230
3. 9: 150
3. 10–39: 150 n. 41, 155
3. 10–14: 149
3. 10–11: 114 n. 120, 221 n. 47
3. 10: 150, 155
3. 12: 129, 150
3. 13: 150
3. 16: 149 n. 39, 150
3. 17: 150
3. 26–33: 150
3. 40–5: 135, 148 n. 38, 150
3. 40–2: 134–5
3. 41: 125, 130, 135, 147 n. 36
3. 42–5: 227
3. 42: 135, 148 n. 38
3. 43–6: 135
3. 43–4: 143 n. 28
3. 43: 211 n. 29
3. 46–7: 150
3. 46: 127 n. 12
3. 284–5: 125
3. 285: 127
3. 286–8: 123
3. 286–7: 127
3. 288: 123, 152 n. 42
3. 290: 63
3. 291–3: 125–6, 225, 227
3. 291–2: 143 n. 28
3. 292–3: 133
3. 292: 126
3. 293: 225
3. 294: 124
3. 295: 123
3. 300: 123

3. 329: 123
3. 339: 124
3. 420: 123
3. 440: 123
4. 1–7: 135
4. 1–5: 123
4. 1–2: 124
4. 2–5: 135 and n. 25
4. 2: 130, 135
4. 6: 63, 134 n. 24, 152 n. 42
4. 62–6: 120 n. 2
4. 62–3: 120 n. 2
4. 62: 123
4. 64: 120 n. 2
4. 116–48: 125
4. 116–17: 140
4. 116: 152 n. 42
4. 118: 141
4. 119: 124
4. 147: 140

4. 219–21: 119
4. 264: 123
4. 315–16: 150 n. 40
4. 315: 129
4. 559–66: 83 n. 42
4. 559–60: 123, 124
4. 559: 124
4. 560–2: 152
4. 562: 134 n. 24
4. 463–4: 152
4. 563: 11, 140
4. 564: 134 n. 24
4. 565–6: 140, 155
4. 565: 155
4. 566: 124, 155

Vita Vergilii Bernensis I: 154

Volcacius Sedigitus, fr. 1. 3: 60 n. 69

INDEX

(For all ancient authors, see also the Passages Cited, above.)

Accius 59
addressee, *see* teacher–student constellation
Aratus 54–8
  in Manilius 119, 232 n. 67
  in the *Georgics* 122
  Latin imitators 60, 201, 212, 222
  see also Callimachus; Cicero
Archestratus of Gela 53–4, 58–9
Aristotle:
  and didactic poetry 2, 29–34, 51
  definition of poetry 7
  on genre 10–11, 28–9
  see also Empedocles
Augustus 14, 62, 154, 170 n. 30, 192 n. 57, 200, 201 n. 11, 202
  see also Octavian

Byron 71 n. 8, 189

'Callimachean' poetics:
  and didactic poetry 55 n. 61
  in Lucretius 87–8, 110 n. 108
  in Manilius 204, 208, 212 n. 32, 213, 215, 227
  in the *Georgics* 126, 133–4, 144, 148 n. 38
Callimachus:
  on Aratus 55 n. 61, 57
chariot metaphor 21–2, 24, 50, 52, 66, 89, 111 n. 110, 154 n. 48, 180–1, 204, 215, 225–30
Cicero:
  on Aratus and Nicander 54 n. 58

  on Lucretius 60
  on Sallustius, *Empedoclea* 60
Coleridge 71–2
creator motif 78–9, 239 n. 89
  see also *poeta creator* motif

didactic intent:
  as a criterion for didactic poetry 36–7
  in Lucretius 69
  in Manilius 198–9
  in the *Ars/Remedia* 159–60
  in the *Georgics* 123
didactic mode 42–3, 44, 46, 48, 49, 50
didactic plot 40
didactic poetry:
  ancient views of 29–34
  as a 'Problem der Poetik' 2, 30
  criteria for 36–41
  Hellenistic 54–57
  idea that all poetry is didactic 36
  Latin, before Lucretius 58–60
  perceptions in the 1st cent. BC 60–7
  relation to epic poetry 29–30, 35, 39, 64, 69–70; *see also* 'epic objectivity'; Lucretius
  'theoretical' v. 'instructional' 41, 123, 199
  works (not) qualifying as 41–3
  see also Aristotle; didactic intent; didactic mode; didactic plot; Effe; poetic self-consciousness; simultaneity,

poetic; teacher–student constellation
Diomedes, *Ars Grammatica* 31–3, 39, 40

Effe, Bernd:
 types of didactic poetry 4, 55 n. 60, 69, 120, 157, 191 n. 55, 197
Egnatius, *De rerum natura* 60
Empedocles 51–3
 Aristotle's opinion of 2, 30, 70–1
 in Lucretius 58, 62–3, 70–1, 76, 84 nn. 43 and 44, 106–7
Ennius:
 Hedyphagetica 58–9
 in Lucretius 87–8, 105–7, 111, 114–15
'epic objectivity' 13, 39, 67, 156
Epicurus:
 view of poetry 94–5
 see also *imitatio Epicuri*

Fish, Stanley 8
'flight of the mind' 90–1, 229–30

Gallus 167–8, 172
Genette, Gérard 28–9, 35
genre 25–6, 34–5, 60–4, and Ch. 2 *passim*
 ancient views of 27–9
 subgenre 35
Germanicus 15, 60, 129 n. 16, 201, 212 n. 30, 217 n. 38
 see also Aratus
Goethe 1

Hesiod, *Works and Days* 44–9
 in the *Georgics* 63, 122, 124 n. 11
Homer:
 in Lucretius 105–7, 114–15

imitatio :

animal contest as a metaphor for 108–11
imitatio Epicuri 86, 105–16
 see also *primus* motif
implied author 190
intentional fallacy 4

Jakobson, Roman 7, 8 n. 4, 9
journey metaphor 20–4
 in Lucretius 88–91
 in Manilius 210–11, 225–34
 in the *Ars/Remedia* 180–2
 in the *Georgics* 133
 see also chariot metaphor; 'flight of the mind'; ship metaphor

Lambinus 109, 111
love elegy, see Ovid
Lucretius Ch. 3 and *passim*
 'Antilucrèce chez Lucrèce' 71 n. 8, 72
 atoms–letters analogy 85–6, 100–5, 239–40
 'discontinuity of symbolism' 93, 97 n. 79, 116–18
 end of Book 6 as a 'test' 81–3
 honeyed-cup simile 96–9
 in Manilius 199 n. 6, 206, 208–9, 211, 214, 217 n. 38, 219, 225, 226 n. 56, 231, 239–40, 242
 in the *Georgics* 122, 126, 130, 131, 137, 140, 143–4, 147, 148, 150
 light imagery 91–3, 112
 reception of 71–2
 repetition in 76, 86–7 n. 50, 103
 the *De rerum natura* not an epic poem 69–71
 see also 'Callimachean' poetics; Cicero; didactic intent; Empedocles; Ennius; Epicurus; Homer; *imitatio*; journey metaphor; Memmius; poetic self-

consciousness; simultaneity, poetic; teacher–student constellation; Venus; writing

Maecenas, *see* Vergil
Malle, Louis, see *Milou en Mai*
Manilius Ch. 6 and *passim*
  address to *Caesar* 200–2
  difficulty of treating the subject matter in poetic form 240–4
  'fatedness' of the poem 216–24, 235–40
  Gemini 220
  'have-one's-cake-and-eat-it-too' principle 208, 222, 233, 242, 244 n. 92, 245
  Hermetism 205 n. 20, 219 n. 43, 220 n. 44, 230
  microcosm–macrocosm argument 205–8, 219
  music of the spheres 235–6
  poetic originality 211–19
  regarded as a second-rate poet 196
  Stoicism 198, 204, 206 n. 21, 207, 215–16, 219, 239–40
  wrong ways of approaching the cosmos 220–4
  see also Aratus; 'Callimachean' poetics; didactic intent; journey metaphor; Lucretius; poetic self-consciousness; simultaneity, poetic; teacher–student constellation; Vergil
Memmius:
  as a historical figure 74
  as an unresponsive student 80–2, 89–90
  'Fading of Memmius' 74–5
Milou en Mai 119–20
mimetic simultaneity, *see* simultaneity, mimetic
Nicander 57
  in the *Georgics* 122
  see also Cicero
nonne uides 76, 130

Octavian 129, 130, 133, 134 n. 24, 150, 152, 154
  see also Augustus
orality, *see* Parry–Lord theory; performance; writing
Ovid, *Ars amatoria* and *Remedia amoris* Ch. 5 and *passim*
  Amor/*amor* 168–73, 177–8
  and love elegy 63, 162–8, 171–3, 178, 186–7
  and the didactic tradition 157–9, 187–8
  elegiac metre 35, 59–60, 163, 193–4
  instructions to the *puellae* (*Ars* 3) 165–6, 184, 194–5
  rejection of divine inspiration 161–2
  the persona a 'failure'? 165, 188–95
  see also Augustus; didactic intent; journey metaphor; poetic self-consciousness; Pythagoras speech; simultaneity, mimetic; simultaneity, poetic; teacher–student constellation; Venus; writing

Parmenides 49–51
Parry–Lord theory 16–17, 44
performance 16–20
  see also Parry–Lord theory; writing
persona 10–12, 188–90, and *passim*
Philaenis 158
Philodemus 94–5, 115
Plato:
  myth of Er 229–30, 235
  on genre 10–11, 28–9, 31–3

poeta creator motif 78–9, 127, 132–3, 184
  see also *creator* motif
poetic self-consciousness, 9–13 and *passim*
  as a criterion for didactic poetry 39
  in Lucretius 83–93
  in Manilius 209
  in the *Ars/Remedia* 161–3, 183, 193–4
  in the *Georgics* 124, 131–9, 156
poetic simultaneity, *see* simultaneity, poetic
poetry, definition of 6–9
Polignac, Cardinal Melchior de 71 n. 8
Porcius Licinus 59–60, 163 n. 15
primus motif 88, 114–15, 149–50, 211–19
Pythagoras speech (Ov. *Met.* 15. 75–478) 64–7, 226 n. 55

recusatio 28 n. 6, 63, 144–5, 148 n. 38, 151, 214
  see also 'Callimachean' poetics
rota Vergilii 154

Sallustius, *Empedoclea* 60
self-consciousness, *see* poetic self-consciousness
Servius:
  on didactic poetry 37–9, 61
ship metaphor 21–2, 24, 40, 66, 180–1, 215, 226
simultaneity, mimetic:
  and 'mimetic poems' 183
  definition 182
  in *Ars* 1 and 2 178–88
  not a feature of *Ars* 3 and *Remedia* 184–5
simultaneity, poetic 13–24 and *passim*
  as a criterion for didactic poetry 39–40
  in Lucretius 84, 104, 105
  in Manilius 209–11, 217 n. 38
  in the *Ars/Remedia* 173–88
  in the *Georgics* 124–5, 132, 139, 144
  student, *see* teacher–student constellation

teacher–student constellation:
  as a criterion for didactic poetry 37–9
  in Lucretius 73–83
  in Manilius 198–209, 231
  in the *Ars/Remedia* 160–1
  in the *Georgics* 123–4, 126–7, 129–39
Tiberius 200–2
Tractatus Coislinianus 31–3, 41, 123

Venus:
  in Lucretius 84–5, 98–9, 117
  in Ovid 161–2
Vergil, *Georgics* Ch. 4 and *passim*
  and contemporary agriculture 120 n. 3, 128, 131 n. 20
  and Vergil's career 152–6
  'deeper meaning' of 120–1
  didactic nature of 122–30, 136–9
  digressions 128–9
  in Manilius 201, 203 n. 14, 211, 214, 221 n. 47, 225, 227, 230
  poem announced in proem 3 150–1
  role of Maecenas 130–9
  sphragis 123, 139–40, 151–2, 156
  see also Aratus; 'Callimachean' poetics; didactic intent; Hesiod; journey metaphor; Lucretius; Nicander; Octavian; poetic self-consciousness; simultaneity,

poetic; teacher–student
constellation
Vergil, *Vitae* 153–5
Volcacius Sedigitus 59–60, 163
   n. 15

Wisdom Literature 44–6, 48, 49
   n. 48, 50–1
writing (v. 'singing') 15, 16
   in Lucretius 85–6, 111–12 n. 114
   in the *Ars/Remedia* 176–8